CanLit Across Media

CanLit Across Media

Unarchiving the Literary Event

Edited by
Jason Camlot
and
Katherine McLeod

McGill-Queen's University Press

Montreal & Kingston • London • Chicago

© McGill-Queen's University Press 2019

ISBN 978-0-7735-5865-6 (cloth)
ISBN 978-0-7735-5866-3 (paper)
ISBN 978-0-7735-5981-3 (ePDF)
ISBN 978-0-7735-5982-0 (ePUB)

Legal deposit fourth quarter 2019
Bibliothèque nationale du Québec

Printed in Canada on acid-free paper that is 100% ancient forest free
(100% post-consumer recycled), processed chlorine free

This book has been published with the help of a grant from the Canadian
Federation for the Humanities and Social Sciences, through the Awards to
Scholarly Publications Program, using funds provided by the Social Sciences
and Humanities Research Council of Canada. Funding was also received from
Concordia University's Aid to Research Related Events Program, administered
by the Office of the Vice-President for Research and Graduate Studies.

We acknowledge the support of the Canada Council for the Arts.

Nous remercions le Conseil des arts du Canada de son soutien.

Library and Archives Canada Cataloguing in Publication

Title: CanLit across media : unarchiving the literary event / edited by Jason
    Camlot and Katherine McLeod.
Names: Camlot, Jason, 1967– editor. | McLeod, Katherine, 1981– editor.
Description: Includes bibliographical references and index.
Identifiers: Canadiana (print) 20190151919 | Canadiana (ebook)
    20190151935 | ISBN 9780773558656 (cloth) | ISBN 9780773558663
    (paper) | ISBN 9780773559813 (ePDF) | ISBN 9780773559820 (ePUB)
Subjects: LCSH: Canadian literature—Archival resources. | LCSH: Canadian
    literature—Research—Methodology. | LCSH: Archival materials—Canada.
Classification: LCC PS8039.5 .C36 2019 | DDC C810.72—dc23

Contents

Figures

Acknowledgments

This book began as an intensive two-day conference held at Concordia University in Montreal, 5–6 June 2015. That event was designed to gather scholars, writers, archivists, and media practitioners for an investigation into the past, present, and future of archiving and unarchiving Canadian literature across media platforms and formats. The conference expanded the methods and research questions that defined a SSHRC Insight Grant–funded project – "The SpokenWeb" – that focused on audio poetry archives, and invited scholars working on other media-diverse archives and collections to join the conversation. In addition to the contributors to the present volume, we would like to acknowledge others who participated in that critical and creative conversation, including Gary Barwin, Michael John DiSanto, Robin Isard, Annie Murray, Eleanor Wachtel, and the late Andrew Bretz. We would also like to acknowledge the 27-plus poets who participated in "All the Poets in Town: A Montreal Poetry Recording Party" – a literary performance associated with the conference. Student research assistants Vanessa Cannizzaro, Lee Hannigan, Erin McDonagh, Clara Nencu, Max Stein, and Adam Van Sertima provided support and assistance in the organization and management of the gatherings and in processes related to the preparation of the manuscript. These events were funded by the Social Science and Humanities Research Council of Canada (through the above-mentioned Insight Grant) and the Office of the Vice-President of Research and Graduate Studies (OVPRGS) at Concordia University through its Aid to Research Related Events (ARRE) Program. A SSHRC Partnership Grant along with a second ARRE grant and an Awards to Scholarly Publishing Program (ASPP) grant helped provide a subvention for the production and publication of this book.

Jason Camlot's chapter, "Archival Spectres and Formats of the Event: The Foster Poetry Conference, 1963," appeared in an earlier iteration, in French (translated by Renaud Roussel), as "Le Foster Poetry Conference, 1963," *Littérature Québécoise: Voix et Images* 40.2 (winter 2015): 59–75.

We are grateful to Mark Abley, acquisitions editor for McGill-Queen's University Press (MQUP), who attended the original conference and provided excellent guidance in developing the research presented there into the present collection. We also acknowledge Finn Purcell at MQUP for her help throughout the process. We are especially grateful to Jonathan Crago who, on top of so many other duties, took on and supported this project, and saw it through the review and approval stages with a steady focus on what was best for the book. We are also extremely grateful to our anonymous peer reviewers who devoted great attention and care to the manuscript, and provided sage advice, from the first draft to the last, on how to improve it. Finally, we acknowledge the ever-important support of our colleagues, friends, and family, who give meaning to this work and make it possible.

CanLit Across Media

Introduction
Unarchiving the Literary Event

JASON CAMLOT AND KATHERINE MCLEOD

This book unarchives acts of literary production. It is about the ways in which archival materials have been structured into forms of meaning, and how they have been transformed into new forms of presentation and experience in the present. The term "unarchiving" refers to the many ways in which the archival structures that inform cultural meaning may be reconfigured, refused, and remade through critical and creative practice, especially as archival materials are remediated and remobilized in public contexts. Our book examines innovative methods of such unarchiving activities enacted upon a range of materials and media formats that have documented and preserved Canadian literature in a wide array of cultural formations since the 1950s. This focus on the means by which literary events have been documented, catalogued, stored, and remobilized allows us to explore the alignment between a boom in national literary production and a McLuhan-esque burst in media technologies. With a consideration of events, performances, and discussions that occurred before live audiences, or that were broadcast on radio, film screen, and television, traces of which are now preserved on media ranging from print publications and documents, drawings, photographs, flat disc records, magnetic tape, film, video tape, and digitized files of such media, this collection examines the complex ways in which media *records* (i.e., the verb) and re-presents literary events, and showcases the range of methods and theories researchers use to engage with such materials.

A core argument of this book asserts that CanLit as a discernible cultural entity emerges through such acts of archival, critical, and creative engagement. Our interest in the production of CanLit as a cultural entity informs our decision to formulate a theory of unarchiving in relation to the ground of CanLit. This ground is not stable and never has been.

The individual contributions in this collection – ranging from chapters on the structure of material or digital archives, the critical work of reconstructing mediated events of the past, and creative works that resituate archival materials in the present – sometimes speak in distinctive terms about the status of CanLit as an entity. However, together, the chapters illustrate the idea that CanLit exists in the institutions, industries, media, events, and theories that declare and instantiate its status as an entity. CanLit emerges as a recognizable phenomenon in the media events that produced it and has been designed, and continues to be designed, as a textual canon in dialectical response to the events as they unfolded from the late 1950s forward. Our book argues that CanLit phenomena become uniquely apparent as ideological productions through critical consideration of the archival structures and media materials that have preserved and documented event-based cultural formations. This thesis, that focuses specifically on the visible emergence of something we can discern as CanLit, is part of a much larger process of historical conceptualization that pertains to the materials and archives we turn to for the construction of our literary past.

The most basic version of this thesis denies the idea that CanLit exists in any specific form of textuality as something permanent or essential. While the existence of Canadian literature may seem undeniable, it is so only after the fact of the institutional and media prerogatives and related critical theories that have made its supposedly synthetic forms and ethos recognizable in the minds of writers, readers, and audiences. This said, something discernible as Canadian literature *does* exist to most of us within a broad field of circulating aesthetic forms and media formats that come to be situated in distinctive contexts, and organized in a great variety of historically specific arrangements, in relation to each other. To deploy a concept used by design theorists, media historians, and literature scholars alike, the productions of CanLit – whether they be poetry readings, palinodes, conference proceedings, or documented forms of oral testimony – emerge and exist within social and cultural contexts according to their inherent formal and mediated affordances. This is not the same thing as saying that they are inherently this or that. Rather, the forms and formats in which they emerge as artifacts we may engage with (think and feel about) inform their possibilities for use and interaction, and consequently for identification and evaluation.

Such claims may seem abstract, so let us define this idea of affordances a bit more before going any further. From the perspective of design theory, "the presence of an affordance is jointly determined by the qualities of the object and the abilities of the agent that is interacting … Whether an affordance exists depends upon the properties of both the object and the agent," (say, the tea cup and the tea drinker, or, to be more Canadian, the mitten and the hand).[1] For the most part, technology theorists concur with this interactive definition of affordance. However, they sometimes stress the force of the "material substratum" in underpinning possible courses of interaction over the agency of the user so that the warp and weft of the artifact and its environments of use give significant shape to consequent actions and experiences (i.e., it is hard to type with mittens).[2] That is to say, there are limits set by the material affordances of a particular technology or medium. For example, while one might try to capture the complexity of a three-volume novel on a three-minute wax phonograph cylinder, the medium will only afford, at best, some very compressed and foreshortened manifestation of that fictional complexity.

Caroline Levine's recent exploration of the concept of affordance in relation to aesthetic form (rather than material or media format, specifically) places the emphasis on the different kinds of actions, thoughts, and feelings that are made possible or impossible due to the affordances of distinctive literary forms. Levine's application of the concept of affordance to literature supports a consideration of the conceptual and historical interaction between literary genres and material affordances, or, to put it another way, between literary form and media format. As she goes on to explain: "The idea of affordances is valuable for understanding the aesthetic object as imposing its order among a vast array of designed things, from prison cells to doorknobs. Literary form does not operate outside of the social but works among many organizing principles, all circulating in a world jam-packed with other arrangements. Each constraint will encounter many other, different organizing principles, and its power to impose order will itself be constrained, and at times, unsettled, by other forms."[3] To think about this relationship between aesthetic form and material format is to articulate a media-historical sociology of texts. Our book's title, *CanLit Across Media*, and its subtitle, *Unarchiving the Literary Event*, already foreground this relationship between aesthetic form and material format. An elaboration upon the critical implications of its key terms will help explain the approach we have in mind. These terms resonate relationally in a networked constellation of practice and meaning and need not be considered within a particular hierarchy or order.

For example, one affordance that Levine identifies as being common to all forms is the quality of portability. As abstract, organizing principles and patterns, "they can be picked up and moved to new contexts."[4] The meaning of texts is established through their mobility within specific media formats, through their migration across media formats, and thereby through the order and effects created in relation to other textual forms and media formats. We might think of an excerpt of a poem from a monograph appearing in an anthology, and then that same excerpt now read as a Tweet or heard as an MP3 file on an iPhone as part of a larger thread or playlist. This mobility of texts and media is signalled by the word "across" in our book's title. In the first instance, "across" is a term designating direction and implying an endpoint beyond a span of some indeterminate distance, traversed. In subsequent instances, and meanings, it signifies communication (getting the message across), position (across the river), movement (across the border), contact (across the head), scope (across a range), and distribution (across Canada), among other possible meanings. We acknowledge these many meanings of across as relevant to our purpose, even as we intend to add to them by figuring the movement and distribution of a culturally complex entity (CanLit) in relation to a diverse range of material formats (media). By "across," we are addressing the possibilities that arise, from the 1950s on, for the distribution, transmission, and circulation of literature and the literary across media forms and formats to new regions, new audiences, and new contexts. Thinking of the movement and distribution (the circulation) of literature (an ideological/aesthetic category) across media formats invites a proliferation of critical terms relevant to literary and media studies. Thus, in addition to "across," we think of adaptation, remediation, migration across platforms, convergence, and differentiation, among other concepts. The portability of forms enabling their movement "across" demands a methodological attention to the historical specificity of their actions and interactions. Again, as Levine summarizes this last point: "We can understand forms as abstract and portable organizing principles ... but we also need to attend to the specificity of particular historical situations to understand the range of ways in which forms overlap and collide."[5] Through these overlapping encounters and collisions, CanLit comes to be recognized as an entity that can, in turn, incite the critical descriptions and theories that instantiate its existence.

The archive itself is a mercurial concept that has its own range of affordances for studying, understanding, and articulating CanLit as a recognizable and meaningful entity. The term "archive" stands in for a diverse range of material, formal, and agential organizing forces – libraries and other brick-and-mortar institutions, archival boxes and acid-free file folders, archival information systems, databases, hard drives, online collections, web servers, musty basements, USB keys, social media platforms, shoeboxes, and archival practices – that have all come to signify methods of preserving and organizing historical artifacts for use in the present and in the future. We work at a moment of significant transition in literary studies, a moment when core ideas about what comprises the literary archive – and the literary itself – are in a state of productive expansion and flux. The conception of the archive has broadened beyond traditional models of authorial structure and provenance to be rediscovered as a wide range of actions and entities: as a repertoire of gestures that hold "traumatic flashbacks ... hallucinations" and other "ephemeral and invalid forms of knowledge and evidence,"[6] as "new genres of expression" in which difficult "feelings are deposited" despite the record's inherent ephemerality,[7] as conceptual instantiations of "an entire spectrum of broadly conceived collections."[8] Feminist scholars have played a particularly important role in this recalibration of our understanding of the discernibility of accumulations of artifacts and actions in archival terms. As Kate Eichhorn has argued, an expanded concept of the archive "as something no longer bound by its status as a repository of concrete materials" has proven necessary for "the possibility of fully investigating how feminist archives have taken shape."[9] Some of the reasons for this include the fact that the materials documenting feminist thought and activism were marginalized by institutional authorities, or deemed too difficult and contentious, or, because potential depositors resisted the more traditional archival institution as an archival home. To mention just one example, Linda Morra provides an account of M. NourbeSe Philip's "act of preserving and withholding her papers from an official Canadian and purportedly 'multicultural' institution in order to forge her own archive" and "as a response to unequal power relations."[10] In this scenario, the archive is a site of ideological recognition and authorization that attributes global political power and the potential for widespread global circulation to those whose traces are present within it.[11]

The archive, as Jacques Derrida defines it in one instance, is a place: "[*arkheion*] a house, domicile, an address, the residence of the superior magistrates."[12] An imagined archive of Canadian literature along the lines of this definition would then constitute a house of national memory. No such place exists – no archive holds such an exhaustive history to the extent that Frye's question of "Where is here?" can ever be answered aside from being *in* the texts that are identified as Canadian, *here* in the actions performed upon them.[13] What do exist are archives, plural, that hold, contain, preserve, store, and record the makings of the nation's literature. These "houses" are not neutral since they contain colonial and other ideological histories within their very structures of containment. One important question for archives of Canadian literature – from institutional to personal to various Web-based – is: under whose terms have these archives been made and to what ends? Further, within our present context of networked digital media, the archive has become associated as much with recirculation and consequent reinterpretation as with material location. As Gabriella Giannachi explains, "over the centuries, archives started to be considered not only as locations or objects but, as media, and communications strategies."[14] Archives in this iteration function less as places that determine a singular form of authorized value than as sites for the possible production of multiple and diverse systems of value. They become subject to what Hal Foster has called an "archival impulse" among artists "to make historical information, often lost or displaced, physically present" in ways that run counter to the original terms under which those archival records were initially housed, through acts of resituating, reordering, and re-*presenting* (both displaying anew and making present, again).[15] It is in this iteration of the archive that the acts of archiving and unarchiving can be said to meet in practices that produce and reinterpret the archive, simultaneously.

Unarchiving, as we began to unpack earlier, refers to the revitalizing impact that arises from the migration of archival materials into public contexts. It also refers to the transformation effect of digital technologies and processes on archival artifacts, and, in fact, to any treatment of archival materials that simultaneously unmakes and remakes the archive. Unarchiving stages a resonant confrontation between structures of the past and the present. Consider, for example, Jordan Abel's erasure poetry – a treatment of Marius Barbeau's ethnographic "preservation" of Nisga'a culture – as a work arising from an archival impulse, in this case to decolonize an archive.[16] Decolonizing the archive is central to any act that aims to unarchive materials held in literary *arkheions* of Canada. Abel's title, *The Place of Scraps*, foregrounds the violence of colonial attempts at preservation that cannot be undone. Scraps, in Abel's hands, are formal traces inciting the memory of place and articulating its relation to the present. Reading *The Place of Scraps* as an act of unarchiving and also as a newly produced archive itself allows for an understanding of archive as something other than a house-like structure. Instead, we have something akin to an eventful occupation of, or dwelling in, the here and now. This version of the archive evokes an analogy to digital media storage platforms and invokes critics to engage with the archive as a moving, shifting medium. Rather than a house, the archive becomes the locus of archival events and the source platform from which new events might arise, beyond the archival collection as it is presently organized. The affordances of any given archival organizing platform will have a noticeable impact upon the meaning of the texts it holds, orders, and circulates. The very nature and existence of CanLit – including our perception of its formal and political properties – depends upon such organizing forces. The literary and political authority of Margaret Atwood as discovered within the structural context of the 414 boxes organized in the manuscripts division of the Thomas Fisher Rare Book Library at the University of Toronto signifies quite differently when it is encountered within the API structure and related hardware platforms of Twitter.

To conceptualize the archive as a platform sets the stage for new ways of describing how texts move across media. Here we can visualize movement through space and time not so much as a totalizing operation, but as a hop from one solid tile to another equally solid but of different material. Nick Montfort and Ian Bogost note that "a platform in its purest form is an abstraction, a particular standard or specification before any particular implementation of it." "To be used by people and to take part in our culture directly," they go on to say, "a platform must take material form."[17] Some of the advantages of thinking about archival structures and literary mediation in terms of platforms is the way it renders the migration materials substantive, and, consequently, how it helps us imagine movement across platforms as changing scenarios of material constraint, form, function, potential use (or usability, to use the language of interface design), and as new ways of presencing the past.[18]

Like other platforms that help shape or afford particular manifestations of the activities and texts of CanLit, the archive becomes a venue that imposes organizing principles upon these texts and consequently works to define the status of its many diverse fragments as events of recognizable social and cultural significance. The archive as traditionally conceived, as an organized collection of records, may thus be understood as one venue, among others, for the literary event – the event that represents, enacts, and instantiates "the literary." Such archives store the records, traces, and pieces of the historical events that made literature exist as an affective, cultural, and social phenomenon at a given point in time. Beyond storing such traces, archives instill meaning and status upon the artifacts they hold through events of archival description. We cannot capture a reader's experience of her immersion (or repulsion) in reading a novel or listening to a poem (although some researchers in the field of cognitive poetics have been working toward such a goal[19]) any more than we can fully capture an author's process of literary creation. What we can do is attempt to reconstruct such experiences – let us call them the events of reading and creation – through our analysis of the documentary traces that were implicated in such processes.

Many established archives use the author as its primary category for ordering the materials in a fonds and for evaluating the provenance and relevance of a material trace for inclusion in a collection. If the material trace is deemed relevant according to the arrangement of a collection – if, for example, it contributes to our conceptual structure of an original order that helps us understand its source, the author or "creator" – that trace will be recorded by the archivist and, in attaining an archival record, will be granted status as an artifact.[20] It is in this way that the archive functions as one site among many where the events of literature occur. Catherine Hobbs makes this point in chapter 5 of this book, asserting that "an archival record can itself be understood as an event that enacts its own inscription resulting in an artifact (be that analogue or digital)."[21] She goes on to say that archival records within established memory institutions have their own histories, thus underscoring the implication of the archive and archival actors (the archivists) in our identification of literary artifacts, and in the ongoing historical creation of the literary. As we move in our analysis of the archive from traditional memory institutions to what Abigail De Kosnik has called "rogue archives" created, usually online, by "amateurs, fans, hackers, pirates, and volunteers," the productive, eventful aspect of archival enactment becomes even more evident.[22] De Kosnik uses the concept of repertoire to describe the acts of human performance – the boxing, filing, processing, uploading, coding, and operating – that define archival labour. Within the context of the Internet-based community and fan archives that she studies, the archival dream of perpetuity has been challenged by the digital, and has revealed the practices, the repertoire of actions, of both professional and rogue archivists as an archival entity of historical significance. As she notes, elements of this repertoire may ultimately have greater claims to perpetuity than the cultural artifacts that mobilize them.[23] Such an intriguing observation suggests that we can learn much about cultural preservation by studying not only the materials preserved but also the preservation practices of the individuals committed to such work. Thus, in describing the practices that have kept certain traces of literary events preserved and in play, we are accounting for the repertoire of concepts and labour practices that have worked to produce and gird the meanings of CanLit over time.

Not all materials assume their eventfully enacted status as historical literary artifacts with equal ease or usefulness for the project of telling stories about the literary, or in the particular case of this book, telling stories about CanLit. As many of the chapters in this collection show, the material traces that persist in non-print media forms, and in the formats of temporal media, especially, tend to be more troublesome for the enactment of archival inscriptions, and, in a more basic sense, for accessing and assessing the shape and meaning of the textual content they hold. First of all, looking at a temporal-media artifact in its material form – for example, a reel of magnetic tape – is not always sufficient to know what exactly one is dealing with or has in hand. We must play a temporal-media artifact to begin to know it. Sometimes that first action of knowing is easier said than done. We may not have the right technology to play it back, or we may justifiably fear that to play it would be to destroy it, resulting in the untenable scenario of activating a temporal moment only by creating a singularly ephemeral moment of that historical sounding in the present. More likely, we will digitize it in our process of preservation and, in doing so, will raise an entirely new set of questions about the artifactual status of the audiotext as it migrates across historically situated media formats. And then, even if we are able to play it, the audiotext that emerges through an archivist's careful transduction of that old tape may raise more questions than it answers. Who is speaking? What is he or she or ze saying? What is happening, or, rather, what do these vibrations in the air suggest might have happened? What is the event that has been captured here, and what historical details on which the tape remains silent could help explain the context of its significance as a literary event, as an event of CanLit? Media artifacts evoke basic questions about our objects of analysis, and challenge us to recognize our assumptions about what it means to read and interpret these objects as instantiations of literary culture.

Our collective focus on mediated events as opposed to books represents a self-conscious strategy by which to establish a degree of critical distance from the ideological processes we wish to analyze, and from the media formats most strongly associated with "literature" and "the literary." The literary, in the sense we use it, draws upon Raymond Williams's parsing of this keyword as it developed in use from the late eighteenth century forward, signifying the idea of a *national literature* as evidenced through particular manifestations of learning and skill in letters such as seriousness, creativity, imagination, and other valued aesthetic qualities, with the post-nineteenth-century bias toward its delivery in printed form.[24] Our more comfortable identification of CanLit with print media (books) organized into canons (anthologies and curricula) gives us a false sense of the fixity of CanLit. To jog ourselves out of such a zone of critical comfort, we turn our attention to the material and theoretical messiness of mediated cultural events.

Event is the spectre that haunts the archive we engage with in the hope of finding answers about past aesthetic experience. We can use event for our purposes as the ineffable term in the equation. It is the unreachable element that incites desire and hope in the researcher. It is the thing (*das ding*) that can never be found in the media traces of event we aspire to decipher. As Derrida asks of the event, in this case the simple event of inscribing something with a signature: "Is there such a thing? Does the absolute singularity of signature of event ever occur? Are there signatures?" The signature as event underscores in graphic form the impossibility of a trace to function as a perfect reproduction of "a pure event."[25] The archival artifact is a partial stand-in for the historical event we hope to recover. A focus on the event soon turns our attention toward the social and ideological contexts in which the literary becomes temporarily instantiated, and away from a hermeneutical decipherment of what is behind the words and generic forms of a given text. A focus on the event takes our noses out of the book and sticks them *elsewhere*. That elsewhere may begin with an archival box, but it quickly expands to encompass a much wider range of possible places, situations, and structures. For as we have already said, the archival box filled with the material and media traces (or tagged artifacts, or hashtagged indices) of CanLit events resides within an institutional structure itself, a structure that is inseparable from those that supported the events in the first place. That elsewhere quickly mutates from box to building or material venue to the critical discourses that give them meaning. The complexity (or messiness) of the mediated literary event occurs in its differential status, its partialness, its material dispersion, and its lacunae.

In its attention to the materials that make up this complexity, our book is not a traditional account of Canadian literature pursued through a series of critical readings and interpretations of literary works. Rather, one of the core contributions of this collaborative study lies in its focus on how the literary in Canada has been produced in cultural activities that are now only apparent to us through a diverse range of media in relation to the archival structures and ongoing acts of remediation that continue to shape their meaning. The first term of our book's title, "CanLit," represents a case study for understanding how an ideology of a literature (any literature defined in terms of national or formal differentiation) comes into being through the literary events that produce it. Those literary events could be live readings, broadcasts, or conferences, or they could be textual, such as in the early appearance of CanLit in the title of Earle Birney's 1962 poem "Can. Lit." Birney's punctuated abbreviation evokes the residue of the full words, perhaps as the slightly more elaborated ghosts that haunt our present condensed metadata version of the acronym, #CanLit. In either case, what makes CanLit recognizable as a cultural entity?

In asking this question, we are not seeking to define CanLit as a rigid category but rather to investigate the institutions and mechanisms that allow for CanLit to be discernible in ways that have social and cultural meaning and value. As much as this question could be situated in a longer, historical account of Canadian literature,[26] our focus on CanLit as a recognizable signifier reframes the question of what constitutes it in terms of cultural capital (Bourdieu) and the interpellating force of the nation (Althusser). These terms of analysis, first taken up and applied to readings of Canadian literary culture by Barbara Godard ("Notes from the Cultural Field: Canadian Literature from Identity to Hybridity") and Smaro Kamboureli (*Scandalous Bodies: Diasporic Literature in Canada*), continue to have resonance and use in approaching the problem of CanLit today.[27] This is most recently apparent in the observation made by Hannah McGregor, Julie Rak, and Erin Wunker in the introduction to *Refuse: CanLit in Ruins* that CanLit is not simply an industry or an academic area of study but is "a complex formation that includes both of these [terms] as well as many other, often unnamed, forces and assumptions."[28] We, too, are integrating these concerns of ideological subject formation and the cultural field of production into the critical vocabulary of this introduction by rephrasing the question once again, this time to ask: In what way does CanLit hail its subject?

The subject of CanLit is constituted by and through a variety of agents: the publishing industry, the academy, mass media, reading publics, and writers themselves – all of which wield radically different degrees of power. Nonetheless, what remains a commonality across these agents is that there is something at stake, for all of them, in defining CanLit, in identifying it when it happens, and in being identified with it. What makes the hail of CanLit further complex is the extent to which, as Kamboureli notes, "CanLit is both firmly entangled with this national imaginary and capable of resisting it."[29] Writers such as Tuscarora writer Alicia Elliott have resisted the hail of CanLit, recognizing that to be a writer in Canada so often entails exposure to CanLit's ontological force: "My literature can never and will never be Canadian. It is forever and always Indigenous, and should be considered such."[30] Even in the most divisive debates within CanLit and in the strongest statements of resistance to it, it is clear that what is constituted as CanLit matters – and, in mattering, it matters for how the category itself is legitimatized, or de-legitimized. Kamboureli observes that the process of inclusion into the category of CanLit must be more than merely symbolic: "With what was illegitimate now legitimatized, CanLit may be in a position to applaud itself for the 'progress' it has made, but it also runs the risk of wrestling difference and otherness into a Canadian trope."[31] Moreover, there has been resistance to an integrated idea of CanLit throughout the history of Canadian literature and criticism: "Canadian criticism is filled with those who have resisted the joys of cohesion and who have imagined new futures, different pasts, and disparate social goods."[32] As a result, CanLit is a "troubled and troubling sign," even though, on the surface, the term CanLit sometimes appears deceptively, perhaps even glibly, cohesive.[33]

In the same way that CanLit as a term and as a discipline is not a monolith, its imagined and real publics are diverse – fragmented, polyphonic, or even prismatic, to cite an adjective used by Kate Eichhorn and Heather Milne.[34] Michael Warner, in his parsing of the difference between an idea of "*the* public" as a kind of "social totality" and "*a* public" suggests that "*a* public" does not exist "apart from the rhetoric through which it is imagined."[35] In this sense, a public is socially imagined "as a relation among strangers that is projected from private readings of circulating texts."[36] Erin Wunker and Travis Mason have mobilized Warner's definition in order to ask how poetry occupies public spaces in Canada and, simultaneously, how it is produced by and through its publics. They make a bold leap from the late-Victorian literary column "At the Mermaid Inn" published in *The Globe* (Toronto) to Sina Queyras's literary blog *Lemon Hound* in order to consider what happens when literature is discussed *in* public, whether that be in a newspaper of 1892 or a present day site on the Internet.[37] These two historically distinct examples address very different publics but are connected by their shared use of a discourse of address to construct relations among strangers. In both cases (the) media form publics discursively. As Warner puts it, publics exist "*by virtue of being addressed.*"[38] The mechanisms and trajectories of such modes of address and their implications for the production of discernible cultural fields become increasingly complex in the context of social media platforms such as Facebook and Twitter. Debates about the status of CanLit, its agents, and its subjects on such platforms are simultaneously powerful, immediately tangible, and potentially ephemeral. As McGregor, Rak, and Wunker have begun to analyze, these platforms enable "perspectives and voices that may not have access to mainstream media platforms" to be heard, and provide new means of cultural labour and production beyond normative hierarchies of CanLit industries and institutions, but at the same time, the "ephemeral nature of social media in particular means this kind of labour is easily lost."[39] Their efforts in *Refuse* to "archive a cultural moment" that captures a "rupture event"[40] of CanLit, by republishing texts first disseminated on social media platforms as a printed book, illustrate the significance of media formats for our understanding of how cultural fields are formed, preserved, and recirculated for use by future publics.

Even if productively indiscernible, it is through the plural publics' consumption of media – and, in the case of this book, through Canadian media – that literature becomes more than the literary and transcends the specificity of its reading audience. By media, another of our keywords, we refer to the materials used to store, deliver, transmit, and circulate information. Media can include "the media" but it has a more expansive meaning; thus, in using media as a term we are attempting to avoid what Gitelman describes as a false assumption that media is a singular agentic entity: "The word media is rightly plural, not singular. Media are. A medium is."[41] While other studies have examined early-twentieth-century print media in Canadian literature,[42] this book takes as its starting point a historical moment when media-as-media took hold of Canadian culture. McLuhan's prophetic statement "the medium is the message"[43] reflected and projected the rapid changes that were taking place in Canadian media during the 1950s and 1960s. These changes occurred at the very same time that CanLit was experiencing its boom, which was the result of a convergence of many factors, including post-war affluence, government programs, centennial nationalism, new emphases in educational institutions, and, media.[44]

By the 1960s, a number of crucial institutional changes and developments were in place as a result of the 1949–1951 Royal Commission on National Development in the Arts, Letters, and Sciences, leading to the Massey Report (1951). The Massey Report's assessment of literature in Canada hailed its subject as an imagined future version of a not-yet-present Canadian writer.[45] The writer in Canada is identified in the Massey Report as a subject who lacks the support required for his proper emergence as an integrated cultural presence and force. Hence, the report made recommendations for public funding through the Governor General's awards, what became known as the Canada Council for the Arts (1957), and, among other recommendations, a push for CBC to continue broadcasting literary works on air. It was in this way that the hailing of CanLit as a literature also hailed forth its publics, or at least its imagined publics.

In 1958 McClelland and Stewart began its mass-market paperback New Canadian Library series; in 1959, the first issue of *Canadian Literature* was published through UBC's Department of English and edited by George Woodcock, who announced the journal as "the first review devoted only to the study of Canadian writers and writing."[46] Small presses were publishing Canadian writing (Coach House; Anansi, Contact, Very Stone); little magazines were flourishing across the country;[47] literary programs on CBC Radio were broadcasting Canadian literature across the nation (see Deshaye on the significance of Robert Weaver's "Anthology");[48] and the national framework already present in the making of print anthologies of Canadian literature, as analyzed and historically situated by Robert Lecker and Janet Friskney,[49] took on the additional force of the centennial of 1967, which was channelled into novels such as Atwood's *Surfacing* (1972), poems such as Lee's *Civil Elegies* (1968), and works of criticism such as George Grant's *Lament for a Nation* (1965) and Northrop Frye's "Conclusion" to *The Literary History of Canada* (1965). One example among the many poignantly told stories of CanLit's emergence during this time period is that Mordecai Richler received $2,000 from the Canada Council to write *The Apprenticeship of Duddy Kravitz* and $2,000 from *Maclean's* magazine to publish a long excerpt from the novel. Nick Mount identifies this as an example of how the government supported the work's production, but a popular media form (the magazine) secured its audience. As Mount puts it: "The book sold about two thousand copies in Canada. *Maclean's* brought Richler half a million readers."[50] The concept of literary celebrity in Canada was growing.[51] Canadian writers were in the media – and continue to be today – but what makes this moment in the mid-twentieth century notable was that it coincided with an increasingly self-conscious attention to media-as-media. Thus, amid the so-called Canadian literary boom of the 1960s, important questions remain to be asked about the alignment of this surge in Canadian writing with a heightened interest in the technological possibilities of media.

Did new media broadcast the same voices as had already been captured on the page? In other words, did new media simply replicate the settler-colonial and hetero-patriarchal power structures that largely determined what was published as CanLit? And what do researchers and readers of CanLit do with dissonant examples of both replication and resistance? As Laura Moss observes: "Exclusion and elitism have always been part of CanLit, as has resistance."[52] Ongoing archival studies, for example, are revealing the structures of media and archivization that have recorded or refused voices most often marginalized for reasons such as race, gender, sexuality, class, or mobility. These archival findings have the potential to unsettle the ground/sound of CanLit by further revealing its exclusions and resistances, such as in the cases of, among other projects, Karina Vernon's *The Black Prairie Archives: An Anthology* (2019) and Deanna Reder's SSHRC-funded project "The People and the Text: Indigenous Writing in Northern North America up to 1992." In the classroom, CanLit can look and sound like the reading list that Laura Moss provides in her refusal to give up on CanLit even while recognizing its history of exclusion: "Over the past twenty years in my Can-Lit classes, I have taught writing by Jeannette Armstrong, Julianne Okot Bitek, Dionne Brand, Nicole Brossard, Sara Jeannette Duncan, SKY Lee, P.K. Page, Eden Robinson, Laura Goodman Salverson, Mary Ann Shadd, Carol Shields, and Rita Wong, among many others."[53] This list is one version of CanLit and a significant one in that it demonstrates what is possible in a future that does not regard CanLit as a fixed entity.

If CanLit stands for a prismatic literature, then what role has media played in conflating the literature and cultural industry as one entity and what do media archives reveal about this complex process? Whether in book publishing, radio broadcasts, multimedia art, or poetry readings, the period of the 1960s onward witnessed an explosive simultaneity in the circulation of works of art across media formats. The implications of this for power, technology, and the nation are taken up by Jody Berland who notes that "the idea that new media abolish relations between center and margin was enthusiastically advanced by McLuhan in the 1960s," thereby arguing that "while print and roads centralize, electronic media decentralize."[54] What, then, as we ask in this book, are the implications of this media-generated decentralization for literature? Although the decentralizing impulse does not exist only in the electronic – one might think of the tactile, material object of Roy Kiyooka's *transcanada letters* with a photo assemblage of out-stretched hands from coast to coast on its cover – the electronic brings new possibilities for connection.[55] Moreover, in terms of our book's title, "across" signifies this kind of decentralizing impulse as manifest in the archive.

Archives call attention to the effects of time-based media upon the writing and recording of history and call attention to the archival practices enacting their preservation and consequent structuring. In asking how media have been implicated in the production and dissemination of CanLit such that it became a discernible entity, our book asks how CanLit continues to be produced and disseminated through and across its many archival platforms.[56] The question of what makes these archives recognizable as CanLit is the same question that Kit Dobson and Kamboureli use as a guiding line of inquiry in their interviews with writers in *Producing Canadian Literature*: "What does it take to produce literature in Canada?"[57] In answer to this question, our book argues that the production of literature in Canada is intrinsically tied to its mediated circulation. The making of CanLit happens as events across media. Consequently, CanLit exists less as a collection of defined artifacts than as a series of mediations and recirculations. To acknowledge such a spectral construction of CanLit is perhaps the best way to understand the possibility of a real CanLit, one that is mediated and one that matters.

Our book unfolds through three sections: Part I: Archives of Canadian Cultural Production focuses on major institutions of Canadian cultural heritage and provides critical analysis of their acts of cultural preservation, dissemination, and reconfiguration. Part II: Archival Lacunae and the Mediated Event gathers chapters that consider the challenges and discoveries about culture and methodology arising from the critic's attempt to reconstruct literary and artistic episodes of live action and mediated occasions from the archives. Part III: Archives of the Present considers the changing meaning of the archive in light of recent activities that either integrate archival materials into contemporary experience or frame events, processes, and occasions as archival occurrences. All three sections provide studies that both ground and expand the theoretical terms and concepts we have discussed in this introduction, and provide answers to the questions: What is an archive? What is at stake in unarchiving materials of diverse media formats in new ways, with new media, and within new contexts? And, what are the implications of such questions for our understanding of CanLit as a field of research and study? This book presents a wide range of scholarly inquiries into archiving and unarchiving as literary and critical acts, and opens a new field of inquiry into the significance of CanLit as a critical category within and across its mediating contexts. In this way, *CanLit Across Media*: *Unarchiving the Literary Event* expands the range of methodologies we may deploy in the study and understanding of CanLit as a moving figure within an ever-mediated ground.

The first section considers how our understanding of Canadian cultural heritage has been shaped and, in effect, produced in relation to the complex nature of the archives that preserve it. As repositories for the materials that document activities of some of Canada's most important cultural agents, the nature and contents of institutional archives inform our understanding of how narratives about CanLit and Canadian culture are constructed, and how the identities of such agents have both shaped and been shaped by the archives that preserve them. Linda Morra, through her case study of long-time CBC producer Ira Dilworth's archives, examines the implications of what she identifies as two sets of CBC Radio archives – a traditional material repository and an online digital "archive." Morra shows how this division reflects two sets of demands, two audiences, and conflicting sets of concerns. Morra argues that Dilworth's tendencies in relation to the safeguarding of his papers parallel those of CBC Radio and that these tendencies emphasize education over preservation. These tendencies also reveal an institution's desire to position itself centrally in relation to Canadian culture, and showcase the CBC's drive toward (and its anxiety about) its relevance in relation to the national imaginary.

Proceeding with a similar motivation to conceptualize the archive as an entity that disrupts fixed notions of culture, genre, and identity, Deanna Fong's "Othertalk" approaches the Roy Kiyooka Audio Archive (a collection of 404 audio recordings made between 1963 and 1988, housed in the Simon Fraser University Library Special Collections and Rare Books) as a multi-format, multi-vocal autobiographical record of one of Canada's foremost artistic and literary figures during a burgeoning period of cultural production. The tapes in Kiyooka's archive are presented as "para-literary" in nature: they capture the voices of prominent experimental writers and artists, including Warren Tallman, Gerry Gilbert, Robert Creeley, George Bowering, and Daphne Marlatt, who speak about poetics, composition, craft, and aesthetics. Most of the tapes are recorded conversations. Following a detailed account of the forms and formats of the collection, Fong proceeds to argue that these tapes present an ontologically different record than the material base that Canadian literary history has traditionally drawn from, namely, monographs, little magazines, formal interviews, and readings. The tapes, she argues, document speaking subjects performing themselves for their contemporaries and for futurity, and manifest what Ann Laura Stoler has called the "affective tremors" of the archive. The archive, in this instantiation, offers a mapping of poetic modernism and postmodernism in Canada that resists the retroactive influence of canonicity and the self-consolidating tendencies of emergent poetic movements. This alternative mapping allows us to trace the imprint of the immaterial labour that constitutes communities and collective subjectivities – labour that is rendered invisible (or inaudible) on the printed page.

Katherine McLeod's chapter examines the archives of poet and broadcaster Phyllis Webb as sites of cultural production. Webb's work for CBC spans across radio and television, including her launch of the CBC radio program *Ideas* (1965–present), her role as host of the CBC TV literary program *Extension* (1967), and her various readings as a poet on CBC literary radio programs (*Anthology*; *Critically Speaking*). McLeod argues that the accessibility, arrangement, and (re)articulation of the CBC archives that document Webb's work obfuscates the real impact that Webb had on CBC literary programming. A once-public intellectual is now housed in virtual obscurity despite holding residence in the archives of a public institution. This argument returns us to questions raised by Morra about the impact of differential archival media formats. For both McLeod and Morra, all archival listening becomes a mode of mediated re-listening. Chapters in this first section exemplify the iterative nature of archives held by well-established Canadian cultural and literary institutions and the implicit and productive tensions that arise when an established archive is mobilized toward new purposes and audiences.

Marcelle Kosman's chapter, rather than unarchiving specific texts or materials, undertakes an unarchiving of genre fiction from within the history of publishing in Canada. Her chapter approaches the formation of CanLit as a discernible cultural entity – and even a discernible genre – by tracing the collapse of Canada's pulp periodical industry and suggesting that the reasons for its collapse are more complex than simply the fear of an Americanization of culture. Concluding the section, Catherine Hobbs's "Voices Kept in Context" explores the traditional archival principles of provenance and *respect des fonds* in relation to acts of unpinning materials from the informative structures of their archival arrangement. She argues that the term "literary archives" describes literary provenance, which in turn implies "the literary activities of creating records and literary content." This implies that even the single isolated literary record reveals a range of literary activities within a network of literary actors. Writing from her perspective as literary and senior archivist for Library and Archives Canada, Hobbs weighs the vivifying gains and historical losses that arise with new conceptions of the archive and outlines what is at stake in the explorations of archival practice that follow.

The book's second section explores the possibilities and perils of the critic's attempt to reconstruct the historical and cultural significance of literary and artistic happenings, scenes, and performances. Jason Camlot's chapter tells the story of the Foster Poetry Conference (FPC, 1963) – a Quebec-government-sponsored gathering of English-language poets in the Eastern Townships – from its conception by English Quebec poets John Glassco, Frank Scott, and A.J.M. Smith to publication of the conference proceedings. While providing a historical account of an all-but-forgotten poetry conference within the context of new forms of government funding for poetry events and the history of Quebec politics and society, the account's parallel focus is on the nature and structure of the archival and print materials available for the reconstruction of what actually happened at the FPC. Drawing upon a robust body of correspondence concerned with the organization of the conference and proceedings housed within an individual author's archival collection, the chapter meditates upon the fact that our reception of the events of the FPC is largely dependent upon the shape of the Glassco fonds held at Library and Archives Canada, and on the textual apparatus of the proceedings of the conference that Glassco prepared in the year after the events took place. In the process of considering how our account of such a literary event is shaped by the archival and publication structures that represent its documentation in the present, Camlot also speculates upon the significance of the fact that tape recordings made of a portion of the event are not accessible to the literary historian at the present time. In considering this archival lacuna – the absence of a temporal-media trace of the event he wishes to narrate – he outlines the significance of the inherent deficiency of archival traces in relation to the scholar's desire for wholeness.

With a similar degree of attention to the disjunction between archival artifacts and the nature of the events they partially preserve, the next two chapters pursue different lines of thinking about how archival materials shape our understanding and incite our affective responses to organized episodes of literary activity. Karis Shearer's chapter on the homemade tapes and film footage that document the Vancouver Poetry Conference (VPC) of 1963 explores the aura of nostalgia that has accrued around such documentary media artifacts, and how the piecemeal and mixed nature of the voices and moments documented – the silences, inaudibilities, and erasures that characterize the VPC tapes in particular – contribute to a listener's deep auditory investment in a motive to achieve coherent historical meaning. Shearer teases out the meaning of this gathering's format by parsing the historical and institutional resonances of the generic categories of "conference," "course," "festival," "seminar," and, finally, "event." She reveals how a pervasive critical tendency to highlight the event's radicality has worked to mask its inherent oppressive hierarchies, in particular, erasures that pertain to the gendered structures of the conference.

Felicity Tayler's study of the Véhicule Art Inc. fonds (1970–83) revisits a locus of Montreal art, performance, and literary publication during the period of a single year (1973) and examines the constraints informing the reconstruction of scenes, happenings, and events that are imposed by the limits of the archive itself. Through her interpretive reading of an archive of photographs that emerged from Véhicule at this time, Tayler tests the ways in which still photographic materials may index the production of an active and eventful space by visual artists, publishers, and poets. In effect, her study performs an answer to the question that asks what we can presume to hear of a historical event from a still, graphic image.

By contrast, Joel Deshaye's contribution considers the limitations that arise from audiovisual archives, focusing on the different kinds of information provided by each of the audio and visual streams of a television broadcast. Deshaye presents his experience of working with Irving Layton's televised interviews and performances, held in audiovisual archives at Concordia University, the University of Saskatchewan, and the CBC headquarters in Toronto. Focusing in particular on Layton's unscripted and un-broadcast dialogue that occurred during commercial breaks, Deshaye explores the implications of our archival access to the private signals of a public broadcast, and considers how our experience of the archive and its authorial subject are affected by the nature of the media stream that is available.

Examining another archival lacuna and working in dialogue with this section's opening chapter, Andrea Beverley reads the ways in which the 1983 Women and Words conference has been "textualized" for posterity. With reference to the fonds in the Simon Fraser University Library Special Collections and Rare Books that contains extensive video and audio recordings of Women and Words, Beverley examines the ways in which "archive-making" necessarily involves editorial choices and prioritizations of some voices or issues over others, and, thereby, raises the important question of whether there is a responsible methodological standpoint from which we might discuss unedited recordings of such events of collective aesthetic and political intention.

Further pursuing this concern with the relationship between mediated texts and cultural and political communities, Dean Irvine's chapter on digital repatriation examines a collaboration with the Street family and the Sepass family of the Stó:lõ First Nation in the curation of a digital exhibit of the Sepass poem cycle. By implementing cultural protocols and traditional knowledge licences introduced by the Mukurtu project, the Sepass exhibit strives to create an online environment in which materials may be curated collaboratively by their source communities. Rather than repeat a narrativization of early modernist literary production in Canada as a form of salvage ethnography, Irvine proposes an exhibit that stages the repatriation of the Sepass cycle in relation to the history of its creation, reception, and preservation, and thus provides an important illustration of what is at stake in the digital structuring of Indigenous knowledge and cultural heritage. Unarchiving, as Irvine explores the concept, involves a process of telling stories about how particular Indigenous knowledges "are transmitted across generations, languages, and cultures and about how the histories of print and audio technologies become part of each telling of these stories."

The third and final section of the book explores the temporal permeability of the archive as a living concept used to describe new processual, digital, and performative formations of materials, data, and information as deployed to engage with topics of immediate currency. In a chapter that directly engages with the present and future impact of an archival document, Clint Burnham approaches the Truth and Reconciliation Commission (TRC) testimony as a remediated event. The testimony was captured on videotape, collected in print editions and ebooks that consist of a combination of text and photographs, and subsequently presented in a variety of ways in digital environments. Burnham argues for the value of keeping this politically, legally and ethically complex archive of human experience "live" by continually reactivating it, thus preventing its death as just another static or hidden government report. Burnham proposes that such reactivation is possible by framing the testimony as a form of "orature," and explores the affective and political resonances that traverse the points of a triad of concepts he works to unpack: archive, event, text.

Where Burnham provides a theoretical critique of the multi-format manifestations of oral testimony, the next two chapters in this section take the concept of the archive even further into the "now" by analyzing contemporary productions of Canadian literature and performance within the informing frame of the living archive. Jessi MacEachern's contribution considers the effects of the palinode, a poetic form of retraction, as a literary mode that affords meditation upon the shape and function of the poet's archive within the context of writing and performance. Through her analysis of Canadian poet Lisa Robertson's 2010 collection *R's Boat*, a work constructed from notebooks held in Simon Fraser University Library Special Collections: Contemporary Literature Collection, in relation to Robertson's media-captured readings of distinct iterations of the poems published in this collection, MacEachern develops an account of literary production as a practice of archival repetition and recantation. MacEachern tells the story of a poet "looking to escape the archive" and, in the process, reveals much about the relationship between the affordances of literary forms, archival structures, and media formats.

Next, in a chapter that selects another alternative literary site for its analysis, Karl Jirgens argues that Canadian installation and sound artists Janet Cardiff and George Bures Miller's "walking tours" emerge as hybrid digital expressions that combine performance art, theatre, literary narratives, and installation art, thereby directly engaging audiences in discovering marginalized archival histories. All of Cardiff and Miller's pieces are digitally stored in their own archive and, thus, their site becomes a meta-archive containing histories within histories. This study of archival performance allows Jirgens to develop an extended, critical account of the nature of the historical event within the multiple temporal frameworks activated by the archive and by creative acts of unarchiving, and to mobilize Gilles Deleuze's theory of the fold as a conceptual framework for the analysis of contemporary, multimedia, avant-garde adaptations of archival and documentary materials in new art productions.

Jordan Abel's chapter, "Excerpt from an Audio Recording (from a presentation at the TransCanada conference at the University of Toronto)," gives compelling and moving form to a critical interrogation of what it means to be an intergenerational survivor of residential schools, to be an urban Indigenous person, to be Nisga'a, to be Indigenous, and of what it means to ask such questions. Presented on the page as a time-stamped transcript from an audio recording of a talk delivered at an academic conference, Abel's text is designed to convey the presence of the speaker in a specifically demarcated time and space, speaking about the complexities of describing and capturing the subject positions that inform his identity as he appears before an audience. The combination of personal narrative, self-analysis, visual illustration, and literary and cultural history is delivered in a manner that highlights the layers of mediation that inform the difficulties of an attempt to speak about, and to speak, one's Indigenous identity. The chapter functions as a powerful textual staging, as a mediated event, of the critical subject acting in a social, institutional, and affective context. Techniques of direct address underscore the chapter's focus on relationality and positionality over authenticating concepts of "identity"; photographic illustration is qualified by personal narration to challenge the evidentiary power and provenance of artifactual evidence in matters of Indigenous identity; and time stamps capture the pacing and affectively charged silences that inform acts of speaking the self. Abel conveys the archival event as something ever alive and in motion.

Finally, as a complementary perspective to Catherine Hobbs's chapter, which closed the first section of our book, and as an appropriate closing statement that reinforces the trajectory of the book as a whole, the concluding chapter is Darren Wershler's "The Archive in Motion." He applies Harold Innis's concept of technological "bias" and the theoretical framework of media archaeology to explore the intricate media and format structures that inform the digital archive's handling of temporality. Because digital media capture time in microscopic samples, infinitesimal slices, and then combine them in a manner that is perceived as temporally fluid, an understanding of the primary structures by which digital media organize and reveal time illuminates some foundational questions about the changing nature of the archive, and our experience of historical and archival materials in the present. Thinking through the "bias" (an Innisian version of "affordance") of digital media forms as they relate to the proliferation of online repositories, Wershler offers a series of probe-like meditations that suggest we temper our enthusiasm for the digital as a storage and preservation medium, and understand its greater potential (and bias) for use in processes of the circulation and transformation of our cultural heritage. Stressing the digital repository as an ongoing, active process – an archive in motion – that "requires a steady electrical current in order to hold anything," Wershler underscores the intertwined relationship between media, culture, and archive, and aptly closes our book with the possibility that the growing archive of the present is yet one more media format within which CanLit, and culture in the broadest sense, will continue to be instantiated, transformed, and re-instantiated on a perpetual basis for the foreseeable future.

NOTES

1 Don Norman, *The Design of Everyday Things* (New York: Basic Books, 2013), 11.

2 Ian Hutchby, "Technologies, Texts and Affordances," *Sociology* 35.2 (2001): 448.

3 Caroline Levine, *Forms: Whole, Rhythm, Hierarchy, Network* (Princeton, NJ: Princeton University Press, 2015), 7.

4 Ibid., 7.

5 Ibid., 7–8.

6 Diana Taylor, *The Archive and the Repertoire: Performing Cultural Memory in the Americas* (Durham, NC, and London: Duke University Press, 2003), 193.

7 Ann Cvetkovich, *An Archive of Feelings: Trauma, Sexuality, and Lesbian Public Cultures* (Durham, NC, and London: Duke University Press, 2003), 1, 7.

8 Kate Eichhorn, *The Archival Turn in Feminism: Outrage in Order* (Philadelphia: Temple University Press, 2013), 18.

9 Ibid., 19.

10 Linda M. Morra, *Unarrested Archives: Case Studies in Twentieth-Century Canadian Women's Authorship* (Toronto: University of Toronto Press, 2014), 151

11 Gabriella Giannachi, *Archive Everything: Mapping the Everyday* (Cambridge, MA: MIT Press, 2016), 8.

12 Jacques Derrida, *Archive Fever: A Freudian Impression*, trans. Eric Prenowitz (Chicago: University of Chicago Press, 1996), 2.

13 Northrop Frye, "Conclusion to *Literary History of Canada*," in *Canadian Literature in English: Texts and Contexts*, ed. Laura Moss and Cynthia Sugars (Toronto: Pearson, 2008), 117.

14 Giannachi, *Archive Everything*, 9.

15 Hal Foster, "An Archival Impulse," *October* 110 (Fall 2004): 4.

16 A particularly resonant example of decolonizing the archive takes place in *The*

Place of Scraps when Abel quotes one of Barbeau's many descriptions of totem poles along the Nass River, and on the next page, Abel has removed all English words, leaving only the Nisga'a words and punctuation; then, on the following page, all words are removed, with only the punctuation remembering the sound that was once present. Jordan Abel, *The Place of Scraps* (Vancouver: Talonbooks, 2013), 47–51.

17 Ian Bogost and Nick Montford, *Racing the Beam: The Atari Video Computer System* (Cambridge, MA: MIT Press, 2008).

18 We deploy the term "presencing" here with reference to explorations of the concept that appear in Gabriella Giannachi, Nick Kaye, and Michael Shanks, "Introduction: Archeologies of Presence," in *Archeologies of Presence: Art, Performance and the Persistence of Being*, ed. Giannachi, Kaye, and Shanks (New York: Routledge, 2012), 1–26.

19 See, for example, Arthur M. Jacobs, "Neurocognitive Poetics: Methods and Models for Investigating the Neuronal and Cognitive-affective Bases of Literature Reception," *Frontiers in Human Neurosience* 9 (16 April 2015), http://journal.frontiersin.org/article/10.3389/fnhum.2015.00186/full (accessed 20 February 2019)

20 For a discussion of the historical origins of the archival Principal of Provenance, see Giannachi, *Archive Everything*, 6–9.

21 Catherine Hobbs, "Voices Kept in Context: Underpinning and Not Unpinning the Recordings Found in Literary Archives."

22 Abigail De Kosnik, *Rogue Archives: Digital Cultural Memory and Media Fandom* (Cambridge, MA: MIT Press, 2016), 2.

23 De Kosnik, *Rogue Archives*, 6–7.

24 Raymond Williams, *Keywords: A Vocabulary of Culture and Society* (New York: Oxford University Press, 1983), 183–8.

25 Jacques Derrida, "Signature Event Context," trans. Alan Bass, in *Limited Inc.*, ed. Gerald Graff (Evanston, IL: Northwestern University Press, 1988), 20.

26 Historical accounts of early Canadian literature have been written by critics such as Carl Klink, Desmond Pacey, and, more recently, W.H. New and Carole Gerson.

27 Barbara Godard, "Notes from the Cultural Field: Canadian Literature from Identity to Hybridity," *Essays on Canadian Writing* 72 (Winter 2000): 209–47; Smaro Kamboureli, *Scandalous Bodies: Diasporic Literature in English Canada* (Waterloo: Wilfrid Laurier University Press, 2000).

28 Hannah McGregor, Julie Rak, and Erin Wunker, "Introduction: Living in the Ruins," in *Refuse: CanLit in Ruins*, ed. Hannah McGregor, Julie Rak, and Erin Wunker (Toronto: Book*hug, 2018), 22.

29 Smaro Kamboureli, "Introduction," *Trans.Can.Lit: Resituating the Study of Canadian Literature*, ed. Smaro Kamboureli and Roy Miki (Waterloo, ON: Wilfrid Laurier University Press, 2007), viii.

30 Alicia Elliott, "Canada 150: Resistance, Empowerment, Calls for Change," *This Magazine*, 29 June 2017, https://this.org/2017/06/29/canada-150-resistance-empowerment-calls-for-change/ (accessed 20 February 2019).

31 Kamboureli, "Introduction," *Trans.Can.Lit*, ix. Jeff Derksen articulates a version of this very point while reminding us of the narratives of resistance as possible even within the neo-liberal state: "Canadian literary critics, even as they cast Canadian literature in perpetual crisis, do not unanimously predict the demise of the nation-state and the folding up of the tent of Canadian literature, or the flipping of the CanLit downtown condo to an offshore owner. Rather, there is a strong current in Canadian criticism toward a critique of the state and towards a questioning of the cultural construct of the nation." Jeff Derksen, "National Literatures in the Shadow of Neoliberalism," in *Shifting the Ground in Canadian Literary Studies*, ed. Smaro Kamboureli and Rob Zacharias (Waterloo: Wilfrid Laurier University Press, 2012), 43. What Derksen's perspective suggests is that the persistence of the "Can" in CanLit is not a hail from the state but rather a critique of the state from within a national literature.

32 Laura Moss, "Notes from a CanLit Killjoy," *Canadian Literature* 228–9 (Spring/Summer 2016): 6–17.

33 Kamboureli, "Introduction," *Trans.Can.Lit*, ix.

34 Kate Eichhorn and Heather Milne, ed., *Prismatic Publics: Innovative Women's Poetry and Poetics* (Toronto: Coach House Books, 2009).

35 Michael Warner, "Publics and Counterpublics," *Public Culture* 14.1 (2002): 50.

36 Ibid., 83.

37 Erin Wunker and Travis Mason, "Introduction: Public Poetics," in *Public Poetics: Critical Issues in Canadian Poetry and Poetics*, ed. Bart Vautour, Erin Wunker, Travis V. Mason, and Christl Verduyn (Waterloo: Wilfrid Laurier University Press, 2015), 3.

38 Warner, "Publics and Counterpublics," 50.

39 McGregor, Rak, and Wunker, "Introduction," 34–5.

40 Ibid., 31.

41 Lisa Gitelman, *Always, Already New: New Media and the History of Data* (Cambridge, MA: MIT Press, 2006), 2.

42 Examples of work done on the intersections of early Canadian literature and print media are Carole Gerson's *Canadian Women in Print, 1750–1918* (Waterloo: Wilfrid Laurier University Press, 2010) and the co-edited collection by Jennifer Blair, Daniel Coleman, Kate Higginson, and Lorraine York, *ReCalling Early Canada: Reading the Political in Literary and Cultural Production* (Edmonton: University of Alberta Press, 2005).

43 Marshall McLuhan, *Understanding Media: The Extensions of Man* (Cambridge, MA: MIT Press, 1964), 7.

44 Nick Mount, *Arrival: The Story of CanLit* (Toronto: Anansi, 2017), 3–16.

45 As the passage in question runs: "the Canadian writer suffers from the fact that he is not sufficiently recognized in our national life, that his work is not considered necessary to the life of his country; and it is this isolation which prevents his making his full contribution. It seems therefore to be necessary to find some way of helping our Canadian writers to become an integral part of their environment and, at the same time, to give them a sense of their importance in this environment." *Royal Commission on National Development in the Arts, Letters and Sciences, 1949–1951,* www.collectionscanada.gc.ca/massey/h5-430-e.html (accessed 25 January 2019).

46 George Woodcock, "First Issue of *Canadian Literature,*" *Canadian Literature* 1 (Summer 1959): 3.

47 Ken Norris, *The Little Magazine in Canada, 1925–1980* (Toronto: ECW Press, 1984).

48 Joel Deshaye, "Anthology on the Radio: Robert Weaver and CBC Radio's Anthology," in *Anthologizing Canadian Literature: Theoretical and Cultural Perspectives*, ed. Robert Lecker (Waterloo: Wilfrid Laurier University Press, 2015) 167–81.

49 Robert Lecker, ed., *Anthologizing Canadian Literature: Theoretical and Cultural Perspectives* (Waterloo: Wilfrid Laurier University Press, 2015); Janet Friskney, "Canadian Literary Anthologies through the Lens of Publishing History: A Preliminary Exploration of Historical Trends to 1997," in Lecker, *Anthologizing Canadian Literature,* 183–208.

50 Mount, *Arrival,* 44.

51 Joel Deshaye, *The Metaphor of Celebrity: Canadian Poetry and the Public, 1955–1980* (Toronto: University of Toronto Press, 2013).

52 Laura Moss, "On Not Refusing CanLit," in *Refuse: CanLit in Ruins*, ed.
    Hannah McGregor, Julie Rak, and Erin Wunker (Toronto: Book*hug,
    2018), 147.

53 Ibid.

54 Jody Berland, *North of Empire: Essays on the Cultural Technologies of Space*
    (Durham, NC: Duke University Press, 2009), 91–2.

55 See Berland on the broadcasting of CBC Radio on railway cars travelling across
    Canada. Berland, *North of Empire*, 107.

56 Within the most recent platforms of social media, CanLit lives and develops in
    accordance with what ethnographers and media theorists refer to as "participa-
    tory culture." As Henry Jenkins notes, "there are strong links between interpre-
    tation, production, curation, and circulation as potentially meaningful forms of
    participation" within the structures of such platforms. Henry Jenkins, Miuko
    Ito, and danah boyd, *Participatory Culture in a Networked Era* (Cambridge,
    U.K.: Polity Press, 2016), 2.

57 Kit Dobson and Smaro Kamboureli, *Producing Canadian Literature: Authors
    Speak on the Literary Marketplace* (Waterloo: Wilfrid Laurier University Press,
    2013), 1.

PART ONE

Archives of Canadian Cultural Production

1

CBC Radio's Digital Archives and the Production of Canadian Citizenship and Culture

LINDA MORRA

A common formulation or understanding of archives finds its origins in the work of Jacques Derrida and Michel Foucault, who argue, in complex and divergent ways, that the archive institutionalizes and centralizes power.[1] As I discovered in the course of my research on Ira Dilworth, a producer at CBC Radio from the late 1930s to the late 1950s, while archival collections may institutionalize and centralize power, they are also forged in relation to the audience for whom the archive seemingly performs. The latter tendency thus affects the shape it assumes. In the case of CBC and specifically Dilworth's papers, I discovered, first, that two separate archives have evolved in relation to its distinct audiences, and, second, that they are peculiarly defined by the forms of preservation assumed and the levels of accessibility permitted. One archive implies the institution's centrality to the evolution of Canadian cultural production; its place and stabilizing power in national discourse, especially when historically contextualized in Canada; and seemingly indicates a commitment to the democratization of knowledge and authority. The other reveals the obfuscation related to its decision-making power about programming and, at some levels, gestures toward the institution's economic instability and its anxiety about its role in such cultural production.

But before exploring this assessment further, it is essential to address the figure who was my portal into CBC's archives: Ira Dilworth. Dilworth was an administrator for the Canadian Broadcasting Corporation/Radio Canada

(CBC Radio) between 1938 and 1962. He served first as the regional director in British Columbia in 1938, then as the general manager of the International Service of the CBC in 1947, and finally as the director of program production for Toronto in 1951, before assuming the role of director of all CBC English networks in 1956. In privileging education and culture via the radio airwaves, he was a key contributor to the shaping of Canadian nationalism in the mid-twentieth century – and yet little scholarly work exists about his substantial influence. When it came to researching his life and career, especially concerning his contributions to Canadian literary culture and as a major player for CBC Radio, I expected to find preserved an extensive and centralized collection of records by him and about his decisions related to programming for CBC Radio, and to read through work-related correspondence that showcased the logic that underwrote these decisions. Instead, records were scattered thinly across several institutions in which CBC archival records are preserved, including Library and Archives Canada in Ottawa, and the CBC holdings in Toronto and Vancouver. Neither he nor CBC Radio have generated a coherent, centralized archive that tracks decisions about broadcasting activities and operations through an accumulation of historical records.

I also consulted CBC Digital Archives, which is located online via a link from the main CBC website. I was struck by this designation, which shapes expectations about the type and range of records that might be offered and yet also begs the question of what a "digital archive" is and what services it performs. During that preliminary search, I observed that CBC Digital Archives appears as a centralized, online repository as distinct from CBC Radio's dispersed physical repositories, which hold audio recordings that form part of CBC Radio broadcasting history but are located in various sites across the country, including Vancouver, Toronto, Montreal, and Ottawa. However, CBC Digital Archives offers no finding aids that allow researchers to gain an overview of the extent or range of its holdings.

The format of the online CBC Digital Archives does give the impression of its wealth of archival material, which focuses on audio copies of the programs themselves. Two years ago, the first page of its website boasted the availability of "hundreds of radio and television clips from the archives of the Canadian Broadcasting Corporation" that are related to the nation's history.[2] Since then, at one point, it showcased "Recommended" pages and, on the right-hand side of the screen, "On this day" – a link to a Canadian historical event that occurred on the same month and day, albeit several years, if not decades, prior. An earlier incarnation of the site included three icons at the bottom of the screen: the first, titled "CBC Programs," linked to the featured program of the day – on the day I visited the site: the National Farm Radio Forum, which aired from 1941 to 1965; the second, titled "Great Interviews," linked to a featured interview; and the third, titled "Guess Who," showcased figures that CBC deemed significant to Canadian socio-cultural and political history.[3]

In both former and recent incarnations, what appears on this site that proclaims itself to be the "CBC Digital Archives" is neither a comprehensive and searchable digital holding, nor a link to a coherent catalogue of its available archival records. Rather, it is an online facility for accessing a selection of programs relating to what CBC views as major Canadian historical events, dates, and literary and political figures, which it then presents to the general public as a popular online resource rather than as a comprehensive guide to its organizational or broadcast history. Further exploration on the CBC Digital Archives home page[4] at one time provided links that led scholars to information about the CBC Broadcast Centre,[5] which housed audio material extending back to Canada's Diamond Jubilee Broadcast on 1 July 1927, and to its collecting mandate to "acquire approximately 135 hours of new programming" every week.[6] These pages have since changed, such that the CBC Broadcast Centre, which I at one time thought might lead to information about past radio programs, is no longer visible on the site, and the "About Us" page simply highlights the fact that "the CBC Archives team has been a unique collaboration of creative teams in Toronto working together with archivists and educational writers across Canada."[7] In both versions of the website that I visited, I could find no further details about operational records surrounding this programming, such as who made decisions about events, persons, and programs that were aired, for example, during the 1930s, 1940s, and 1950s. Certainly, I found little at all about Dilworth.

By these initial observations, I realized that there are two distinct types of CBC archives, each of which confirms the CBC's historical agenda and mandate related to the education and production of Canadian citizens, even as each archive reveals inconsistent record-keeping practices. The first consists of more traditional holdings that contain broadcast recordings and other operational records, which are housed within official CBC Radio buildings in various Canadian cities and within other institutions across the country, and which are of significant interest to researchers. The second is an online, digital archive that showcases how CBC Radio is invested in appealing to and educating the masses, a generalized audience rather than a scholarly one. Even as CBC Digital Archives has greater reach and popularizes key historical events and persons, it reinscribes its role in the service of the education and production of national citizens.

However, the radio broadcaster's latent anxiety about its place in the national fabric is revealed by the fact that, while it offers past recordings about national occurrences or persons, it does not render more transparent its *role* in documenting such occurrences and persons and showcasing the management of its broadcasts. In other words, the technicians of Canadian identity and their decisions about content have been rendered invisible, perhaps because there was a lack of consciousness about or appreciation for the value of these decisions. By comparison with the BBC digital archives, for example, the CBC emphasizes major historical Canadian events it reported on, rather than, as in the case of the BBC, examining "how attitudes and broadcasting have changed" over the years.[8] BBC explicitly arranges some of its website material, for example, in relation to programs offered throughout the decades, such that one can see what topics were discussed (and regarded as priority) during such programs and how these priorities have shifted over time. In part, of course, CBC's dispersed and uneven archive is also related to the marginal positioning of its archival material in state-driven institutions, such as Library and Archives Canada (LAC), and the neglect and erosion of specialized folios, of which CBC is one; that position is complicated by its status as a Crown corporation rather than as a clearly defined, state-funded institution. This problem is further exacerbated by the fact that the acquisitions backlog for the CBC is immense.[9] Still, the development of CBC Digital Archives in isolation confirms the broadcaster's renowned urge to locate itself centrally in relation to the production of Canadian culture, offers a way of restaging its political and cultural significance, and addresses its potential loss of cultural capital in the context of federal cuts to the national broadcaster, and therefore to its more traditional archival repositories, under the Harper government.[10]

To consider further its two forms of archives, I returned to definitions of what constitutes archives and what services they perform. The Archives Library Information Center (ALIC) in the United States asserts that archives may be defined as the "noncurrent records of an organization or institution preserved because of their continuing value"; as the institution "responsible for selecting, preserving, and making available records determined to have permanent or continuing value"; or as the actual "building in which an archival institution is located."[11] CBC's archives, both its digital and non-digital holdings, conform to the first part of the definition provided by the ALIC. These records clearly have a value related to Canadian socio-political culture and to the institution's place in that culture. Other parts of the ALIC's definition are also applicable, including the fact that archives traditionally involve "institutions responsible for the long-term care of the historical records of the organization or institution of which they are a part."[12] CBC Digital Archives is presumably an investment in such "long-term care" of its broadcasts: its online presence advances the values that the institution espouses, those related to national culture and to the education of its citizens.

Significantly, the ALIC also asserts that, "archives acquire historical material through the action of law or through internal institutional regulation or policy."[13] Neither of these applies to the CBC, but rather to those institutions that have participated in acquiring papers *from* the CBC, including LAC. Also, archives usually house an organization's records, which "typically might include copies of letters, memoranda, accounts, reports, photographs, and other materials produced by the organization as well as incoming letters, reports received, memoranda from other offices, and other documents maintained in the organization's files."[14] Even though several sound broadcasts of Dilworth's have been preserved in the archives of CBC Radio in Vancouver and in LAC in Ottawa, exceedingly few letters and other documents from or to Dilworth have been preserved – and none by his own determination, with the exception of correspondence that pertains to writer and artist Emily Carr. This tension between the disparate nature of Dilworth's papers and CBC's pedagogical/nation-building agenda flags the importance attributed to the cultural content that was featured over the airwaves but not to the decisions rendered about that content. In part, this dearth of materials at the Vancouver branch may be related to its peripheral status on the West Coast. Thus, the records that have survived are usually the result of an individual CBC employee's actions, such as those of journalist Elspeth Chisholm. On her own initiative rather than as part of an institutional mandate, she preserved copies of all her institutional records for posterity.[15]

In one of my exchanges with an employee of CBC Radio concerning operational documents related to Dilworth, I discovered that there is no explicit policy or institutional regulation that governs archival practices within CBC, nor has there ever been one. Colin Preston, former library coordinator at CBC Vancouver Media Archives, explained that there was an unofficial, tacitly understood practice of keeping broadcasts related to CBC Radio. In March 2013, after my research trip there, he explained by e-mail that there was considerable "practice, staff and resources directed to the archiving and preservation of CBC and Radio-Canada-produced material." However, he added, "there is not and never has been a policy to that effect."[16] He further indicated that the lack of policy regarding preservation of documents related to its broadcasting operations was probably connected to the fact that CBC and Radio-Canada had been "tasked with producing material," not preserving it; therefore, management had not been preoccupied with either understanding or communicating the "value of their collection and staff to ongoing CBC production."[17]

Despite the challenges of locating suitable records related to the broadcasting operations of CBC Radio, navigating CBC Digital Archives, and gaining a more accurate understanding of what its holdings might contain, I recognized that in comparing these two forms – the analog and the digital – CBC's emphasis on the performative value of education remained consistent. Unlike one of its counterparts, the National Film Board of Canada, for which collection management activities form "a core component of its program activity architecture," CBC Radio consistently privileged its production and broadcasting over the systematic preservation of documentation about those activities.[18] On the one hand, its limited preservation practices mean that the accessibility and availability of records render it more challenging for researchers to understand the inner workings of the institution in the modern period. On the other hand, that same difficulty can be thought indicative of the extent to which CBC Radio has steadily highlighted its educational role within a national and socio-cultural context. This practice is an implicit comment on its perceived values, which elevate audio programming over broadcasting practices: that is, the administrators of CBC Radio likely perceived the *content* or subject of its broadcasts as "high culture," as valuable, and as worthy of preservation, which is why they chose to focus the program on the said subject, but not on its own activities related to the medium of radio broadcasting itself. This practice is an implicit comment on its perceived values, which elevate audio programming over broadcasting practices: that is, the administrators of CBC Radio likely perceived the *content* or subject of its broadcasts as "high culture" (which is why the said subjects were chosen for programs) and therefore valuable and worthy of preservation but not so its own activities related to the medium of radio broadcasting itself.[19]

Thus, both CBC Digital Archives and the historical mandate of CBC Radio, as Preston suggests, coalesce to reflect an agenda that paralleled Dilworth's own in the modern period and thereafter: both are invested in civic education and culture, in the performance and production of the broadcasts themselves. By performance and production, I refer to the radio broadcasts that were planned as part of CBC Radio's mandate to instruct Canadian citizens by disseminating various forms of high culture and programs of educational material. Indeed, the online Digital Archives underscores the fact that CBC Radio continues to see its role as preoccupied with the formation of Canadian citizenship and culture grounded in immediacy, rather than with the preservation of the evidence of its role as an educational force for Canadian citizenship and culture over time.

This interest in Canadian citizenship and culture and CBC's urge to locate itself centrally in relation to this agenda evidently undergirded the inception of radio in Canada. As several scholars have noted, national broadcast radio was produced in response to a keen desire for cultivation of national unity and national identity, especially in relation to the threat of Americanization.[20] Prior to the 1920s, Canadian broadcasting had been regulated for "technical, not cultural, reasons." By the late 1920s, however, a "combination of regulatory and economic difficulties" and the "perceived cultural threat from the United States" prompted the government to set up a royal commission on radio broadcasting in Canada and eventually to "foster the development of national broadcasting."[21] The public radio system grew out of the implementation of the recommendations of the 1928 Aird Commission, "appointed by Prime Minister Mackenzie King to advise the government on broadcasting policy."[22] By 1929, as Sheila Latham notes, the Royal Commission on Radio Broadcasting was established and recognized the civic role of that new medium as "a great force in fostering a national spirit and national citizenship."[23] The Commission recommended that broadcasting "be placed on a public-service basis" and "its status and duties ... correspond to those of a public utility."[24] By 1932, under the term of Prime Minister R.B. Bennett, the Canadian Radio Broadcasting Commission was founded, and by 1936, under the direction of the Liberals, the Canadian Broadcasting Corporation was launched. From the outset, Canada's cultural elite perceived radio as central to Canadian democracy because of its potential to offer "unparalleled means for widespread education, information dissemination, and cultural edification."[25] It was believed that radio programming could be developed that would have greater reach in terms of educating its citizens and, therefore, would contribute to and "improve public taste over the long term."[26] Prime Minister Bennett particularly believed that a "public broadcasting company ... could be the longed-for twentieth-century equivalent to the CPR [Canadian Pacific Railway], utilizing the latest communications technology to unite and bind the nation."[27] In moving for the appointment of a Committee of the House to address the issue of public broadcasting, he argued that "properly employed, radio can be a most effective instrument in nation-building, with an educational value difficult to estimate."[28]

In *Radio, Morality and Culture: Britain, Canada, and the United States, 1919–1945*, Robert S. Fortner observes that radio broadcasting was effective in its contribution to nation-building, because it "took 'intelligence' more widely into remote areas and constructed larger and more inclusive audiences."[29] On the one hand, such inclusion was seen in positive terms because radio "increased the potential both for cultural enlightenment and political participation";[30] on the other hand, it was seen as a "class leveler" in its democratization of cultural life, which was also seen to have "moral consequences."[31] Since national culture was regarded as the purview of the elite, radio was seen as a potential threat to those who had an exclusive hold over what constituted high culture. As a result, the means, content, and ends of radio communication became hotly contested. At that same time as questions were raised related to who was to safeguard the moral and aesthetic values of the period (the elite or the masses), questions were raised related to political and economic interests, and the control and operation of radio stations.

As a primarily state-funded institution, radio in Canada had a definite role in and influence upon stimulating "the ideals, myths, and history that Canadians saw as distinctive in their own experience," and also fostering Canadian print culture.[32] Latham argues that the "CBC encouraged the production of original texts by Canadian writers, developed an audience for programs featuring books and authors, transmitted unpublished and published texts over radio airwaves, published some texts under its own imprints or in collaboration with independent publishers, and celebrated original literature with awards."[33] That attitude has been consistently entrenched in the legal system over the decades. The Broadcasting Act of 1991, for example, "stipulates that Canadian broadcasting is a public service, comprised of public, private, and community elements," that it must "contribute to shared national consciousness and identity," and that broadcasters must air programming that reflects "Canadian attitudes, opinions, ideas, values and artistic creativity."[34]

However, the mandate that governed programming and production did not necessarily extend to long-term preservation of documentation related to the corporation's broadcasting history. The value (or lack thereof) that CBC Radio itself places on that documentation is made clear in its budgetary response to the constant threat from changing governmental policies and declining financial support.[35] "Weakened by years of budget cutting," the CBC has "continued its downward spiral," notes David Taras; it was particularly evident in 2000 when the corporation "imposed further budget cuts and underwent yet another of a long series of 'transformation' and 're-engineering' exercises."[36] That same year, its president, Robert Rabinovitch, asserted before the Standing Committee on Canadian Heritage that the broadcaster would be obliged to address its structural problems – or face bankruptcy.[37] Marc Raboy and Taras observe that such cuts have amounted to $400 million "over the last decade."[38] They argue that "public broadcasters are still essential instruments of identity and statehood," and that the "financial, regulatory, and political pressures have wounded the public broadcaster to the point where its future is in jeopardy"; even as "public broadcasting has re-emerged as a vital tool for national and democratic expression, the CBC dangles close to the edge of extinction."[39] In view of those cutbacks, developing its archives, digital or otherwise, becomes additionally challenging. Although a more recent, keener interest in generating archives in federal institutions and a clearer recognition of their importance to Canadian cultural history has developed – a distinct change from attitudes in the modern era in Canada – the resources to do so have become scant. As federal funding cuts to CBC increase, the investment in preservation of records related to its operations and even to preserving its programs may become precarious, because such preservation is a costly endeavour.[40]

That threat to CBC's identity and role is complicated by the fact that, historically, broadcasters themselves "rarely saved their programs, especially their everyday 'typical' programs."[41] My research on Dilworth confirms this practice. Even as he steadfastly believed in the CBC's role in the production of Canadian citizens, Dilworth himself saved neither audio programs nor his own institutional records. His practice suggests the lack of value he attributed to his own papers, a gesture that was reiterated within the institution itself. He did, however, retain his personal correspondence with writer and artist Emily Carr: close to 300 of her letters written between 1939 and 1945 survive and have been preserved as part of the Emily Carr fonds at the British Columbia Archives and Records Service in Victoria, British Columbia. Significantly, that correspondence was not preserved as part of a CBC archive, even though CBC Radio is frequently a subject of discussion between the two and Dilworth's letters were often typed by CBC support staff and written on CBC letterhead. Moreover, the Dilworth/Carr correspondence took place during the period when he worked as the manager for the British Columbia branch of CBC radio. The diligence Dilworth showed in preserving that correspondence when he discarded so many other records related to his place of employment makes plain that in general he valued artists more, and specifically regarded Carr as an important Canadian cultural figure, than those letters that would have documented his decisions related to his work at CBC Radio. He may have also preserved these letters because they were written to him personally rather than as a representative of CBC Radio. Their exchanges, as often as three times a week with increased frequency in the last two years of Carr's life, reveal a great deal about Dilworth's commitment to CBC Radio and its role in constructing a national imaginary, but not to preserving his own investment in the institution.

As his surviving letters to Carr show, Dilworth attempted to promote the work of those he conceived of as important cultural figures. He cultivated relationships with those writers and artists who he believed would contribute to a national aesthetic or were worthy of a national audience, and integrated them into CBC Radio programming. His instincts as a teacher were deployed in this setting as he adopted similar methods to instruct and develop a national audience via the airways. From reading the literary works of those such as writer and artist Carr and poet and bureaucrat Duncan Campbell Scott in public broadcasts to interviewing artists (and so increasing their cultural capital) to inviting them to speak directly to the public, Dilworth carefully gathered a body of writers and artists he believed to be worthy of national attention.

His significant role in the development of programs for broadcast is also made plain in his correspondence with Carr. Letters show that his interactions with other writers, artists, and musicians were more formally arranged at CBC Radio in at least two specific programs he developed: the weekly *Our*

Canada: The Arts Grows Up and *Sanctuary*. For the former, which aired on 3 January 1943, Dilworth contacted poet Dorothy Livesay to ask if she would participate with "a number of people outstanding in literature and painting and music" already scheduled to speak. Apparently, Livesay agreed, as did member of the Group of Seven Lawren Harris and Duncan Campbell Scott. Dilworth spoke on Carr's behalf. The latter program "was aired on Sunday evenings, during which time Dilworth would read selections of poetry. The poems were to provide a psychological retreat or "sanctuary" from "the turmoil of everyday life."[42] His selection is evidenced in Carr's own "sanctuary": this cloth-bound notebook, preserved in the Emily Carr fonds at the British Columbia Archives and Records Service, is where she collected the poetry that Dilworth read over the air and that he sent to her. It is the sole surviving document about this interaction related to this specific literary broadcast, aside from references to this program that they made in their letters. Dilworth apparently read poems by "literary greats," such as William Shakespeare, Robert Herrick, John Keats, George Meredith, Robert Browning, Walt Whitman, and others – perhaps modelled after T.S. Eliot's own literary broadcasts related to Tudor prose made for the BBC, which extended over thirty-five years.[43] Selections of the poems Dilworth chose were also later included in his publication *An Anthology of Twentieth Century Verse*, which Oxford University Press published in 1945 and which was presumably for general circulation. The two radio programs showcase the dual impulses that informed Dilworth's decision-making: on the one hand, showing support for the arts in Canada and the development of a national aesthetic, and, on the other hand, maintaining proper reverence for the international literary tradition out of which he believed Canadian art and literature grew and to which he believed it must necessarily respond.

According to P.W. Luce, Dilworth had "a sublime faith in the future" of CBC Radio, and "an assurance that it would prove a tremendous power in the diffusion of education and culture."[44] He also clearly saw himself as pivotal to the creation and dissemination of a particular idea of Canadian culture when he began to work at the CBC. For this reason, among others, he must have been considered an appropriate candidate for general supervisor of the International Service, the "department which, [first had] the responsibility of interpreting the Dominion to foreign countries and which, [second,] serve[d] as a constant link of communication with the rest of the British Empire."[45] In this capacity, he developed one talk that has survived, titled "Radio and World Affairs," which he gave on 18 October1946 and during which he addressed the new program *The Voice of Canada*. Although he suggested it was small in scope compared "with BBC's Overseas Service" and the "Voice of America," he suggested that its importance resided in a primary mandate that extended beyond national cultural education "to project the life and culture of the people of Canada overseas in a friendly, honest, true, interesting fashion. It makes no attempt to say that ours is the only way of life or necessarily the best way. It is just a way of life that we have developed and have found good for ourselves and that we should like to invite others to understand and, if they will, share." Dilworth's remarks reveal that he felt Canada did not need to make an apology for its status or achievements, and that he endorsed a "way of life" that was distinct from other national cultures.[46]

Dilworth thus offers a specific example of what is a general practice, both historically in relation to the institutional mandate and in relation to CBC Radio's archives. As Austin Weir notes about Dilworth, "no one else … quite so accurately mirrored the conscience of the CBC."[47] Dilworth was instrumental at seeing the pedagogic possibilities of radio and endeavouring to forge a national heritage through a relatively new public medium that was in its crucial formative years. Poet Anne Marriott would later claim that Dilworth was responsible for inspiring her own poetic endeavours: his reading of T.S. Eliot's *The Waste Land* "turned her interest toward modern poetry."[48] By 1948, Dilworth was seen as having done so much for both "the province and the country at large, as teacher and scholar, as protagonist and promoter of the arts and education, in the classroom, on the public platform, and in his direction of an important part of [the Canadian] broadcasting system" that he was awarded an honorary Doctor of Laws by the University of British Columbia.[49] During his address to convocation, Dilworth made two points that were also pivotal to his role at CBC Radio. He highlighted the humanities' "vital relation to life" and addressed the dangers of "specialization" if one did not pay heed to what he considered a fuller picture: "We have allowed – and many educators must here take their full share of responsibility – we have allowed fragmentation and specialization to run rampant among us with the result that much of our work has been carried on without a clear conception of purpose."[50] These moments render clear that he was committed to educating the nation about its cultural life during his tenure with CBC Radio.

These conclusions about CBC Radio and Dilworth's tendencies to privilege education over preservation became immediately clear while conducting research related to Dilworth and his engagement with major Canadian literary figures represented over the airwaves in the modern period, and ultimately explain the need for the creation of two kinds of archives. Dilworth's individual tendencies are consonant with the institution's focus on education and citizenship, on production and dissemination rather than preservation of operational materials within the institution, even as there is a tension between his own archive as a broadcaster and the papers that were preserved. CBC's online Digital Archives reiterate and extend this tendency, as they also challenge traditional or methodical safekeeping of materials and suggest that two forms of archives may coexist. CBC Digital Archives showcases its ongoing preoccupation with the promulgation of Canadian cultural education and with situating the institution of CBC as integral to that culture and appeal to a broader, popular audience. Despite seeming to create a coherent storehouse, CBC Digital Archives presents a narrative of Canadian history through the records of its programming rather than a reflection of the CBC's broadcast or operational history.

However, a truly effective digital archive for scholars might work by linking to and representing broadcast records that are currently preserved in various locations across the country – in archives at universities, in federal institutions, and elsewhere. Such an archive might centralize power, in ways that Derrida and Foucault critique, as it would allow for a more comprehensive or global understanding of how the CBC functioned at mid-century and perhaps how its agenda was being shaped and produced. Digital mediations and representations might enhance the coordination and understanding of formulations of national identity, even as such digital access would likely carry significance well beyond national boundaries. Even so, digitization, which lends itself to the perception of longevity, is subject to obsolescence. Traditional rather than digital archives have been regarded as more unstable and subject to forms of governmentality; however, as Tara McPherson notes, digital archives equally shape what "can be seen or enunciated" and "become more explicit, revealing and disrupting, not exhaustive classification, but instead, the relentless processing of an informatic age."[51] Thus, what becomes digitized will have a bearing on, and will ultimately shape and control, manifestations and interpretations of national identity.

Still, in researching about Dilworth and his own archival legacy, it would have been useful to have a comprehensive understanding of where his papers related to his decisions for the programming of CBC Radio might be found. As it is, surviving archival materials about Dilworth that appear in the more traditional archives of CBC Radio are either focused on the audio programs themselves or reveal an irregularly developed cache of operational documents, such as institutional letters or transcripts of radio broadcasts saved by former employees rather than the CBC itself (thereby highlighting the fragility of CBC Radio's own historical records). Such irregular preservation speaks not only to anxiety about its role in cultural production but also perhaps to a lack of understanding that certain imperatives and tacit assumptions shaped such production, as the preservation of operational papers would have revealed. Inconsistent safeguarding of archival records also suggests how cultural content was seen to be of far greater importance than broadcasting practices – that the former offered real educational advantages that the latter did not. The audio programs that form part of the online Digital Archives are no doubt an excellent resource – but they are only a partial archive that elides those who made the decisions and how decisions were made about what constituted material worthy of CBC Radio's educational mandate. Researchers, therefore, must face the challenges of having to use CBC Digital Archives by additionally calling upon the records related to broadcasting operations dispersed in various other institutions in order to reconstruct the dynamics related to CBC Radio's broadcasting history. This dispersal is a reminder that archives are not necessarily centralized forms of power, as Derrida or Foucault might suggest, but rather a register of the struggles for and about cultural identity and significance.

Acknowledgments

I acknowledge Katherine McLeod, with whom I co-presented an early version of this paper at the Archives Futures Research Network workshop in Montreal (21 June 2013); her part of the paper focused on CBC producer Robert Weaver. I also acknowledge the contributions of L-G Harvey, who critiqued an early version of this paper, and Jason Camlot and Katherine McLeod, who hosted the Can Lit Across Media Conference (Concordia University, 5–6 June 2015), at which I gave a more expanded version of that initial conference paper.

NOTES

1   See Jacques Derrida, *Archive Fever: A Freudian Impression*, trans. Eric Prenowitz (Chicago: University of Chicago Press, 1995) and Michel Foucault, *The Archaeology of Knowledge & The Discourse on Language*, trans. A.M. Sheridan Smith (New York: Pantheon, 1972).

2   CBC Digital Archives, www.cbc.ca/archives/ (accessed 1 June 2014, 6 June 2016).

3   Ibid.

4   Ibid.

5   CBC Digital Archives, www.cbc.ca/beta/arts/archives/welcome-to-the-canadian-broadcasting-centre-1.3292598 (accessed 1 and 6 June 2014, June 2016).

6   "CBC Digital Archives: About Us," www.cbc.ca/archives/about/ (accessed 26 July 2014, June 2016).

7   Ibid.

8   BBC Archive, www.bbc.co.uk/archive/ (accessed 26 July 2014).

9   I am grateful to Catherine Hobbs for making these observations about the erosion of specialized folios and the acquisitions backlog at the CanLit Across Media Conference (Concordia University, 5–6 June 2015).

10 This situation may change, of course, in view of the fact that the Liberal party under the leadership of Justin Trudeau has replaced the Conservative party, headed by Harper.

11 Maygene F. Daniels, "Archives and Records Management Resources," *Archives Library Information Centre*, National Archives, 1984, https://www.archives.gov/research/alic/reference/archives-resources/terminology.html (accessed 20 February 2019).

12 Ibid.

13 Ibid.

14 Ibid.

15 "Programming: Talks and Public Affairs Broadcasts. Program Speakers and Topics: Elspeth Chisolm," 1945–1960. File 11-18-11-28. Collections Canada, Library and Archives Canada.

16 Colin Preston to Linda Morra, e-mail, Untitled Subject, 12 March 2013.

17 As Preston noted, analog radio forms and technologies presented distinctive problems to a researcher not only because of the form itself but also because this form and its associated technologies have been increasingly mediated by and "situated alongside and within digital forms, in complex and intertwined

arrangements." He noted that it was "important to remember how cumbersome [and] complicated the analog material was. Early Radio 'artifacts' were fragile [and] unwieldy," which further complicated the preservation process (Colin Preston to Linda Morra). As I was to discover when I arrived, the erratic patterns of preservation and the unstable nature of the preserved materials greatly impeded the process of research: in the depths of this archive, I was presented with some vinyl records that preserved some of the internal broadcasts made, some of which had been apparently found and preserved in the basements of former employees of CBC. I was able to listen to three recordings that had aired in the 1930s and that were listed in a database to which Preston had access and which he kindly searched on my behalf.

18 *Evaluation of the NFB's Collection Management* (National Film Board of Canada: October 2013), 3, http://onf-nfb.gc.ca/wp-content/uploads/2013/10/Oct.-2013_Final-Evaluation-of-NFBs-Collection-Management-ENG.pdf (accessed 25 February 2019).

19 This practice may also suggest that the relatively late development of the civil service in Canada may have contributed to the lack of a coherent archival preservation policy.

20 Mary Vipond, *The Mass Media in Canada*, 3rd ed. (Toronto: James Lorimer & Company Ltd, 2000).

21 Ibid., 26. See also Mary Vipond, "Whence and Whither: The Historiography of Canadian Broadcasting," in *Communicating in Canada's Past: Essays in Media History*, ed. Gene Allen and Daniel J. Robinson (Toronto: University of Toronto Press, 2009), 234, and Vipond's *Listening In: The First Decade of Canadian Broadcasting, 1922–1932* (Montreal and Kingston: McGill-Queen's University Press, 1992), in which she describes how the CBC was to become "a major cultural force" that emerged from a network of private broadcasting. Further, see also Frank W. Peers, *The Politics of Canadian Broadcasting, 1920–1951* (Toronto: University of Toronto Press, 1969).

22 Paul Litt, *The Muses, the Masses, and the Massey Commission* (Toronto: University of Toronto Press, 1992), 124.

23 Sheila Latham, "CBC Radio and Anglophone Authors," in *History of the Book in Canada*, vol. III: 1918–1980, ed. Carole Gerson and Jacques Michon (Toronto: University of Toronto Press, 2007), 154–5. According to Robert Fortner, such discourse emerges directly from the Aird Commission, which reported to Parliament in 1929; its members had been "impressed by the work of the British Broadcasting Corporation (BBC) and wanted to achieve the same

level of cultural achievement for Canada." The Commission also believed that the radio might be regarded as a vehicle for the "creation and maintenance of a Canadian identity separate from the American." Robert S. Fortner, *Radio, Morality, and Culture: Britain, Canada, and the United States, 1919–1945* (Southern Illinois: Southern Illinois University Press, 2005), 136. Also of key importance to the emergence of such discourse was the Canadian Radio League: "Its interests in radio were purely to assure that Canadian airwaves would belong to Canadians, and that the Canadian people would be able to use this new medium to build a strong national identity – capable of standing up to the Americans to their south. One of the three principals of the league, Graham Spry, eventually became known as the "Father of the CBC." Fortner, *Radio, Morality and Culture*, 134.

24 E. Austin Weir, *The Struggle for National Broadcasting in Canada* (Toronto: McClelland and Stewart, 1991), 110.

25 Litt, *Muses*, 123.

26 Ibid., 131.

27 Vipond, *Mass Media*, 41.

28 Weir, *Struggle for National Broadcasting*, 110.

29 Fortner, *Radio Morality*, 2.

30 Ibid.

31 Ibid., 6.

32 Ibid., 13. By comparison, radio was more "stodgy" and played a less significant role in England, where literary culture was already well established; it was used with "abandon" in the United States, where it was a form of "commercial entertainment business." Ibid., 129.

33 Ibid., 155.

34 Marc Raboy and David Taras, "On Life Support: The CBC and the Future of Public Broadcasting in Canada," in *How Canadians Communicate II: Media, Globalization and Identity*, ed. David Taras, Maria Bakardjieva, and Frits Pannekoek (Calgary: University of Calgary Press, 2007), 88. They note that the Lincoln Committee in 2003 recommended multi-year funding to assist the CBC to fulfill its mandates (101). See also Joe Friesen, "Harper's CBC Views Draw Fire," *The Globe & Mail* (20 May 2004): A7, and Michael Posner, "How Did It All Go So Wrong at the CBC?" *The Globe & Mail* (27 October 2005): R3.

35 As federal funding cuts to CBC increase, the investment in preservation and a more coherent representation of CBC's broadcasting history will be more challenging. See "CBC Budget Cut by $115M over 3 years," CBC *News* (29 March

2012), www.cbc.ca/news/politics/cbc-budget-cut-by-115m-over-3-years-1.114
7096 (accessed 28 August 2017).

36 David Taras, *Power and Betrayal in the Canadian Media* (Peterborough, ON: Broadview Press, 2001), 237–8.

37 Ibid., 228.

38 Raboy and Taras, "On Life Support," 90.

39 Ibid., 84–5. They add that the CBC has been vulnerable to the interests of governments who have stacked the CBC's board of directors with those affiliatedwith the governing party (94).

40 See "CBC Budget Cut by \$115M over 3 years."

41 Vipond, *Mass Media*, 238. She adds that historical neglect was also related to the fact that "radio and television were too *popular*, and too *American*."

42 Linda Morra, ed., *Corresponding Influence: Selected Letters of Emily Carr & Ira Dilworth* (Toronto: University of Toronto Press, 2006), 49, n44.

43 Michael Coyle claims that "Eliot's commitment to the BBC proved one of the most sustained and principled engagements in modern literary history, inseparable from his interest in radio itself." Michael Coyle, "'This Rather Elusory Broadcast Technique': T.S. Eliot and the Genre of Radio Talk," ANQ 11.4 (Fall 1998): 33.

44 P.W. Luce, "Music His Passion," *Saturday Night* (10 August 1940): 2.

45 He was appointed because, aside from his fidelity to both a national and British audience, Dilworth was seen to have embodied the range of qualifications and characteristics that were required: "much diplomacy, a thorough knowledge of world affairs, a broad cultural background, and a sympathetic attitude towards conflicting viewpoints." Luce, "Music His Passion," 2.

46 As he moved upward in the administrative ranks of the CBC, however, he was also required to address those criticisms that he at least regarded as barriers to the role CBC might play in national education. His aversion for popular demands made by what he deemed as whimsical, "uncritical listeners," for example, was registered in the mandate upon which he insisted: that the CBC was designed for a national audience, and, while it was all-encompassing in terms of reaching all listeners and of fostering national unity and harmony, it was also to uphold a standard of "good taste." His emphasis on what constituted "good taste" relates to his use of the literary traditions to which I alluded earlier while developing a national aesthetic; however, he took a surprisingly different tack in relation to *how* one relayed material over the CBC.

47 Weir, *Struggle for National Broadcasting*, 277.

48 Anne Marriott, *The Wind Our Enemy* (Toronto: Ryerson, 1939), 11.

49 Ira Dilworth, *And We Are Here: An Address Delivered at the Autumn Congre-gation of the University of British Columbia* (Vancouver: University of British Columbia, 1948), 1.

50 Ibid., 3.

51 Tara McPherson, "Post-Archive: The Humanities, the Archive, and the Database," in *Between Humanities and the Digital*, ed. Patrick Svensson and David Theo Goldberg (Cambridge, MA: MIT Press, 2015), 490, 488.

2

____

Othertalk
Conversational Events in the Roy Kiyooka Digital Audio Archive

DEANNA FONG

On 26 June 1982, Roy Kiyooka and Trudy Rubenfeld had the following conversation over a cup of coffee:

ROY: I think to hear your own voice means working through all that, consciously or unconsciously. It's an interesting experience. It just … I don't know. It's the ear's equivalent of the mirror. You look at yourself in a mirror for visual affirmation or negation.
TRUDY: It must have the equal amount of distortion.
ROY: Yes. That's right. […] Hey, I think this is the first time I've ever made coffee for you. You've made coffee for me hundreds of times.
TRUDY: That's right, Roy.
ROY (laughs): See? Things are changing, Trudy.
TRUDY (laughs): Yeah.
ROY: Things are changing.
TRUDY: Oh, they are! It is a time of change.
ROY: In every sense. I see it all over the place, in everybody's lives.
TRUDY: Isn't it incredible?
ROY (gasps): It's devastating. It makes me tremble sometimes.
TRUDY: Oh, it's wonderful!
ROY: Yeah, sure it is.
TRUDY: Everybody needs trembling.

2.1 "Summer Backdoor Rain" cassette tape from the Roy Kiyooka Audio Archive.

ROY: Because, uh, the shape of whatever these changes are about is not
a given. It's a breaking out, it's –
TRUDY: Well, that's what's exciting.
ROY: Yeah, right. Yeah. I agree. (pause) I agree. (00:06:05.52)[1]

Here we have all the makings of a tiny event: an occurrence, a shift in perspective, a trembling. The tape, labelled "Summer Backdoor Rain, June 26,
'82/ Trudi & I, Talking" [*sic*], is one of the hundreds of audio artifacts in
the Roy Kiyooka Audio Archive housed at Simon Fraser University's Special
Collections in Vancouver, BC. Recorded on a variety of audio media formats
(cassettes, minicassettes, and reel-to-reel tapes) between 1963 and 1988, they
capture the voices of many prominent members of the West Coast artistic,
musical, and literary avant-garde, including Alvin Balkind, Taki Bluesinger,
George Bowering, Judith Copithorne, Robert Creeley, Maxine Gadd, Carole
Itter, Daphne Marlatt, Al Neil, John Newlove, Rhoda Rosenfeld, Trudy
Rubenfeld, Warren Tallman, and Fred Wah. They also record voices of men
and women with no particular claim to fame in either of those communities:
the unidentified yet resolutely present voices of people who happened to be

there, at a specific intersection of time and place. Kiyooka brought his tape recorder with him almost everywhere, setting it in the middle of the dinner table (or bar table), propping it up on the back of the couch, slinging it over his shoulder in its leather case. The tapes in his archive are *kind of* literary; that is, their content is not all matter of an obvious literary nature like readings and lectures. Some of them touch upon matters of poetics, composition, craft, and aesthetics, but most are just conversations – some funny, some painfully personal, some idle, some heated and polemical. What do these tapes record, and how do their form and content shape history – personal, communal, literary, or otherwise? What kinds of techniques in listening and interpretation are needed to encounter and engage with conversational artifacts such as these, which register the affective tremors of the archive?[2] The tapes document speaking subjects performing themselves, both for their contemporaries and for futurity; they try on different ideas and registers, opening themselves to omission and self-revision. They narrate their own movement through the event as it unfolds, voicing their thoughts aloud, exteriorizing them in a register that strikes us as strange: they anticipate an audience of a scale that exceeds the people in the room. What we hear is not quite conversational; something else is there.

This "something else" marks the recording itself as a kind of event, caught between spontaneous performance and the scenario of its documentation. In turning my attention to Kiyooka's vast set of recordings, I focus on how the event is registered, and so constituted, by both speech and its attendant material document: the audio recording. Over the past several years, I have built a digital repository and interface through which users can access and interact with these recordings. In the process, I have grappled with a number of practical, legal, and ethical questions: How might I go about identifying the many voices, especially on tapes that are unmarked? How could the interface meaningfully represent the community relationships that the tapes record, at both a granular level and en masse? How much contextualizing information – biographical, bibliographical, and/or geographical – would a user need to make sense of what they are hearing, and where should this information appear in relation to the recording when presented online? How do we approach the question of copyright when recordings like these so clearly fall outside the purview of laws designed to protect the interests of commercial music? Does a conversation become a protectable work simply by being fixed in a stable, material form? And, finally, should I even be listening to these tapes, let alone making them an object of study, when their content is so personal? All of these questions deserve serious attention in their own right. However, before we can even enter into a conversation about a work's discursive or legal status, we must first attend to the ontological status of the event that produced it, sounding out the relationship between its emergent properties and its incomplete material record. The tapes in the Kiyooka archive provide a compelling case study to think about the ontology of media. Their form and content, both structured by lack, mirror the constitutive lack in the interwoven systems of cognition and social organization, and thus provide a material site to think through questions of eventness and being.

I take this cue from separate (though not unrelated) questions posed by Martin Heidegger and Mladen Dolar half a century apart: What does it mean to be? and What is the voice?[3] That both these terms appear universal and self-evident belies the fact that their consistency dissolves under close scrutiny, incommensurate with the jagged particularity of material instantiations. The more we try to pin down a definition of the voice, the more it escapes us: it is neither the exclusive territory of language nor the body, neither a guarantee of interior presence nor an autonomous force "out there" in the world. It originates in a set of complex physiological processes, but can be absented from the body via acousmatic technologies, such that it forms what Kiyooka calls "the ear's equivalent of the mirror" for acoustic self-reflection, or rather an "acoustic mirror" to use Kaja Silverman's term, which both affirms and negates a sense of selfhood.[4] So, too, is the case with being as such: its use in the everyday sense suggests a suspended, transhistorical position: something is, without articulation to the grammatical components that ground it in a specific time and place; yet, as Heidegger reminds us, "being is in each instance comprehensible only in regard to time."[5] The experience of time regulates existence and gives it its shape. Audio recordings resist neutral definitions of voice and being by carrying a disembodied sound across a striated temporality. They are a point at which both physical and metaphysical distinctions break down. Such recalcitrant objects require a creative swerve from the standard positions on representation, experience, presence, mimesis, and originality. The impasse that audio recordings pose for theories of performance and mediation opens out onto the messy structure of eventness, in which documents are never fully complete at the moment of their arrest, and performances are never fully present in the moment of their liveness.

To think through the relationship between voice and document, being and event, I turn first to the field of performance studies, an area of theory that interrogates these categories across a number of cultural sites, among them performance art, dance, theatre, and film. Specifically, I am interested in how liveness enters into a differential relationship with reproduction, documentation, and registration. This opposition is expressed through a number of antinomic terms. Writing in 1993, Peggy Phelan's Lacanian-feminist treatise *Unmarked: The Politics of Performance* opposes performance to reproduction, insisting on their mutual impossibility as ontological categories. Once the live performance enters into the economy of reproduction it ceases to be performance. For her, "performance's only life is in the present. Performance cannot be saved, recorded, [or] documented"; it "plunges into visibility – in a manically charged present – and disappears into memory … where it eludes regulation and control."[6] The invisibility or "unmarking" of performance is given an emancipatory potential that aligns it with a feminist political project. By becoming itself through disappearance, performance disrupts the desire and appropriative incursions of the gaze – a gaze most often turned upon the female body in the visual media of photography and film. Philip Auslander picks up these threads in *Liveness: Performance in a Mediatized Culture* (2002). Like Phelan, he opposes liveness to mediatization, but rejects their status as self-evident ontological categories. Liveness, he insists, must be examined "not as a global, undifferentiated phenomenon but within specific and cultural social contexts."[7] His particular focus is on mid-twentieth century American theatre and the spectacular live events of sport and rock music, where performance increasingly mimics the mediated features of broadcast television. In Auslander's view, mediatization "colonizes"[8] liveness. He rebuffs Phelan's claim that performance resists legal inscription and insists that all transmissive media are "locked in combat for cultural and economic dominance"[9] and that "our current cultural formation is saturated with, and dominated by, mass media representations."[10]

At first glance, these accounts of performance seem irreconcilable. Yet a moment of critique exposes a shared affinity: in the final chapter of *Liveness,* Auslander rejects Phelan's claim that performance is transitory, evanescent, and as such resistant to commodification and codification. Drawing upon two spheres of jurisprudence – evidence law and intellectual property – he shows how even memory is subject to the invasion of law. In the case of the former, Auslander demonstrates how the legal system strongly prefers live testimony to pre-recorded video deposition – in fact demanding it in the Confrontation Clause of the Sixth Amendment to the U.S. Constitution. The act of memory retrieval, publically performed in front of a jury at a trial, is viewed as more authentic, immediate, and truthful than one given outside the spatial and temporal event of the courtroom. In the case of copyright law, he analyzes the unusual case of *Bright Tunes Music Corp. v. Harrisongs Music, Ltd.* (1976), in which George Harrison was sued for copyright infringement because the melody of his song "My Sweet Lord" closely resembled that of an earlier tune, "He's So Fine," composed by Ronald Mack and performed by the Chiffons. Harrison claimed he never heard the other song, and so could not be guilty of infringement. The courts, however, reasoned otherwise: while it is possible that Harrison had not deliberately plagiarized "He's So Fine," they nonetheless ruled that "his subconscious knew… a song his conscious mind did not remember"[11] and that such "unknown knowledge" (to use Slavoj Žižek's phrase) is subject to the same legal limitations as the "known knowledge" of conscious thought.[12] These two legal examples show not only how memory can be pressed into the service of the law but also, more importantly, how it is objectified even in its immaterial form, making it actionable in its own right. Here, Auslander creates a hypertrophic one of representation: liveness, like mediatization, is always already representative in nature. No perceptual reality exists independently of its meaning under the law. Such a statement aligns with Alain Badiou's notion of the "state of the situation," whereby the entities present in a given situation are re-counted, acknowledged, and confirmed by the state, in the process affirming the state's power as the one that imposes the count.[13] Auslander's unhappy conclusion is that our current cultural moment is characterized by radical closure: in order to escape regulation, he writes, "performance must not only disappear but be excluded from memory."[14] While he aims to contradict Phelan's claim, Auslander in fact exposes a common supposition that they both hold, namely, that performance, whether live or recorded, is always already inscriptive in nature and therefore imbued with a positive, knowable ontology. For Phelan, live performance is inscribed in the unconscious, where it is sheltered from the law and thus given revolutionary potential; for Auslander, the only writing is the writing of the law – there is nothing outside legal inscription. Both theorists deal exclusively in what Jacques Lacan might term the symbolic dimensions of the event, ignoring the pre-subjective or pre-inscriptive horizon from which it emerges. These accounts are problematic for two reasons. They present us with a false choice between authentic and inauthentic inscriptive media that actually only differ in degree, not in kind. And they create a deadlock in which all experience must be assimilated into one of two a priori categories – live experience or mediatized reproduction – and thus do not recognize these categories as events in their own right.

Antinomic accounts of presence and absence, liveness and documentation, presentation and representation seem insufficient to explain what we hear on the Kiyooka tapes. In every instance, there is something sensible beyond what is positively inscribed on the tape – something that speaks to us through sheer absence, pointing to a kernel of unrepresentable matter. Take, for example, the "Pacific Rim Express" recording, which documents a trip that Kiyooka and seven other poets (George Bowering, Brian Fawcett, Dwight Gardiner, Gerry Gilbert, Gladys [Maria] Hindmarch, Carole Itter, and Daphne Marlatt) took to Prince George for a public reading in April 1974.[15] The tape is an audio letter addressed to Penny Chalmers (Penn Kemp). In the background, we hear the sound of a train whistle, indiscernible conversation, and the clatter of typewriter keys. Marlatt and Kiyooka take turns narrating:

> DAPHNE (laughs):Are we going to start the tape for Penny?
> ROY:Yes, I think we should start the tape for Penny.
> DAPHNE: Okay. Penny, you are being spoken to from a couple of turquoise seats on the first coach of the British Columbia Railway, formerly the Pacific Great Eastern, now the "P" Pacific, "G" Grim, Grime, Rim, Rhyme, "E" Express. (Roy laughs.)
> ROY: Hi, Penny. Daphne's on my left. Across from her and one seat up is George. To the right, beside George, is Glady. In front of Glady is Brian. George is interjecting here. In front of me – I'm on the window side – is Dwight. He's got the shades half drawn. Beside Dwight is Gerry, his nose buried in a sheaf of paper, typewriter on his lap. Two seats up and to the right is Carole, sitting beside all the media paraphernalia […] You can't hear Daphne smile on this little machine. Shall I describe it to you? (laughs)
> DAPHNE: How would you describe it, Roy?
> ROY (pause) (laughs): She, uh … She, uh … She …(laughs) She …?
> DAPHNE: Penny, you can hear the feet of men walking in the aisle past my left shoulder. You can hear the door slam. When the door opens

2.2 "PRE" cassette tape from the Roy Kiyooka Audio Archive.

you can hear the moving wheels on the track. You can hear Gerry typing in short, sporadic bursts. You can hear George reading. You can hear the long hoot of the train as it turns the next curve (train whistle sounds). You can hear minds working phenomenally, writing what is, as Roy would say, nominally, a story. (00:00:37.04)

There are a few curious features here that turn around equivocation and absence. First, the tape defies generic classification: it is at once the document of a live performance, correspondence, stream-of-consciousness composition, and recitation (after the "letter" portion, Marlatt goes on to read from some current work). Crucially, the tape recorder not only registers the results of these different literary and theatrical products but also produces them: the performance of describing the space around them – people's actions, proximities, colours, textures, and sounds – uniquely compensates for the fact that the listener does not have access to the visual and haptic dimensions of the event that the tape records.[16] It is not that the tape neutrally documents some activity that is happening "outside" or independent of the act of recording; rather, the tape itself creates the very occasion that it records.[17]

Second, the tape records what Friedrich Kittler terms "the bodily real"[18] that escapes symbolic notation. As a space- and time-based medium, sound recording picks up meaningful sound and unintentional noise indiscriminately, omitting and transducing only according to the "will" of the recording device's specifications. No longer bottlenecked through subjective, symbolic representation, the "physiological accidents and stochastic disorder of bodies"[19] recorded on the tape become as audible as purposeful speech, threatening to unseat logos as the sole conduit of meaning. There are many "accidental" sounds on the tape that are extralexical but not extrasemantic: the thrum of the train engine, the speakers' spontaneous laughter, hesitation, and stammering. Though they do not refer to ideas and objects in the same way as language, environmental and bodily sounds nonetheless shape the ways that we receive, interpret, and imagine what we hear. To me, however, the most resonant aspect of the real in a recorded sound event lies not in incidental sound, but in what we simply cannot hear. As a third feature, then, the tape evocatively traces what Alain Badiou calls the "subtractive" nature of ontology: "If ontology is the particular situation which presents presentation, it must also present the law of all presentation – the errancy of the void, the unpresentable as non-encounter."[20] More simply put, for something to exist in a given situation (i.e., in reality), the pure multiple – noisy, unstructured, multitudinous existence – must be suspended or bracketed by symbolic representation. This subtractive process creates an operational sense of coherency between subjects and objects. The subtractive process is the threshold through which things become sayable and knowable and works as a contract that secures the possibility of meaning. The elements foreclosed by representation do not disappear (at least not fully), but persist as blank signifiers or as a set of nonentities that attach themselves as void to the underside of every act of signification. Thus, representation, as the very law underwriting the structure of reality itself, produces an excess over what is named or symbolically counted within that structure. It counts, but does not account for the law of its own counting. As a result, the void is not just a lamentable absence, nor an incidental by-product of reality. Rather, it is the very condition that permits transformation and radical change. In isolating the non-representable element in any situation, we expose something about the logic or organization that dictates what counts as meaningful, as sensible, as extant. For this reason, we must take very seriously Kittler's claim that media "define what really is"[21] rather than merely transmit content from one point to another. Intertwined with both subjects and social reality, media artifacts are haunted by what they exclude or bracket out. Each medium is marked by a gap or point of impossibility – analogous to the Badiouian empty set – which points to, without representing, the foreclosed dimensions of the pure multiple. Badiou's theory of ontology is Jacques Lacan's theory of the subject written socially: the representational structure of the state corresponds to the symbolic order of the laws, institutions, morals, practices, and traditions of society that are entwined in various ways with language. The subject's lack emerges with his induction into the symbolic order, whereby articulation fails and a remainder or *objet a* persists as an inassimilable symbol of the Real. In Lacanian terms, this *objet a* is both the object and the cause of desire. On the one hand, it is the series of objects that serve as placeholders for the void itself, the metonymic slide of desiring one thing after another, none of which ever succeed in closing the gap. But at a more fundamental level, the object is nothing other than the insatiable void itself, what Lacan (after Freud) terms the drive.

On the tape, this gap (or lack) opens up around the object of Daphne's smile, which is a little piece of the Real that the tape recorder can't convert into electromagnetic signals, and that Kiyooka can't translate into words. Daphne's smile defies representation, yet is still somehow present in that absence – something manifest in Kiyooka's stuttering voice and nervous laughter.[22] Contrary to Auslander's notion that everything is inscriptive, the smile-as-object points to something that is symbolically unassimilable in both the live event and its document. Neither does the smile fall within the ambit of Phelan's inscriptive memory. It is something wholly different, an absence at the very heart of live presence. This is the critical point of every ontological situation: the instruments that we use to register reality – whether the faculties of our bodies (sight, hearing, touch, memory) or mechanized prostheses (writing, painting, photography, sound recording) – act as frames that bring certain elements of the pure multiplicity of the event into focus – and thus into being – at the expense of others.[23] In this way, media are not subordinate or incidental to what we call reality, but rather agents in establishing the possibility of its constitution. By dispensing with the categorical opposition of materiality and immateriality – that is, performance and representation, liveness and mediatization, repertoire and archive – we can refocus our attention on the specific losses that attend each medium, and how these losses in turn direct or script our engagements with these artifacts when we encounter them. Dispensing with these binaries helps us understand how temporal-media artifacts make evental sites that open onto the void or gap that exists in every structured situation. The promise of such gaps is that they expose something about the logic of the situational structure itself, revealing the logic of how something comes to count as a discernible entity. The experience of hearing is most acute at the threshold where sound vanishes. The mediality of the audiotape is most evident in what it fails to record. But even more than simply revealing the limits of experience, this void is the site where the radical event can occur. As Badiou explains, "there, the activist constructs the means to *sound*, if only for an instant, the site of the unrepresentable, and the means to be thenceforth faithful to the proper name that, afterwards, he or she will have been able to give to – or *hear*, one cannot decide – this non-place of place, the void"[24] [emphasis added]. What would it mean to imagine the audio recording as an event? Or, more to the point, what kinds of events are made possible through the particular gaps of audio recordings? How do they engage the retroactive structure of the event described by Badiou and Slavoj Žižek that fastens together past, present, and future? Žižek defines an event as "something shocking, out of joint, that appears to happen all of a sudden and interrupts the usual flow of things; something that emerges seemingly out of nowhere, without discernable causes, an appearance without solid foundation at its being."[25] To recognize an event as something relies upon "a circular structure in which the eventual effect retroactively determines its causes or reasons,"[26] and yet somehow remains in excess of those causes or reasons. Žižek illustrates the tenuous relationship between cause and effect when he writes about the inexhaustible exercise of explaining why he loves someone. In the end, it is some unassignable factor x (or, more specifically *objet a*) that is to blame; I love "that which is 'in you more than you' and thus makes me desire you."[27] Void and event are thus part of the same undecidable situation; they are the intersection of the object and the excess of symbolizing activity intended to cover up its absence or instability. Every gap opens up a space in which future symbolization may "hook" back syntactically onto the signs that preceded it and, in the process, alter the present structure of the situation.[28] The reasons for falling in love fasten back onto the event of the falling itself – they change the inflection of what it means to love in day-to-day reality – but they can never quite explain the mysterious object of love itself. Rather, the object's absence requires constant symbolic suturing, such that past and present temporalities stitch together and shape one another's consistency. The symbolic activity of the present changes the very frame through which we access the events of the past.

The retroactive loop is a salient feature of tape recordings that either directly or implicitly hail a future audience that will interpret – and be interpellated by – their content. Rebecca Schneider invites us to think of material artifacts not as the finite products of a "non-returning time, but instead as situated in a live moment of encounter that they predict, through their articulation as gestures or hails."[29] Drawing from Louis Althusser's notion of the hail as a subjectivizing gesture – the moment we identify ourselves in the policeman's call of "Hey, you there" – Schneider insists that media artifacts operate in much the same way, directing our attention and, in a certain sense, scripting how we should interact with the past. This pronouncement resounds with Darren Wershler's observation in his chapter of this volume that archives are as much defined by their circulatory practices in the present as they are by their originary moment of inscription. We get a palpable sense of the hail when speakers acknowledge the presence of the tape recorder, when its symbolic futurity bends time around it in a recursive way.

On a second tape recorded the same day as his conversation with Rubenfeld, Kiyooka speaks to the tape recorder in a dreamy, legato monologue. There is no immediate human recipient for his musings, only the whirring device in front of him and the rain falling softly in the background. He speaks: "Saturday, June the twenty-sixth. Rained. A light. When at last … A real drench after three intense weeks of silences. Summer, hot summer silences. That's the first sky I can see sitting here, turned toward Powell Street. That silver sliver. That silver sliver of sky I can see beguiles me. […] I've started doing things again. I'm doing it at this moment. This very moment. Can you hear all those lovely slits of sky? Can you hear them?" (00:16:13.05).

Twenty-four years pass between the issue of the question and its answer in the present (at least this *present* present when I, on another rainy Vancouver day, listen to his words and type this chapter). I am unavoidably situating myself as the intended "you" of the recording. I *can* hear it – that is, I can physically and affectively sense the past moment he describes in an odd moment of times touching. More vividly than most media, audio recordings demonstrate how a gap is always also a hail, perpetually suspended between the moment of utterance and the moment of acknowledgment or receipt. In their acts of hailing, material artifacts not only invite the engagement and interpretation of future interlocutors but also depend upon this engagement to actualize their content in repeated, performative encounters. To mobilize Alexander Galloway's useful terms, the event of the tape recording is not only decisional but also relational. On the one hand, it is a "cutting off," a "more or less conscious action … willed into existence by someone or some catalyzing agent."[30] On the other hand, it is "a relation between two moments in time, or between two states of affairs."[31] Tape recordings are events in both senses: they "cut off" wilfully and decisively, both through the medium's affordances and the producer's conscious acts of framing, and they also "bring back," looping discrete temporalities together dialogically and affectively.

To consider the interplay of these two evental modes, I turn to a final example, one of the most cacophonous recordings in the Kiyooka archive, which captures conversations at the Cecil Hotel, a now-defunct bar in downtown Vancouver, on 22 October 1970. The recording is shot through with exuberance and energy. Voices swim in and out of the hum of background conversation. There are peals of laughter, clinking glasses, fugues of song and poetry, speculations on the war in Vietnam. The recording quality is poor, and it is often impossible to tell what is being said, let alone who is saying what. When Roy is asked, "What are you doing here, anyway?" (regarding his practice of taping conversations), he responds: "What I've been doing all night is I'll let it run through for thirty minutes, and then I'll get the buzzing signal that tells me it's at the end. I play it back and listen to it a bit then I rewind the whole thing, and then do it again, and again, and again, and again, cancelling out each successive thirty-minute stretch. I can do that at the Cecil because the nature of what occurs as conversation is that thing. It is not discriminatory, it never stops, and it is totally impartial as to what is uttered or said" (00:12:54.00).

In either a swerve of serendipity or a deliberate act of self-documentation, the extant portion of the tape captures Kiyooka's description of his own process, pointing toward the subtracted dimensions that brought it into being. The tape can only record thirty minutes of sound, and thus imposes an arbitrary frame on its contents. The tape is "not discriminatory" in what it records when activated, but only records when it is made to move. If conversation "never stops," then the tape must capture it, portion it, cut it off arbitrarily. Kiyooka's description of his process points to the absence of the other thirty-minute segments that had to be destroyed in order to

2.3 "Cecil Hotel" cassette tape from the Roy Kiyooka Audio Archive.

produce the tape in its current form – one of the necessary conditions of the tape's subtractive ontology.[32] The recording also foregrounds the subtraction of the haptic, visual, and proprioceptive dimensions of the event required to produce a sonic object. We get no sense of how many people are present, who they are, what they look like, or where they are positioned in the room or in relation to each other (as we do from the details supplied by Marlatt on the "Pacific Rim Express" tape). We also lack the visual semantic cues that condition speech, such as facial expressions, posture, and eye contact. Yet another major gap in the tape is its implicit address to a future recipient. Kiyooka holds the microphone up to a friend and entreats him to "say a few words to the folks" (11:28). An unnamed male speaker exclaims, "Roy, you are going to have an absolutely fantastic tape!" (12:47), which seems retroactively ghosted with the question: fantastic for whom? Listening to this recording forty-five years later, one cannot escape the uncanny feeling that the voices captured speak directly to us, the "folks" intended to receive it, as though the site of our future encounter with the tape were already pre-inscribed in the previous site of recording. The speakers imagine the tape's future reception even as they produce it, such that its future reception becomes the excessive cause or reason for the effect of its production. In this way, the evental site of the recording remains open long after the tape itself concludes.

Ultimately, the audio artifacts in Kiyooka's archive foreground the medium's lacking properties, defined as much by its particular affordances (thirty minutes per side) as the author's conscious choices to frame the material he records. Unlike other temporal media – say, commercial music recordings or spoken word intended for broadcast – these artifacts do not claim to reproduce reality with any degree of verisimilitude (contra the media ideological discourse of "fidelity" that Jonathan Sterne outlines in *The Audible Past*).[33] Rather, as is evidenced in Kiyooka's description of his own process – of cancellation, overwriting, splicing, and cutting – the tapes point us toward the subtractive ontology of media objects, which mirrors the subtractive ontology of the subjects that create and behold them. The tapes show how theories that privilege the exclusively live, as well as those that privilege mediatization are insufficient to account for the looping, performative dynamic that these tapes enact. The mediated voice pours into our living ears, speaking to us, reverberating inside us, across space and time. Refusing a binary distinction between the live and the mediated and instead focusing on the interplay between decisional lack and relational excess offers a new way to conceive of literary history – its narratives, its sequence, its values, and its temporality. Rather than rely on teleological narratives that make an unbroken line between past and present, mediation has us rethink history as a continuously and recursively unfolding event, whose multiple voices, contradictions, and anxieties speak to, and through, the present.

NOTES

1   All audio recordings transcribed and edited by Deanna Fong. Trudy Rubenfeld is a Vancouver-based artist. Roy was her painting teacher. Detailed biographical information and a full transcript of the recording are available on the Roy Kiyooka Digital Audio Archive: https://roykiyookaaudioarchive.wordpress.com (accessed 20 July 2017).

2   I borrow the phrase "affective tremors" from Laura Ann Stoler's *Along the Archival Grain* (Princeton and Oxford: Princeton University Press, 2009),

which deals with the intersections of affect and materiality at the site of the colonial archive.

3 Martin Heidegger, *Being and Time* (Albany: State University of New York Press, 2010), 3–12; Mladen Dolar, *A Voice and Nothing More* (Cambridge, MA: MIT Press, 2006), 13–14.

4 Silverman uses the term "acoustic mirror" to describe the voice's capacity to be simultaneously "emitted and heard, sent and received … by the subject himself" (80). This confusion of interiority and exteriority conditions, but also confounds, the separation of subject and object upon which subjectivity depends.

5 Heidegger, *Being and Time*, 18.

6 Peggy Phelan, *Unmarked: The Politics of Performance* (Florence, KY: Routledge, 1993), 148.

7 Philip Auslander, *Liveness: Performance in a Mediatized Culture* (London and New York: Routledge, 2008), 3.

8 Ibid., 13.

9 Ibid., 1.

10 Ibid., 9.

11 Quoted in Ibid., 178.

12 Žižek develops a fourfold epistemology around knowing and not knowing, revelation and obfuscation in his 2008 *In Defense of Lost Causes*: "In March 2003, [Donald] Rumsfeld engaged in a little bit of amateur philosophizing about the relationship between the known and the unknown: 'There are known knowns. These are things we know that we know. There are known unknowns. That is to say, there are things that we know we don't know. But there are also unknown unknowns. There are things we don't know we don't know.' What he forgot to add was the crucial fourth term: the 'unknown knowns,' the things we don't know that we know – which is precisely, the Freudian unconscious, the 'knowledge which doesn't know itself,' as Lacan used to say." Slavoj Žižek, *In Defense of Lost Causes* (London and New York: Verso, 2008), 457.

13 Badiou's use of the word "state" gestures to the full range of its semantic possibilities: it is the "state of things" – that is, things as they are, or as they exist in the world, but also the State and the structural systems of power that it maintains and which subtend it.

14 Auslander, *Liveness*, 181.

15 The occasion of the trip was a poetry festival that Barry McKinnon and Gerry Gilbert organized at the College of New Caledonia. Marlatt's *The Story, She*

Said was the product of artistic and material collaboration on the trip. See Daphne Marlatt, "Correspondences," *Line* 13 (1989): 10–12.

16 We might consider Kiyooka and Marlatt's performance on this tape as operating in the tradition of the "descriptive sketch" characteristic of some of the earliest spoken recordings made. See Patrick Feaster: "Framing the Mechanical Voice: Generic Conventions of Early Sound Recording," *Folklore Forum* 32 (2001): 57–102; and Patrick Feaster and Jacob Smith, "Reconfiguring the History of Early Cinema Through the Phonograph, 1877–1908," *Film History: An International Journal* 21:4 (December 2009): 311–25.

17 Jonathan Sterne is adamant about this point in his chapter, "The Social Construction of Sound Fidelity," in *The Audible Past*. Writing about the production of early commercial music recordings, he insists that "the 'original' sound embedded in the recording – regardless of whether the process is 'continuous' – certainly bears a causal relationship with the reproduction, but only because the original itself is an artifact of the process of reproduction. Without the technology of reproduction the copies do not exist, but, then neither would the originals … 'Original' sounds are as much a product of the medium as are copies – reproduced sounds are not simply versions of unmediated original sounds." Jonathan Sterne, *The Audible Past: Cultural Origins of Sound Reproduction* (London: Duke University Press, 2003), 219.

18 Friedrich Kittler, *Gramophone, Film, Typewriter*, trans. Geoffrey Winthrop-Young and Michael Wutz (Stanford, CA: Stanford University Press, 1999), 12.

19 Ibid., 16.

20 Alain Badiou, *Being and Event*, trans. Oliver Feltham (London: Bloomsbury, 2013), 57.

21 Kittler, *Gramophone*, 3.

22 One might argue that the smile would have been captured by another medium – photography or video, say – but this is beside the point. There is always something lacking within a given situation, because this lack is the foundation of its very structure, pointing out the limit of representability itself. Video, for example, is structured by spatial limits (the camera's visual field or frame) and temporal limits (the maximum duration of a recording). The tape also points to other such objects that elude representation: the act of writing (the activity par excellence of the Lacanian sinthome – "that which does not cease to write itself"), the other as object, figured as "minds working phenomenally," etc.

23 We might usefully think of the physiological faculty of audition as a metaphor for this process, which brings the sound into being out of the undifferentiated

world of vibration. In *The Audible Past,* Sterne notes that sound exists only as a *process* of registering vibrations – pressure changes in a conductive medium, like the air. Vibrations are asemantic in and of themselves; they have no positive content and, as such, model the contingent element of the event. They can be registered by a number of human senses and prostheses, including hearing and touch, but they do not exist in the world *as sound* before their registration. As Sterne rightly points out, "the hearing of the sound is what makes it." Sterne, *The Audible Past,* 11. By this logic, all acts of hearing are necessarily events. Crucially, materiality is not subordinate or incidental to the constitution of reality: rather, it is *the* pivotal component of the event's retroactive structure.

24 Badiou, *Being,* 115.

25 Slavoj Žižek, *Event: Philosophy in Transit* (London: Penguin, 2014), 2.

26 Ibid.

27 Žižek, *Defense of Lost Causes,* xviii.

28 Bruce Fink's discussion of the Lacanian *point de capiton* as a syntax is helpful here. For example, a sentence such as "Jack and Jill were exposed to …" hinges on the final word that indicates to what they were exposed (radiation, their uncle, French culture …). In each case, the sense of the ultimate word fastens back upon the sentence that precedes it, retroactively determining the meaning of the verb "exposed," while foreclosing the semantic possibilities of the other two words. Bruce Fink, *Lacan to the Letter: Reading* Écrits *Closely* (Minneapolis, MN: University of Minnesota Press, 2004), 90.

29 Rebecca Schneider, *Performing Remains: Art and War in Times of Theatrical Reenactment* (London and New York: Routledge, 2011), 141.

30 Alexander Galloway, *Laruelle: Against the Digital* (Minneapolis, MN, and London: University of Minnesota Press, 2014), 73.

31 Ibid.

32 Indeed, subtraction resounds at a meta-level, too: two of the five tapes from the "Pacific Rim Express" were so brittle that they were destroyed in the process of digitization.

33 As Sterne writes in the chapter "The Social Genesis of Sound Fidelity": "Within a philosophy of mediation, sound fidelity offers a kind of gold standard: it is the measure of sound-reproduction technologies' product against a fictitious external reality. From this perspective, the technology enabling the reproduction of sound thus mediates because it conditions the possibility of reproduction, but, ideally, it is supposed to be a 'vanishing' mediator – rendering the relation as transparent, as if it were not there." Sterne, *The Audible Past,* 218.

3

Poetry on TV
Unarchiving Phyllis Webb's CBC-TV Program, Extension (1967)

KATHERINE McLEOD

"Where Have All the Poets Gone?," a documentary made by Sook-Yin Lee for CBC's *The Exhibitionists*, opens with a story of Lee finding CBC-TV footage of a host with "a giant beehive hairdo" interviewing two sound poets.[1] Over the course of the program, Lee learns not only that this beehive-sporting host was poet Phyllis Webb but also that Webb left the CBC and Toronto shortly after this program was filmed to lead a more private life on Salt Spring Island, British Columbia. The footage that Lee found was from *Extension*, a thirteen-episode program about Canadian poetry that aired in the summer of 1967. After speaking with Webb in a phone interview that is part of the documentary, Lee asks herself: where is this kind of innovative programming on CBC today? Her question results in the second half of "Where Have All the Poets Gone?" in which she records conversations with poets bill bissett, Samantha Bernstein, Ronnie Clarke, Stephen Collis, Liz Howard, Shad Kabango, Vivek Shraya, Lena Suksi, and Elana Wolff. At some point in their conversation, each poet reads or recites a poem. Thus, Lee's program puts poets on TV, or rather, it broadcasts poetry on a mix of TV/radio/digital platforms. Lee's single program is not the same as a serial program of thirteen episodes about poetry on TV, as was the case with Webb's *Extension* (see "Appendix" to this chapter, below). Nevertheless, "Where Have All the Poets Gone?" raises the question of why poets are *not* more present today on mainstream media platforms. The online promotional material for Lee's show frames this issue in terms of "uncovering the past to make room for today."[2] However, I would take this further to suggest that it is an uncovering of the past to make room, publicly, for the question of where poetry *is* in mainstream media. Specifically, is its presence or lack thereof related to the public perception of poetry, or to the medium of TV itself? Why is there not a television program like *Extension* today? Or would a comparable program be broadcast on YouTube or Netflix? Is Lee's documentary an attempt to create such programming?[3]

The broadcasting of Lee's program across platforms – radio, TV, and digital – reveals much about how we consume popular forms of literary culture today compared to the 1960s. Rather than looking for poets on television, one might look to digital spaces of social media, such as Instagram for bestselling poet Rupi Kaur, to 'find' today's poets. Even a digitization of Webb's *Extension* would end up producing a hybrid form of a television program broadcast on a digital platform, a result that would disseminate the work and yet would create a complex remediation in that audiences would be watching poets-on-television-on-the-Internet. An extension of an extension.

Lee's program title, "Where Have All the Poets Gone?" asks a question that many would argue is redundant.[4] After all, "the Poets" are here. They have not gone anywhere. One simply needs to listen in order to hear them, which is what Lee does in the second half of the program with present-day poets. Lee asks bill bissett about his painting; she speaks to Shad about poetic rhythm and hip-hop lyrics; Samantha Bernstein talks about her father Irving Layton; Liz Howard recites a poem from her soon-to-be Griffin Prize–winning collection; Vivek Shraya recites a poem at the Art Gallery of Ontario; Lena Suksi talks about poetry on a street in Toronto. The documentary concludes with Elana Wolff speaking about her poetic collaboration with the late Malca Litovitz, whose poetry Lee discovered in a box in her partner's basement, leading her to the conclusion that the poets have been here all along. In one sense, the title of Lee's show perpetuates the relegation of poetry to the sidelines of cultural media (not unlike Ben Lerner's recent title, *The Hatred of Poetry*, or Marianne Moore's opening lines to the poem "Poetry": "I, too, dislike it"). However, in the case of Phyllis Webb, the poet did go somewhere – in fact, I would argue that she went to two places: she herself moved out of the public eye to Salt Spring Island, and her public CBC persona as represented on *Extension* moved into the CBC archives, away from the public eye as well.

With Webb's move out of the public eye of media, one might argue that the poets also went somewhere, considering the presence of poets on television in *Extension* and the absence of poetry on television today. However, *Extension* was not simply a program of poetry readings. Each episode represents an experiment in the staging of poetry in distinct contexts and manners, with poetry presented through film, theatrical readings, conversations at a table and even at a piano, and then a traditional "reading" as the final episode. With such stagings in mind, this chapter argues that unarchiving the audiovisual footage of poets on CBC television in 1967 teaches us as much about poetry in Canadian public culture of the 1960s as it does about the mediatization of poetry and its writers. This book defines unarchiving as the transformational effect enacted by digital technologies and processes upon archival artifacts, along with the impact of other modes of revitalization that arise from the migration of archival materials into public contexts. In this chapter, I focus on both aspects of this definition by examining the archives of a television program of poetry, and its migration from old to new media platforms. I watched and listened to the thirteen episodes of *Extension* in order to ask what happens to poetry when it is put on TV, and to speculate on the public, new media platforms where poetry *can* be found in the present. *Extension* was an innovative (re)mediation of CanLit not only because it put poetry on television but also because it called for Webb to perform on TV *as* a poet.[5] As Webb says to Leonard Cohen after he sings "Hey, that's no way to say goodbye" as his first poem 'read' on *Extension*, "Well, I could go on listening to those for a long time, but, this is a program mainly about poetry, and so let's talk about the poems for a while."[6] That is exactly what Webb did: talk about the poems for a while on television.

Here, Now, and Then

Extension aimed to give viewers "a range of Canadian poetry: here, now, and then." This phrase, spoken in the first episode, became the subtitle for *Extension. Here, Now, and Then* aptly conveys the urgency of Webb's effort to put poets on television (in "the present" of 1967) while also providing a sense of context (*then*) for poetry in Canada.[7] Webb presented her program as a cohesive pedagogical resource. In the first episode, she makes it clear that *Extension* is about poetry as an art form rather than simply a collection of poetry readings (an anthology, like Robert Weaver's CBC radio show

Anthology): "In my craft or sullen art exercised in the still night – the sullen art Dylan Thomas referred to was, of course, poetry. For our purposes here I prefer to call it a lively art. One of the liveliest in Canada today. And this program is the first of thirteen devoted to modern Canadian poetry. You've just heard Irving Layton and Frank Scott reading poems they crafted in the forties, where this series begins." Webb returns to these words of Thomas throughout *Extension* to such an extent that they become an argument for poetry as "a lively art" and an argument that Webb could not make except through an audiovisual medium.

Extension begins with a historical and educational overview of Canadian poetry in the 1940s to 1950s. Why start then? Webb explains that the 1940s was a time in which modern Canadian poetry, the subject of her programs, began to flourish. After these opening comments, there is a one-minute collage of images from the 1940s in Canada before the camera returns to Webb and her guests: Irving Layton, Frank Scott, and Miriam Waddington. Rather than Webb 'starting' the conversation, the camera lingers on Layton and Scott, who are candidly talking about the writing they did in the 1930s. (I say candidly rather than casually because, although Layton appears relaxed, leaning to one side, Scott sits rather stiffly in the middle of the couch, between Layton and Webb while Waddington sits in a chair to the right of Webb.) Webb observes that they are talking about the 1930s even though this program is supposed to be about the 1940s, which prompts Layton to comment on how he was still writing nature poetry in the 1930s and only in the 1940s did he begin "to reflect on things happening in the world." At one point, Waddington interjects that she and A.M. Klein had written poems about the Spanish Civil War in the 1930s while at university, thereby countering Layton's suggestion that the earlier poets were not as political. (In fact, although she is not mentioned here, Dorothy Livesay, a guest on a later episode of *Extension*, among others, also wrote Spanish Civil War poetry during the 1930s.) When Webb asks of the poets, "Did the war generate a truly political commitment of the poets?" the conversation turns to the impact that the 1940s had on poetry. The poets agree that there was a palpable turn toward the political during this period in Canadian poetry.

The conversation about poetry in the 1940s would have surprised listeners expecting a program of poetry readings. Such surprise was Webb's intention. As though anticipating criticism from viewers expecting to hear more poetry on a poetry program, Webb foregrounds the fact that she wants to subvert such expectations. She concludes the third episode with: "Today's look at the sixties brings us to a close for our brief and biased living history of poetic activity in Canada during the forties, the fifties, and this far in the sixties. You may feel that there's been too much talk and not enough poetry on these programs. Good … Next week though we go directly to poetry with an anthology of poems selected to give some idea, to give a range of Canadian poetry: here, now, and then. I've called the program, 'A Lonely Music.' I think you'll like it." But calling the next episode "A Lonely Music" does not prepare the viewer for the experimentalism of the episode. After Webb announces the title of the next episode, the Beatles sing "Ah, look at all the lonely people" and "Eleanor Rigby" plays during the credits. This sonic marker firmly places the program in the mid-'60s, or as Webb calls it, "this far in the sixties," but the episode "A Lonely Music" is a long way from the pop aesthetic evoked by the Beatles song. "A Lonely Music" begins with a minimalist aesthetic – three readers wearing black, holding white pages of paper, and standing on podiums in a starkly lit theatrical setting. The camera pans around to Webb, seated on a chair onstage with the readers, and her introduction to the episode immediately foregrounds the loneliness in its title: "I've called this program 'A Lonely Music' perhaps because I was touched by what Rilke said to a young poet: Works of art are of an infinite loneliness and with nothing to be so little touched as with criticism, only love can grasp and hold and fairly judge them. Our title 'A Lonely Music' does refer to Canadian poetry but also to the art of poetry itself. First 'The Lonely Land.'" A.J.M. Smith's poem "The Lonely Land" is then read out loud by one of the readers standing on a podium.[8] Listeners may recognize lines in this poem (such as "the pine trees lean one way," inspired by the Group of Seven painter Tom Thomson) but the names of the poems and poets do not appear until the credits at the end of the episode. Webb occasionally comments between poems, such as her words introducing "The Lonely Land," but an audience unfamiliar with the poem might not realize that she is stating the poem's title, especially since she does not cite the author of the poem. In fact, one might not even realize that Webb has read one of her own poems until the credits roll at the end, a significant event given that this episode is the only time Webb reads one of her poems on television. It is her poem "Mad Gardener to the Sea." The camera differentiates between the poet and the program host. As the poet reading, the camera films Webb in profile from the side. This angle makes her look like a different person from the host who had just before faced the camera directly. Reading this poem, alone, she makes a lonely music. The last word of the poem, "solitaire," is embodied in the solitary presence Webb conveys as she reads, alone.

The episode "A Lonely Music" moves from one poem to the next with little commentary from Webb as host. When she does interject, she is less a host than a poet immersed in a performance, even when providing brief context for the poems: "I am afraid. I said that. I said that to you. Lines from one of my own poems, 'Walking in the Dark.' Fear whatever it results from, an unknown threat, the madman at your back or the madman in you. At least one of the poet's functions in society is to give speech to the unspeakable. The deep ambiguous footprint in the sand moves into the next group of poems to be defined more clearly in the universal patterns of guilt, innocence, and exile. The voice of forsaken man." It is difficult to express in writing the affect of hearing and watching Webb speak these words, and I have punctuated this transcription to capture the pacing of her voice. This affect constitutes a version of what Webb means when she says that the poet gives "speech to the unspeakable" in the sense of the unspeakable as that which eludes language. But in suggesting that this moment eludes the written speech typed on this page, do I become complicit in perpetuating an equating of performance with disappearance, as articulated through Peggy Phelan's argument (as described in Fong's chapter) that live performance is defined by its own disappearance and thus eludes leaving an archival trace? Watching this episode on a computer screen today is far from the experience of watching this program 'live' on television in 1967, but I would argue that there has always been an underlying liveness – even in this mediated experience – to the extent that, as Philip Auslander argues, mediatized performance is modelled on a live one.[9] Watching *Extension* involves unarchiving a digital remediation of a live television broadcast that shows a performance of poetry on a TV sound stage. This distance from the "original" broadcast does not render it less affecting.[10] It is deeply affecting to watch (here, now, and then) – despite the fact that a viewing in the present necessarily entails watching this particular clip while sitting at a computer workstation in the media library on the third floor of the CBC building in Toronto. When Webb says, "I am afraid. I said that. I said that to you. Lines from one of my own poems," she foregrounds the fact that her words have predicted this moment of encounter with "you" that is constructed in the past as a live event. It is her poetry and that of the poets whose work she presents in this program (and whose work she has just characterized as speaking the unspeakable) that allows her to speak of this fact of encounter. What is further unspeakable (now, from the perspective of the archival researcher accessing and unarchiving this poetry TV show) is the experience of watching Webb speak these words. Just as this affective experience exceeds writing, so too do numerous other moments throughout the series that can only be experienced by watching and listening.

The entire episode with James Reaney takes place standing at a piano with composer John Beckwith speaking with Reaney and Webb about musical collaborations for Reaney's poetry and playing a few pieces as demonstrations. In another episode, Al Purdy lies on a couch to be psychoanalyzed by Webb as host. In the second part of that same episode, Webb introduces Margaret Avison through a short film that was made by Timothy Findley: "One afternoon in winter Margaret Avison and I recorded a long conversation in a radio studio. We talked quietly. There were long pauses and silences. She answered my questions in that reticent accurate language which you'll hear in a moment." This is another moment in which Webb mediates our encounter with the artifact. In this case, the remains of her conversation with Avison take the form of a short film played before the camera returns to Webb. By that point, Avison is sitting next to her. But what is harder to explain is the affective experience of watching the short film's cold scenes of snow paired with the deep pauses in Avison's words, all the while knowing that they were recorded by Webb in a radio studio before the two of them went out into a winter storm. The digitized audiovisual archive exceeds what can be expressed here on the page. In remediating the audiovisual archive onto the page, the temporal experience of watching and listening cannot be replicated. Although a replication of the archive is not what is being attempted here, to speak about the liveness of the archive is one of the purposes of this chapter. To pursue this purpose entails speaking about the production of affect – affect that is not fully unarchivable and yet, for this user of the archives, affect that informs archival practice. There is an experiential element to watching and listening to these performances of literature, and one cannot help but be moved by this experience. And while this experience is personal, it reminds one that remediated performances continue to be affecting, as though live each time they are replayed.

A Lively Archive

In the process of watching Webb's *Extension* in the CBC media library, what became deeply apparent to me as a viewer and researcher was the difference between the archival descriptions in the CBC database and the episodes themselves. Archival description will always be an approximation of the nature and content of the artifact described; however, in this case, the archival descriptions are what are most readily available to the public (even though viewing them requires a visit to the CBC building itself). Consequently, the sharpness of *Extension*'s content as literary criticism ends up getting lost in the archives. This loss is due especially to the subtlety of Webb's carefully crafted public-private poetic voice. The on-air mode of criticism provides an important and singular forum for Webb to perform as public poet and as public literary critic. The on-air role she develops and assumes could be compared to the written critical voice Webb presents in *Nothing but Brush Strokes: Selected Prose* as part of the "Writer as Critic" series of NeWest Books, but with an important difference that in the case of *Extension*, the "writer as critic" is also playing a performative role as host. Archival records can only approximate the temporally based moments in which they were made and the archival object can only be described through metadata. Metadata describes the archival artifact for the purposes of discovery in a digital database, and for interoperability with an access repository system. The metadata in the CBC archives search for *Extension* includes program details of its broadcast (title, city, date, time); technical information about the format of its preservation; and a brief description of its contents, including the writers involved, whether directly or indirectly (i.e., responsible parties), and the material discussed (i.e., content). The most pronounced gap between the particulars of the archival artifacts that comprise the *Extension* collection and the archival description used to capture information about those artifacts is the complex role that Webb plays as host, poet, and literary critic. This gap is well exemplified by the metadata for the *Extension* episode from 7 May 1967 (see Figure 3.1). Furthermore, in the case of this episode, there remains only an audio recording, not a visual record, which only further accentuates the archival lacunae between the episode and its metadata because of all the information lost without the visual referent.[11]

For an audience that has neither seen nor heard of *Extension*, the archival description of this episode of *Extension* appears to provide a great deal of

---

670507-10
Pgm. Title: EXTENSION
Program City: UNKNOWN
Broadcast Date: MAY07-1967   Broadcast Time: 12:30:00
Series Title:
MODERN CANADIAN POETRY
1t, format: digital, type: DAT

Network: CBLT
TV audio of an anthology series devoted to modern Canadian poetry.

Host Phyllis Webb interviews Canadian poets Louis Dudek, George Johnston and Michael Gnarowski. They discuss the poetry scene of Montreal in the 1950s and the influence of Ezra Pound, Frank Scott and Dylan Thomas, on Canadian poetry.

The following letters are read:
(a) Louis Dudek to Raymond Souster, New York, 1951.
(b) Ezra Pound to Louis Dudek, Washington, 1951.
(c) Raymond Souster to Louis Dudek, Toronto, 1951.
(d) Louis Dudek to Raymond Souster, New York, 1951.
(e) John Sutherland to Louis Dudek, Montreal, 1951.
(f) Sid Corman to Raymond Souster, Boston, 1952.
(g) Louis Dudek to Raymond Souster, Montreal, 1952.
(h) Sid Corman to Raymond Souster, Boston, 1952.
(i) Robert Creeley to Raymond Souster, Majorca, 1952.
(j) Louis Dudek to Raymond Souster, New York, 1952.
(k) Kenneth Patchen reads his own poetry to jazz.
(approx. 04:00).

The program concludes with general discussion on the influence of American beat-poetry, and the critiques of Northrop Frye on the development of Canadian poetry.

3.1 CBC catalogue record for 7 May 1967 episode of *Extension*.

information, including the names of the poets who read, the general topics of discussion, the archival correspondence read aloud during the episode, and the fact that only the audio signal from this audiovisual media event is now available in the archive. Only when comparing the experiences of listening to the episode and of reading the archival description does one realize how much is left out of the latter. While there are certainly numerous actions and nuances that are necessarily absent from any archival description, I would argue that the most significant lacunae in this particular textual record are the qualities and meanings implicit in Webb's performance as mediator of the episode's conversation. Her critical work in making the conversation and archival documents of the letters converge can be gleaned only by experiencing the audio document itself. For instance, the archival description notes that Webb and her guests (Louis Dudek, George Johnston, and Michael Gnarowski) "discuss the poetry scene of Montreal in the 1950s and the influence of Ezra Pound, Frank Scott and Dylan Thomas, on Canadian poetry." One might further ascertain from the description that this discussion makes reference to the letters as primary sources that archive the conversations that poets were having about poetry and the influence of the poets Ezra Pound, Frank Scott, and Dylan Thomas. However, it is impossible to ascertain, except from the program itself, that Webb makes the following argument regarding the influence of these poets on Canadian poetry: "Dylan Thomas opened up our ears, so that, when Ginsberg started reading his great long howl of protest, there was nowhere to run to. With the violent gesture of his language, he accomplished, in one poem, what Irving Layton, back in 1952, claimed poetry must do, especially in Canada." Webb builds toward this argument through audible sound editing, starting with "Howl" read by Allen Ginsberg – "I saw the best minds of my generation" – and then shifting from Ginsberg to Webb. Webb's voice takes over reading Ginsberg's lines, "Who were expelled from the academies for crazy and publishing obscene odes on the windows of the skull," before she changes the tone of her voice to introduce the theme of tonight's episode of *Extension*: "The opening lines of Allen Ginsberg's famous poem, 'Howl,' the poem that howled its way across America and Canada, and is still making it around the world. But this isn't a program about Allen Ginsberg, patron saint of the beat movement. What I want to say is that that poem of his was a major poetic event in the fifties. A breakthrough." But were audiences ready to hear this breakthrough? Webb says, yes, because, as she argues, "Dylan Thomas opened up our ears." Moreover she aligns the force of Ginsberg with Layton in Canada in that he broke down barriers of what constituted 'poetry' and shook up more conservative listeners.

After making this argument, Webb transitions to her guest Louis Dudek by turning to the publication of Layton's *Cerberus*, the first book published by Contact Press and a book that presented Layton's work with fellow poets Louis Dudek and Raymond Souster: "These three poets were out to change the world in 1952 as much as they were out to change poetry." The on-air conversation then begins about this time in the 1950s (recalling that this program aired in 1967, which was not far from that decade), and the poets all agree that the 1950s were times of change and momentum: "It was a very confident time in the 1950s ... One felt one knew what poetry needed." Following this statement made by Dudek, the poets begin to list names they recall as important figures, starting with Webb's comment that "there was a genuine sense of community" and then continuing with her list: "I think I began to believe in the terrific importance of poetry because I was moving with people like Irving Layton, Louis, Frank Scott, Leonard [Cohen] was around ... Avi Boxer was there ... Eli Mandel ... Doug Jones." Improvised and unscripted, they pause amid the listing of names and comment on how some poets were "movement" poets and others were not (noting Margaret Avison as an example of the latter), which leads Webb to pose the question: "Is there any importance in a group or is there a negative value?" In response, [Dudek] replies, "I would think that a group would be kind of a nice thing. There's lots of excitement." At this point, a beverage is poured (on set) and one hears these interjections: "Thank you – oh you're welcome!" along with the sound of pouring liquid into a cup, which I describe audibly because only the audio is available for this particular episode. One could argue that "a group" has formed here in this audio document of a televised conversation, and even though they are being filmed, the setting is very much like the sort of meetings over coffee that they talk about as being part of the 1950s poetry scene in Canada. This episode then captures the making of poetic communities even while staging an unarchiving of those makings through the reading of letters and through a conversational reconstruction of these communities. The layers of mediation that inform this archival performance of community, past and present, exceed the archival description of this episode. Ironically, this act of unarchiving, and the performative production it entails, can only be heard *in* the archives themselves or, rather, during the temporal moments when the archival materials are replayed in the present, thereby revealing, as in the case of Webb's opening argument (regarding a line of influence rooted in the oral-aural from Ginsberg and Thomas to Layton) an archival lacunae of poetry and poetics waiting to be made lively again.

Readings on TV: "Take Off Your Mask, Bill, and Join the Group"

The most publicly accessible episode of *Extension* is the one in which Webb interviews bpNichol and bill bissett, originally broadcast on 2 July 1967. The reason for this is its uploading to YouTube by bissett, who curates a

YouTube channel of videos of his past readings. This episode of *Extension* appears in full, divided into Parts I and II, with a black screen where commercial breaks occurred. Interviewing Nichol and bissett in 1967 means that Webb taps into the aura of experimentation associated with the sound poetry and concrete poetry that both Nichol and bissett were exploring at the time. Artwork decorates the walls of the television-stage set, a record player is on hand (for when Nichol plays one of his sound experiments), and soft jazz music plays as an announcer's voice welcomes viewers to this episode of *Extension*. "This is the death of the poem, as I have faithfully reported it, November 29, 1966," begins the first reading by Nichol, and then bissett's and Webb's voices join, chanting "obituary obituary obituary." *This* is the poetry reading that viewers across Canada encountered if they tuned in on that summer day in Canada's centennial year.[12] The reading of "this is the death of the poem" is a chaotic polyphonic chant. Enacting a version of the poetic disruption she heard and admired in Ginsberg or Layton, Webb brings a performative poetics of avant-garde sound poetry onto the television sets of Canadians. After this "reading," she says to bissett, "Take off your mask, bill, and join the group" (as he had been wearing a painted mask with surreal, exaggerated facial features and a fake knife through the throat during the opening group reading). With this instruction, Webb symbolically unmasks the strange identity of the new Canadian avant-garde. She then proceeds to meditate upon the strangeness of the Canadian avant-garde for a CBC audience by conducting a conversation about poetry with two living specimens from the fringe of Canadian cultural content while also engaging in avant-garde practice herself.

Webb guides the audience through the intricacies of Nichol's and bissett's poetry – educating viewers about concrete poetry and concepts of border-blur, such that the conversation flows naturally, just as the set design appears 'natural' in a Barthesian sense of knowing that its naturalness is staged. Sitting at a table, the poets sip coffee and smoke cigarettes, discuss what a poem is, and occasionally read a poem as an example, as though the audience is sitting there with them in that fourth space at the table. At one point, all the poets become listeners as they attend to a recording of Nichol's own experimental sound poem played on a tape player. The media technologies of poetic sound are all around them, thereby staging the act of listening through these objects and also situating themselves and their poetry among the technologies that have both created and inscribed their poetry (the typewriter and the pen and paper) and that can be used to listen to it (the tape player and the record player).

From bissett and Nichol, the final episode of *Extension* moves to the opposite end of the spectrum of what constitutes a poetry reading. It was filmed on location in Toronto's Parliament Street Public Library as a traditional poetry reading, or the kind of reading that Frank Lazer has called "the more standardized and university-accredited poetry reading."[13] Even though *Extension* ends with this more traditional reading format, all of the other episodes push the boundaries of what constitutes a literary reading. With *Extension*, Webb expanded the format of both a television program *and* a poetry reading.

Christine Mitchell and Jason Camlot have argued that "the poetry reading series, as a literary and performance genre and temporal entity, demands special emphasis as it resists straightforward classifications and modes of presentation."[14] One could make the same argument for the poetry reading itself as a form of event. According to Charles Bernstein, "the reading is the site in which the audience of poetry constitutes and reconstitutes itself. It makes itself visible to itself."[15] In the final episode of *Extension*, the staged audience quite literally "makes itself visible to itself" and to the viewing public, which constitutes yet another audience for this poetry reading. Webb hosts the broadcast of a poetry reading by "six new poets" – Margaret Atwood, Robert Hogg, Harry Howith, Roy Kiyooka, Michael Ondaatje, and Joe Rosenblatt. As Camlot and Darren Wershler note, "From the 1950s on (at least), the reading series has been implicated in an existential ethos that values presence, and a hermeneutical ethos that values context."[16] This final episode of *Extension* presents a televised staging of such existential values of presence and liveness. It is a reading staged for television, a performance of a poetry reading. Several factors make the constructed liveness for television more apparent. Nearly all of the applause is edited out. Webb addresses the camera more than the audience as she announces each reader. The camera work of the episode focuses closely on the active reader and occasionally pans across the faces of audience members. In fact, I would call this a poetry watching as much as a poetry reading to the extent that the camera presents the people in the studio audience on screen watching the poets read their poetry. As in all film-based media, the camera becomes a focalizing character of its own. The camera even makes ironic choices about who to focus on during the reading: for example, when its gaze seems to have become distracted by two women sitting behind the reader and lingers on them for a full thirty seconds. The length of this lingering segment was so noticeable it prompted me to count the seconds, and then to note that it occurs while Ondaatje reads the word "scowl" and that these two women could very much be described as scowling even if what they were doing was intently listening. By framing the way in which we watch a reading, the camera influences how we perceive it. In this episode, this influence is most explicit in the way the footage is edited to match particular lines read to audience responses. For example, while Atwood announces that her poem is "about the Boston Strangler," the camera zooms in on a man who smirks, as though the camera 'reads' his reaction as part of the poem. Even though we as viewers are in a similar position to those audience members in the Parliament Street Public Library, our watching of the reading is mediated through the camera lens and the televisual medium that it records. As a result, even this seemingly more traditional reading takes on more dimensions as a mediated literary event. The staging, editing, and camera angles draw our attention to the making of this event such that we, as viewers, read and interpret how the event has been recorded as much as we attend to the readings themselves.

Extension

The title *Extension* was directly informed by Webb's poetics and her work for the CBC. I make this claim because, in 1963, Webb recorded a series of interviews at the 1963 Vancouver Poetry Conference that were intended for broadcast on the CBC literary radio program *Anthology*. Although the interviews were never broadcast, they reveal Webb's intense interest in the poetics articulated at that conference – a conference that featured American poets Robert Creeley, Robert Duncan, Allen Ginsberg, Denise Levertov, and Charles Olson. Importantly, at the time of these interviews and of the conference, Creeley had made his oft-quoted statement in a letter to Olson: "Form is never more than an extension of content."[17] By calling the poetry program *Extension*, Webb invokes Creeley and aims to extend her own experiments in the relationship between form and content (in *Naked Poems* [1965], for example) to her media production. If we follow this line – this poetic line – of thought, then how is form an extension of content in the case of this program? For nearly all the episodes, the form takes the shape of Webb mediating conversations with poets about poetry. Readings are often interspersed within these conversations, particularly when readings offer examples of the kinds of poetry under discussion. Within this mix of conversation and poetry reading, Webb functions as the extension. She links the poetry and the audience by crafting the program and by contextualizing the poems when read out loud. She concludes her series with comments that, again, reinforce the idea of poetry as a medium – as a lively, mediated art. Webb has crafted an argument for poetry as a lively art through all of the preceding episodes, and in this final one, the attentive listener cannot help but notice that she has returned to the same poet mentioned in the first episode: Dylan Thomas. She concludes *Extension* and the filming at the public library by reading a poem – Thomas's poem "In my Craft or Sullen Art." In reading another poet's poem out loud and in choosing to read this particular poem, Webb makes a statement about poetry (her own "craft") without seeming to. Ostensibly, she is simply reading a poem, doing nothing different than the other readers in this last episode. Yet her choice of poem speaks volumes: it continues the argument that she proposes in the first episode of *Extension* when she rephrases Thomas's "sullen art" to describe poetry as "a lively art." A close assessment of the *Extension* series in its entirety reveals that Webb has made this argument for poetry as a lively art through all thirteen episodes and, moreover, that she has developed this argument through a medium that constructs an illusion of liveness on screen. The final episode in which the poetry reading looks as though it were filmed live – with an audience listening and poets reading at the podium on stage – and yet which cuts the applause and directs our gaze with camera work and editing, the mediated nature of the liveness, and liveliness, of the event underscores the art of poetry.

As the credits roll at the end of this episode, the medium of television poignantly asserts itself. As Webb reads "In my Craft or Sullen Art," the credits start to appear. First, the word "Extension" partially covers the face of Margaret Atwood, who is sitting in the audience. Audibly, Webb reads the poem (the lively art), and as the credits continue, the camera (mediating the live art) focuses on poets in the audience. One medium extends from the other in what I would argue *is* an extension. With the words, "Nor heed my craft," the camera rests upon the faces of Atwood, Howith, and Ondaatje. The viewer of the program watches poets hearing Webb's voice reading a poem by another poet (Thomas) that reflects upon poetry – "my craft" – at the end of a reading that the viewer has both been part of and distanced from. It is a *mise en abyme* effect that I would argue mimics an archival structure in which the audiovisual recording is not at home in one place but, rather, in its fact of circulation – in the multiple acts of watching and listening that constitute it. In other words, the archive in question is not 'at home' in a preservation of the original broadcast but rather in its extension outward. The audiovisual archives of the CBC have shifted from being understood as static locations or objects to being understood "as media and communications strategies," to cite Gabriella Giannachi's account of the contemporary archive.[18]

To close, I am interested in combining Giannachi's claim with the opening question of Lee's program – "Where have all the poets gone?" – and my own suggestion at the start of this chapter that they have not gone anywhere. The poets – of here, now, and then – are here in the world and in the audiovisual archive. The archival status of the *here* is one of extension. *Extension* as a television program resisted a fixed format. The experimental form of the program leads us to recognize that its archival 'home' is not in the CBC building in Toronto but rather in its mechanisms of circulation. The fact that one must go to the CBC in order to watch the program puts it at odds with the circulation it so desires and deserves as "a lively art."

In the final seconds of the last episode of *Extension*, the camera shifts away from the poets listening and Webb reading the poem, and, as though playing a trick on the TV viewing audience, settles on the same female audience members who had caught the camera's attention during Ondaatje's reading. This time the two faces are not looking at the camera but, instead, in the direction of Webb herself reading the final words of Thomas's poem. The camera remains focused on these two faces through a full five seconds of silence. In these seconds, the fact that this is a taped reading becomes wholly apparent: the reading is over but the camera is still rolling. This moment reveals that the reading we have been watching has always been an archive of a literary event, even in its "original" format. In other words, it was never candidly live but rather a staged presentation of what resembles a live event. However, the status of the program as a staged recording of a live event does not mean that there is no liveness to be found in this archive. It is, in fact, a lively archive. And within this lively archive, there are even moments that exceed the recording and reveal its status as a staged record of time. "This has been a CBC presentation": these final words of *Extension* appear on the screen while the two audience members continue looking in the exact same direction they have been throughout the episode – even though the reading has ended. Just as the camera holds its gaze upon them, they appear to hold theirs on Webb – here, now, and then – as though everyone is posed, paused, waiting for someone to say that this taping of a lively art is over.

Appendix: *Extension* Poets: Here, Now, and Then

The following condensed list of broadcast dates and guests on *Extension*, hosted by Phyllis Webb, was compiled from the CBC archival database.

30 April 1967 F.R. Scott, Irving Layton, and Miriam Waddington

7 May 1967 Louis Dudek, George Johnston, and Michael Gnarowski

14 May 1967 Earle Birney, George Bowering, Victor Coleman, and bpNichol

21 May 1967 Poems by A.J.M. Smith, Jay MacPherson, L.A. MacKay, A.M. Klein, Alden Nowlan, F.R. Scott, Patrick Anderson, Anne Marriott, Gwendolyn MacEwan, Roy Daniells, Flora Clark McLaren, Eli Mandel, George Bowering read by Irena Mayeska, Gillie Fenwick, Timothy Findley, Claude Miguet, and Phyllis Webb

28 May 1967 Irving Layton

4 June 1967 Louis Dudek and Raymond Souster, with a film by Timothy Findley

11 June 1967 Margaret Avison and Alfred Purdy, with a film by Timothy Findley

18 June 1967 Gwendolyn MacEwen and Leonard Cohen

25 June 1967 Earle Birney and Miriam Waddington

2 July 1967 bill bissett and bpNichol

9 July 1967 James Reaney, John Beckwith, and Dorothy Livesay

16 July 1967 P.K. Page and A.J.M. Smith

23 July 1967 An edited version of a live reading at the Parliament Street Library in Toronto by six poets: Michael Ondaatje, Roy Kiyooka, Margaret Atwood, Robert Hogg, Harry Howith, and Joe Rosenblatt

NOTES

1   Sook-Yin Lee, "Where Have All the Poets Gone?" Exhibitionists, CBC, online, https://www.cbc.ca/player/play/2685222968, 25 March 2016.

2   Ibid.

3   See the work of Albert Moran on the evolution in television formatting and its impact on the medium. Karina Aveyard, Albert Moran, and Majbritt Jensen, eds, *New Patterns in Global Television Formats* (Chicago: Intellect, 2009).

4   The title "Where Have All the Poets Gone?" has been used before, such as in Juan Vidal's questioning of where the voice of poetry has gone from political protest: "Why do I bring this up? Because I'm wondering why the words of today's poets don't pack the same weight and influence as works like 'Howl.'" Juan Vidal, "Where Have All The Poets Gone?" NPR, online.

5   The emphasis on poetry makes *Extension* stand apart from other television programming and even from other literary programming on Canadian airwaves. CBC Radio programs such as *Anthology* and *Critically Speaking* have included poetry, both as content and as a topic of discussion, but there was not a program specifically devoted to poetry on air until *Extension*. Thus, to create this poetry program on a public broadcaster was a significant step, let alone discuss and enact literary criticism of poetry on the airwaves.

6   This quotation and all other quotations that follow from *Extension* are transcribed from audiovisual recordings of the program in the CBC Archives, Toronto. They will be cited in my text without further reference. My thanks to Keith Hart and Arthur Schwartzel for their help in accessing these materials.

7   "Television is instrumental in the everyday narrativizing of the nation," writes Marusya Bociurkiw, in relation to more recent television programming in Canada, but nonetheless relevant. Marusya Bociurkiw, *Feeling Canadian: Television, Nationalism, and Affect* (Waterloo: Wilfrid Laurier University Press, 2011), 43. When listening to *Extension*, each time one of the recordings included the advertisements that preceded it, I was deeply aware of its 1967 context: nearly every one was related to the Centennial. Before the episode with Earle Birney and Miriam Waddington, an image of a turkey appears with the following transcribed audio advertising CBC's Country Calendar: "It's agricultural week, and this afternoon at 1:30, Country Calendar presents a special national edition of its show direct from Expo 67 in Montreal. Four CBC farm commentators will show us many of the fine displays of Canada's resources. That's this afternoon at 1:30 on Country Calendar. See it in colour." This was what

preceded Webb's program on Canadian poetry: nationalism, agriculture, media commentary, and the promise of all of it in colour. Moreover, this advertisement reveals the organizational structure of television programming that greatly differs from the on-demand streaming of digital media, in which the media event is still time-based and yet almost timeless in not being fixed to a rigid broadcast schedule. In the particular episode of *Extension* that follows this advertisement, Earle Birney reads a poem that criticizes billboards, and Webb comments, "You'll be glad to hear there are no commercials on this program, Earle." In this comment, we might recall that there had been an advertisement (albeit for the CBC) before the program, but we also think about the program itself as resisting the construct of the commercial as a site of affect. Viewers would experience *Extension* both through this affective frame of the nation and through the affordances of television as a medium to either (re)produce or resist this frame. Furthermore, *Extension* was one of the CBC's Centennial projects and had received funding for that reason, which, as Webb explained, was also why the program did not continue since it was not part of regular programming. Phyllis Webb, interviewed by Katherine McLeod, Salt Spring Island, BC, 28 July 2017.

8   I refer to the readers as readers because they read the poems, but they are more like actors due to their staged placement and anonymity during the performance itself. They are not identified until the credits, which list the readers as Irena Mayeska, Gillie Fenwick, Timothy Findley, and Claude Miguet, with Findley being the most recognizable of the group.

9   Philip Auslander, *Liveness: Performance in a Mediatized Culture* (New York: Routledge, 1999).

10   Here, I am reminded of Ann Cvetkovich's *An Archive of Feelings*, but I am also aware of how Webb's archives, even if relatively inaccessible, have an institutional legitimacy that differentiates them from the marginalized archives of queer trauma and their relation to the public and the private through affect. Ann Cvetkovich, *An Archive of Feelings: Trauma, Sexuality, and Lesbian Public Cultures* (Durham: Duke University Press, 2003).

11   All episodes were available to view except for this one and the episode with Gwendolyn MacEwen and Leonard Cohen (18 June 1967). The CBC archives were not able to locate any copy of these two episodes in the television archives. However, the radio archives hold audio recordings of all episodes; therefore, I was able to listen to these two episodes for their audible content.

(See Deshaye's chapter 9 in this book on Layton and CBC audiovisual archives for a similar encounter with an audio recording of a television program.)

12 The centennial represents an important context for such a broadcast of cultural content. For instance, the advertisement that played just before this episode reminded viewers that the CBC would be broadcasting episodes from the Royal Tour throughout its coverage of Expo and Centennial events. That this advertisement appears on the recordings of the program held in the CBC archives but not before bissett's YouTube version of the broadcast (which has been posted online by the author himself and not by the CBC) reveals the significance of watching and listening to CBC programs within the context of their original broadcast as much as possible. However, one might argue, too, that bissett's YouTube version also exists within a readable platform and that the advertising panels and comment section, among other features, are just as important when understanding the remediation of this program.

13 Frank Lazer, "Thinking Made in the Mouth: The Cultural Poetics of David Antin and Jerome Rothenberg," in *Picturing Cultural Values in Postmodern America*, ed. William G. Doty (Tuscaloosa: University of Alabama Press, 1995), 119.

14 Jason Camlot and Christine Mitchell, "The Poetry Series," *Amodern 4: The Poetry Serie*s, http://amodern.net/issues/amodern-4/ (1 June 2014).

15 Charles Bernstein, "Introduction," *Close Listening: Poetry and the Performed Word* (New York: Oxford University Press, 1998), 22.

16 Jason Camlot and Darren Wershler, "Theses on Discerning the Reading Series," *Amodern* 4 (2015), http://amodern.net/article/theses-reading-series/ (1 June 2014).

17 Robert Creeley and Charles Olson, "Monday/June 5 (1950)," in *The Complete Correspondence, Vol. 1*, ed. George F. Butterick (Santa Barbara: Black Sparrow Press 1980), 79.

18 Gabriella Giannachi, *Archive Everything: Mapping the Everyday* (Cambridge, MA: MIT Press, 2016), 9.

4
____

Canadian Pulp Fictions
Unarchiving Genre Fiction as CanLit

MARCELLE KOSMAN

In the wake of the 2011 Scotiabank Giller Prize nominations, the *Globe and Mail* ran a column asking, "Are Canadian writers 'Canadian' enough?"[1] The column's author, John Barber, premised his query with the assumption – what he proposes to be "an article of national faith" – that "Canadian literature is good because it tells Canadian stories to Canadians." Specifically referencing a dearth of overt Canadian settings on each of the country's major literary award short lists, Barber wrote: "Even the jury for the Governor-General's Literary Award, traditional bastion of national literary taste, could only find two identifiably Canadian novels to recommend on a short list of five contenders." Though the column quotes scholars who positively identify the trend of setting Canadian literature outside Canada as "confident," "cosmopolitan," and "a faithful reflection of the ethnic diversity of modern Canada," Barber's column as a whole laments an imagined, uncomplicated history of high cultural production in which Canadians told (good) stories *about* Canada *to* Canadians.

A question so inherently exclusionary as "Are Canadian writers 'Canadian' enough?" is inextricable from intersections of colonialism, sexism, and white supremacy. These intersections shape the constitution of English-Canadian literature as an industry so fundamentally that the absence of genre fiction from the canon might well seem to be the institution's least urgent concern,[2] but an understanding of the history of genre literature in Canada can help us recognize the formation of CanLit as a discernible cultural entity. In particular, an examination of the collapse of Canada's pulp periodical industry is instructive in its revelation of the process by which genre was prevented from infiltrating English-Canadian literary culture in the first place and, indeed, of the zeitgeist that motivated and shaped what we have come to call CanLit. That is, the erasure of Canada's brief experiment with genre fiction publishing and accompanying archive of comics, pulp magazines, and mass-market novels underscores how CanLit itself was shaped into a genre. To demonstrate this, I analyze the rise and collapse of Canada's pulp magazine industry during the 1940s and early 1950s using a historical materialist approach and conduct a symptomatic reading of several Canadian pulp magazines and key government documents. The juxtaposition of the assertively leftist pulp magazines against the moral conservatism expressed in House of Commons debates, bills, and acts reveals the operational political antagonism motivating the Canadian government's allocation of resources exclusively in support of highbrow cultural production. The erasure of pulp magazines from both the cultural landscape and cultural memory was a desired outcome – not merely an incidental side effect – of the manufacturing of middle-class anglophone Canadian culture so methodically represented by CanLit.

The question of whether Canadian writers are "Canadian" enough, as well as eschewing matters of racial and gender-based discrimination, which exceed the focus of this chapter,[3] takes for granted the widely accepted convention of CanLit as generically uniform: novels and short story collections that overwhelmingly abide by the principles of realism (if written by men) or the sentimental and autobiographical (if written by women). In fact, stereotypes of what constitutes CanLit are so consistent that they inspire comical parodies on social media. For example, Canadian feminist blogger Anne Thériault produced a series of tweets describing "Every historical novel set in Nova Scotia," including: "The Sea Is A Metaphor for God/ fate/death/ a woman's love/how much we hate Ontario."[4] Perceptions of Canadian poetry fare no better; in February 2016, BuzzFeed featured an article about a Tumblr collection of "imagined" Canadian poetry volumes, highlighting the invented titles: "Canadian Poetry: a well-meaning people and a noble genre," "Soul of a Monarch, Dream of the Zephyr: Modern Canadian Poetry," and "The Night Isn't Going to Call Itself 'Luminescent' on Its Own, Is It?: Canadian Poetry 1967–2015."[5] Clearly there exists a tacit understanding of what constitutes CanLit. As a result, readers and cultural critics rarely wonder, "Is it 'Canadian' enough?" of science fiction, fantasy, or hard-boiled detective fiction.

The generic uniformity of the literatures called CanLit is the legacy of decades of canon-formation practices motivated by the report of the Royal Commission on National Development in the Arts, Letters and Sciences (commonly known as the Massey Commission) issued June 1951. Despite numerous critical interventions in the canon since its institutionalization in the 1960s and 1970s, the qualities of CanLit (the *CanLit*-ness of CanLit so easily taken for granted by readers and cultural critics) have remained relatively consistent. In fact, the works making up the Canadian canon are so generically similar that, while provocative, it is not inaccurate to refer to CanLit as a *genre*. Donna Bennett's essay "Conflicted Vision: A Consideration of Canon and Genre in English-Canadian Literature" compellingly demonstrates how the construction of a Canadian literary canon in English has been obstructed by preoccupations with genre.[6] Bennett's analysis indicates that the works occupying the canon are not canonical because they exemplify the *best* of Canadian writing, but because they are so sufficiently similar in generic qualities as to form a cohesive list. It is in this sense that we can refer to CanLit as a literary genre with identifiable cultural and social implications and resonance. Or, to put it provocatively, CanLit is genre literature.

The Massey Report takes for granted that a singular, national culture is not only feasible but also necessary for national unity, arguing vehemently that Canada suffers a dearth of recognizably Canadian culture. While literature is only one among numerous cultural enterprises championed by the Commission, the report identifies government investment in literature as imperative in preventing an American mass culture invasion: "we do think it important to comment on the efforts of those literary groups belonging to various schools of thought which strive to *defend* Canadian literature against the *deluge* of the less worthy American publications. These [publications], we are told, *threaten* our national values, *corrupt* our literary taste and *endanger* the livelihood of our writers"[7] (emphasis added). The language of security and defence deployed by the Massey Report is deliberate; the Commission's investigation into the state of Canadian culture was a nationalist project undertaken during the Cold War and initiated by Canada's then minister of defence Brooke Claxton.[8] A review of House of Commons debates on popular reading practices concurrent with the Commission's investigation makes clear that the "American publications" in question were pulp periodicals. The House of Commons debates over Davie Fulton's (member for Kamloops) private member's bill to categorize the depiction of crimes in pulp magazines and comics as "obscene" is illustrative. Members of the House make numerous references to the need not only to control the circulation and content of pulp periodicals but also to supply fiction-hungry readers with "good literature."[9] Further, these debates show that for the political elite even pulp periodicals written and produced in Canada were considered American.

The relationship between federally supported Canadian culture and nationalism is well documented.[10] Of particular relevance here is the obligation cultural nationalism imposed on English-Canadian literature to articulate a mature, secure, unified nation.[11] It is thus useful to remember Robert Lecker's charge in 1995 that the books taken for granted today as the early works of the Canadian canon were selected arbitrarily.[12] Likewise, we might recall that in 1998 Nick Mount added that the canon's early texts aren't even very good.[13] And, importantly, John Metcalf's polemical assertion in 1982, preceding both Mount and Lecker, that the works of CanLit are "largely crappy."[14] If an *arbitrary* collection of *not very good*, perhaps even "largely crappy," books could articulate the nation, how much worse could pulp magazines have been that even their Canadian-authored stories weren't accepted as Canadian? What, precisely, about these "less worthy American publications" was so threatening to Canada's cultural and political elite that it warranted state intervention? My research suggests that the federal government's manoeuvres to control pulp magazine circulation in Canada during the 1930s, 1940s, and 1950s was only superficially a matter of cultivating taste and can more credibly be understood as a strategy to forestall a socialist revolution (though it succeeded at both).[15]

Scholars have reasonably documented the Canadian elite's anathema for pulp magazines and comic books as symptomatic of the pre-canon anxiety about the Americanization of Canadian culture, particularly literature. Archival research conducted by John Bell, Carolyn Strange and Tina Loo, Michelle Smith, and Will Straw[16] demonstrates the phenomenal popularity of American pulp periodicals in Canada during the early to mid-twentieth century. Smith's research, for example, puts pulp magazine circulation in Canada "at 1 million issues per week" in the 1920s and 1930s, accounting for "one-tenth of American sales."[17] Evidently, Canadians were consuming

American popular culture en masse, thereby channelling a significant share of Canadian funds into the pockets of American cultural producers. When in December 1940 the Canadian government introduced the War Exchange Conservation Act to keep Canadian dollars in Canada, pulp magazines and comic books were included among a substantial catalogue of embargoed items. While Strange and Loo remark that the embargo specifically "restricted periodicals that featured 'detective, sex, western, and alleged true or confession stories,'"[18] even magazines dedicated to science fiction and the supernatural were stopped at the border,[19] suggesting that no border control agents differentiated pulp magazine genres; pulp materiality alone signalled its prohibition. Working backward from the eventual criminalization of pulp magazines in 1949, both Strange and Loo and Smith make compelling claims for the classist nature of the embargo on pulps, noting that the Act permitted the continued importation of American "slicks," the shorthand for middle-class and elite magazines like *The Saturday Evening Post* and *Colliers*.[20] In fact, the phrasing of the Act gives the minister of national revenue discretion over which items are "desirable" and may therefore be afforded a permit to enter Canada,[21] thus indicating that American culture is only undesirable when it is low class.

Smith attributes the classist stigma against pulp magazines to the periodicals' perceived readership, a demographic believed to be mainly white, male, working class, and "often immigrant."[22] Drawing on the American pulp industry, where magazine publishers sold pulps to bankroll the costly production of slicks, Smith argues that pulp magazine production sustained "high culture" by serving as both "a lowly 'other' against which elite culture could structure itself" and an exploitable "base commodity that funded high culture, much the same way that the mass labor of typical pulp readers supported the power and elitism of the upper classes."[23] An excellent example is the American hard-boiled detective pulp magazine *Black Mask*, whose sale by co-owners H.L. Mencken and George Jean Nathan for a substantial profit on their original investment after a mere eight published issues, allowed Mencken and Nathan to "subsidise their elite magazine, *The Smart Set*."[24] Smith's research shows that, overtly, the War Exchange Conservation Act capitalized on "the inferior class status of the pulps" combined "with the belief that the pulps promoted moral degeneration"[25] and thus enabled the pulp embargo to serve both moral and economic ends. Covertly, however, the Act allowed "the Federal Government of Canada [to control] the reading matter of Canadian citizens who possessed the least degree of economic and social power."[26] That is, the Act demonstrated to working-class readers their political insignificance to those in power.

While research affirms that the stigma associated with pulp fiction results from the pulps' perceived readership, it is crucial to note that there is no reliable evidence that periodical reading can be segregated by class. Aritha van Herk reminds us that the figure of "the reader" is one "so adamantly slippery that we can no longer be clear [if we ever could have been] about the who/what/how of that reader."[27] Andrew Thacker identifies "the interplay between high and low circulations, between mass and minority publications, or between 'pulp' and 'slick' and 'quality' magazines" as evidence that a binary between high and low publications is "too crude to capture the diverse field of American periodicals."[28] Faye Hammill and Michelle Smith's work on magazine publishing in Canada likewise indicates that the boundaries between the main tiers of periodicals (pulps, slicks, and avant-garde publications called "little magazines") are so porous that "it is perhaps more useful to think in terms of a continuum rather than a fixed hierarchy."[29] Indeed, members of Parliament in debates over the censorship of pulp magazines make references to their own children reading the pulps.[30] The slipperiness of "the who/what/how" of the pulp reader by no means invalidates Smith's or Strange and Loo's claims about either the classist nature of the embargo or the Canadian government's subsequent efforts to eliminate pulp magazine production in Canada. Rather, it urges a re-evaluation of what the Massey Commission members meant when they claimed the pulps threatened our national values, corrupted our literary taste, and endangered the livelihood of our writers.

As has been noted by Bell, Strange and Loo, Smith, Straw, and others, the War Exchange Conservation Act triggered the emergence of a Canadian pulp magazine industry to fill the gap left in the periodical market. This industry, scholars contend, only fortified governmental fears of the Americanization of Canadian culture irrespective of the distinctiveness of the Canadian magazines' content.[31] Though Straw demonstrates the rampant plagiarism in the Canadian pulp magazine industry,[32] my research aligns with that of Bell, Strange and Loo, and Smith, who show that publishers like Alval and Superior went to tremendous lengths to market the new magazines as one hundred per cent Canadian products. For example, the back cover of the second issue of *Science Fiction*, a short-lived publication devoted entirely to reprints of American science fiction stories, states: "This magazine is an all-Canadian product, printed and published in Canada and distributed by a Canadian distributing firm. By the purchase of this periodical you are giving Canadians employment, Canadians who are paying taxes, buying War Savings Certificates and Victory Bonds, doing their bit to preserve a free Canada and to maintain our prosperity."[33] Further down the cover, this promise is reiterated: "Ours are truly all-Canadian magazines, conceived, edited and written in Canada by Canadians, adding to our country's business."[34] Smith explains that even though Canadian pulps were saturated with nationalist rhetoric, they were designed to be "indistinguishable from the American [pulps] that could no longer be purchased in Canada."[35] She provides a case study of one publisher, Alec Valentine, whose magazines were "so similar to their American counterparts that at one point [Valentine] became entangled in a dispute over the copyright of one his titles."[36] The particular confluence of American mass culture and Canadian nationalism found in Canadian pulp magazines, Smith argues, "drew out fears about the Americanization of Canadian society" because "American culture was being replicated within the borders of the Canadian nation in a manner that eroded distinctions between American and Canadian literary culture."[37]

Canadian anxiety about Americanization is a well-documented cultural phenomenon and the 1949 House of Commons debates over Fulton's criminal code amendment to censor pulp magazines are excellent examples of this. Fulton's private member's bill, which would criminalize the production of comics and pulp magazines and thereby catalyze the collapse Canada's entire pulp periodical industry, was introduced to address the circulation of crime comics given the alleged threat they posed to the moral development of children. However, careful examination of House records makes clear that the bill's adoption was only superficially about censoring depictions of crime. Robert Ross "Roy" Knight (member for Saskatoon), for example, declares: "The comic book and comic strip business originated in the United States … this is an American institution … The fact that we copy these things is an illustration of something I said the other day. In the matter of literature we seem to be copiers rather than originators. The sooner we change that attitude the better it will be not only for the adults but for our children."[38] Keeping in mind that these debates occurred while the Massey Commission undertook to inventory cultural production in Canada, it is clear that this was a period of cleaning house, culturally speaking. Criminalizing crime comics provided members of the Canadian government who were concerned with literary culture an opportunity to get rid of the entire pulp industry.

Smith is reluctant to make a causal link between the passing of Fulton's bill and the end of Canada's pulp magazine industry. Though she recognizes the bill's influence, as well as the "political and social anxiety" that motivated it, Smith points to the cheap paperback novel as the ultimate culprit in the demise of Canadian pulp magazines: "The content of the novels was similar to that of the pulps, but the format offered more fiction at a cheaper price than pulp magazines. Changes in material production and consumer tastes, in conjunction with political efforts to stamp out crime pulps and define mass culture as counter-Canadian, ended the predominance of pulp magazines in Canada."[39] Strange and Loo, too, in their work on Canadian true crime pulps, stop short of blaming government intervention for the industry's collapse. They argue that "Canadian publications dwindled not because of moral campaigns but as a result of changing business practices, shifting tastes and increased competition. The reappearance of bigger and glossier U.S. magazines in the late 1940s … and the rise of the pulp novel industry (a phenomenon that ultimately overwhelmed the U.S. pulp magazine business as well) all contributed to the decline."[40] While the end of Canada's pulp magazine industry certainly resulted from a variety of factors, it cannot be overstated that government intervention sought to suppress rather than support this small but vibrant Canadian cultural industry. Strange and Loo themselves remark that "had Fulton and his supporters turned their attention to Canadian true crime magazines they might well have called for government subsidies to save this arm of Canada's publishing industry in an era of growing concern over the Americanization of Canadian culture."[41] Building from Smith's thorough investigation, then, we can put pressure on the notion that government intervention in the pulp periodical industry was concerned simply with "Americanization"; in so doing, we can further reconsider the impact of that intervention on the industry's demise.

Much as it is the case that Fulton's criminal code amendment was passed to curb the circulation of "unwholesome literature,"[42] it is also the case that Canada's pulp magazine industry destabilized the authority and dominance of high culture itself. During this period of aggressive cultural nationalism, when cultural and national sovereignty were made mutually constitutive, the Canadian elite would certainly have recognized the threat that a self-sustaining mass culture industry posed to Canada's interconnected cultural and economic class hierarchies. Unlike its American counterpart, for instance, Canada's pulp magazine industry operated autonomously. When the War Exchange Conservation Act embargoed American pulp periodicals, it wasn't Canada's established magazine industry that took advantage of the void in the periodical market; it was a handful of upstarts and opportunistic newspapermen who came out of the woodwork to capitalize on the massive demand for pulp magazines. They set up small-scale publishing operations, produced scores of lowbrow periodicals completely independent of the Canadian magazine trade, and – prior to government intervention – were tremendously successful. Alec Valentine's Alval Publishers of Canada Ltd, for example, the subject of Smith's 2006 case study, grew to have numerous subsidiaries and was one of the last pulp publishers to survive the return of American imports. Smith writes that "at the publishing house's peak in 1943–45, Valentine was publishing up to forty-four different titles on a monthly basis."[43] Whereas American pulp magazine sales subsidized slick magazine production, Canadian pulps provided no economic benefit to middle-class or elite cultural producers. Publishers like Alval and Superior were purely purveyors of lowbrow entertainment and their profits supported exclusively the expansion of their respective publishing enterprises. The success of this rogue cultural industry thus established a viable alternative to Canada's existing economic and class stratification.

Another compelling example of the industry's threatening influence is the nationalist rhetoric that gilded pulp magazines inside and out. Patriotism was carefully deployed in a manner that championed the working class as consumers and producers of Canadian culture. Smith claims that "the ways in which the magazines represented their own processes of production suggested that the magazines supported the labor of Canadian workers, the pulp and paper industry, and Canadian authors."[44] She quotes a blurb from one of Alval's true crime magazines as evidence: "*True Gangster Crime Cases* is edited and printed in Canada by Trade Union Workmen on Canadian paper."[45] The same blurb is also found in the men's magazine *Stag*,[46] discussed below. For Smith, these blurbs and the deployment of patriotic, wartime rhetoric in general "set up the pulps as not only a socially legitimate reading practice, but also a way of patriotically participating in Canadian society."[47] Uplifting the value of the working class may not strike the contemporary reader as a threat to post-war Canadian society, but in 1949 the government's aversion to communism was formidable. Recalling the wide circulation of lowbrow periodicals and the moral panic over the pulps' supposed influential power, these magazines' championing of the working class as capable producers of Canadian culture was a subtle but meaningful political position that called into question existing class-based social hierarchies.

The most compelling evidence to prove that the pulp industry served as a viable threat to Canada's established cultural and economic hierarchies is the fact that Valentine, one of the biggest players in the Canadian pulp periodical industry, was publishing socialist editorials and revolutionary fiction in his magazines. Library and Archives Canada's digital exhibition of Valentine's pulps, "Tales from the Vault!" draws attention to the men's magazine *Stag*, published initially by Daring and then by the Norman Book Company, both subsidiaries of Alval Publishers. The website remarks that throughout the 1940s, "*Stag*'s editorial position ... reveals a definite sympathy for left-wing and socialist principles," and describes the magazine's "socialist-themed cartoons," its criticism of "American 'lunacy laws,'" and its editorials that expressed "admiration for socialism and the Soviet Union." [48] Valentine's *Uncanny Tales*, too, was a site of political agitation. Published by Adam Publishing[49] until May 1942, then by the aforementioned Norman Book Company through its final issue in September/October 1943, *Uncanny Tales* was the only Canadian science fiction pulp magazine to produce more than a handful of issues. It was edited by Melvin Colby, a man described as a "strong leftist" with connections to the Futurians,[50] an American science fiction association known for its revolutionary communist politics. According to self-described anti-communist Sam Moskowitz, a writer and literary agent who headed the New York branch of the Science Fiction League (the fan association from which the Futurians had split due to political differences),[51] Colby conspired with the Futurians to keep anti-revolutionary science fiction out of circulation in Canada.[52] Moskowitz had observed the appearance of Futurian reprints in *Uncanny Tales* and, being "a prime antagonist of [Donald] Wollheim [one of the founders of the Futurians] on political grounds," Moskowitz contacted Colby to inquire if *Uncanny* would accept science fiction manuscripts "from non-revolutionary quarters."[53] Colby replied enthusiastically, so over the course of several months Moskowitz sent Colby about 100,000 words of reprints, unsold stories, and original manuscripts to be printed in *Uncanny*.[54] Colby, unbeknownst to Moskowitz, threw these manuscripts away, having neither published nor paid for them. Meanwhile, according to Moskowitz's account of his encounter with Wollheim's associate, John B. Michel, the Futurians had been supplying Colby with material for *Uncanny Tales* free of charge. As Moskowitz recalls, Michel claimed that "Colby was a strong leftist and didn't at all like the intimation he got from you that you were anti-communist."[55] This, combined with the Futurians' willingness to supply the editor with free material for the magazine, allowed Colby to withhold and eventually destroy any manuscripts that Moskowitz sent him.

Thus, Canada's major science fiction pulp magazine was edited by a "strong leftist" who not only filled the magazine's pages with stories by known socialists and communists in the American science fiction field but also strategically withheld from publication works of science fiction that were ideologically non-revolutionary. On its own, Moskowitz's account does not prove that Valentine was a communist sympathizer, nor that Canada's pulp periodical industry was a hothouse for radical politics. But when we consider in tandem the industry's independence from established Canadian cultural enterprises, the proud references in Valentine's magazines to employing "trade union workmen," and the federal government's strategic framing of the pulp industry as *un*-Canadian, suddenly the political leanings of Valentine's network of pulps seems a more convincing explanation for the anti-pulp sentiment expressed by late-1940s Canadian politicians than the vague claim that the pulps were "American."

If put under pressure, the argument that pulp magazines were a *specifically* American form of mass culture is unsupportable. Middle-class slicks, as demonstrated above, were never demonized as "un-Canadian" for sharing material similarities with their American counterparts. That the pulps originated in the U.S. is true,[56] but the pulps were no more "American" than novels are "British." Nor was the cheap paperback novel perceived as having a nationality or posing a threat to the autonomy of Canadian literature.[57] Rather, Canadian writers laud the paperback for making Canadian literature accessible for classroom study,[58] and numerous academics attribute to it Canadian literary studies as a field.[59] In framing mass culture as *un*-Canadian, Canada's political and cultural elite tied cultural production to national loyalty. In David Ketterer's words, "realism and naturalism were tools of nationalism. To describe the Canadian reality was, supposedly, to create the Canadian reality."[60] From this attitude came a self-perpetuating literary tradition in which Canadian writers overwhelmingly published their non-realist writing in American (and sometimes British) venues. For example, Ketterer provocatively states that Canadian author Phyllis Gotlieb considered her science fiction career to be "somehow un-Canadian, maybe even treasonable."[61] Gotlieb, Ketterer explains, whose poetry had been published in Canada, found that "the only outlets for her SF were American."[62] Frank Davey's material analysis of the Canadian canon supports Gotlieb's experience. Davey explains that "texts published by British and American publishers tended to … foreground internationally popular generic conventions" whereas "texts published by Canadian publishers tended to focus on internal Canadian events and issues" and, further, that "prizes awarded by [Canadian] publishers rewarded consumable 'realist' texts."[63] Davey's analysis demonstrates a consistent preference for realist and naturalist literatures across Canada's various "canon-constructing actors."[64]

The sustained marginalization of pulp periodicals as "American" suggests that there were no tropes or characteristics of Canadian genre fiction unique to Canadian pulp writers, but this assumption is disproven by the texts themselves. Strange and Loo identify two genres that stand out as characteristically unique to Canadian writers: the true crime arm of the Canadian pulp industry and a genre of "identifiably Canadian stories" that had been produced since the early twentieth century called "'Northerns' – fictional accounts of the high north, typically involving heroic Mounties on the hunt for scoundrels."[65] Both genres, Strange and Loo explain, served to promote values consistent with conservative Canadian nationalism. The Northerns, for example, "served imperialist ends: civilization always wore a scarlet [Mountie] uniform and spoke the Queen's English when delivering the benefits of empire to the hostile Indian, lawless American, or ignorant foreigner."[66] Likewise, Strange and Loo document a similar "moralism" of Canadian true crime magazines: "A detailed analysis of these crime narratives illustrates how Canadian pulps persistently conveyed the moral that sinfulness leads to earthly punishment: every crime sprang from pride, envy, anger, greed or lust. True crime stories were narrated with edgy dialogue and gumshoe argot, but they remained within and helped define the boundaries of heterosexuality, the racist tropes of moral hierarchies and the certitude of explicable crime."[67]

Building from the research conducted by Strange and Loo, Smith investigates the differences in American and Canadian pulp crime fiction, arguing that the latter "presented criminal activity as a problem that occurred in one of two places: either Canada's untamed spaces, or the cities south of the border. In using American locations, Canadian crime stories projected modern social problems onto a culturally similar 'other' so that such problems might be viewed from a comfortable, and comforting, distance."[68] Providing a case study that compares a short story by Canadian Niel Perrin with American Raymond Chandler's novel *The Big Sleep* (originally published in the American pulp *Black Mask*), Smith echoes Strange and Loo, stating: "The central message of the story is simple: order and justice are made possible by the co-operation of the law-abiding community with the official purveyors of law and order, while those who choose to break the law are punished for their actions. In this way, Canadian crime pulps worked in a manner directly opposite to the American pulps."[69]

Strange and Loo and Smith acknowledge that many Canadian pulp magazines reprinted and sometimes plagiarized stories by American writers. Nevertheless, their respective research agrees that the Canadian-authored works abided by conservative nationalist tropes consistent with the project of Canadian cultural nationalism itself: "While most stories explored the underbelly of Canada's colonial legacies and its more recent immigration trends, cases involving Asian or black victims or perpetrators were rarities. Pulp writers pandered to English Canadians' anti-Native prejudices and fears of European 'foreigners,' but they simultaneously reassured readers that law and order Canadian-style was there, ready to right any and every wrong."[70] Clearly, nationalizing the materiality of pulp magazines as "American" mass culture was a means of marginalizing genre fiction and its presumed audiences, in particular excluding working-class citizens from conversations about "Canadian culture." Although this dispossession from cultural capital is in no way unique to Canada,[71] the long-term ramifications of sidelining popular writing out of Canadian culture are worth attention.

Between 1949 and 1951, the Massey Commission brought the matter of Canadian cultural production into public discourse and, following its report in 1951, introduced a variety of government-sponsored institutions and funding bodies to support cultural production – but only *high* culture. According to Maria Tippett, a great deal of cultural production in Canada had become Americanized after the First World War, including music, theatre, and writing.[72] That is, like Canada's pulp magazine industry, high culture was greatly influenced by American cultural industries. With concentrated government support, however, most notably the Canada Council for the Arts established in 1957, these American-influenced arts could be adequately Canadianized and would eventually make Canada an internationally acclaimed producer of arts and culture. But there were no efforts to secure the viability of Canada's pulp magazines, comic books, or even mass-market fiction published in paperback form. Fulton's Criminal Code amendment had not only successfully marginalized pulp magazines and comics as "American" culture undeserving of government support but also degraded that particular iteration of American culture as immoral and, therefore, criminal.

Interestingly, Fulton would testify as to the inefficacy of Canada's anti-pulp legislation before the U.S. Senate Subcommittee on Juvenile Delinquency in the spring of 1954. According to Amy Nyberg's analysis of the hearings, "the law to ban the sale of crime and horror comics had proven ineffective in Canada. After it passed, that type of comic was replaced by what Fulton termed 'salacious' material, and within the year, the crime and horror comics were back on the stands as well. Canadian law enforcement officials proved reluctant to prosecute retailers and distributors under the law, *and the publishers were American* and therefore not subject to Canadian law"[73] (emphasis added). Thus, the outcome of the Fulton bill was not the elimination of crime comics and pulps from Canada, but only the elimination of Canada's pulp magazine and comics industries. In halting the potential for a Canadian tradition of genre writing, Fulton's bill ensured that the mass culture circulating in Canada would remain dominated by American producers, ultimately bringing to fruition the elitist characterization of mass culture as "American."

When we look at the Massey Commission's findings in context with the War Exchange Conservation Act in 1940 (which, in stopping pulps at the border, catalyzed Canada's pulp boom) and the 1949 Fulton bill (which then stifled that boom), it is clear that the project of "establishing" a Canadian literary culture was absolutely intolerant to the inclusion of lowbrow fiction. Pulp fiction was scapegoated as "the garbage of the literary world"[74] and Canada's political and cultural elite sought to ensure that neither it nor its producers had any place within the nation's cultural narrative.

As shown above, it is generally accepted by scholars that the demise of pulp magazines in the 1950s was brought about mainly by the rise of the paperback novel. In Canada, however, the rise of a *specific* collection of paperback novels was championed at arm's length by the federal government thanks to the Massey Report's calls to action. McClelland and Stewart's New Canadian

Library (NCL) series of existing Canadian-authored novels reprinted in cheap paperback form was launched in this climate of federally sanctioned handwringing over cultural production. Moreover, adoption of the series for the instruction of English-Canadian literature throughout the country has directly contributed to its canonization despite many of the books having "no claim to public interest."[75] Eventually, through the Canada Council, the Canadian government would actively (if still at arm's length) support producers of literary culture such as NCL-published novelists and magazines, including "literary periodicals of high quality and permanent interest which provide a valuable outlet for Canadian writers."[76] By contrast, writers of genre fiction and popular periodicals like Valentine's pulps were privy to no financial support. In fact, Smith's research shows that unlike American pulp fiction, "no Canadian fiction ever made the transition from pulp story to novel. American crime pulps produced a group of writers who were re-published by big-name literary publishers like Knopf and have not been out of print since – most notably Hammett and Chandler – but the majority of Canadian pulp writers languish in obscurity."[77] It is useful here to reassert Lecker's,[78] Mount's,[79] and Metcalf's[80] earlier-cited criticisms of the early works of the English-Canadian canon, lest the temptation to speculate on the talents of these obscured Canadian pulp writers proves too tempting to resist.

Conclusion

The collapse of the Canadian pulp magazine industry effectually exorcised genre fiction qua genre fiction from the English-Canadian literary landscape. The CanLit tradition that followed was sufficiently dominated by realism and naturalism to not only restrict Canadian writers to publishing their genre fiction internationally but, further, to make commonplace the mutually exclusive relationship of genre and CanLit. Founder of cyberpunk William Gibson is an excellent example. Despite being a major figure in the science fiction tradition, Gibson is not patriotically celebrated as a Canadian author. Although CanLit darling Margaret Atwood seems to have made science fiction tolerable to the English-Canadian literary industry, it is worth considering why science fiction novels by Hiromi Goto, Nalo Hopkinson, and Larissa Lai[81] have had less fanfare than Atwood's work.[82] These science fiction novels are all comparably political, but only Atwood's speculative dystopias fit comfortably in the (realist and naturalist) CanLit tradition. Returning to *Globe and Mail* columnist John Barber's call for Canadian novels to be "identifiably Canadian," we might well consider the ways in which Atwood's exceptional success as a *Canadian* science fiction writer has been made possible by her recognizability – and representability – as a Canadian author. (No one has ever asked, "Is it 'Canadian' enough?" of a Margaret Atwood novel.) Thus while CanLit can be said to be increasing in unrecognizability, it remains that a Canadian writer of genre is not necessarily the same thing as an author of CanLit.

Acknowledgments

I wish to gratefully acknowledge the editorial feedback and support of this collection's editors, Jason Camlot and Katherine McLeod, through the numerous iterations this chapter has taken. I want also to remember and honour my friend Andrew Bretz, alongside whom I presented this chapter in its nascent form as part of Katherine McLeod's 2014 ACCUTE Conference Panel, "Can Lit On Air: Audiences and Archives." Andrew's companionship and enthusiasm accompanied me through the evolution of this chapter since its humble beginnings as my first academic conference paper.

NOTES

1   John Barber, "Are Canadian Writers 'Canadian' Enough?" *The Globe and Mail* (updated 29 October 2011), www.theglobeandmail.com/arts/books-and-media/are-canadian-writers-canadian-enough/article4183161/ (accessed 20 February 2019).

2   The intersections of colonialism, sexism, and white supremacy – visible in every corner of the CanLit industry – facilitate so much hostility toward BIPOC writers, especially women, that throughout 2017 and 2018, writers and critics took to describing the state of CanLit as "a dumpster fire." While not the subject of this chapter, it is worth acknowledging that the issue of *what* constitutes CanLit generically is ultimately inseparable from *who* constitutes CanLit culturally. For further reading, see Jen Sookfong Lee's "Open Letters and Closed Doors: How the Steven Galloway Open Letter Dumpster Fire Forced Me to

Acknowledge the Racism and Entitlement at the Heart of CanLit," *The Humber Literary Review* (2017), http://humberliteraryreview.com/jen-sookfong-lee-essay-open-letters-and-closed-doors/ (accessed 13 June 2017) and Scaachi Koul's "On Glibness and Diversity in Canadian Media," *BuzzFeed* (updated 12 May 2017), www.buzzfeed.com/scaachikoul/so-hows-that-whole-diversity-in-media-thing-going?utm_term=.ssnJgNYBk#.mrDrqbWDQ (accessed 13 June 2017).

3 This conversation has been taken up in Hannah McGregor, Julie Rak, and Erin Wunker, ed., *Refuse: CanLit in Ruins* (Toronto: Book*hug, 2018).

4 Anne Thériault (anne_theriault), "Every historical novel set in Nova Scotia," Twitter, 13 April 2016, 5:48 p.m., https://twitter.com/anne_theriault/status/720398370351812608.

5 See Craig Silverman's "This Canadian Poet's Tumblr Is Filled with Hilarious Fake CanLit Book Covers," *BuzzFeed* (updated 23 February 2016), www.buzzfeed.com/craigsilverman/a-well-meaning-people-and-a-noble-genre?utm_term=.lvyrZbd67#.slWEeZ8Bm (accessed 20 February 2019).

6 Donna Bennett, "Conflicted Vision: A Consideration of Canon and Genre in English-Canadian Literature," *Canadian Canons: Essays in Literary Value*, ed. Robert Lecker (Toronto: University of Toronto Press, 1991), 131–49.

7 Government of Canada, *Report: Royal Commission on National Development in the Arts, Letters and Sciences 1949–1951*, Library and Archives Canada (1951, updated 27 January 2001), 226, www.collectionscanada.gc.ca/massey/index-e.html (accessed 20 February 2019). My assessment of both the Commission and its report are grievously brief. For thorough and dedicated considerations of the Commission and its impact on Canadian cultural production, see Karen Finlay, *The Force of Culture: Vincent Massey and Canadian Sovereignty* (Toronto: University of Toronto Press, 2004); Paul Litt, *The Muses, the Masses, and the Massey Commission* (Toronto: University of Toronto Press, 1992); and Maria Tippett, *Making Culture: English-Canadian Institutions and the Arts before the Massey Commission* (Toronto: University of Toronto Press, 1990).

8 Litt, *Muses*, 11.

9 Government of Canada, Parliament *House of Commons Debates*, 21st Parl, 1st Sess, vol. 1 (4–6 October 1949), 585.

10 See, for example: Robert Kroetsch, *The Lovely Treachery of Words: Essays Selected and New* (Toronto: Oxford University Press, 1989); Kevin Dowler, "The Cultural Industries Policy Apparatus," in *The Cultural Industries in Canada: Problems, Policies and Prospects*, ed. Michael Dorland (Toronto:

James Lorimer & Company Ltd, 1996), 328–46; Zoë Druick, "Remedy and Remediation: The Cultural Theory of the Massey Commission," *Review of Education, Pedagogy, and Cultural Studies* 29.2–3 (2007): 159–74; and Sabine Milz, "Canadian Cultural Policy-making at a Time of Neoliberal Globalization," ESC 33.1–2 (March/June 2007): 85–107.

11 Milz, "Canadian," 89.

12 Robert Lecker, *Making It Real: The Canonization of English-Canadian Literature* (Toronto: House of Anansi Press, 1995), 168.

13 Nick Mount, "In Praise of Talking Dogs: The Study and Teaching of Early Canada's Canonless Canon," *Essays in Canadian Writing* 63 (1998): 92.

14 John Metcalf, *Kicking against the Pricks* (Downsview: ECW Press, 1982), 149.

15 This chapter elaborates on research that I conducted for my dissertation and that I delivered as a keynote address in May 2018 at the annual conference of l'Association des bibliothécaires du Québec Library Association (ABQLA).

16 See: John Bell, *The Far North and Beyond: An Index to Canadian Science Fiction and Fantasy in English-Language Genre Magazines and other Selected Periodicals* (Halifax: School of Library and Information Studies, 1998) and *Invaders from the North: How Canada Conquered the Comic Book Universe* (Toronto: Dundurn Group, 2006); Carolyn Strange and Tina Loo, "From Hewers of Wood to Producers of Pulp: True Crime in Canadian Pulp Magazines of the 1940s," *Journal of Canadian Studies/Revue d'études canadiennes* 37.2 (Été/Summer 2002): 11–32 and *True Crime, True North: The Golden Age of Canadian Pulp Magazines* (Vancouver: Raincoast, 2004); Michelle Smith, "From 'The Offal of the Magazine Trade' to 'Absolutely Priceless': Considering the Canadian Pulp Magazine Collection," ESC 30.1 (March 2004): 101–16, "Guns, Lies, and Ice: The Canadian Pulp Magazines Industry and the Crime Fiction of Raymond Chandler and Niel Perrin," *Dime Novel Roundup* 47.1 (2005): 1–17, and "Soup Cans and Love Slaves: National Politics and Cultural Authority in the Editing and Authorship of Canadian Pulp Magazines," *Book History* 9 (2006): 261–89; and Will Straw, "Constructing the Canadian Lowbrow Magazine: Periodical as Media Object in the 1930s and 1940s," *The Journal of Modern Periodical Studies* 6.2 (2015): 112–33.

17 Smith, "Soup Cans," 286n18.

18 Quoted in Strange and Loo, "Hewers," 12. See also Government of Canada, *Journals of the House of Commons*, 19th Parl, 2nd Sess, vol. 81, no. 21 (6 December 1940), 88.

19 Numerous letters published in the Canadian pulp magazine *Uncanny Tales*

between 1941 and 1942 describe being unable to buy copies of American science fiction pulps, like *Weird Tales*.

20 Smith, "Soup Cans," 267.

21 Government of Canada, Parliament *Journals of the House of Commons*, 19th Parl, 2nd Sess, vol. 81, no. 21 (6 December 1940), 85.

22 Erin A. Smith, *Hard-boiled: Working Class Readers and Pulp Magazines* (Philadelphia: Temple University Press, 2000), 16.

23 Smith, "Soup Cans," 266.

24 Faye Hammill and Michelle Smith, *Magazines, Travel, and Middlebrow Culture: Canadian Periodicals in English and French 1925–1960* (Edmonton: University of Alberta Press, 2015), 23–4n1.

25 Smith, "Offal," 103–4.

26 Ibid., 104.

27 Aritha Van Herk, "Introduction," in *The Canadian Postmodern: A Study of Contemporary Canadian Fiction*, ed. Linda Hutcheon (Don Mills: Oxford University Press, 1988), n.p.

28 Andrew Thacker, "Magazines, Magazines, Magazines!" general introduction, in *The Oxford Critical and Cultural History of Modernist Magazines. Vol. 2: North America 1894–1960*, ed. Peter Brooker and Andrew Thacker (Oxford: Oxford University Press, 2012), 12.

29 Hammill and Smith, *Magazines*, 25.

30 See, for example: Ernest George Hansell's (Member for Macleod) discussion of his "file" on "unwholesome literature" in Canada, Parliament *House of Commons Debates*, 21st Parl, 1st Sess, vol. 1 (4–6 October 1949), 517–18.

31 Strange and Loo, "Hewers," 14.

32 Straw, "Constructing," 112–33.

33 *Science Fiction* 1.2 (November 1941): n.p.

34 Ibid.

35 Smith, "Soup Cans," 267.

36 Ibid., 268.

37 Ibid., 269.

38 Government of Canada, Parliament *House of Commons Debates*, 21st Parl, 1st Sess, vol. 1 (4–6 October 1949), 586.

39 Smith, "Soup Cans," 285.

40 Strange and Loo, "Hewers," 14.

41 Ibid.

42 Government of Canada, Parliament *House of Commons Debates*, 21st Parl, 1st Sess, vol. 1 (4–6 October 1949), 517.

43 Smith, "Soup Cans," 267.

44 Ibid., 268.

45 Ibid.

46 See Library and Archives Canada's digital archive *Tales from the Vault: Canadian Pulp Fiction, 1940–1952*.

47 Smith, "Soup Cans," 268.

48 "'Peek-a-boo Bangs and Global War': Bachelor Magazines, World Politics and Socialism," Library and Archives Canada, last modified 26 August 2005, www.collectionscanada.gc.ca/pulp/027019-1430-e.html (accessed 5 October 2018).

49 Tellingly, Adam Publishing is the same publisher Valentine used to commission the book *Red Ally: An Estimate of Soviet Life and Soviet Power*. According to "'Peek-a-boo Bangs,'" "the book, with a cover that features the faces of Churchill, Roosevelt, and Stalin, is presented as a long-overdue appraisal of Canada's new military ally."

50 Sam Moskowitz, "Canada's Pioneer Science-Fantasy Magazine," *Science-Fiction Studies* 17 (1990): 90, 88.

51 For more information, see the Wikipedia entries "Futurians," Wikipedia (updated 14 May 2018), https://en.wikipedia.org/wiki/Futurians (accessed April 13, 2018); "Sam Moskowitz," Wikipedia (updated 10 July 2018), https://en.wikipedia.org/wiki/Sam_Moskowitz (accessed 13 April 2018); and "Donald A. Wollheim," Wikipedia (updated 22 September 2018), https://en.wikipedia.org/wiki/Donald_A._Wollheim (accessed 13 April 2018).

52 Sam Moskowitz recounts his interactions with Colby in "Canada's Pioneer Science-Fantasy Magazine," *Science-Fiction Studies* 17 (1990): 84–92.

53 Ibid., 88.

54 Ibid., 90.

55 Ibid.

56 There is some debate as to the official start date of pulp as a form, but Frank Munsey's periodical *Argosy* is universally considered to be the first pulp magazine.

57 Harlequin Books (now Harlequin Enterprises) is the exception that proves the rule of the Canadian pulp industry. For dedicated accounts of the romance publisher, see Archana Rampure, "Harlequin Has Built an Empire," in *History*

of the Book in Canada, vol. 3, ed. Carole Gerson and Jacques Michon (Toronto: University of Toronto Press), 185–8; and Paul Grescoe, *The Merchants of Venus: Inside Harlequin and the Empire of Romance* (Vancouver: Raincoast, 1996). The paperback giant was founded by three men with social prestige and publishing acumen: Doug Weld of Toronto's Bryant Press; Jack Palmer, sales manager for the Curtis Circulating Company, responsible for circulating "heavyweight periodicals" like *Saturday Evening Post* and *Ladies' Home Journal* (Grescoe, *Merchants*, 28); and Richard Bonnycastle, the "well-born, properly educated" (ibid., 20) managing director of Advocate Printers who went on to "become mayor of metropolitan Winnipeg and chancellor of the University of Winnipeg" (Rampure, "Harlequin," 186), and who, according to Grescoe, got into the business of publishing for *fun* (*Merchants*, 29). Grescoe quotes Bonnycastle's personal assistant, Ruth Palmour, who explains that "Harlequin was a filler for a nice, steady business" (ibid., 29). Of course, the company's lowbrow product and emphasis on reprinting well-known American and British authors (ibid., 33) would keep it on the outskirts of Canadian culture; however, Harlequin's business connections were such that the company flourished without government support. These origins align Harlequin's success with the American pulp business model described above; that is, Harlequin was intended to be a low-stakes money-making business venture to bolster the incomes of several already successful businessmen.

58 Charles Steele, *Taking Stock: The Calgary Conference on the Canadian Novel* (Downsview: ECW Press, 1982), 148.

59 For example, see Lecker, *Making*, 154–5 and Janet Friskney, *New Canadian Library: The Ross-McClelland Years, 1952–1978* (Toronto: University of Toronto Press, 2007), 3.

60 David Ketterer, *Canadian Science Fiction and Fantasy* (Bloomington: Indiana University Press, 1992), 2.

61 Ibid., 1.

62 Ibid.

63 Frank Davey, "Canadian Canons," *Critical Inquiry* 16 (Spring 1990): 676.

64 Ibid.

65 Strange and Loo, "Hewers," 12.

66 Ibid.

67 Ibid., 14.

68 Smith, "Guns," 8.

69 Ibid., 9.

70 Strange and Loo, *True Crime*, 7.

71 See Pierre Bourdieu, *Distinction: A Social Critique of the Judgment of Taste*, trans. Richard Nice (London: Routledge, 2010), 387–9.

72 Tippett, *Making Culture*, 127–9.

73 Senate Hearings, 160–1, qtd. in Amy Nyberg, *Seal of Approval: The History of the Comics Code* (Jackson: University Press of Mississippi, 1998), 78–9.

74 Smith, "Soup Cans," 276.

75 Lecker, *Making*, 55. See, for example, the list of "the most important ten works of various genres" (List C) voted on in advance of and debated at the Calgary conference (Steele, *Taking Stock*, 154). The list is primarily comprised of Canadian "classics" that, Robert Lecker claims, even "well-read, literate people who follow Canadian writing" would not have heard of (*Making*, 13).

76 Canada Council, "Second Annual Report," *The Canada Council Second Annual Report to March 31, 1959*, 32, http://canadacouncil.ca/about/governance/corporate-reports (accessed 1 September 2016).

77 Smith, "Dime Novel," 10.

78 Lecker, *Making*, 168.

79 Mount, "In Praise," 92.

80 Metcalf, *Kicking*, 149.

81 See: Hiromi Goto's *The Kappa Child*, Nalo Hopkinson's *Brown Girl in the Ring* and *The Salt Roads*, and Larissa Lai's *When Fox Is a Thousand*, *Salt Fish Girl*, and *The Tiger Flu*.

82 Bruce Miller's television adaptation of Margaret Atwood's *The Handmaid's Tale*, for example, has reignited literary interest in the 1985 dystopian novel. McClelland and Stewart released a television tie-in edition in 2017 and a graphic novel edition adapted by Renée Nault was released in March 2019 by McClelland and Stewart.

5

____

Voices Kept in Context
Underpinning and Not Unpinning the Recordings Found in Literary Archives

CATHERINE HOBBS

In 1978, archival theorist Hugh Taylor made the following McLuhan-inspired statements about how archivists should handle records of differential media formats: "We should perhaps work to ensure that those who draw sustenance and insight from archives feed on a balanced diet of media and are aware of the effects. We should be more conscious of the power of media hybrids ... We must also develop the insight to choose the medium of the record which is most appropriate to a given situation. Above all, we must learn the 'languages' of media without the benefit of syntax and with the grammar still uncertain. Only then will we be able to do full justice to our documents and our profession in the twenty-first century."[1] Taylor's views prompted the (then) Public Archives of Canada (now Library and Archives Canada) where Taylor worked between 1971 and 1977 to make the radical move of splitting recorded sound, film, broadcasting, documentary art, and photography into working sections separate from those for textual records. During this period, the National Photography Collection, National Arts Archives, National Sound Archives and National Film Archives were formed, followed by a merger of the National Film, Television and Sound Archives in 1980.[2] The resulting structure enabled media-specific expertise to flourish, facilitated the brilliant careers of a number of archivists specializing in particular media such as photography and documentary art, and benefited the collection on an item basis.[3] It also established a rift between media-specific expertise that continued into the early 2000s and subsequently became the focus of the "integrity of the fonds" discussions and initiative within Library and Archives Canada (LAC) in 2004, an institutional approach to re-centring an archivist's work on entire fonds rather than media speciality.

The implications of the rift between archival structures based upon media specificity and a more holistic, contextualizing conception of the archives persist to this day. Most literary archives are comprised predominantly of textual records.[4] As an archivist who spends most of her time with archives that are predominantly text-based, a number of problems and issues around sound and video recordings in their broader archival contexts have struck me repeatedly over the years. No doubt, this is because I look at literary archives holistically and with literary scholarship in mind, rather than from the specialized perspective of expertise in recording media. A primary aim of this chapter is to illustrate why it will be useful to literary scholars and archivists alike to explore more fully the present misalignment of approaches to audio and video recordings/film with the archival approaches we use for textual materials. For example, there are a number of interpretive approaches to personal archives that can enlarge possibilities for our understanding of the place of recordings within an archival fonds. I argue for the importance of understanding how a writer's personal or aesthetic concerns often fold back on the recordings in her archives, and how those concerns layer these recordings with additional interpretive possibilities that arise from the many sides of the originating literary life. What can literary analysis bring to bear on a sound recording if we are guided by what we know of its originator's understanding and approaches to literary creation? How does a critical awareness of the positioning and archival treatment of records inform our understanding of the materials we study and the literary historical narratives we develop?

I pursue answers to these questions with reference to a series of specific archival examples, ranging from the organization-developed fonds of the International Readings at Harbourfront Centre to the authors' archives of Daphne Marlatt, Jan Zwicky, Robert Bringhurst, and Phyllis Webb. These examples will demonstrate how knowledge of the archival structures that comes from the originating organization or creator, knowledge of the creator's personal networks and predilections, and knowledge of the originator's attitudes toward media itself, can reveal important information about the significance of records in an archives. In a broader sense, each example demonstrates how the nature of an archives can reveal important information about its contents, and how holistic models of archival interpretation can help incite such revelations.

Within the profession, a holistic interpretation of archives has gradually replaced the earlier emphasis on "literary manuscripts" or "literary papers." These earlier terms focus on paper-based records. Within the so-called manuscripts tradition in the U.S., which dominated from the nineteenth to the mid-twentieth century, records were often acquired individually by curators and venerated because of their associational value.[5] After the first half of the twentieth century, this emphasis on the importance of particular records was replaced in many countries by methods that sought to give contextual value to records collectively. In Canada, the official adoption of the concept of the fonds in the 1990s, where records were acquired from a single individual or organization as their source, focused on maintaining context and largely overcame the former sensibility of venerating documents without regard for their archival context.

The term "literary archives" has gradually replaced the earlier terms "papers" and "manuscripts" as this contextualizing approach came to permeate the archival profession. The sense of holism and contextualization is explicit in Canadian archival practices. Still, as I have already noted, we continue to live out some effects of separation by media. The term "literary archives" is not subject based. Rather, it refers to literary provenance, which, in turn, implies the literary activities of creating records and literary content. Even in the case of a single isolated literary record, the implication is that the record signifies a range of literary activities within a network of literary actors. Consequently, a record that does not, at first glance, seem at all literary can be integrated into literary archives due to this sense of provenance and context. The emphasis on paper-based text within literary archives remains predominant for the time being, not because the archivist focuses exclusively on paper records but because the majority of literary records created by authors are still paper based.

Recordings do not simply duplicate original literary happenings nor do they simply "add value" to text. Because literary scholarship is still primarily text focused, scholars would benefit from more refined methodologies when approaching recorded sound, film, or video. This would be the case for scholars using recordings for research and for those collecting and storing recordings, as with several recent academic projects crossing the line between scholarship and custodianship.[6] A more refined approach to studying recordings requires using what we know about archives and then seeing how the recording can "play" or "play out" within these archival conceptions. To achieve this archival refinement to methodology, I will first outline some of the commonly conceived ideas of archival context and consider how and why sound recordings have not been well served by these models. I will then consider how certain ideas that inform our understanding of personal context serve to *underpin* and, at the same time, sometimes to *unpin* these meanings of archival recordings, providing fruitful expansive shifts in what we might consider the identity, status, and contents of the recordings themselves.

The Idea of Context

From an archival perspective, contextual evidence drapes itself around recordings of literary events both in Canadian archival repositories and outside the archives. Archivists and scholars alike should want to underpin recordings with their archival context as we would for any other type of archival documentation. In a broad sense, archives are a multi-faceted, multi-generational attempt to leave traces: a legacy we leave for the future. The more threads of evidence we leave showing, the greater the number of possible avenues of inquiry and understanding we leave open for use in the future. Likewise, repurposers are also implicated in this practice of creating possibilities. Archivists, un-archivists, anarchivists, and any other people dealing with "stuff" (archaeologists, museologists, forensic investigators, for example) will usually have but one chance to do justice to archival documentation, that is, to "hinge" the stuff correctly to its context, at the front end. At the other end, users of these archives need to know how to trace the contextual side of the records they are working with, even if they are not yet aware of how an acquired understanding of the contextualizing and hinging processes that have been applied to the research materials will be relevant to their paths of inquiry.

The idea of context in archives is grounded in the foundational concepts of "provenance" and "original order."[7] Provenance serves to ensure that all archives from a single source (or "creator") are kept together and not mixed with records of another provenance. Original order is there to ensure that the order of the documentation during the time of its creation and use is preserved *in order* to retain the added information that the records have in relation to one another, and within their respective groupings.

If you were to strip a sound recording of its archival context, you might transform it from a record bearing robust evidence into an isolated recording, and the contents of that recording into disembodied voices or something approximating unprocessed data from an unknown source.[8] Digital records and audiovisual records on magnetic media have qualities that make them more readily repurposed and potentially divorced from their context-specific meanings (i.e., they are easily copied, sampled, or redacted using technology). Furthermore, many sound and video recordings (analog or digital recordings on physical carriers) are not found physically together with the textual records in a cardboard folder. They are often stored in separate cabinets or on separate shelves. Consequently, the correlation of all the records in a fonds is not always clear. A photograph of poet George Bowering's grandfather's grave was found next to the annotated page proofs for the poem "Rewriting My Grandfather."[9] Their relationship to each other is clear by virtue of their physical proximity in his archives: the paper proof and the photographic print on paper were found together because they were kept together by Bowering. Unfortunately, original physical arrangement that provides contextual links between texts and photographs is rarely present in the case of audio and video recordings. Such a disconnect in physical arrangement can prove problematic for archivists who are used to relying on physical proximity to sort out intellectual elements of arrangement, which then further informs how an archivist might delimit file units or decide the parameters of a series.[10]

Beyond this issue of physical arrangement and its subsequent implications for the contextualization of audiovisual materials, we (in a Western European literary tradition) have had some historical difficulty in linking the aural and the written. This difficulty is usually overcome in the structuring of archives only when the intellectual links between these two categories are very clear. Such is the case with the connections made between Daphne Marlatt's oral history interviews on tape and the recordings of the CBC dramatization *Steveston* with drafts of her poetry book *Steveston*, and with drafts of *Steveston Recollected: A Japanese-Canadian History* (her published oral history project) in her archives.[11] In this exceptional example, different archival records are not just linked by "topic" but also present different stages of the production of related projects by Marlatt. The nature of the relationship between Marlatt's work in oral history and her poetic practice has resulted in archives that present the relational evolution of her work.

A common use of archival non-textual media (including audio, video recordings, film, and photographs) involves trying to glean the texture or grain of the literary event by looking for/listening for non-textual cues. For example, one might use the photographs in the Daphne Marlatt fonds of the 1963 Vancouver Poetry Conference[12] to explore the many happenings of the conference that took place in Warren and Ellen Tallman's house. The viewer of the photographs can gather what this unofficial side of the conference looked like, what the house looked like, what the Tallmans and other participants looked like – including what Ginsberg looked like in the morning when he got himself breakfast in the Tallmans' kitchen. This is precisely the type of use made of these photographs in the film about that Vancouver Poetry Conference, *The Line Has Shattered*.[13] Further to the context of the photographs themselves, the series of photos (according to Marlatt's memory) were taken by Karen Tallman and were given to Marlatt at some later time.[14] It is fairly easy to agree on why an understanding of the content and staging of a recording would interest a researcher in a similar way. In the case of recordings, one would want to identify the voices, the ambient sounds, the venue, the sets, and the people or organizations involved in production. and then deploy these elements to demonstrate or interpret literary, social, political, and other aspects of the originary event in ways that text cannot. One must bear in mind that the originary event is where the creators, the site of creation, the ambient noises, technology, and other mitigating factors formed both the event and the recording of the event.

An archival record can itself be understood as an event that enacts its own inscription resulting in an artifact (be that analog or digital). Archival records have their own histories. The more we attend to those histories, the more we can understand the structures that underpin our own historical assertions about the records we study and the processes by which they were produced and then stored.

In addition to enabling the testing of the "grain" or qualities of a happening, evidence of archival context offers even more nuanced possibilities for understanding. From such evidence we can develop an awareness of the hints of the originating context and later contexts that affect the recording, from its creation and use by the creator to subsequent "archival events" of creation and custodianship, as it were. Many archivists would argue that the discovery of a recording that has not had its history of creation and storage traced is equivalent to finding it in a dumpster. In other words, a document, photograph, or recording is not truly archival without its accompanying provenantial and contextual information. The circumstances of creation control what gets produced and the circumstances afterward, and the choices of organizations and individuals control what is kept. Additionally, the habits, predilections, and priorities of creators when making recordings, and their opinions about technology, will also play a role in the subsequent fate of their records, and the records' situation within an archives.

Unfortunately, archival context has not been so easily understood by archivists for literary recordings or for recordings in general. There is a long-standing and widespread practice of what archivists call "item-level treat-ment" for sound and video recordings and for regarding them as a last priority. It seems that archivists were not able to put together a firm concep-tion of original order for these media even though it has been acknowledged for decades that archivists are supposed to be media agnostic in their under-standing of records, and that archivists are meant to acquire records in the form in which they were created, used, and kept, and are supposed to keep them this way. This is becoming commonly understood as archivists grapple with different aspects of born-digital archives.[15] Seeing a recording as isolated is the archival equivalent of not seeing the forest for the trees. This "indi-vidual item" thinking has slowed, if not impeded our understanding of what recordings were in terms of their full identities and in contextual relation with one another.

The Contextualizing Value of Archival Arrangement

It appears that the researcher may encounter a less than comprehensive con-textualized treatment of sound recordings in any literary archives. At LAC, there is a single database detailing audio, video, and film from the archives of private individuals and organizations (originally created or kept for their uses), as well as official recordings of public broadcasts and commercial films. This database retains an emphasis on versions, broadcast, cast, and rights, thereby reflecting the needs of commercial interests like feature film and the broadcasters to sample or reuse recordings, rather than reflecting a more comprehensive archival sense of situating materials contextually for research. For example, the term "series" in the database is not used in the typical archival sense but instead indicates a series of broadcasts. While this approach has significant utility for the reuse of recordings vis-à-vis copyright and repurposing, it also thins out the linkages with other useful forms of archival description. From the database, one can glean high amounts of detailed recording-specific information, although one does not know exactly how x recording relates to the fonds of y writer. Presumably one is expected to guess the links using the content, subject matter, or production credits of the recordings.

In the rest of the country, we also see perpetuated a tendency to leave media until last during processing, or to provide only item-level access for such materials. Series called simply "Recordings" (where it is unclear if the archivist is acting on the storage arrangement of the donor or simply grouping records by media) and precedence given to text over other media formats within fonds are very common.[16] This leaves an impression that paper is privileged within literary archives. While this focus on text certainly also relates to prioritizing archival work within situations of insufficient resources, one significant result is that archivists often do not situate their media holdings within informative archival contexts. Recordings would be better served by archival analysis yielding specific file or series links or, in some cases, with firm justifications of media-specific series based on analysis of original physical and intellectual arrangement elements.

In 2010, I acquired the International Readings at Harbourfront Centre fonds for the LAC.[17] This fonds contains a moderate amount of paper records, as well as photographs of each Harbourfront literary event (usually a podium shot and a signing shot) totalling about 7,650 photographs or negatives of international literary figures. In addition, there are 8,760 audio and video recordings: one of each reading (with few exceptions).[18]

In terms of added elements of archival context, seeing the recordings together as a whole has complementary value. One of the great advantages of seeing lists of all the audio and video from Harbourfront together is locating recordings of various authors appearing at the festival many different times: for example, Margaret Atwood features in seventy-four recordings, beginning in 1978 when the first international festival was held (although in considering this number we should bear in mind that in the 1990s, audio and video were recorded for the same event). Therefore, by assessing the entire series together, it is possible to trace such trends among invitees and event programming.

I first visited Harbourfront in 2006 and then in 2010. Staff kept the audio and video in orderly cabinets in a small storage room, alongside artwork, posters, signed book bags, etc. The storage room held anything that was not in the main office. The files of textual records and photographs used to prepare future events or to create displays/publicity were kept in the main office space. During these site visits, Harbourfront's record-keeping practices were discussed, which helped me to understand what *they understood* they were doing and the qualities of their actions toward the records. I learned that each reading event can be counted on to be approximately the same length, that the venues rarely changed, that the event formats or genres were consistent (reading, panel, interview, or special event), and that the media of choice to record these events had evolved over time: from magnetic reel-to-reel and cassette tape, Betamax, and VHS videotape toward Digital Audio Tape (DAT) and later digital audio and video formats on CD-Rom. Over the course of their activities, Harbourfront also – thankfully – had a well-developed sense of the archival value of the recordings themselves: they had a number of spreadsheets for many (though not all) years of the festival and reading series beginning in 1998. These spreadsheets were used to locate the recordings in-house and to lend them informally to other outlets, such as the CBC. This also accounted for a few recordings not being locatable at the time of deposit (these appeared to have been loaned out and not retrieved).

Knowing which materials were catalogued by Harbourfront and which by LAC has some value for study. It tells us what was considered a priority by Harbourfront or perhaps, at least, when Harbourfront began to take this cataloguing seriously and when the organization developed its archival sensibility. Such knowledge indicates how and when Harbourfront placed value on the records in-house, when they began housing their own photographs in archival enclosures, and when they began self-conscious cataloguing – which tale is also told by their internal investigation of suitable digital recording formats for the purpose of documenting festival activities. In other words, by developing an informed understanding of how the organization functioned and how it carried out actions upon its documentary materials, we can glean a useful sense of context for the recordings and of their meaning to the creator.

An Excel spreadsheet drafted by Harbourfront is a document with certain advantages for gaining such insight: for each event, it details everyone who appeared, the month of the event, and the room in which it occurred. From this data, researchers can learn what Harbourfront considered to be an event and which search categories were deemed valuable. If we extend our view further, we can get a sense of the inherent historic value attributed to the reading series throughout its duration. Cross-referencing the spreadsheets from different times can also provide telling evidence of staff turnover because the same information is captured slightly differently each time. In the case of Harbourfront, the information demonstrates a traditional notion of archival context; that is, it shows how records relate to the activities of the creator in the original site of production, as well as to the creator's information practices.

The Role of Individuals in Archival Creation

Individuals, too, have a role to play in archival creation. We can look to retain traces or reflections of individual agency in our interpretation of the structure of the archives. Unlike Harbourfront's concerted information-gathering practices, there is often a frailty to that kind of information within personal archives. Sometimes individual contributions to informal recordings are not noted down. Sometimes the information can be gleaned from notes made on recording labels and boxes or from other sources such as notes, letters, and diaries. An archivist would, of course, want to be careful to show and not deny traces of agency when performing her work.

The recently acquired second accession of poet Jan Zwicky's archives includes tapes of music that accompany rich correspondence between Zwicky and her (now) husband, poet and linguist Robert Bringhurst.[19] The thirty-five cassettes in this accession had been stored by Zwicky separately from their accompanying letters, but during acquisition she provided a note to underscore their connection to other documentation in her archival fonds, indicating that an intellectual rather than physical arrangement links them together. The cassettes themselves are of well-known commercial recordings, predominantly of classical music: for example, Arvo Pärt, John Cage, Bartok, Taverner, Haydn, a lot of Schnittke, Die Kunst der Fuge of Bach, and (evocatively) one cassette with Britten on one side and a gamelan recording on the other. There might be archivists or others who would dismiss these recordings as redundant because they are relatively modest homemade copies of commercially available music. In effect, any valuing of such tapes hinges on how one identifies and values the events or realizations that this particular set of recordings depends upon, either to identify or connect them to their context.

What kinds of values might one attribute to these tapes to contextualize them within the larger archival fonds? One such value might be the concept of listening itself, and the qualities of reciprocal listening as explored in the letters of each individual correspondent: Zwicky the violinist, poet, and philosopher and Bringhurst the poet, linguist, translator, polyphonist, and typographer. Zwicky is a poet whose poetry "has always been acutely musical (and sensitive to the silence out of which music comes)"[20] and, for Bringhurst, the title of the recent book of criticism on his oeuvre of work, *Listening for the Heartbeat of Being*, speaks volumes as to the centrality of listening as informing his writing practice. Here, the archivist asks herself: What shades of context rub off on the thirty-five innocuous-looking cassettes that Zwicky and Bringhurst made and then mailed to each other? What do I need to know to see (and hear) what the recordings mean? How do personal artifacts signify as they relay evidence of the creator and the originating contexts of creation, use, and keeping?

The Zwicky/Bringhurst correspondence[21] is a dialogue in which the two writers are honing their ears and together interpreting the music they exchanged. In the letters, they trade remarks about the qualities of one recording over another and apologies for poor sound quality alongside brilliant insights about performance and music history. As a whole, the cassettes combined with the letters display tremendous cohesiveness and present a deeply significant dialogue between these two poets. Approaching the recordings, letters, and other documents as a cohesive element of an archival fonds allows us to delineate a series of letter writing and invisible listening events in which the cassettes played an integral role, both physically (as they were sent through the mail, received, played, and experienced) and intellectually.

Attitudes toward the Media of Creation

As said above, in order to understand personal record, we need to investigate the attitudes, habits, and predilections a creator has toward making the records *and* toward the media of creation. I think this precept holds equally true for sound and video recordings, and in the case of writers, this precept intersects with how the aesthetic approach affects our interpretation of the archival records. A strong example of how the attitudes of the creator of the records (or a participant in a recording) might shift the interpretation of that recording is found within the fonds of the interlocutor on the other side of Zwicky's correspondence: Robert Bringhurst.

In much of Bringhurst's writing, literature is presented as a human response to *what is*. He argues that the creation of complex literature pre-exists print culture, and yet, Bringhurst has remarked that literature has a better home in print than in recorded sound.[22] In this line of thinking, he reasons that writing "leaves a lot of things out as well as putting a lot of things in," but the printed text allows fruitful space to literature because it is performative when it is read, whereas recording media deliver "the same performance each time."[23] Bringhurst's notion of recording media is weighted by the history of cultural anthropology that he is well acquainted with through his translations of North American Indigenous literatures that so often began with transcriptions of oral storytelling, as in the case of *A Story as Sharp as a Knife*.[24] As he explains, "the tape recorder, as usually employed, reduces all oral poets to mimics" while a "good transcription, just because it requires more involvement from the reader, is in some sense different every time you read it. That doesn't replicate the richness of a living oral culture, but at least it bows in that direction."[25]

If this conception (i.e., Bringhurst's attitude toward the media of creation) is brought to bear on recordings of his voice or any other recordings in his own archives (of which he is termed the creator in the sense of *amassing* his own archives), it alters their meaning by negating or problematizing some aspects of the recording we would otherwise take for granted. Here, for example, the idea of responsible recording that recognizes the circumstances of its own production (such as is proposed among proponents of oral history recordings) is no longer enough. The creator (Bringhurst) indicates that the richer copy of a work is a print version, one that can be revived and relived through recitation or enacting in the theatre of the mind, which we call "reading," because literature is "a thing in itself with a life of its own." According to this thinking, print allows the imagination a more conducive space to engage literature.[26]

Bringhurst's alignment with performativity resists attempts to capture his voice with recording technologies. It grates against any simple notions concerning the recording of his polyphonic works, such as were made by the CBC of *The Blue Roofs of Japan* or any other recordings of *New World Suites* and *Ursa Major*, etc., that may be out there.[27]

It is somewhat of a paradox, then, that Bringhurst's progression with polyphonic literature was formed by listening to a recording – specifically, that of Glenn Gould's polyphonic radio documentaries. As he put it in the essay "Singing with the Frogs" in *Everywhere Being is Dancing*, "in 1986, when the CBC recorded *The Blue Roofs of Japan* – a poem of mine scored for two simultaneous voices – Dennis Lee brought Gould's 'documentary' poems to my attention."[28] Here he is referring to Glenn Gould's *Solitude Trilogy*: three voice-collages created for CBC between 1967 and 1977, the first of which is titled *The Idea of North* (1967). Bringhurst continues: "The only way to hear Gould's trilogy then was acoustic samizdat – pirated tapes of the radio broadcasts – but these were easy enough to obtain. In the three or four years between writing *The Blue Roofs of Japan* and *The New World Suites,* I did a lot of listening. I began, then, to understand that Gould was the most colossally improbable of all Canadian poets – and that he was, more improbably still, one of the greatest."[29] As an individual recording, this is the sole recording of Gould's work (a work Bringhurst calls poetry) that Bringhurst could find at the time and one that made him progress in his exploration of polyphony. The individual cassette recording in Bringhurst's archives – in a eureka moment for the researcher – suddenly takes on vast meaning: this very cassette is the "pirated tape of the radio broadcasts" of Gould that informed the structures of what became Bringhurst's polyphonic poems. Moreover, Bringhurst describes elements that may allow us to at-tribute several kinds of event-ness to the recording: the first is the event of Gould's purported *poetry* sensation broadcast on the CBC; the second is the event of Dennis Lee bringing the broadcast to Bringhurst's attention and then Bringhurst obtaining the tape; this awareness is followed by the event of Bringhurst's listening and then his prolonged meditation on the work, which is perhaps even a fourth event (or an *event-smear* that trails after the precipitating events and seeps into new literary composition). All such reso-nances contrast Gould's own complex conception of recording media.[30] Gould broadcast *The Idea of North* four years after publishing an essay called "The Prospects of Recording,"[31] which is Gould's dislodging of two of the pins that had been working to secure an idea of an event in time and space (with a date and a perception of authentic singularity), making his concerns in that essay enfold important questions about the literary nature of event-ness itself.

In "Singing with the Frogs," Bringhurst makes a further remark regarding his attitude to technology when he states: "I find it easier to think that industrial technology is short-lived and finally irrelevant than to think that it is either evil or good." Such a comment plays directly off of Gould's celebration of the splice in a rejection of the perceived authenticity of the concert hall. As Bringhurst continues in this line of reflection: "Still, to me, the thought that full-fledged polyphonic literature might be dependent on the microphone, the tape deck and the splicing bar is not completely welcome. Nor does it comfort me to know that such machinery is already obsolete. I'm told that no such worries haunted Gould, but they haunt me. I use fancy tools when they're here, but only on condition that I live at least part-time in the older world, where I do my work without them."[32] Bringhurst, then, has a conditional relationship to technology, and he tells us that his work is also created *elsewhere*. This conditional relationship to technology and this elsewhere haunt my own listening to Bringhurst's recordings, as does his view that creative acts are not solely confined to our species, implying that to listen in the spirit of the creator's conception is to hear these human voices as one of many sounds produced by species that, as he says, "participate in being."[33] Clearly, listening in the spirit in which performances were created elicits ideas and debates about the status, identity, and content of a recording. Further, the conditions surrounding this particular cassette set off a series of questions that ricochet against Gould's conceptions of what *he* was doing.[34] The cassette's conditions set off a creative reflection on creation that in turn sets off parallel track conceptions of event-ness concerning when and where creation properly takes place.

Archives' Personal Meanings

In addition to the more traditional idea of archival context (Zwicky), we are also able to interpret archives from the contexts of personal meaning of their creators, including the creators' own attitudes toward technology (Bringhurst).[35] Central to this approach is how the records relate to the moral imperative we struggle with in connection with the creator's life and aesthetic – even, sometimes, how the records reflect infinitely within these concepts of evidence (evidence of a life and evidence of an aesthetic). In taking such an approach, we need to pose the question: how is the status of this document repositioned or shifted by what we know about its personal context with this individual creator? I am interested too in those Möbius strip–like movements where interpretation is turned inside out: in other words, the point where a personal meaning or aesthetic overturns aspects that normally stabilize the meaning of an archival document. This is exemplified in the fonds of poet Phyllis Webb.

In 1969, Phyllis Webb left her job at the CBC in Toronto to return to British Columbia, but the sound recordings in LAC consist mostly of recordings that she made after this retreat from public broadcasting.[36] Specifically, there is a recording of an interview she did, as a freelancer working for the CBC, with cultural anthropologist and museum curator Wilson Duff about his exhibition *Images Stone B.C.: Thirty Centuries of Northwest Coast Indian Sculpture*, which took place in 1975 at the Art Gallery of Greater Victoria.[37] Webb's later aesthetic development and personal context can be seen to shade this recording, which predates the publication of Webb's 1980 work, *Wilson's Bowl*. The "Artifacts" section of *Wilson's Bowl* reflects her interest in Duff and her friendship with Lilo Berliner, who left Webb her correspondence with Duff after Duff's suicide and shortly before Berliner herself committed suicide by "walk[ing] into the sea."[38] The sound recording of the Webb interview with Duff is inextricable from this net of contextual meaning by virtue of its being part of Webb's experience and part of her own creative expression that plays out as a dialogue with Duff's ideas and concerns. Here, the Möbius movement ensues, as the placement of this particular recording within Webb's artistic development plays back into Webb's personal relationships and the influence those relationships had, in turn, upon her artistic ideas. To interpret this example of the interview requires that we see it as revealing her aesthetic positioning at a moment in her historical development and, at the same time, as absorbing Webb's considerations of Duff. Put another way, the full significance of this sound recording's placement within her archives is contingent. In fact, it might be very difficult to preserve an idea of a single event or context for this recording in relation to Webb. The archival recording, in this instance, is positioned within several contexts among the archival texts that surround it and can be understood to interact with and disrupt its contextualizing elements in a kind of perpetual interpretive motion.

Also in the Webb fonds is a recording of her performance of the poem "The Tree Speaks." Written by Webb to protest logging in Clayoquot Sound, she recited it in 1993 in front of the BC Parliament Buildings, during a Writers for Clayoquot Sound event. As such, the recording of a poem told as the voice of a tree is an excellent example of a literary reading event imbued by its place of creation. Consider how the content of the recording (the poem "The Tree Speaks") is extended by the conjunction of place and politics found in this particular protest event. That poem will not be read in the same way when one has knowledge of the event and the political context that occasioned it. The poem makes repeated reference to an "old woman poet," situating us with the spectators seeing Webb read on the steps of the Parliament Buildings and hearing her play, as the "old woman poet" does, with the concept of the speaking "I":

> Listen to me now,
> talking out of character like
> a member of the human race,
> look what you've brought me to,
> so low that I'm only a foolish
> projection of some old woman poet.[39]

The concepts of speaking, voice, and silence are resurgent in Webb's work. As she said in the foreword to *Wilson's Bowl*: "My poems are born out of great struggles of silence. This book has been long in coming. Wayward, natural and unnatural silences, my desire for privacy, my critical hesitations, my critical wounds, my dissatisfaction with myself and the work have all contributed to a strange gestation."[40]

The 2014 launch of *Peacock Blue: The Collected Poems of Phyllis Webb* at the Vancouver Writers Festival featured sound recordings of Webb's voice. These recordings were to be played between readings of her poems by Webb's fellow poets, including Daphne Marlatt, Sharon Thesen, and George Bowering. Webb had retired from writing and public appearances in the late 1990s, so it surprised no one that she had declined to speak at the launch. Instead, the clips of her voice (from recordings of her readings, interviews with her, and her interviews of others) were meant to "enact the role of her voice" between the readings of her poems by her friends. We might say that these recordings are re-inscribed by their performance in the context of

Webb's launch (by way of final selection made by Brian Brett and the Vancouver Writers Festival staff). We might say that the reading shifts again the meaning of these poems and interviews. As Phil Hall said at the end of an ecstatic review of *Peacock Blue*, "she has engendered her full scope – by silences – by retreats – unto a woman's lyric authority."[41] But perhaps interpretations of her silence will not reign or, indeed, "have the last word." Webb chose to read again publicly in April 2015, from *Peacock Blue*, on Salt Spring Island with Brian Brett. This engagement with public performance bounces against these negotiations with silence. All of this interplay between voices and silences can also enfold any recorded public performance by her.

Conclusion

As I hope I have demonstrated, understanding literary archival recordings requires us to invest time in understanding the personal and organizational meanings found in the contexts of individual sound and video recordings. Adhering to this requirement will present more multi-layered interpretations of recordings, and will give rise to substantive research and debate into the arrangement, origins, and contexts of recorded sound and video.

Underpinning the archives of literary events entails an understanding of the creator's role and the creator's personal meaning in relation to the records we study. Such work of underpinning creates a ground from which we are able to engage with the level of complexity and the alternate meanings that a creator's context of creation, keeping, and values may place upon such archives. At the same time, however, investigating the creator's meanings can complicate the notion of a strictly single event or a stable record. In this action, investigation can unpin the recordings as well by adding a range of interactive meanings that shift or complicate our notions about the recordings and recording events themselves. By adding a range of personal meanings, we are securing our relationship to the archival components of these recordings in their originating circumstances. Moreover, we are establishing ground for entirely new ecologies of meaning and horizons for debate around what a life and creative text can mean and where the personal interaction with the non-textual can shift our sense of the textual and the media recording, and even touch the ontological.

NOTES

1   Hugh A. Taylor, "The Media of Record: Archives in the Wake of McLuhan,"
    in *Imagining Archives: Essays and Reflections by Hugh A. Taylor*, ed. Terry
    Cook and Gordon Dodds (Lanham, MD: Society of American Archivists and
    Association of Canadian Archivists and Scarecrow Press, 2003), 72.

2   Jean T. Guénette, *National Film, Television and Sound Archives* (Ottawa:
    Public Archives of Canada, 1983 General Guide Series), 1.

3   In his essay "Hugh Taylor: The Far Away Archivist," Gordon Dodds com-
    ments, "[Taylor] always justified these changes as necessary to redress the
    imbalance of resources typically given over to the care and access of written
    records in archives. Critics would counter that concentration on media can
    obscure or at least distort the provenance or context of records that should be
    linked in a unified way for every medium to their creator and not divided into
    media empires within archives. Of course, Hugh didn't intend that, for he al-
    ways had a holistic vision of archives, but perhaps naively trusted that archival
    managers would share his vision rather than being more intent on protecting
    their turf." Gordon Dodds, "Hugh Taylor: the Far-Away Archivist," in
    Imagining Archives, 11.

4   For further comments on the relation between literary archives and the unique
    domain of production of creative text, see Hobbs, "New Approaches to
    Canadian Literary Archives," *Journal of Canadian Studies/Revue d'études
    canadiennes* 40.2 (2006): 109–19, and "Personal Ethics: Being an Archivist
    of Writers," in *Basements and Attics, Closets and Cyberspace: Explorations
    in Canadian Women's Archives*, ed. Linda M. Morra and Jessica Schagerl
    (Waterloo, ON: Wilfrid Laurier University Press, 2012), 181–2.

5   See Richard Pearce-Moses, "Manuscripts Tradition," in ed. Luciana Duranti
    and Patricia C. Franks, *Encyclopedia of Archival Science* (Lanham, MD:
    Rowman & Littlefield, 2015), 241–3.

6   The trend toward combining study centres with custodial/collecting projects is
    becoming prevalent. Some examples include the SpokenWeb research program
    led by Jason Camlot at Concordia University (spokenweb.ca), as well as the
    Pathfinders project led by Dene Grigar (Washington State University Vancou-
    ver) and Stuart Moulthrop (University of Wisconsin–Milwaukee) (http://
    dtc-wsuv.org/wp/pathfinders/). Projects such as these seek to not only study
    but also collect the media of study and to develop parameters for preservation
    and cataloguing.

7   For core definitions of these foundational concepts, see Heather MacNeil, "Archival Theory and Practice: Between Two Paradigms," *Archivaria* 37 (Spring 1994): 6–20; Michel Duchein, "The History of European Archives and the Development of the Archival Profession in Europe," *American Archivist* 55 (Winter 1992): 14–25; and Terry Cook, "Mind over Matter: Towards a New Theory of Archival Appraisal," in Barbara L. Craig, ed., *The Archival Imagination: Essays in Honour of Hugh A. Taylor* (Ottawa, 1992), 38–70. These foundational concepts have also wrought fruitful debate within archival circles, examples of which are found in Laura Millar, "The Death of the Fonds and the Resurrection of Provenance: Archival Context in Space and Time," *Archivaria* 53 (2012): 2–15, and Tom Nesmith, "The Concept of Societal Provenance and Records of Nineteenth-Century Aboriginal-European Relations in Western Canada: Implications for Archival Theory and Practice," *Archival Science* 6.3 (2007): 351–60.

8   I am referring here to the archival notion of data to signal disconnection from context, that it is (as the Society of American Archivists' Glossary puts it): "Facts, ideas, or discrete pieces of information, especially when in the form originally collected and unanalyzed … Data often is used to refer to information in its most atomized form, as numbers or facts that have not been synthesized or interpreted, such as the initial readings from a gauge or obtained from a survey. In this sense, data is used as the basis of information, the latter distinguished by recognized patterns or meaning in the data. The phrase 'raw data' may be used to distinguish the original data from subsequently 'refined data'" (Society of American Archivists' Glossary, "data," www2.archivists.org/glossary/terms/d/data (accessed 3 March 2019).

   Any interaction with sifting and restructuring of data as such is outside of archival treatment of context, that is, it would ignore provenance and integrity to the activities of their creator in context (precisely the kind of treatment that has historically occurred for sound recordings that were hived off from fonds: see the discussion of Hugh Taylor and the public archives).

9   These documents are found in George Bowering fonds LMS-0115/R11712, accession 2006-01 Box 21 f.2.

10 There are always decisions and potential conflicts for archivists around whether or not to use physical or intellectual elements to determine final physical and intellectual arrangement for the archives they are arranging and describing. Essential to my discussion here is the idea that, whichever element indicates an

arrangement, the decision-making of the archivist is based on an assessment of elements of original order rather than an unexplained, imposed (artificial) final arrangement that remains undisclosed to the researcher. Physical cues in original order are best taken note of on-site at the time of acquisition, and intellectual cues to original order can be gleaned by asking the right questions of a living donor or an estate about the relationships among records.

11   These documents are found in the Daphne Marlatt fonds LMS-0200/R11776 in the 1st accession (1985–08) Series E. Published Works and Series F. Oral History and in the Audio Cassette Tapes series; and the 2nd accession (1993–13) Series D. Published Works.

12   These photographs are found in Daphne Marlatt fonds LMS-0200/R11776 (1985–08) Box 30 f. 3.

13   *The Line Has Shattered* is a documentary film by Robert McTavish released in 2013 and featuring narration by Phyllis Webb. The film explores the importance of the 1963 Vancouver Poetry Conference, which brought American poets Robert Creeley, Charles Olson, Robert Duncan, Allen Ginsberg, and Denise Levertov to Vancouver.

14   Based on an e-mail exchange between the archivist and Marlatt, where she explained this origin and her custodianship of the photographs. These details are included in the custodial history note and the credit notes to the fonds-level record for the Marlatt fonds in the Library and Archives Canada catalogue.

15   Digital records are currently presenting some issues to this relating to the migration and storage of viable formats. It is generally understood among a number of practicing literary archival programs that attempting to retain original formats and wrestling with issues of look and feel are important considerations for literary archives, in particular. Most larger archives do have a highly respected expertise in sound and video preservation, involving older playback technologies and extensive labs.

Media archaeology labs are becoming more prevalent in university contexts with Lori Emerson's founding in 2009 of the Media Archaeology Lab (Boulder, Colorado) and UBC Okanagan's AMP Lab, among other examples. Digital repositories such as the bpNichol archive project (www.bpnichol.ca/) and the Pathfinders project mentioned in n5 have found innovative ways of "going deep" to preserve all elements of certain platforms and works. Archival repositories have generally not developed media archaeology labs in-house. This could be a symptom of the library/archives/museum divide where published works are treated separately from unpublished (archival) documents and the lack of convergence between these two and the world of museum objects (of which the hardware can be seen to be part). It is probably also a symptom of the late emergence of approaches to born-digital archives and the even slower mobilization of many archival repositories toward addressing the digital. I am not aware of a robust partnership between a media archaeology lab and a public or even university repository for archives, although the benefits would be enormous (and I suspect this will emerge). There are also many possibilities here for cross-disciplinary discussions between archivists and digital conservation professionals.

16 I am basing these statements on a sampling of online finding aids from literary archival collections (in English) from across the country and my professional experience with other archives. A full study of the national scope of this approach is not the intent of this chapter.

17 International Readings at Harbourfront Centre fonds R13150 held at Library and Archives Canada.

18 These recordings were dumped automatically into the database described above to create simple item-level records and additional details about arrangement were added in the finding aid.

19 See Recordings Discussed by Zwicky and Bringhurst, MISACS numbers 486966 to 487001 relating to Vol. 64 files 1–14 and Vol. 65 files 1–17, Jan Zwicky fonds LMS-0239/R11836, 2nd accession (Reg. 2014-0289).

20 Jan Zwicky, *Chamber Music: The Poetry of Jan Zwicky*, ed. Warren Heiti and Darren Bifford (Waterloo: Wilfrid Laurier University Press, 2014).

21 Correspondence found in Jan Zwicky fonds LMS-0239/R11836, 2nd accession (Reg. 2014-0289), Vol. 64 files 1–14 and Vol. 65, files 1–17.

22 Because Bringhurst has such clear thoughts on the origination and transmission of literature and the morality of good design, I invited him to clarify the question directly. His full response (via e-mail, 11 November 2016) was the following:

> Audio recordings were enormously important to me as a young poet, because I grew up in a world where poetry – especially contemporary poetry – was not often spoken aloud. It came only in scrubby little pamphlets and paper-back books. So hearing the voices of writers I'd read – when they finally came my way on scratchy records or cassette tapes – made a great impression. This was true even for low-voltage readers like T.S. Eliot, and more true for oratorical wonders like Dylan Thomas. But if that poetry had come to me initially

through live readings or audiotape, I'm confident the printed versions would have been an equally powerful revelation, and in the long run a more useful one.

When I was older, I lived for a time in a world where poetry readings were frequent. I learned then that a poem could seem powerful on first hearing but might seem much less so when I had a chance to study the published text.

Tape recordings were also vitally important to me when I was learning my way around Haida oral literature – even though the available recordings were not of the authors or texts I was actually studying. (I've written about this in the afterword to the 2nd edition of *Sharp as a Knife*.) The recordings helped me immensely to get my bearings – in much the same way as recordings of Pound, Eliot, and Dylan Thomas had twenty years earlier. Still, the thing I needed most was what I had already: the transcribed Haida texts.

In a real oral culture, you quickly learn the difference between the mimics and the real tradition-bearers (who are also, of course, tradition-creators). The mimics have learned their routines, and they perform the same stories in pretty much the same way regardless of context or circumstance. The real oral poets don't repeat themselves in this way, even though they also tell "the same" stories many times. If you're lucky enough to find yourself in the company of such a person, you can learn a great deal every time a story is told, *especially* if it's a story you've heard before.

The tape recorder, as usually employed, reduces all oral poets to mimics in this sense, by delivering exactly the same performance every time the switch is turned. A good transcription, just because it requires more involvement from the reader, is in some sense different every time you read it. That doesn't replicate the richness of a living oral culture, but at least it bows in that direction.

A transcription of an oral work in another language – ancient Greek epic or recent Cree or Haida myth-telling – is like a long-distance message, never perfectly transmitted or perfectly received. You get what you can. The same is true of a printed work from the past, even if it's composed in your native language. Languages, like people, are constantly changing, so that vital organ called the imagination always has to be brought into play. But I think the crucial thing is this: a work of literature is *not* just a message. It's a thing-in-itself, with a life of its own. It isn't enough just to hear it or read it. To get what it has to offer, we have to give it a place to live. That can't be done until the imagination becomes involved – and imagination needs room to maneuver.

'To the letter,' we say, because written texts are proverbial symbols of precision and dependability. But writing leaves a lot of things out as well as putting a lot of things in. A written text, like a living voice, often gives the imagination more of the fruitful room it needs – and maybe more encouragement as well – or so it seems to me.

23 This is linked to the sense that the text may act as the musical score for polyphonic work, in his essay "Licking the Lips with a Forked Tongue," which ends: "The printed text should be as fine as it can be, but it should never be the final incarnation. A book must be a place where things begin." That is, for Bringhurst, a book of poems is a place of being, and a beginning in that it is the site of a human response to the world evoking "that quality in things – I like to call it poetry – that calls language into being," as he puts it in the essay "The Typographic Mind." Robert Bringhurst, *Everywhere Being Is Dancing: Twenty Pieces of Thinking* (Berkeley: Counterpoint, 2008), 219.

24 For a critical assessment of the public debate about Bringhurst's translations, see Nicholas Bradley, "At Land's End: *Masterworks of the Classical Haida Mythtellers*," in *Listening for the Heartbeat of Being: The Arts of Robert Bringhurst*, ed. Brent Wood and Mark Dickinson (Montreal and Kingston: McGill-Queen's University Press, 2015), 194–223.

25 See full citation in n21, above.

26 For more on this, see Hobbs, "Personal Ethics: Being an Archivist of Writers."

27 Including the few recordings of Bringhurst's voice we have in his archives (Robert Bringhurst fonds LMS-0114/R11716).

28 Robert Bringhurst, "Singing with the Frogs," in *Everywhere Being Is Dancing*, 51.

29 Ibid.

30 Here I would like to acknowledge a very engaging exchange with my colleague, music archivist, academic, and harpsichordist Rachelle Chiasson-Taylor, about *The Idea of North* and Gould's approach to technology. Many thanks to Rachelle for pointing me in the direction of Gould's essay.

31 Glenn Gould, "The Prospects of Recording," in *The Glenn Gould Reader*, ed. Tim Page (New York: Alfred A. Knopf, 1984), 331–53.

32 Bringhurst, "Singing with the Frogs," 51–2.

33 Bringhurst explains, "Songbirds sing. That is a fact, not metaphor. They sing in the forest every morning … The polyphonic music and the polyphonic poetry and fiction humans make is an answer to the world. It is mimicry of what is as much as statements of what might be … But night after night in Indonesia I have walked between the village, where the humans boomed and chirped with their bogglingly complex polyphonic tuned percussion, and the rice fields,

where the frogs, just as earnestly and skillfully, were polyphonically croaking." Bringhurst, "Singing with the Frogs," 37.

34 Here I am indicating the ricochet effect between Bringhurst's and Gould's use of technology. Whether or not Bringhurst feels that Gould's revolutionary use of recording media overcomes in some way the way "the tape recorder, as usually employed, reduc[ing] all oral poets to mimics" (as stated in n25) would be a fruitful avenue for discussion with him. I do not mean to imply that this door is closed, just that Bringhurst's and Gould's approaches imply further questions. Certainly, Bringhurst's comment that Gould might "contest 'poetry' as it is now written" implies there is more to be asked here.

35 For further discussion of these matters, see Hobbs, "Personal Ethics: Being an Archivist of Writers."

36 Katherine McLeod considers Webb's sound recordings outside of Library and Archives Canada in "Listening to the Archives of Phyllis Webb," in *Moving Archives*, ed. Linda Morra (Waterloo: Wilfrid Laurier University Press, forthcoming).

37 Phyllis Webb fonds LMS-0098/R11841, accession 1983-17 Cass 771 "WILSON DUFF – P. WEBB, Images Stone B.C."

38 Webb dedicates "Artifacts" in *Wilson's Bowl* to "Lilo, who walked into the sea." *Peacock Blue: The Collected Poems of Phyllis Webb*, ed. John Hulcoop (Vancouver: Talonbooks, 2014), 263.

39 Phyllis Webb, "The Tree Speaks," in *Peacock Blue,* 476.

40 The "Foreword" is dated 16 June 1980. Phyllis Webb, "Foreword," in *Wilson's Bowl* (Toronto: Coach House Press, 1980), 9.

41 Phil Hall, "Rev. of *Peacock Blue*," *The Malahat Review* 190 (Spring 2015): 79–83.

PART TWO

Archival Lacunae and the Mediated Event

6

Archival Spectres and Formats of the Event
The Foster Poetry Conference, 1963

JASON CAMLOT

The main concern of this chapter is the nature and meaning of a single, all-but-forgotten English-language poetry event that occurred in Quebec in 1963, and how the material traces (manuscript and print documents) that survive the event inform the narrative that I will construct about its significance. I focus on this particular poetry event – the Foster Poetry Conference (FPC) – in order to make an argument about a lost trajectory that might have defined the future of anglophone poetry events, and a subsequent anglo-Quebec poetry scene, in the late 1960s and beyond. The FPC event was organized by an older generation of English Quebec poets – namely, John Glassco, Frank Scott, and A.J.M. Smith – in an attempt to define what English Quebec poetry had accomplished up to that point, and where it should be going. It was also planned with the explicit hope of steering the development of the English Quebec poetry scene in the direction of greater interaction and communication with the poetry scenes of French Quebec.[1] How do we develop and define arguments about the significance of events and scenes after they have taken place? How is our present understanding of events shaped by the archives, media, and documents that preserve traces of their occurrence?

Spectres, Archival Structures, and Precedents

The tape recordings of the conference readings were made by FPC participant Ralph Gustafson. This we know from Gustafson's correspondence with Glassco.[2] But the tapes themselves have yet to reveal themselves, if they ever will. I begin and end this chapter with speculation on the situation and import of this lacuna.

Recently, a colleague from Bishop's University provided me with a box of original tapes as well as CDs containing digitized copies of Gustafson's extensive tape recording collection. While this box was received with great hope that *my* tape would be found there, it was not among the fourteen reels (thirteen 7″, one 5″) of magnetic tape, thirteen audio cassette tapes, and four VHS tapes that comprise the analog media contents of this collection.[3] Jack Eby, a professor of music history and literature at Bishop's, received a grant from the Eastern Townships Resource Centre in 2001 to research, organize, and digitize the collection (held in the aforementioned box). His work reveals Gustafson's life-long implication in the use of sound recording technology in his practice as a poet and critic, and explains why Gustafson would have been the one to make the recordings of the FPC readings that we can no longer hear. The Gustafson recordings collection is substantial and includes early transcription recordings of ABC radio broadcasts (1933–1944) and CBC broadcasts from the 1960s and 1970s; tape recordings of live readings Gustafson gave in a variety of venues (mostly universities); two reels of Gustafson reading thirty poems (3 February 1977) at the invitation of Robert Hayden for the Library of Congress in connection with the Washington Symposium on 20th Century Canadian Culture; numerous recordings that Gustafson made of himself reading poems in sequence from his latest books; recordings made for use by Gustafson in his teaching of poetry and music, which include his own lectures as well as compilations of other poets' recordings; and a series of home recordings that Gustafson made of other Canadian poets, such as Irving Layton and A.M. Klein, reading their own work. This still virtually inaccessible collection of Gustafson's homemade recordings is a valuable example of an audiophile-poet's engagement with tape-recording technology as a facet of his personal, archival documentation and performative practice from the 1930s to the 1990s. It deserves to be rescued from the banker's box that presently holds it and warrants the development of a robust online platform to enable critical access to the many hours of literary historical sound it contains. But, unfortunately, the Gustafson collection is silent on the questions I wish to pursue here.

I have chronicled at some length the contents of this adjacent collection – even though, ultimately, it has no direct bearing upon the story of the FPC that I am telling – because it informs us of the will that existed to capture the FPC event in a non-print medium with the aim of disseminating literary activities of perceived national import to a wider public. In this way, Gustafson's work as recordist links a meeting that may seem, in retrospect, parochial with a much wider national and international interest in the use of sound recording technologies for literary dissemination and practice, and stands as a quite early example of such interest. Perhaps even more importantly for my subject, the knowledge that such tapes existed but cannot be heard in the present represents an occasion to speculate upon the symbolic import of temporal media capture for the study of literary events. What does it mean to know that a sound recording of an event *existed*, but, for the practical purpose of writing history in the present, *no longer exists*? There is a certain degree of magic associated with a sound recording of an event that arises from the time-critical nature of the medium. The real-time quality of sound recording, the fact that sound recording as a temporal medium puts us *into* time that has already passed and, in this way, opens a tunnel connection with the past, triggers what philosopher Wolfgang Ernst has called "the drama of time critical media."[4] An encounter with a tape-documented sound unfurls as an experience of real time: the listener has the sense that the temporal process one is hearing is living in the present, replicating the *live* signal, of which it is apparently a real-time reproduction. Sound recording works on human perception itself and, in particular, on our perception of time. Ernst's argument about the strange drama of sound recording is based, in part, on his idea that we are not cognitively equipped to process events from two temporal dimensions simultaneously. When we immerse ourselves in real-time sound, we perceive it as "live" and this jars our awareness of time.

The drama associated with temporal sound recording media seems particularly resonant when the medium is applied to the documentation of an occasion of live reading, that is, an event of sonic performance that would otherwise have resulted in an ephemeral experience of listening. Don Ihde, in his explorations of sound phenomenology, observes that, "insofar as all sounds are also 'events,' all the sounds are within the first approximation, likely to be considered as 'moving.'" Ihde, in this instance, imagines sounds as divorced from visible objects, existing as auditory presences within the horizons of silence that surround them.[5] Historical sound seems to present itself as a unique kind of artifact because its non-visual presence may make us experience it as more ephemeral than other kinds of visible, material artifacts, like manuscripts, for example, and because its presence depends upon controlled temporal movement. Whether or not the recording of the FPC poetry reading would have revealed anything significant about the historical event itself is to some extent irrelevant in relation to the symbolic power of the absent sound recording. The absent recording casts the spectre of a lost wormhole to the region of FPC space-time that is my historical concern. It projects the mirage of a portal to the eventfulness my narrative seeks to recover and suggests a wide range of sonic clues to affective and tonal relations and quotidian occurrences that I will never hear. I am left, instead, like most literary historians, with traces of an event set down on paper, in ink, and the apparitional hiss of tape sounding in the back of my mind.

One key source for my account of the FPC is the robust body of correspondence concerned with the organization of the conference and proceedings found in the John Glassco fonds, held at Library and Archives Canada. The archive of letters (and the published proceedings to be discussed below) reveal that the shape of the conference was determined by a vision of pan-Canadian, bilingual and intergenerational representations, models of literary conferences that preceded it, and the immediate unfolding of political events that would determine the level of financial support available. However, to discern this vision from the materials held in the archive entails working against an ordering structure that obstructs the immediate perception of a multi-party event, organized as it is in relation to the production activities of a single author. Historically, the application of the archival principles of provenance were introduced within administrative contexts in the late nineteenth century and were innovative for their stress upon capturing the administrative conditions of a collection's emergence in time, in another place.[6] Within the context of archives of the state and other organizations, these principles worked well to capture administrative activities as they occurred, and to present organizations as complex, functioning organisms. The persistence of such principles within an author-based archive like the Glassco fonds are designed to present the author himself as the developing organism, but do not provide an obvious bridge toward understanding communal activities as they may have unfolded.

The archival materials pertaining to the FPC are segregated within the much larger Glassco fonds, thus isolating the author's activities in relation to documents pertaining to the event. Correspondence folders within this event-themed section of the Glassco fonds provide insight into communications channels that run between individual authors in an isolated manner at the expense of capturing the movement of more complex communications circuits that involved lateral interference from multiple parties. More specifically, the FPC correspondence consists of 199 letters (112 composed by Glassco and 87 others written by 25 distinct correspondents) arranged into folders alphabetically by corresponding author, with Glassco's own letters interspersed chronologically within the alphabetically arranged structure. This authorial arrangement with temporal sub-arrangements divulges the event, initially, as twenty-five siloed negotiations between two individuals: Glassco and a young poet, Glassco and a long-time friend, Glassco and a member of the National Assembly, Glassco and an editor of a university press, etc. In addition to the letters, the Glassco fonds contains five folders of materials organized according to document categories, namely, Cataract Accounts of the Foster Poetry Conference, Financial Documents, Proceedings, Clippings, and Miscellaneous.[7] A key task in transposing this archive into historical narrative involves desegregating the contents from the alphabetized, authorial arrangement and the document categorization, with the aim of remixing these discursive materials to reveal other shapes and networks that explain the event.

Beyond these materials in the archive, our reception of the FPC is largely shaped by the textual apparatus of the proceedings that Glassco edited, published as *English Poetry in Quebec* by McGill University Press (MUP) in 1965. These proceedings were prepared in the year after the events took place. The published "proceedings," a historical genre dating back to the late eighteenth century, were structured to assemble narratives and documentation of historical activities, procedures, membership, mission, research, and resolutions of scientific associations. The proceedings bear an interesting resemblance to the archive of administrative institutions insofar as both aim to organize the records of complex, motivated organizations. Proceedings were associated with the public communication of events and discussions of learned societies,[8] and functioned as the first source within a wider communications network, as newspapers and other print media circulated accounts and reports based upon the documentation presented in these official publications.[9] The proceedings as a genre of publication often presented oral forms of communication – scientific papers or "talks" that were originally delivered aloud before an audience, discussions, debates, and sometimes the minutes of association meetings – in print form. Proceedings thus represent a historical form of remediating and formatting oral communication into print.

In the case of the FPC proceedings documents, our access to the events is filtered by the editorial plan and principles that Glassco, Scott, Smith, and their MUP editor (Lloyd M. Scott) finally agreed upon. Early on in the editorial process, A.J.M. Smith wrote to Glassco stating that he felt the proceedings of the conference should "be modeled on Whalley's Macmillan editing of the Kingston Poetry Conference report."[10] George Whalley's *Writing in Canada: Proceedings of the Canadian Writers' Conference, Queen's University, 28–31 July 1955* thus provides one template that informs our ultimate reception of the format of the FPC as an event.[11] The very title of Glassco's proceedings – *English Poetry in Quebec* – functions as a generically specified, and geographically localized, rendering of Whalley's report on the 1955 conference. Whalley's book provided a systematic and collectively developed representation of the Canadian Writers' Conference (CWC) according to its three primary themes – The Writer, The Writer's Media, The Writer and the Public – including reproduction of the papers that were delivered as sub-topics for each of those themes, and summary accounts of discussion groups as compiled by discussion chairs. Scott wrote in his introduction to *English Writing in Canada*, "the theory and composition of the Conference meant that it was not so much a *writers'* conference as a conference on writing and its dissemination."[12] It was, in short, a true academic conference. In line with Whalley's publication model, Glassco tried on several occasions to convince Scott and Smith to write an introduction, but none was delivered and so Glassco's meandering, "factual but frothy" preface is the only critical frame provided for the FPC proceedings.[13] Also according to Whalley's precedent, Glassco tried to delegate the summary of seminar discussions (there were no chaired discussion groups at the FPC), but few of the participants obliged in sending him anything that was publishable.

The mere attempt of Glassco to replicate aspects of Whalley's model for conference proceedings indicates some desire on the organizers part toward comprehensive engagement with questions surrounding contemporary poetry. The ultimate failure of *English Poetry in Quebec* to repeat the more coherent account provided in Whalley's *Writing in Canada* can be attributed to the fact that, in contrast to Scott's introductory description of the CWC, the FPC was primarily a *writers'* gathering combined with some critical discussion. The inconsistent structure and contents of the FPC proceedings – with critical essays of differing lengths, sporadic reproduction of delegate discussion, and a large anthology of poetry comprising the last third of the book followed by a list of "Resolutions" forwarded by the participants of the conference – may be read as a textual trace of the discursively divided nature of the activities of the FPC itself: a combination of formal scholarly discussion followed by poetic performance. Not quite engaging in the spontaneous mixture of readings, interviews, and artist statements that was characteristic of poetry events in the 1960s and 1970s, the scheduled activities of the FPC imposed a more rigid distinction between the function of poetic and critical discourse. For example, rather than have poets on stage discussing their conceptions of process and poetics through a combination of reading, self-analysis (in the form of preambles consisting of lengthy explanations and statements of poetic process and principles), and publicly staged poetic conversations (like the ones presented at the 1963 Vancouver Poetry Conference), the FPC format designated the problem of "The Creative Process" to one discrete seminar (led by Irving Layton) as just a single topic among those deemed important for critical treatment. The FPC also seems to have been designed according to an ethos of social responsibility, as if the gathering was ultimately meant to develop public policy surrounding the situation of poetry in Quebec and Canada. The resolutions published at the end of the proceedings reinforce this perception. No doubt this apparent ethos was connected to the fact that the Quebec government had sponsored the conference.

The publication of the proceedings themselves was steeped in wrangling about the significance of a published account of an English-language poetry event as a political document within the Quebec context. The proceedings were approached as a public, archival account of a government-sponsored event. The initial plan, at the request of Quebec government official Glendon Brown, was to pursue publication of the proceedings with the Quebec Department of Cultural Affairs rather than with MUP, in effect, making the proceedings of the poetry conference an official government document.[14]

Glassco and Scott were enthusiastic about this idea to have the proceedings "printed by the Queen's Printer in Quebec and distributed by the Quebec Government to libraries, universities, etc. throughout the world as well as put on sale at all English booksellers in Canada."[15] They felt this arrangement would be rewarding "from the point of view of both operation and prestige."[16] But continued discussion in the Quebec Department of Cultural Affairs led to the withdrawal of this offer and to a series of subsequent "virtual promise[s],"[17] delays, and cancelled offers around government funding of the publication.[18] The Quebec government initially promised to print it themselves, then to provide full funding (over $3,120) for its publication with MUP, then to provide a reduced amount ($2,000); finally, the government contributed $500 to the publishing endeavour.[19] The importance of having the Quebec government's approval of such a publication is apparent in MUP editor Lloyd M. Scott's statement to Glassco that while the exact amount of the grant from Quebec wasn't a deal breaker, "failure to work in some sort of partnership with them on this project will cause disappointment and even embarrassment."[20] In 1963, common sense dictated that a book explicitly addressing the state of English poetry in Quebec required consent from Quebec's minister of cultural affairs. In the end, the reduced contribution from Quebec was supplemented by Canada Council funding to make the publication of *English Poetry in Quebec* possible.[21] It is somehow fitting that a publication documenting the format and contents of a poetry event devoted to the topic of English-language poetry in Quebec in 1963 should have been partially sponsored by both the provincial and federal governments.[22] It underscores the ambiguity surrounding the very idea of English poetry in Quebec as a problem to consider within the national context.

English Poetry in Quebec

The year 1963 was an important one for poetry gatherings in Canada. On the west coast, there was the Vancouver Poetry Conference, organized by Warren Tallman and Robert Creeley at the University of British Columbia. Consisting of a series of discussions, seminars, readings, and house parties, it has become legendary as a foundational moment for the development of avant-garde poetics in Canada.[23] On the east coast in the fall of that year, the equally ambitious, yet arguably far less impactful, FPC was organized and held at the Glen Mountain ski resort just outside of Knowlton (Lac

Brome) in Quebec's Eastern Townships. This eclectic meeting of English-speaking poets and intellectuals was initially conceived as a meeting of French and English Quebec poets but, for political reasons, was reformulated as a public sounding of the state of English-language poetry in the province as it related to the rest of the world. Reporting on the conference for *The Canadian Forum*, Alan Pearson summarizes the events as having been "divided between seminars for the daytime and an address for the evenings, with a climactic marathon poetry reading on Sunday afternoon (Ralph Gustafson presiding at the tape recorder), consisting of new work by almost all the poets present."[24] With seminars and papers on such topics as "The Poet and the Nuclear Crisis" (A.J.M. Smith), "The Creative Process" (Irving Layton), "The Poet in Quebec Today" (Frank Scott), "The Reviewer of Poetry" (Milton Wilson), "The Little Magazine" (Louis Dudek), "Revolution and Poetry" (George Whalley), and poetry readings by established poets (including Smith, Layton, Scott, Dudek, and Ralph Gustafson) and younger ones (Leonard Cohen, D.G. Jones, Seymour Mayne, and K.V. Hertz) – the "elders" and the "children" as Glassco called them[25] – this conference stands as a confident and insulated attempt to set the course for English Quebec's continued leadership at the vanguard of Canadian modernism.

The FPC was planned as a gathering to discuss and sound the future of Canadian poetry, whereas the Vancouver Poetry Conference pursued a broader sounding of North American poetics. Whereas the models informing the Vancouver meeting as framed by Creeley and the American literature professor Tallman focused on the importance of innovative and open-form American poetics, the poetic inclinations of the organizers of the FPC were rooted in a taste for the polished poem. Further, and most importantly for the present discussion, the Foster conference was explicitly concerned with the significance of French-language poetry as it might relate to the future of Canadian poetics. The conception of the FPC was informed by an awareness of a recently manifested Quebec-based nationalist poetry, which the Vancouver conference showed little knowledge of or concern for.

This is not to say that ideas of nationalism were not important to contemporary discussions of Canadian literature in a broader sense. There are dozens of articles from the period that address questions about what makes (or might eventually make) Canadian literature distinct.[26] Many of these turn their attention outward, against the immediate influence of American language and culture upon that of Canada, and articulate a hope that the

Canadian poet's uniqueness would emerge either as a result of the conditions of her geographical location (as Atwood would argue in *Survival*) or (and this is the most relevant point for our purposes) from the combined uniqueness of its two founding cultures. For example, in his article "The Two Traditions: Literature and the Ferment in Quebec," published just a year before the Foster Poetry Conference, Louis Dudek articulates such concern. Here the future of Canadian literature depends upon a developed synthesis of both founding cultures: "Canadian literature, if we understand it, becomes the whole literature of France and the whole literature of England standing behind the literature of French Canada and the literature of English Canada. We must conceive of it in this large, dramatic frame, if we are to escape from provincialism and if we are to create a new complex civilization in the north. This, and nothing less, must be our aim."[27] While the FPC was not conceived with any such specific argument about the necessary fusion of the French and English traditions as the sole course to ensure the future of Canadian literature as a distinct entity, there is no question that the conference was initially conceived as a potential occasion to initiate what was seen (from the perspectives of Glassco, Scott, and Smith) as an absolutely necessary rapprochement between English and French Canadian poets. If the first idea for the conference was that of a modest gathering of a few English Quebec poets, the promise (in May 1963) of $3,000 from Glassco's local member of the Legislative Assembly Glendon P. Brown led the three organizers to imagine a more ambitious kind of conference, a bilingual gathering of poets on a large scale.

In the first instance, Brown the politician – in conversation with his colleagues from the Quebec office of Cultural Affairs – seems to have imagined the conference as a great opportunity to promote contact between French and English Quebecers through the decidedly non-political occasion of a poetry gathering, and he wrote to Glassco with that idea.[28] To this news conveyed by Glassco, Smith replied, excitedly: "Urge acceptance of offer for conference which must be bilingual,"[29] and Scott wrote back a day later: "This is looking very interesting and naturally I heartily support it."[30] Between mid-May, when Glassco first heard the news about substantial funding, and late June, things got interesting in unexpected ways and the plans for a full-fledged bilingual poetry conference would have to be changed. Suddenly, what had been seen as a usefully "non-political" opportunity for the Quebec government became a potential threat to national security. In fact,

Glassco's announcement of the funding offer to Scott and Smith was sent on 18 May, the same day of the FLQ mailbox bombings in Westmount (perhaps the news hadn't reached Knowlton yet). Further bombings on the Island of Montreal, including one on Victoria Day, and the capture of certain leaders of the FLQ would dominate the national headlines over the next month.[31] By the end of June, Glassco would have to write to his co-organizers with an update on the funding situation, explaining that "we may really have to restore it to its original unilingual status" because "the Quebec govt. are worried over its possible (now don't laugh) infiltration by FLQ-ers, Castroites and Communists."[32]

Accepting the fact that the FPC must become a smaller event with less funding (now just $1,000), Glassco reiterated to Guy Frégault (deputy minister of Cultural Affairs) his hope "that this conference will be merely a starting-point from which will develop a thoroughly bilingual gathering, in accordance with what we believe to be a genuine need of our common Canadian culture."[33] This would remain a goal for the FPC organizers even after the conference had concluded and they discussed plans for a second poetry gathering, tentatively scheduled to take place in North Hatley under the direction of Ralph Gustafson. As Glassco mused in a letter written to Smith in April 1964 (a year after the FPC) about the formidable force of Quebec nationalist poetry and the ongoing need for rapprochement between English and French Quebec poets, "if we try to bring it [rapprochement] about (as I think we should very soon) it will have to be done privately, i.e. not with Quebec money."[34] The letter indicates that the idea of any large-scale bilingual poetry conference that might have been planned as a follow-up to the unilingual FPC would be politically "impossible" to stage, because of the violence and radicalism associated with Quebec nationalist poets as well as an apparent ill-will toward the promotion of anglophone cultural activities at this time (according to Glassco, at least).[35] So, when Gustafson, in the process of considering the organization of a follow-up to the FPC, asked Glassco, "Would you tell me whether such a conference would attempt again to include French-language poets? Or would it follow last autumn's pattern?"[36] Glassco replied, "I am still all for it, but unfortunately Quebec mistrusts the French-language poets almost as much as it did last year. I spoke to Brown last night and he said there's no chance of getting *anything* for a bilingual conference. It's tragic, but there it is. He suggested that a few French poets whom any of us know personally and who are not connected with the FLQ might be invited. This might be a way of breaking the ice. We have all got to get together some time."[37]

In summary, the conference was originally conceived by Glassco, Scott, and Smith as "a means to bridge the two linguistic groups" by including both French and English Quebec poets. However, FLQ violence set off a series of negotiations with the government funders of the event that resulted in conditions stating that "the Foster Poetry Conference was to be unilingual, it was not to be publicized," and the name of Glendon Brown, the MNA who secured funding for the conference, was not to be mentioned.[38] One version of the FPC, based upon a vision of CanLit as a synthesis of the descendants of two European nations, exists only in the cultural imaginary of Glassco and his fellow organizers. Had the political context been such that this vision could be realized, the material traces of that non-event would have differed radically from what history has left us to examine.

Format of the Event

The format of the FPC was steered by the political perspective of the representatives in the Quebec Department of Cultural Affairs, who ended up reducing the initial grant by two-thirds. The waffling over how much would be granted to the FPC left Glassco and his fellow organizers in the position of needing to conceptualize and implement a plan quickly. As would be the case with the preparation of the printed proceedings of the FPC, Glassco and company turned to the Canadian Writers' Conference (CWC) held at Queen's University in 1955 for ideas. The CWC had, in turn, been modelled after poetry conferences held at Harvard in 1950 (attended by Frank Scott, A.J.M. Smith, and A.M. Klein) and McGill in 1951 (led by Scott).[39] Thus, the fallback template for the revised structure of the FPC was rooted in institutionally authorized frameworks for discussions of modernism previously held at two of North America's most prestigious institutions. There would be no time to commission formal papers from scholars (as Whalley did in organizing the CWC), so instead, by mid-September, just one month before the FPC took place, Glassco, Scott, and Smith developed "a tentative programme of six subjects for informal discussions."[40] They could not afford, nor did they have time, to bring in poets representing regions across Canada (as Whalley had done), but a few out-of-province poets were sought to broaden the perspective of the conference. For example, invited participant Milton

Wilson (professor at Trinity College, University of Toronto) wrote to Glassco recommending Eli Mandel, who had just moved to York University after time in Alberta, as one who "would help to broaden our perspective west of Ontario and Quebec."[41] Glassco, Scott, and Smith were also seeking younger participants, an important element insofar as the gathering, among other things, was intended to establish an identifiable lineage for English Quebec poetry and to plant seeds for the future. David McFadden was considered as a representative "young poet" from Ontario, but in the end, budget constraints required the organizers to settle on the "Cataracters" – editors of the little magazine entitled *Cataract* – including Seymour Mayne, Leonard Angel, K.V. Hertz, and Henry Moscovitch, as well as English Quebec poets D.G. Jones and Leonard Cohen, who, while certainly well established, were still less-old-garde than the three conference organizers.[42] There were no women on the program. This fact not only captures the gender-limited imagination of the organizers, and the conception of the Montreal poetry scene in predominantly masculine terms, but also indicates the existence of entrenched social hierarchies that were related to ideas about poetic tradition and form. In chapter 7, Karis Shearer addresses the nature and implications of such hierarchies as manifest in the organization of the Vancouver Poetry Conference. Overall, the FPC seems to have worked by mixing the elements of a more formal academic conference with the atmosphere of a gathering of writers debating ambitious topics, like their role in a nuclear age; practical topics, like the state and function of reviewing in Canada; and questions of technique and process.

Concerns about the immediate significance of the Quebec context for English-language writing, so ubiquitous in the correspondence surrounding the planning, and aftermath, of the conference were also integrated explicitly into the conference programming itself. Frank Scott's seminar, "The Poet in Quebec Today," argued that "Quebec is in the midst of a period of 'accelerated history'" and that the rise in nationalist politics provided the French Canadian poet a more solid subject for poetry than English poets in Quebec who "though living in the same province … do not appear to feel that it is their revolution which is taking place."[43] Scott's talk as reproduced in the proceedings is not followed by a summary of discussion as is the case with accounts of some other seminars, but Alan Pearson's report on the conference in *The Canadian Forum* suggests Scott's argument that the French Quebec poets had a more immediately visceral and concrete source for their poetry incited "some of the most uninhibited rebuttals and agreements that one is likely to hear at a public conference."[44] On one side, arguments stated that poetry was no place for politics and the Québécois poets' focus on local politics would render their work "parochial and boring," and rebuttals warned that such criticisms would only work to fuel "an already inflammatory situation." As Pearson concludes in his summary of the discussion: "By the end of this seminar no one could fail to be more aware both of the explosive potentialities within some of the most (apparently) personal and even reactionary French Canadian poetry of the past and of the extent to which such potentialities had been coming into the open in the poetry of the last few years.[45] As my discussion up to this point has shown, the "potentialities" that Pearson refers to were certainly on the minds of the government officials who funded the FPC. The Quebec government's concerns about the political affiliations of the French-speaking poets whom Glassco had planned to invite had a significant impact on the amount granted to the event and, consequently, on the format and scope of the poetry conference as it actually took place.

Poetry Readings

What of the poetry readings themselves? Soon after the FPC, Ralph Gustafson wrote to Glassco: "You remember at the Conference I suggested that the readings that afternoon would make a good anthology with some editing? Having listened to the tape again, I felt this conviction borne in upon me again. I remember hearing that Mr Brown suggested printing some record of the sessions. Do you think he plus the Quebec Government would like to memorialize the Conference in this way?"[46] There was subsequent discussion among the organizers and Gustafson on several occasions about sending recordings of the readings to Bob Weaver to be played on his program CBC *Wednesday Night*. While that plan does not seem to have been realized, it is clear that the idea of rendering the reading as a print anthology was conceived early in the process.[47] Consequently, our access to this poetry-reading event is dependent upon the decisions of presentation made by Glassco, Scott, and Smith in preparing the proceedings of the conference. Glassco and his co-organizers made their selections based upon their own well-rehearsed categories of literary taste and judgment.

In letters written during the selection process, Glassco refers to the tension surrounding the selection of poems to be included in the proceedings. These controversies occasionally resulted from the complaints of individual poets about the omission of specific poems but, in a broader sense, they pertained to the documentary function of the proceedings as a representation of a live poetry-reading event. Dudek complained forcefully about the selection process, saying that "no poem should be omitted if it was read at the conference, unless we can say firmly that it is simply incompetent by any standards. Otherwise the whole principle of democratic inclusion is lost."[48] Dudek wished the anthology to function as an accurate printed record of the readings as they had occurred. This approach would have had the anthology function as a printed surrogate for the event as it had been captured on magnetic tape, albeit without the effect of actual transcription, which would have required relineation of the poems according to the patterns in which they were delivered orally. Glassco's response to Dudek's argument noted the "monstrous imbalances": total inclusion would entail "giving Leonard Cohen top linage position with 240 lines, compared to Doug Jones in second place with 145, and an over-all average of about 75 lines for every other poet – including tripe of varying degrees of badness."[49] From this note, and related correspondence, we learn not only that Cohen read for approximately twice as long as most of the other poets but also that Glassco's priority in representing the poetry reading in print was not to capture a documentary rendering of the event but to salvage as strong a print anthology as possible from the poems read at a live performance. The result was a fifty-page anthology comprising more than one-third of the book, *English Poetry in Quebec*. The section of the proceedings was titled "Selection of Poetry Readings" and included a subtitle stating, "This selection was made jointly by A.J.M. Smith, F.R. Scott and John Glassco."[50] It is interesting to note that Whalley's proceedings of CPC did not reprint poems that were read at his conference, but rather included a "Report on the Poetry Readings" written by Jay Macpherson. Her report provides some information about who read poems and which poems were read, but mainly it provides an account of the structure, tenor, and pacing of these readings, a summary account of what occurred at the readings as a poetry event. The report represents an alternative approach to rendering an ephemeral historical event – a reading – for posterity, an approach that has more in common with the historical genre of association proceedings than that of the poetry anthology. Macpherson tells us that the readings were informal and included interruptions, comments, and general discussion as part of the process. She goes on to consider the impact of poetry when it is read aloud by delivering a few "close listenings" (to use Charles Bernstein's phrase[51]) of several of the readers and "attempting to account for the excitement the readings generated."[52] In this instance, Whalley's book was not a formal precedent for the FPC proceedings. Glassco would remain notably unimpressed with recitation as a facet of poetic practice, remarking that while listening to a poem may be nice, "so often we discover, on reading the poem later for ourselves, it was a bad poem."[53] Glassco and his organizers held firm on their decision to select poems and to produce a miniature anthology to which they could attach their names with a print bias that may have contributed to the foreclosure of non-print access to the event. This approach to presenting the reading in print suggests that the actual reading event functioned as an "audition" of the participating poets before the elder poets who organized the conference, and who would subsequently select which poems looked (rather than sounded) good enough on the page to make it into the anthology that would comprise a significant part of the published proceedings. The amount of effort Glassco gave to the selection of poems, as compared to the papers and discussions, suggests that he placed greater weight on a traditional anthology then on criticism as a means of securing the legacy of English Quebec poetry within the context of Canadian letters. From this perspective, the tape recording of the poetry reading – the archival lacuna that haunts the current chapter – continues to wield its influence on the legacy of the event, despite its present absence as a historical artifact to be considered.

Poetry Resolutions

The conference ended with the adoption of three lengthy institution and media-oriented resolutions, which, in summary, moved (1) to commend the Province of Quebec's support for Quebec-based poetry as a model to be emulated by other provinces in Canada, (2) to request grants from the Humanities Research Council of Canada to support lecture and reading tours by Canadian poets, and (3) to urge the CBC to provide "adequate opportunities for the presentation of Canadian poetry on its television facilities."[54] Just as the influence of English-language poetry in Quebec was waning, the organizers formulated ideas for disseminating poetry across other, more wide-reaching media, namely, public events, radio, and television. The resolutions were meant to accomplish actual results, as delegates were assigned the task of forwarding specific resolutions to designated offices and government officials. In a 12 October 1963 letter, Eli Mandel reminds Glassco of his obligation to "forward to the appropriate people the resolution commending the Department of Cultural Affairs" and says that he will "look after the CBC and Humanities Research Council resolutions."[55] Glassco fulfilled this obligation soon after by transmitting the first resolution to the Quebec minister of cultural affairs, Georges-Émile Lapalme.[56] All three resolutions are addressed to government agencies, underscoring the function of the Quebec government–funded poetry conference as a meeting that was concerned with cultural policy as well as poetry. These "unacknowledged legislators" understood the strategic value of commending the government institutions that made their meetings possible, and felt that their vocations as poets and intellectuals warranted their intervention in matters of cultural affairs by consulting on the best use of government funds and the instruments of national media.

What one takes away from all three resolutions and from the materials representing the conference as a whole is the continued confidence among the participants in English Quebec poetry's centrality to poetry in the rest of Canada. Dudek's much-quoted phrase about "the dominant role of Montreal as a center of activity and a source of new poetry" in Canada, penned in 1957, continued to inform the tone of the participants, and their bold motions signalling their significant role in defining the future.[57] Glassco's preface to the proceedings remarks that plans for the second conference (which, as we recall, was to be hosted by Gustafson in North Hatley) were already underway, and that "it is hoped that the Foster Poetry Conference was only the beginning"[58] – the beginning, as we now understand, of a true rapprochement with the poets and poetry of French Quebec, and of policies concerning the mobilization of radio and television media designed to promote and secure the import of the printed word in the process of disseminating CanLit to the future.

The Spectral Media Event

In closing, I return to the question of what the tapes would have revealed for our historical understanding of the events that occurred on 12–14 October 1963 in Foster, Quebec. What would access to the tapes of the Foster Poetry Conference have provided in the form of historical experience, information, and possible critical insight into the nature of that event, in the present? How would the temporal listening tube, the perception of access to the unfolding of a historical (if not historic) event, have been different? One thing that is missing is the frisson of temporal connection afforded by the sound-recording medium, and our inclination to understand it as indexical of a previous span of time. We are time-sensitive creatures, not equipped ontologically to perceive the sound of two spans of time simultaneously. This element alone, without even taking into account the information that the documentation of the event might have provided, is significant enough to identify as a difference. In that case, I would have faced the task of communicating the sense of difference arising from a temporal-media document within the print medium of scholarly publication. This might have been accomplished through the development of alternate descriptive and methodological techniques, an opportunity that the present state of the John Glassco archive denies me, practically speaking. Still, to imagine the impact of such additional archival materials, I will conclude by identifying some of the possible losses in the critical narrative I have been able to produce with the materials I had at hand.

First, there is the loss of a temporal portal to the events in question and its importance for a consequent perception of presence that I have already mentioned. Second is the loss of information perceptible within the media documentation itself – the sound of the event – which includes the following: The ambient sounds that evoke the materials and spatial horizon of the en- vironment. The sound of the fabric and the bodies that we might have heard as ghostly signals, that is to say, as vocalic and sonic bodies.[59] The semantic information *and* the social implications of intonations heard in the non- poetic speech that would have been recorded, including the introductions of readers, the poet's comments, and explanations during the reading, as well as interjections and responses from the audience. (Such sonic information might have revealed important social dynamics pertaining to gender, class, and ethnicity, among other factors.) The timbre of the poet's voice for clinical hints of the physical state of the poet's speaking body. The timbre and into- nations of the poet's reading voice for the aesthetic motives that might be deciphered from the poet's oral interpretation of a word, a line, a pause, a breath, a poem. A third category of loss is one of perceptible access to the fact that the media technology used to document the event entailed physical action, labour, technical understanding, and, less obviously interpretable, some kind of motive for recording a poetry reading. Connected with this category is the loss of a perceptible sense of that motive's connection to the media technology used and the possibilities for historical documentation that it afforded. This last point in the spectral reading, the lost reading I am imagining, is particularly interesting to consider in relation to the FPC resolutions to generate extensive media productions of their performances and presence, and ultimately (although they do not mention it) to have those media productions preserved for posterity as new forms of cultural heritage artifacts, in a new kind of archive – an archive that preserves and structures the performance of printed literature and its corresponding events in temporal-media formats.

NOTES

1　To be clear, in stating that the FPC failed to steer the trajectory of English Quebec poetry toward rapprochement with Francophone Quebec poetry, I do not wish to suggest that bilingual and multilingual poetry events have remained an impossibility in Quebec since that time. Many such events are discussed in Victoria Stanton and Vincent Tinguely's oral history, *Impure: Reinventing the Word: The Theory, Practice, and Oral History of Spoken Word in Montreal* (Montreal: Conundrum Press, 2001). My point in focusing on the FPC is to trace the sense of difficulty such a meeting of poets represented to a certain generation of poets, within a government-funded context, in the early 1960s.

2　Letter from John Glassco to Louis Dudek, 11 December 1963, John Glassco fonds MG 30 D163, Vol. 1, Folder: Foster Poetry Conference Correspondence, Folder: Angel – Lapalme 1963–1964 (1 of 2).

3　Jack Eby, "The Recorded Archives of Ralph Gustafson," unpublished catalogue. I am grateful to Linda Morra for facilitating my acquisition of the original tapes as well as Dr Eby's unpublished catalogue and CDs of the digitized recordings.

4　Wolfgang Ernst, "Temporalizing the Present and Archiving Presence: The Impact of Time-Critical Media Technologies" (public lecture, Concordia University, Montreal, Quebec, Canada, 26 September 2014).

5　Don Ihde, *Listening and Voice: A Phenomenology of Sound* (Athens: Ohio University Press, 1974), 53.

6　Gabriella Giannachi, *Archive Everything: Mapping the Everyday* (Cambridge, MA: MIT Press, 2016), 153.

7 Anne Godard and Francis Mansbridge, John Glassco fonds, MG30-D163, Finding Aid No. 892, (1992, 2004): 4–12.

8 Henry Fotherby, *Scientific Associations: Their Rise, Progress and Influence* (London: Bell and Daldy, 1869), 38–9.

9 Louise Miskell, *Meeting Places: Scientific Congresses and Urban Identity in Victorian Britain* (London and New York: Routledge, 2013), 112.

10 Postcard from A.J.M. Smith to John Glassco, 10 February 1963, John Glassco fonds MG 30 D163, Vol. 1, Folder: Foster Poetry Correspondence Scott – Wilson.

11 George Whalley, ed., *Writing in Canada: Proceedings of the Canadian Writers' Conference, Queen's University, 28–31 July, 1955* (Toronto: Macmillan, 1956). George Whalley was an invited participant in the FPC.

12 Frank Scott, "Introduction," in *Writing in Canada*, 3.

13 Letter from John Glassco to Frank Scott, 19 February 1964, John Glassco fonds MG 30 D163, Vol. 1, Folder: Foster Poetry Correspondence Scott – Wilson.

14 Letter from John Glassco to Ralph Gustafson, 30 October 1963, John Glassco fonds MG 30 D163, Vol. 1, Folder: Foster Poetry Conference Correspondence, Folder: Angel – Lapalme 1963–1964 (2 of 2).

15 Letter from John Glassco to Frank Scott, 25 October 1963, John Glassco fonds MG 30 D163, Vol. 1, Folder: Foster Poetry Correspondence Scott – Wilson.

16 Letter from John Glassco to Glendon Brown, 29 October 1963, John Glassco fonds MG 30 D163, Vol. 1, Folder: Foster Poetry Conference Correspondence, Folder: Angel – Lapalme 1963–1964 (1 of 2).

17 Letter form John Glassco to Frank Scott, 19 February 1964, John Glassco fonds MG 30 D163, Vol. 1, Folder: Foster Poetry Correspondence Scott – Wilson.

18 For the first stages of this negotiation, see: Letter from John Glassco to Frank Scott, 3 November 1963, John Glassco fonds MG 30 D163, Vol. 1, Folder: Foster Poetry Correspondence Scott – Wilson, and Letter from John Glassco to Frank Scott, 20 November 1963, John Glassco fonds MG 30 D163, Vol. 1, Folder: Foster Poetry Correspondence Scott – Wilson.

19 Letter from Guy Frégault to John Glassco, 5 February 1964, John Glassco fonds MG 30 D163, Vol. 1, Foster Poetry Conference Correspondence, Folder: Angel – Lapalme 1963–1964 (2 of 2).

20 Letter from Lloyd M. Scott to John Glassco, 13 February 1964, John Glassco fonds MG 30 D163, Vol. 1, Folder: Foster Poetry Correspondence Scott – Wilson.

21 Letter from John Glassco to A.J.M. Smith, Easter Monday [15 April] 1964, John Glassco fonds MG 30 D163, Vol. 1, Folder: Foster Poetry Correspondence Scott – Wilson.

22 The Quebec government was not alone in sponsoring poetry-related activities at this time. The Canada Council (established in 1957) entered the business of funding public poetry readings in 1959 when it decided to grant funds to The Contact Poetry Readings and a reading at Le Hibou, both in Ottawa, then to The Sir George Williams Poetry Series in Montreal, and finally, series and festivals all across Canada. Between 1959 and 1975 (the year when the Sir George Williams series ceased because its application didn't receive money), the funding envelope for readings expanded from $845 to over $80,000, and the number of events funded went from one to nearly one hundred. For an extended account of Quebec-based poetry events in the early 1960s, see Jason Camlot, "Le Foster Poetry Conference," *Voix & Images* 40.2 (2015): 62–3. For an overview of the Sir George Williams Poetry Series, see Jason Camlot, "The Sound of Canadian Modernisms: The Sir George Williams Poetry Series, 1966–74," *Journal of Canadian Studies/Revue d'études canadiennes* 46.3 (Fall 2012): 28–59. For an account of the funding of poetry events by Canada Council, see Cameron Anstee, "Setting Widespread Precedent: The Canada Council for the Arts and the Funding of Poetry Readings in Canada, 1957–1975," *Amodern* 4 (2015), http://amodern.net/article/setting-widespread-precedent/ (accessed 20 February 2019).

23 See Robert McTavish's film, *The Line Has Shattered: Vancouver's Landmark 1963 Poetry Conference*, which premiered at Simon Fraser University in Vancouver, 21 March 2013. Recordings of the events made by Fred Wah are now available via the Slought Foundation (http://slought.org/toc/Vancouver1963/).

24 Alan Pearson, "Foster Poetry Conference: A Report," *The Canadian Forum* (November 1963): 178.

25 John Glassco, "Preface," in *English Poetry in Quebec*, ed. John Glassco (Montreal: McGill University Press, 1965), 6–7.

26 To note just a few here: James Reaney, "The Canadian Imagination," *Poetry* 94.3 (1959): 186–9; Margaret Avison, "Poets in Canada," *Poetry* 94.3 (1959): 182–5; Desmond Pacey, "The Canadian Imagination," *Literary Review* 8.4 (1965): 437–44; Arthur R.M. Lower, "Canadian Values and Canadian Writing," *Mosaic* 1.1 (1967): 79–93; William H. New, "A Wellspring of Magma: Modern Canadian Writing," *Twentieth Century Literature* 14.3 (1968): 123–32;

Desmond Pacey, "The Outlook for Canadian Literature," *Canadian Literature* 36 (1968): 14–25; Eli Mandel, "Modern Canadian Poetry," *Twentieth Century Literature* 16.3 (1970): 175–83.

27 Louis Dudek, "The Two Traditions: Literature and the Ferment in Quebec," *Canadian Literature* 12 (1962): 49.

28 Letter from John Glassco to Frank Scott, 18 May 1963, John Glassco fonds MG 30 D163, Vol. 1, Folder: Foster Poetry Correspondence Scott – Wilson.

29 Handwritten note, A.J.M. Smith to John Glassco, 21 May 1963, John Glassco fonds MG 30 D163, Vol. 1, Folder: Foster Poetry Correspondence Scott – Wilson.

30 Letter form Frank Scott to John Glassco, 22 May 1963, John Glassco fonds MG 30 D163, Vol. 1, Folder: Foster Poetry Conference Correspondence Scott – Wilson.

31 David Oancia, "Montreal Suburb Rocked," *The Globe and Mail* (18 May 1963): 1; David Oancia, "Victoria Day Fearful One in Montreal," *The Globe and Mail* (20 May 1963): 1; David Oancia, "8 Held as FLQ Terrorists," *The Globe and Mail* (3 June 1963): 1.

32 Letter from John Glassco to Frank Scott, 25 June 1963, John Glassco fonds MG 30 D163, Vol. 1, Folder: Foster Poetry Correspondence Scott – Wilson.

33 Letter from John Glassco to Guy Frégault, 19 July 1963, John Glassco fonds, MG 30 D163, Vol. 1, Folder: Foster Poetry Conference Correspondence, Folder: Angel – Lapalme 1963–1964 (2 of 2).

34 Letter from John Glassco to A.J.M. Smith, Easter Monday [15 April] 1964, John Glassco fonds MG 30 D163, Vol. 1, Folder: Foster Poetry Correspondence Scott – Wilson.

35 Ibid.

36 Letter from Ralph Gustafson to John Glassco, 4 February 1964, John Glassco fonds, MG 30 D163, Vol. 1, Folder: Foster Poetry Conference Correspondence, Folder: Angel – Lapalme 1963–1964 (2 of 2).

37 Letter from John Glassco to Ralph Gustafson, 11 February 1964, John Glassco fonds MG 30 D163, Vol. 1, Folder: Foster Poetry Conference Correspondence, Folder: Angel – Lapalme 1963–1964 (2 of 2).

38 Brian Busby, *A Gentleman of Pleasure: One Life of John Glassco, Poet, Memoirist, Translator, and Pornographer* (Montreal and Kingston: McGill-Queen's University Press, 2011), 186–8.

39 George Whalley, "Preface," in *Writing in Canada: Proceedings of the Canadian*

Writers' Conference, Queen's University, 28–31 July, 1955, ed. George Whalley (Toronto: Macmillan, 1956), vii.

40 Letter from John Glassco to Louis Dudek, 17 September 1963, John Glassco fonds MG 30 D163, Vol. 1, Folder: Foster Poetry Correspondence, Folder: Angel – Lapalme 1963–1964 (2 of 2).

41 Letter from Milton Wilson to John Glassco, 7 September 1963, John Glassco fonds MG 30 D163, Vol. 1, Foster Poetry Conference Correspondence, Folder: Scott – Wilson.

42 Letter from Milton Wilson to John Glassco, 7 September 1963, John Glassco fonds MG 30 D163, Vol. 1, Foster Poetry Conference Correspondence, Folder: Scott - Wilson.

43 Frank Scott, "The Poet in Quebec Today," in Glassco, *English Poetry in Quebec*, 48.

44 Pearson, "Foster Poetry Conference: A Report," *The Canadian Forum* (November 1963): 178.

45 Ibid.

46 Letter from Ralph Gustafson to John Glassco, 21 October 1963, John Glassco fonds MG 30 D163, Vol. 1, Folder: Foster Poetry Conference Correspondence, Folder: Angel – Lapalme 1963–1964 (2 of 2).

47 I would like to thank Katherine McLeod and CBC archivist Keith Hart for their assistance in searching the CBC holdings to determine whether recordings from the FPC poetry readings had aired on the CBC. While there is no evidence that they *aired* on the CBC, this does not rule out the possibility that the recordings were sent to the CBC for consideration.

48 Letter from John Glassco to Louis Dudek, 9 April 1964, John Glassco fonds MG 30 D163, Vol. 1, Folder: Foster Poetry Correspondence Scott – Wilson.

49 Letter from John Glassco to Louis Dudek, 9 April 1964, John Glassco fonds MG 30 D163, Vol. 1, Folder: Foster Poetry Correspondence Scott – Wilson.

50 John Glassco, F.R. Scott, and A.J.M. Smith, "Selection of Poetry Readings," in Glassco, *English Poetry in Quebec*, 89–135.

51 Charles Bernstein, "Introduction," in *Close Listening: Poetry and The Performed Word*, ed. Charles Bernstein (New York and Oxford: Oxford University Press, 1998), 3–26.

52 Jay Macpherson, "Report on the Poetry Readings," in *Writing in Canada*, 137–8.

53 John Glassco, "A Real Good Noise: The Poet As Performer," in *The Insecurity*

of Art: Essays on Poetics, ed. Ken Norris and Peter Van Toorn (Montreal: Véhicule Press, 1982), 59.

54 Glassco, *English Poetry in Quebec*, 136.

55 Letter from Eli Mandel to John Glassco, 24 October 1963, John Glassco fonds MG 30 D163, Vol. 1, Folder: Foster Poetry Conference Correspondence, Folder: Layton – Saint-Germain (1 of 2).

56 Letter from John Glassco to Hon. Georges Lapalme, minister of cultural affairs, Quebec, 22 October 1963, John Glassco fonds MG 30 D163, Vol. 1, Folder: Foster Poetry Conference Correspondence, Folder: Angel – Lapalme 1963–1964 (2 of 2).

57 Louis Dudek, "The Montreal Poets," *Culture: A Quarterly Review* 18 (1957): 149.

58 Glassco, "Preface," in *English Poetry in Quebec*, 8.

59 The concept of the vocalic body is borrowed from Stephen Connor who writes: "The principle of the vocalic body is simple. Voices are produced by bodies: but can also themselves produce bodies. The vocalic body is the idea – which can take the form of dream, fantasy, ideal, theological doctrine, or hallucination – of a surrogate or secondary body, a projection of a new way of having or being a body, formed and sustained out of the autonomous operations of the voice." Stephen Connor, *Dumbstruck: A Cultural History of Ventriloquism* (Oxford, U.K.: Oxford University Press, 2000), 35.

7

"It's All a Curious Dream"
Nostalgia, Old Media, and the Vancouver Poetry Conference, 1963

KARIS SHEARER

> … we go to Vancouver where,
> Thanks to friends Warren and Ellen Tallman,
> I get a job teaching at the University of British
> Columbia. It's all a curious dream, a rush
> To get out of the country before the sad
> Invasion of the Bay of Pigs, that bleak use
> Of power.
> – Robert Creeley, "Yesterdays"[1]

> I stay home and listen to tapes; for which, praise be.
> – Warren Tallman, "Letter to Robert Creeley"[2]

From 24 July to 16 August 1963, the University of British Columbia sponsored what is now commonly referred to as the "1963 Vancouver Poetry Conference." Featuring guest-instructors Margaret Avison, Robert Creeley, Robert Duncan, Allen Ginsberg, Denise Levertov, and Charles Olson, the "conference" has been described as a "landmark"[3] event, "a major early manifestation of the Sixties West Coast Zeitgeist"[4] and "a germinal event moment in the development of the Canadian avant-garde."[5] Many of the then-emerging young poets who attended have referred to it as a pivotal point in their creative development (George Bowering, Larry Goodell, Daphne Marlatt, Michael Palmer, and Fred Wah). An event remarkably well documented at the time in a wide range of media (photography, film, reel-to-reel, journals, and letters)[6] that have since been published in re-mediated forms, the Vancouver Poetry Conference has more recently become the subject of its own documentary film, *The Line Has Shattered: Vancouver's Landmark 1963 Poetry Conference* (2013). While these documentary forms do offer us valuable materials for engaging with the Vancouver event, I argue that there is a tendency toward nostalgic focus on the event's radicality that masks the ways in which the event and its subsequent representations have erased and/or reproduced oppressive hierarchies.

As many have pointed out, the word "conference" – a term that appears to have taken up a permanent place in the contemporary discourse around the 1963 events in Vancouver – is something of a misnomer: at the heart of the event was a three-week summer course titled "ENGL 410 – Poetry Writing" offered through the UBC Department of English, and as a non-credit course offered by the Department of University Extension.[7] And yet, as Fred Wah observes, it was not strictly a course either. Instead, Wah offers us the term "event": "There was a very communal kind of thing; it wasn't like 'Gee, here's a bunch of students going to school.' It was an event. I still have a hard time thinking about it as a course. It was an event that was just an intense event with these great intense people where you had panels in the morning, classes, workshops in the afternoon – the workshops weren't like writing workshops that they have in creative writing now. They were, they'd talk about ideas. That's all. They would talk about poetics, they would talk about what they're doing, maybe talk about a poem."[8] Although formally, the event had three official components – twelve morning lectures, three sets of afternoon writing workshops, and nine public poetry readings, running from 24 July to 16 August 1963 – it exceeded either a typical "conference" or a university course in its structure and concept.

Beyond the official tripartite structure were the unofficial, "informal off-campus parties, readings and discussions at the Tallman, Reid and Wah homes," all of which opened up liminal spaces of learning outside the limits of the institution.[9] The poetics discussions, for instance, spilled over into a party at the apartment of Wah and Butling where, with some "eighty people in [their] two-bedroom apartment," Olson took up a place on the double bed, while Ginsberg "spent most of the evening sitting on the landing at the apartment entrance chanting mantras with a group of his followers" before the police eventually showed up.[10] Similarly, George Bowering recalls the "impromptu classes" and "public readings both at the university and all over town."[11] It was these liminal spaces of pedagogy and festivity that Pauline Butling has referred to as the "founding moments of my life as a reader/writer/critic of contemporary writing."[12]

Flying a fairly radical event focused on open-form poetics under the guise of a university course or "writing conference" and at the expense of UBC and the Canada Council[13] can be linked to the liberatory narrative of the anti-establishment U.S. American Beat culture, in which the establishment (in this case the University of British Columbia and its English and Extension departments) is a site from which one liberates resources. This kind of counterculture activity had already been seen on campus as early as 1961 with some of the undergraduate TISH poets having "liberated" at least one copy of Donald Allen's *New American Poetry* from the UBC bookstore, as well as paper and postage stamps from the Department of English and the student society offices at Brock Hall to produce and circulate their little magazine.[14] The Vancouver event performed a similar irreverent gesture on a larger scale: it brought radical "New American" and Beat poets into contact with registered UBC students and registered individuals for the non-credit components at a time when the English department privileged literature from England or the work of American poets like Robert Frost and "hardly any professors in the USA or Canada had heard of the poets in the Allen anthology"; it also made their poetry readings available to a larger Vancouver public.[15] How did this happen?

The "Con" in the "Conference"

In an 8 April 1962 letter to Bobbie Louise Hawkins and Robert Creeley, the latter with whom he was co-organizing the event, American-born UBC English professor Warren Tallman began outlining plans. Using his position within the university and the privilege that went with it, he lay the ground for what he called a "jamboree," one he hoped would "get out of hand as to formal arrangement but be real" – a "big open house with everybody available to everybody and it all swinging."[16] The notion that the event would be a formal "conference" comes under scrutiny in the very first letter: "I usually disbelieve in such affairs if only because of all the phoniness" and instead he envisions an event that must "if it is going to be a conference, be big and wild."[17] For Tallman, there appeared to have been two main goals for the event. The first was to put Vancouver on the North American literary map: "It MUST be big because that is the only way to get writing students from way on out, over and down, to come so far west." The second was to connect students to writers Tallman considered to be significant and whose names had serious literary currency: "I don't care if Kerouac just wants to sit still in a corner or any damn thing, if we could get Olson, [Robert] Lowell or [Theodore] Rothke, [James] Baldwin and [Jack] Kerouac, we'd have made it. That is, students would say WOW."[18]

The liberatory, anti-establishment ethos is evident in the language Tallman uses to describe the event in his letters to Creeley: "jamboree" and "open house," "big and wild" suggest anything but a serious academic literature course. In his tracing of Tallman's terminology, Frank Davey shows that after his early correspondence with Creeley, Tallman, in his subsequent writing, almost never referred to the event using the academically legitimizing term "conference." Instead, Tallman writes of the "festival," "seminar," or "month-long poetry klatsch,"[19] terms that can be said to perform the "kind of nose-thumbing gesture toward the genteel literary establishment that prevailed in early 1960s English Canada" by refusing institutional labels.[20] Such was the notoriety of this anti-establishment event that word of it reached border control before many of the American participants had even crossed back into the United States.[21]

But the organization of such a "big and wild" event needed institutional support, and this involved appealing to a number of different interests, as well as navigating internal academic politics. To that end, Tallman saw himself as needing to "con" a number of members of the establishment, from his English-department colleagues to having "to con the EXTENSION DEPARTMENT, who run the summer show."[22] Tallman's earliest list of potential guest-writers reflected what Frank Davey, in his essay "The Conference That Never Was," has called a certain "gamesmanship" designed to satisfy various parties. Davey explains: "Lowell and [Saul] Bellow were being proposed in order to make Olson and [Louis] Zukofsky more palatable to professors [Elliott] Gose, [Tony] Friedson, [Jake] Zilber, and [Earle] Birney, whom Tallman unfavourably perceived as 'academic.' Layton was being proposed to please Birney, and Kerouac to impress the Extension Department and prospective students."[23] Tallman's strategy also involved inviting a poet who filled the role of "the Academic." In the end, the game proved both easier and more difficult than Tallman had imagined: Birney left UBC to take up a position at the University of Toronto, so there was no need to navigate around him (30 May 1962); however, there was also less funding available than Tallman had anticipated and "for money reasons" he needed to reduce the scope from month-long, multi-genre courses to a poetry-specific event with fewer guest-writers (21 May 1962). By 30 May 1962, he was able to write to Creeley that "the boat is AFLOAT," despite some steering still required to "avoid snags, snits, snarls and snafus."[24]

As for meeting the goals Tallman had set out, the event was an enormous success. In addition to having 48 students officially enrolled in ENGL 410 (Bowering, Butling, Judith Copithorne, Gladys [Maria] Hindmarch, Robert Hogg, and Wah among them), Tallman created a space that drew, as he had hoped, "writing students from way on out, over and down, to come so far west" – 118 registered in the non-credit panels[25] and at least 70 individuals participated in the event's other components, some of whom hitchhiked across the United States to attend. As Wah recalls, "people like John Keys and Drummond Hadley and Clark Coolidge and Michael Palmer showed up. So here all of a sudden were our contemporaries from the states [*sic*]. Some of them hitchhiked, however they could get here, they came to Vancouver for this, and gee, they wrote poetry, too, and they published magazines, too!"[26] Tallman's other objective – to draw major names – was also a success. Creeley had already been hired by UBC and would be a co-organizer. Tallman also secured Charles Olson, as he had hoped for from the beginning; Robert Duncan, who had already made a trip to Vancouver to lecture in Tallman's basement in 1959; Allen Ginsberg, who already had a following and returned from India to attend; Denise Levertov ("a leading New York poet" [Tallman to Creeley 8 June 1962]); and Margaret Avison, who had won a Guggenheim Fellowship in 1956 and a Governor General's Award in 1960. Tallman had his big-name poets.

"You Put the Microphone on the Table"

The success of the event was also its demise. If Tallman's con had surprised his English-department colleagues that year, it was not to happen again, as he writes in a post-event letter to Creeley: "The summer was entirely too successful, i.e. created amongst the many drones around here the firm if covert conviction that they mustn't let *that* happen again. So Vancouver as new frontier has closed up shop."[27] There was, however, one consolation: "I stay home and listen to tapes; for which, praise be."[28] The tapes to which Tallman refers were the reel-to-reel recordings he had asked Fred Wah to make on his personal Wollensak. Although Tallman envisioned professional recordings of the Vancouver event in a variety of media, including film,[29] it was the series of amateur recordings he commissioned from Wah that Michael Davidson argues are "among the most crucial 'texts' for contemporary poetics."[30] Wah recalls:

> Warren knew I was interested in recording and he had bought, or his father-in-law had bought for him, a brand new 4-track tape recorder that we were going to record the Conference with, the readings anyways. And it broke down the very first night or the very first day and I had to use my own Wollensak to do that. But in any case, recording in those days was pretty simple. You have a tape recorder and you have a microphone. You put the microphone on the table and you had this long cord and you sit off to the side with headphones on listening, you know, just recording it. And I had known nothing about recording it and certainly wasn't very professional. So my whole experience of the Conference, of all the readings anyway, was that I was off to one side just paying attention to the recording level and then I'd put it away at the end of the evening and then on to the next.[31]

Portable reel-to-reel recorders such as the Wollensak were just becoming popular in the early 1960s, leading to the proliferation of amateur recordings of poetry events – in this case, using 4-track, recorded at the speed of 3¾ ips, with one microphone.[32] If Wah's recordings allowed Tallman to indulge in a nostalgic reconnection to the event as he listened to them in his home, the tapes were also poetics documents – copied several times and circulated – with which he and many others could critically engage.[33]

The Vancouver event was, as Aaron Vidaver notes, largely ignored in Canada, while the "panels and readings are seen, south of the border, as primary documents of the New American Poetry and subsequent developments."[34] However, the same cannot be said of the event's status in Canada today. It has gained retrospective significance within the field of Canadian literature as the site marking the end of the first TISH era at the University of British Columbia. In other words, as the poetry careers of then-students Fred Wah, Daphne Marlatt, and George Bowering have gained national significance, there is all the more reason to look back at the Vancouver Poetry Conference as a shared site of creative formation. Moreover, contemporary considerations of the event have been facilitated by the digitization of Wah's reel-to-reel recordings by Aaron Levy (7–16 March 2002), which are publicly available on the Slought website, and more recently, via PennSound (2014), for educators, poets, scholars, and the like. In recent years, Bowering, Davey, Marlatt, and Wah have all themselves published or republished texts that identify the event as one of some significance (see Bowering's "Poetry Summer" chapter in *Words, Words, Words* [2012]; Wah's 2013 Garnett Sedgewick Memorial Lecture, published as *Permissions: TISH Poetics 1963 Thereafter* – [2014]; selections of Marlatt's journals in the Lost & Found reprint series [Series 1, 2010]; Davey's *When TISH Happens: The Unlikely Story of Canada's Most Influential Little Magazine* [2011]). However, by far the most sustained engagement with the old media generated from the event has been Robert McTavish's documentary film *The Line Has Shattered*.

Before turning to McTavish's film, however, I want to argue here that trends in the discourse that has emerged in response to the Vancouver Poetry Conference have replicated some of the oppressive hierarchies present during the event itself. Looking to the margins of this discourse can produce a less comfortable but equally important critical narrative.

"Who Is She?"

The received narrative of the Vancouver Poetry Conference has tended to privilege the oral histories, memoirs, and critical discourse of those who celebrate the liberatory ethos of the event and its New American open-form poetics. However, nostalgic celebration of this landmark event risks obscuring the fact that "radical literary communities are not immune from enacting the 'symbolic violence' (Bourdieu) of oppression, exclusion, and subordination that is more often associated with mainstream groups."[35] Butling's chapter "Who Is She? Inside/Outside Literary Communities" in *Writing in Our Time: Canada's Radical Poetries in English (1957–2003)* is, to date, the most important critical intervention on the early 1960s poetry community in Vancouver. In it she draws attention to the hierarchies within radical literary communities that often go unnoticed by "their members because of an assumption that aesthetic innovation goes hand in hand with progressive social relations."[36] Gender hierarchies informed the 1950s Beat culture, reducing women to the role of muses, but as Michael Davidson has noted, their marginalization from "centres of artistic and intellectual life in general in the 1950s" was, in fact, "a structural necessity for the liberation of new male subjects."[37] In the case of the Vancouver event, the tendency to focus on the subversiveness of the event draws attention away from problematic gender issues that inform its planning and actualization, as well as the retrospective representation of it.

Butling's own lived experience is a case in point: after tracing her history of performing (often gendered) labour that goes on behind the scenes of literary events – the "thousands of hours" in which she "organized poetry readings, hosted visiting writers, helped plan workshops and conferences, cooked party meals and cleaned up party wine spills, made posters, wrote press releases, helped with magazine production" – she finds herself "often invisible" in the historical record.[38] Although rarely acknowledged in the accounts of the Vancouver poetry event, Butling had, as well, "a part-time job assisting Tallman with the pre-conference paper work, which also gave [her] free admission to the course."[39] Of this time, she recounts: "I went to all the morning lectures and evening readings (though not to the writing workshops). I was excited, exhilarated (or so I thought) by these events." I want to take Butling's lead and rethink the gender hierarchies in the Vancouver poetry event's "liberation" narrative.

Coincidentally, "Who Is She?" – the title of Butling's autobiographical chapter – is also echoed in the wording of an editorial note written into the margin of the typescript of Warren Tallman's post-event essay "Poets in Vancouver 1963":[40] "'*Who's she?*' the editor comments, '(This to be read by readers in several countries.)'" [emphasis added]. Here, the unknown editor refers to the one Canadian poet amongst the invited writers, Margaret Avison. Often marginalized within the Vancouver Poetry Conference narrative, Avison is acknowledged for having attended, but her presence is at odds with the "New American and Beat poets come to Canada" narrative.

Avison had a lengthy correspondence with Cid Corman and had work published in *Origin* (issue 20, 1957), giving the perception at the time, perhaps, that she was affiliated with the Black Mountain poets, but she never considered herself to be so affiliated.[41]

Tallman's letters contain no details about what motivated the invitation to Avison[42] specifically. However, it seems likely that her affiliation with Corman, her publication in *Origin*, her recognition in the U.S. by a Guggenheim Fellowship in Chicago (1956), and her recent Governor General's Award (1960) for the book that had resulted from the manuscript developed in Chicago, *Sunblue*, gave her the American-endorsed prestige and perceived Black Mountain affiliation that satisfied Tallman's sense that there ought to be a Canadian[43] poet invited: "it may come down to one Canadian as a concession to national whatever pride" (30 May 1962). Later, having read this letter, Avison would comment, "O you Americans!"[44]

Avison's presence at the Vancouver Poetry Conference is all but irreconcilable with the dominant received narrative of the event. Her presence challenges, for example, the way in which the event's radicality has been framed around notions of anti-establishment, freewheeling activities. Avison has recalled being aware at the time of her separateness: "The Americans were old friends whose conversation was in a context of many prior explorings of ideas and literary discoveries. I was aware of being separate, Canadian, more formally dressed, and often in awe. The great gain from such discomfort was the fact that Denise Levertov and, oddly, Charles Olson perceived this. They often manoeuvred me back into the circle of talk, inconspicuously."[45] Also underscoring this sense of separateness was Avison's recent religious conversion: early in 1963, Avison had a religious epiphany,[46] which led to her writing from a Christian world view. It was this world view that she keenly felt was at odds with the general assumptions of those at the Vancouver event: "Between sessions and at meal times, the talk among ourselves made it evident that Robert Duncan and Denise Levertov were intrigued by current ideas that somehow bothered me ... All this seemed freewheeling and speculative; was it the sixties-ethos [*sic*] or the post-Christian climate? ... Only eight months earlier, my stance had been theirs."[47]

Avison left Vancouver early, owing to the sudden death of her father in Ontario, and therefore did not spend the same amount of time at the conference as the other writers. However, to see Avison as merely an anomaly, to dismiss her as unimportant to the central received narrative, and to suggest that the Vancouver event was unimportant to Avison herself is simply incorrect.[48] In fact, Avison draws the very title of her autobiography, *I Am Here and Not Not-There*, from a comment she made during a panel discussion at the Vancouver conference, having been asked, "what makes a poet's language distinctive?" Her response was: "It is saying I am here and not not-there" (5 August 1963). As a statement, "I am here and not not-there" – an assertion of the poet's presence carefully aware of the dangers of ego – is an apt response to those who have overlooked her. It is also an invitation to return to the tapes to locate her. Avison participated on panels on 5 August and 7 August 1963 in discussions that totalled 269 minutes of recordings; in addition, there is the 59-minute recording of her poetry reading. However, the recordings of the Vancouver poetry readings, as presented on the Slought website, are described as "recordings by Fred Wah of readings, lectures, and discussions by notable New American poets."[49] Once again, Avison's participation in these events is incompatible with its contemporary framing.

If Avison's presence itself challenged the received narrative of the Vancouver event, so too do her recollections of it. First, Avison's letter of 2 August 1999 to Aaron Vidaver calls into question the event's originality. The event has been celebrated for having brought together "for the first time, a decisive company of disregarded poets," and yet, as Avison points out, in Toronto, "before 1963 we had already had readings by Olson, twice, by Levertov, Corman, Leroi Jones, Zukofsky, Enslin, Creeley, and Leonard Cohen who has become international. You will understand that these prior contacts make it difficult to disentangle the specific influences of the Conference."[50] Attention to other readings and events that saw Black Mountain poets read north of the Canada-U.S. border challenge the assumption that the Vancouver event was unique in its recognition of the New American poets.[51]

Avison's recollections of the event itself also shift away from the dominant narrative in another important way. In her autobiography, Avison writes mainly about the hospitality shown to her during her visit and about the women who extended that hospitality; in this, her memory narrative is a radical departure from that of many male writers. Her attention in *I Am Here and Not Not-There*, for example, is to the graciousness of Professor Helen Sonthoff, who invited her to dine at her home with writer Jane Rule and who also helped arrange all of Avison's travel, "even the final details of my packing," after news of her father's death arrived, and to being driven to the city for "a delightful coffee with George and Angela Bowering."[52] Here again, Avison's focus is on the connections established with other women: Angela's "feather-touch of wit, the gift of listening she showed that day, our instant ease with one another, were unusual, peaceably low-keyed."[53] Ultimately, Avison's presence, her questioning of the event's uniqueness, and her privileging of the women who played key parts in hosting roles peripheral to the discussions and readings challenges the way in which this event has been traditionally framed. It also raises important questions about which other women have been marginalized or omitted.

These include Ellen Tallman, who Vidaver suggests "should be considered a co-organizer" of the Vancouver event.[54] A professor of English at UBC, Ellen Tallman is rarely mentioned in her organizing capacity, yet it was through her connection to San Francisco's anarchist movement and literary scene, which included Jack Spicer, Marthe Rexroth, Kenneth Rexroth, Robin Blaser, and Henry Miller, that her husband Warren Tallman met many of the Bay-area writers. It was "at Ms Tallman's invitation, [that] many of them made their way to the UBC campus and to the Tallmans' front door."[55]

Also marginalized is Carol Bergé, an American writer who attended the conference and wrote the highly critical *The Vancouver Report*, published in New York by Fuck You Press (1964), in which Bergé by and large expresses her disappointment with the conference: "I don't think anything bright or sharp or new came through, as it might have if the poets had another stance there, or if there had been dissonant voices brought there to provide stimulation or contrast."[56] As Frank Davey notes, contemporary responses to Bergé's report on the conference have been "unkind."[57] Among these responses, he notes Larry Goodell's dismissal of *The Vancouver Report* as "a totally unfair slam of the event" and Vidaver's characterization of Bergé "not as having criticized but having 'complained.'" Davey rightly, I think, suggests that both men's comments may be grounded in their objection to her "having found fault with an event appreciated most deeply by its male witnesses."[58]

"Our Overall Purposes Would Probably Be Better Served If an English Bloke Were on the Scene"

The marginalization of women is not limited to the post-event reception of the Vancouver Poetry Conference; it is systemic in the event's very conception. At first glance, the lineup of guest-writers appears to have female representation that one might expect of the time: two women to four men – a better ratio than many poetry anthologies of the period. But Tallman's correspondence with Creeley reveals that there was no intention initially to include women writers in the event. On the contrary, the potential ten writers to invite were all presumed to be "ten men"; further references include "three fiction men," "15 students per man," "poems ... are sent on to the men prior to arrival," and so on (8 April 1962). As early as the second letter to Creeley, Denise Levertov is mentioned as a possibility – in the most tentative language: "maybe Denise Levertov perhaps" (30 May 1962). But in later correspondence, she is considered in the context of her influence as an editor rather than as a writer: "kindly remember that Levertov, as poetry editor of Nation ... would have pull for students, but that our overall purposes would probably be better served if an English bloke were on the scene."[59] Michael Davidson's observation that the marginalization of women from "centres of artistic and intellectual life in general in the 1950s" was, in fact, "a structural necessity for the liberation of new male subjects" describes the situation of the radical Vancouver Poetry Conference of 1963.[60]

In Robert McTavish's documentary *The Line Has Shattered: Vancouver's Landmark 1963 Poetry Conference*, the marginalization of women is directly addressed in a short series of present-day interview segments, immediately preceded by a 1963 recording of Margaret Avison reading from "Unspeakable." In the first of the interviews, Daphne Marlatt comments: "I'm very conscious of the fact that I haven't mentioned Margaret Avison and Denise Levertov yet ... She doesn't stay in my mind as a presence there, which was unfortunate because she was the only Canadian" (38:42–39:07). Marlatt attributes this to what she speculates to be Avison's preoccupation with her father's illness. Fred Wah is more direct in identifying the marginalization of Avison and Levertov as a structural issue: "I mean, this was pretty much a male, Black Mountain – this was pretty much Olson-Creeley-Duncan, and with Ginsberg kind of there to stir things up. And Levertov and Avison were, uh, fairly on the outside of that" (39:08–39:27). Butling recalls: "It was pretty boysie" (39:28–39:29). Altogether, approximately three minutes and thirty seconds of *The Line Has Shattered* are explicitly devoted to the topic of the marginalization of women (specifically Avison and Levertov) at the event.

The film goes some distance to address this issue, recuperating and presenting documentary media made by or featuring women. For instance, as Pauline Butling describes Levertov's presence and her powerful reading of "Hypocrite Women," the film cuts to an animated historical sound recording of Levertov reading an excerpt from the aforementioned poem and then offers us both archival still images and footage of Levertov at the event, making her present for viewers through the simultaneous recollection voiced by Butling and the presentation of historical media. McTavish also recovers Webb's radio program "Five Poets," commissioned but never aired by the CBC, featuring excerpts of her interviews with the poets in the film's soundtrack. *The Line Has Shattered* also brings a woman's voice into a place of prominence by featuring Webb as its framing narrator.

While the film takes these important steps to both address the marginalization of women and recover their voices and images, it is ultimately far more interested in participating in the received narrative that focuses on (1) the event's radicality and (2) the event as a site where the New American poets crossed the border and influenced a group of younger (mainly) Canadian writers. For example, immediately following the three and a half minutes devoted to the topic of women's erasure, the film focuses on the closing of the conference and presents a series of anecdotes about the transgressions of the event's participants, including the arrest of one student for marijuana possession, and about the transgressive reputation of the course having reached the Canada-U.S. border by the time its American participants were on their way home (42:17–42:22). With the film's investment in the narrative of the New American poets coming north – the "Line" of its title is both the poetic line and the borderline between the U.S. and Canada – it is unable to reconcile Canadian Margaret Avison's presence at the event and, as a result, erases her at the same time as it recuperates her. This is reinforced by the film's DVD cover, which features hand-drawn sketches (courtesy of the CBC) of the faces of Robert Creeley, Robert Duncan, Allen Ginsberg, Denise Levertov, and Charles Olson; Avison is conspicuously missing.

Gender hierarchies can be observed in the planning, in the actualization, and, even more problematically, in the subsequent memory narratives and critical discourse constructing the Vancouver Poetry Conference, in which women's labour and their participation are minimized at the expense of nostalgic recollections of the event's radicality. Perhaps unsurprisingly, this erasure is characteristic not just of the 1963 event but also of the Vancouver literary scene in the early 1960s. Marlatt, for example, observes that "although they've been omitted from literary histories of that scene, there were other women involved in TISH and the Writers Workshop then. Gladys Hindmarch was very present, and Pauline Butling was there, as well as

Ginny Smith, Carol Johnson. And Maxine Gadd and Judy Copithorne ... It's only the filter of history that says I'm the lone woman."[61] That "filter of history" or the received narrative of the 1963 Vancouver Poetry Conference has done much to mask the participation of women. Now, at a moment when the crisis in higher education and the pedagogical challenges that come with it may invite nostalgic indulgence in the event's narrative of radicality, writers and critics need to rethink the way they engage with this event and its archival documents.

NOTES

1   Robert Creeley, "Yesterdays," *The Collected Poems 1975–2005*, vol. 2 (Berkeley: University of California Press, 2008), 595.

2   Warren Tallman, letter to Robert Creeley, 7 December 1963, *Minutes of the Charles Olson Society* 30 (April 1999): 3–14, www.charlesolson.org/Files/ Minutes30.pdf (accessed 20 July 2016). All subsequent quotations from letters between Tallman and Creeley are from this publication.

3   Robert McTavish, *The Line Has Shattered: Vancouver's Landmark 1963 Poetry Conference,* film, Inferno Media, 2013.

4   Fred Wah, interviewed by Robert McTavish, *Journal of Poetics Research*, http://poeticsresearch.com/article/fred-wah-in-conversation-with-robert-mctavish-vancouver-2009/#fn1 (accessed 30 November 2016).

5   Adam Beardsworth, "Vancouver 1963: Crossroads of the Canadian Avant-Garde," www.grenfell.mun.ca/academics-and-research/Pages/Bachelor-of-Arts/English/Faculty-and-Staff/Adam-Beardsworth.aspx (accessed 26 November 2016).

6   The course notes or journals of Daphne Marlatt, Pauline Wah, George Bowering, and Clark Coolidge were published in OLSON: *The Journals of the Charles Olson Archive* 4 (Fall 1975). Bowering published a second set of notes in "Poetry Summer" in *Words, Words, Words: Essays and Memoirs* (Vancouver: New Star, 2012).

7   Daphne Marlatt, interview by Ashley Clarkson, *SpokenWeb*, 12 September 2014, http://spokenweb.ca/oral-literary-history/daphne-marlatt-interview-september-12th-2014/, 26:40 (accessed 20 July 2016); Aaron Vidaver, "Warren Tallman: 'Poets in Vancouver' (1963)," online, https://vidaver.wordpress.com/ 2009/08/10/warren-tallman-vancouver-1963/ (accessed 17 June 2016); Frank

Davey, "The Conference That Never Was: The 'Landmark 1963 Vancouver Poetry Conference,'" http://publish.uwo.ca/~fdavey/VancPoetryConfPaperDr.pdf (accessed 12 February 2016).

8 Fred Wah, interviewed by Robert McTavish.

9 Aaron Vidaver, "Warren Tallman."

10 Pauline Butling and Susan Rudy, *Writing in Our Time: Canada's Radical Poetries in English (1957–2003)* (Waterloo: Wilfrid Laurier University Press, 2005), 145.

11 George Bowering, "Poetry Summer," 118.

12 Butling, *Writing in Our Time*, 145.

13 Ibid., 144–5.

14 Butling, "TISH: The Problem with Margins," in Butling and Rudy, *Writing in Our Time*, 53.

15 Bowering, "Poetry Summer," 117.

16 Warren Tallman, "Letters to Robert Creeley, 1962–63," *Minutes of the Charles Olson Society* 30 (April 1999): 3–14, www.charlesolson.org/Files/Minutes30.pdf (accessed 20 July 2016).

17 Ibid., 6.

18 Ibid., 5.

19 Davey, "The Conference That Never Was," 8.

20 Butling, "TISH," 53

21 In *The Line Has Shattered*, Clark Coolidge recounts travelling back into the United States and being questioned about the purpose of his stay in Canada: "by the time we crossed the border to come back, we were worried, you know, because the word had gotten out and I remember – it was hysterical in a way – as I recall, Allen and Phil drove back and they were all, you know, bearded, you know, and kind of sloppy looking and they were in some kind of little camper or something. And also had all kinds of, you know, illegal substances, I think, in the car and somehow went whistling through the border, you know. And said 'we were hunting up north,' you know. And when *we* got to the border, the American side, they asked us where we were coming from and we said UBC. They said, 'what were you doing there?' We said 'summer course.' They said 'what's the number of the course?' We said '410.' They said, 'pull over.' And they stripped the car. And, they went through everything. It was a real hassle. But we were prepared. We weren't carrying anything. We were expecting that. That was the word " (42:29–43:30).

22 Tallman, "Letters," 6.

23 Davey, "The Conference That Never Was," 4.

24 Tallman, "Letters," 3–14.

25 Vidaver, "Warren Tallman."

26 Wah, interviewed by Robert McTavish.

27 Quoted in Vidaver, "Warren Tallman."

28 Ibid.

29 "Do you have any idea, if all these poets were collected here, what it would cost to have someone like [Stan] Brakhage do a half hour film like Poetry on a Summers [*sic*] Day?" he asks Creeley in his second letter, 21 May 1962. And again later, "Re: Stan Brakhage, the Festival people do a Film Festival as part of their program … Who knows maybe we can con a half-hour film thing too. No use letting all that talent wander around for 24 days without using it" (30 May 1962). In the latter letter, Tallman also imagines the potential for a spectacle, in which Duncan is provoked by Snodgrass to the point of "dancing on the tables, flinging his arms overhead, eyes crossed 8 ways, while all the rest of you poets try to carry on SERIOUS discussions. And if there was a camera around!"

30 Michael Davidson, "'By ear, he sd': Audio-tapes and Contemporary Criticism," *Credences* 1.1 (1981): 111.

31 Wah, interviewed by Robert McTavish.

32 Wah, Statement, "Vancouver 1963 Poetry Conference & Miscellaneous Readings," Slought Foundation, https://slought.org/resources/wah_conference_discussions (accessed 15 December 2016).

33 For example, Michael Davidson's preface to his 1997 book *Ghostlier Demarcations* begins: "One impulse for writing this book on the material text can be traced to my hearing, sometime in the late 1960s, a tape recording of the 1963 Vancouver Poetry Conference in which Robert Creeley and Allen Ginsberg discussed their work." Michael Davidson, *Ghostlier Demarcations: Modern Poetry and the Material World* (Berkeley: University of California Press, 1997), xi. Warren Tallman's unpublished essay "Poets in Vancouver (1963)" engages directly with the tapes and has been made available by Aaron Vidaver (https://vidaver.wordpress.com/2009/08/). Frank Davey also suggests the circulation of the sixty-three "conference" tapes included copies for Duncan and that Duncan created copies for Levertov. Davey, "Tape-recorded Poetry in the 60s #media archaeology #poetry," *Open Mic Poetry*, 22 July 2013, www.londonpoetry-openmic.com/frank-davey-blog/tape-recorded-poetry-in-the-60s-mediaarchaeol ogy-poetry (accessed 16 February 2016). Davey himself had copies of the tapes, which he cited in his 1968 doctoral dissertation. Frank Davey, "Theory and

Practice in the Black Mountain Poets: Duncan, Olson, and Creeley," dissertation (University of Southern California, 1968), 11.

34 Vidaver, "Warren Tallman," fn 2.

35 Butling, *Writing in Our Time*, 142.

36 Butling, "TISH," 41.

37 Quoted in Butling, *Writing in Our Time*, 141.

38 Butling, *Writing in Our Time*, 141–2.

39 Ibid., 145.

40 Vidaver, "Warren Tallman."

41 Robyn Sarah, "Introduction," in Margaret Avison, *The Essential Margaret Avison* (Erin, ON: Porcupine's Quill, 2012), http://store.porcupinesquill.ca/essential_margaret_avison (accessed 10 June 2016).

42 In her 2 August 1999 letter to Aaron Vidaver, Avison believes it was likely Professor Roy Daniells, UBC English department chair, who suggested her name.

43 In an 8 June 1962 letter to Creeley, Tallman writes: "we thought that the third of the one-week poets ought to be out of Toronto-Montreal or some Canadian place. Problem here is that we now feel Layton is more or less ruled out – that is he'd be more likely to come out only in order to split, and this leaves one Alden Nowland [*sic*], or Dudek, or a prairie poet, Wilfred Watson or a Toronto area academic name of James Reaney."

44 Margaret Avison, 2 August 1999 letter to Aaron Vidaver.

45 Margaret Avison, *I Am Here and Not Not-There: An Autobiography* (Erin, ON: Porcupine's Quill, 2009), 145.

46 Ibid., 142.

47 Ibid., 145–6.

48 Her marginalization is even written into Noreen Shanahan's obituary for Avison, where the poet is remembered for having "attended an inspiring writing workshop at the University of British Columbia, where she worked with Black Mountain poets Robert Creeley, Charles Olson, and Denise Levertov," not as a guest-poet but "as part of her studies," as though she were one of the students.

49 "Vancouver 1963 Poetry Conference & Miscellaneous Recordings," Slought Foundation, https://slought.org/resources/wah_conference_readings (accessed 11 June 2016).

50 Avison, *I Am Here*, 145–6.

51 Frank Davey, too, observes that "unlike many of the U.S participants [the TISH poets] had already met Duncan and Creeley and heard readings and lectures by them." Davey, "The Conference That Never Was," 16.

52 Avison, *I Am Here*, 144.

53 Ibid.

54 Tallman, "Letters," 3–14.

55 Noreen Shanahan, "Canadian Turned Two Epiphanies into a Career of 'Staggering Impact,'" Margaret Avison obituary, *The Globe and Mail*, 14 August 2007, http://rampantmemories.com/wp-content/uploads/2012/11/avison-margaret-aug-14-07.pdf (accessed 20 July 2016).

56 Carol Bergé, *The Vancouver Report* (New York: Fuck You Press, 1964), 16.

57 Davey, "The Conference That Never Was," 19.

58 Ibid.

59 Tallman, "Letters," 11.

60 Quoted in Butling, *Writing in Our Time*, 141.

61 Brenda Carr, "Between Continuity and Difference: An Interview with Daphne Marlatt," *West Coast Line* 25.1 (1991): 102.

8

Linguistic Therapy c. 1973
Archival Traces from Véhicule's Press

FELICITY TAYLER

the place where your ideas/fantasies/forms/works can become reality
lieu ou vos idées/fantaisies/formes/oevres peuvent se réaliser
– "Véhicule: Alternative Space, Alternative Attitude,
New Situation," *Médiart*[1]

Véhicule Art opened its gallery doors in Montreal on 13 October 1972, at a temporal midpoint between the federal imposition of the War Measures Act in 1970 and the passing of the Official Language Act (Bill 22) in 1974 by the Liberal leadership in Quebec. When the federal government invoked the War Measures Act as a response to the perceived threat to civil peace from the Front de libération du Québec (FLQ), the arrival of the military on city streets was accompanied by the censorship of print and other news media. Prominent writers, artists, intellectuals, and labour activists were arrested or held for questioning without charge during the October Crisis. Widely perceived as an unwelcome imposition on the autonomy of Quebec provincial powers, the War Measures Act simultaneously fuelled nationalist causes driven by conflicts over language use and caused disillusionment with federal restrictions of civil liberties.

This chapter discusses a group of publications, exhibitions, and mediated events that complicate the narrative of bilingualism and biculturalism, or the "two solitudes," determining most histories of Canada and Quebec in this period. In chapter 6, Jason Camlot outlines the vexed position English-language poetry held within the language and cultural politics of modernism in Quebec in 1963. By contrast, I want to unarchive a series of books and literary events that took place a decade later at Véhicule Art gallery (between 1972 and 1975) that encourage present-day readers to imagine a fleeting, affective "linguistic space" generated between the gaps of networked media technologies and photo-mechanical grids. I argue here that Véhicule Art gallery could be thought of as a space where architectural structures, administrative protocols, a printing press, and intermedial and process-based conceptualisms combined to function as countermeasures to both the lingering effects of the October Crisis and a media space dominated by ongoing coverage of competing federal and provincial language legislation.

Unarchiving the linguistic space at Véhicule Art means working through the tension between the two kinds of "archive" described by Jacques Derrida in *Archive Fever*. As Katherine McLeod and Jason Camlot outline in greater detail in their introduction, for Derrida, the "archive" describes an institutionally held collection of documents, but also points to a process of psychic inscription, as historically situated acts of interpretation confer literary status upon artifacts. The textual documents, photographs, books, and magazines discussed below all bear the mark of institutional holding places, such as the Concordia University Library, Concordia Records Management and Archives, or Artexte, a documentation centre for contemporary art. These marks are a sign of the archive as a regulating filing system and institutional record for the corporate entity Véhicule Art Inc., which ceased to exist in 1983. While taking into account the imposed ordering of these collecting practices, this chapter emphasizes events that mark the early 1970s as a moment when cultural codes were naturalized as attributes intrinsic to a nation or people.[2] This tension is important in respect to Véhicule Art because in 1975, Fernande Saint-Martin, then director of the Musée d'art contemporain de Montréal,[3] argued that the systems- or communications-based work associated with Véhicule Art was not a form of cultural expression originating from Quebec. She stated it was "un art du non-lieu" – which translates loosely as, an art originating from no-place.[4] The assertion that language-based visual art originates nowhere has a utopian ring to it, but it also positions this work as external to Québécois neo-nationalist projects of the 1970s. This position is similar to that taken around the same time by art historian Barry Lord, the former editor of *artscanada* magazine and curator of the *Painting in Canada* exhibition in the Canadian Pavilion for Expo 67. Like Saint-Martin, Lord drew upon Maoist theory to argue that conceptual art was antithetical to left-leaning strains of Canadian cultural and economic nationalism because it was an aesthetic form issuing from "the latest stages of decadence in US imperialist culture."[5] From this shared perspective, the linguistic turn of conceptual art was authentic to neither Québécois nor Canadian modernisms. As this chapter shows, this misalignment of conceptualism with cultural nationalist projects has obstructed from view material and social relations of import to both the localized development of language-based conceptual art practices across Canada and to related literary genres and figures studied within a field known as CanLit.

Tom Dean's *Beaux-Arts* magazine (1972–73), Allan Bealy's *Davinci* magazine (1973–79), and the series of poetry chapbooks Bealy issued under Eldorado Editions (1974) were conceptual projects produced at Véhicule Art that engaged with image and text as signifying fields aiming to cultivate affective relationships between identity and community. Instead of proposing an outright negation of the nation-state, these works imaginatively engage their readers in the affective process by which inclusion or exclusion from cultural groups is experienced, that is, as an internalized response to external linguistic structures and cultural codes. Likewise, the exhibition *Sound as a Visual/Visual as Sound* (1973) organized by Suzy Lake and Allan Bealy and Roy Kiyooka's *Poetry/Video/Text* (1973) both extend the play with cultural codes into performance, sound, and architectural space. These publications and events also engage with Véhicule Art's location at the intersection of Sainte-Catherine Street and Saint-Laurent Boulevard (the Main) as an imaginary site where political positioning occurred through the articulation of desire.[6]

The publications, photographs, and scraps of ephemera that I bring together here are material artifacts of a "linguistic space" in which a politics of *eros* disrupted official narratives of unified national identity in the post-Centennial period. As critic Susan Sontag observed at the time, the neo-avant-garde revived surrealist strategies in order to redefine the body's sensorium through a countercultural "erotics of art."[7] Art historian Jonathan

Katz has more recently argued that the politics of *eros*, as enacted in the transitional moment between the late 1960s and early 1970s, is not identity-based but rather derived from a collective belief in the universality of psychic drives.[8] For this reason, a polymorphous celebration of affective experience and erotic desire presented a counterposition to heteronormative national citizenship. The linguistic space produced at Véhicule Art gains further complexity when studied in relation to *Médiart* magazine, published as part of the course work undertaken by students in the Groupe de recherche sur l'administration de l'art (GRAA) at the Université de Québec à Montréal (UQÀM). *Médiart* printed content supplied by Véhicule Art, or reviews and interpretive texts written by students, some of whom would later assume administrative positions at the gallery.[9] Curator Normand Thériault and art historian Yves Robillard acted as faculty advisers to the GRAA students, using exhibition and publishing projects to familiarize the younger generation with publications such as *Parti-pris* (1963–68) and *Mainmise* (1970–78), which combined psychoanalysis and cultural expression with a political message, ultimately reaching a mass audience.[10] This chapter takes the mutability of language and texts as a starting point, recognizing that the ability to assume multiple forms, and to migrate from one place to another through citation, reprinting, translation, or remediation is key to the politics of *eros*, all of which combine to produce the linguistic space of Véhicule Art.

Véhicule's Press: Véhicule d'Idées

Tom Dean published the "Special Pornography Issue" of *Beaux-Arts* magazine on the press at Véhicule Art gallery in 1973. Like other magazines in the pornographic genre, the *Beaux-Arts* issue includes a provocative centrefold. A close-cropped image depicts a woman's legs spread across the Canadian maple leaf flag; the focal point is her generous thatch of pubic hair. Titled "Maid in Canada," this sexy "beaver" sits atop a recently born symbol of Canadian nationhood.[11] Slim fingers with brightly lacquered nails casually suspend a pair of sunglasses before the bushy region, suggesting this national vision is libidinally driven. The grainy half-tone pattern of the printed image and a pulsing colour combination of purple and pink ink further transports the reader into an altered state. When the magazine was first published, it was distributed in a Vaseline-smeared plastic wrapping.[12] Other pages in the magazine include a scrapbook-like series of snapshots and handwritten notes titled "Love, Drugs and Faggotry" and a collage-essay of tabloid news clippings titled "LSD and the National Bulletin." Artie Gold's poetics begin with the question/statement, "Have you ever wished to embrace your double in the evening set," followed by a disorienting litany of conflicted internalized sexual roles. As a way of shifting the affective bonds linking national identity to language and territory, Tom Dean's *Beaux-Arts* magazine binds together contributions from multiple authors, which contrast ideal forms of citizenship to countercultural explorations of sexual difference.

Dean's appropriation of the visual tropes of a pop-culture title, such as the centrefold image of *Playboy* magazine, performs "linguistic therapy," a term used by Herbert Marcuse to describe a countercultural strategy for social transformation by aesthetic means.[13] Marcuse argued that words and concepts considered "obscene" by political or corporate entities were being reclaimed and repurposed by individuals who sought to redirect their erotic drive toward cultural subversion. In the early days at Véhicule Art, the social life of the gallery was closely bound up with the material objects of expanded literary forms, intermedial practices, and the "linguistic turn" of conceptual art. This convergence of materials and practices produced a space that fostered mutable sexualities and destabilized corporate identities. The messy and haphazard collection of materials and mental conditions in *Beaux-Arts*, for instance, is only formally recognizable as a "magazine" because it is held together by the conventions of a typographic grid and the sequential structure of bound pages. Likewise, Véhicule's press is only identifiable as an incorporated publisher because it is listed in a masthead beginning with the insolent phrase "Beaux-Arts is published and blah blah blah."

Such a cavalier tone indicates that the linguistic space at Véhicule Art operated with a self-conscious awareness of exhibition-making, publishing, and archiving as discursive practices. Founding member Suzy Lake recalls, "we wanted to have an archives, we wanted to have a printing press so that books could be done."[14] When Dean used publishing as a conceptual strategy, it reflected his desire to engage with the discursive effect of print media as it defines or influences the production and reception of art. More specifically, he tested the limits of fine art as an autonomous sphere of activity, and as distinct from mass-culture forms such as magazines. In chapter 10, Andrea Beverley reflects that such reflexive acts of self-archiving were widely practiced in this period as part of artists' and poets' engagement with the documentary modes of lens-based media technologies. Self-publication or self-archiving were two methods through which artists could gain visibility in local and international networks by leveraging the recognition afforded corporate identities such as a publisher or non-profit gallery. As a mode of cultural politics, publishing and archiving were a means to build upon and reorient the connotative meaning of pre-existing cultural myths that understood aesthetic styles to be an expression of national cultures. A visual record of this elusive linguistic space is also partially accessible through the textual files and anonymous photographs held in the Véhicule Art Inc. fonds at the Concordia University Archives.[15] Rescued from obscurity in 1983 by Nancy Marrelli, then the head of these archives, the original order reflecting the gallery's artist-run organizational culture has since been augmented by captions inscribed on the back of photographs, press clippings added to exhibition files, a finding aid, chronology, and recorded interviews that serve as supplements to these files. Consulting these materials is no longer a direct encounter with the archive as an aesthetic experience that artists had reflexively produced and conceived of as a work of conceptual art.

As I attempt to attenuate the effects of this mediation and return to an earlier moment of artistic reflexivity, my eye perceives the photographic remnants of Véhicule's space to be consistent with conceptual photography's mimesis of documentary modes. Likewise, the administrative papers, such as meeting minutes, mimic conceptual "aesthetics of administration."[16] When defining this mode as a movement, critic Lucy Lippard has remarked that conceptualist strategies transformed exhibitions and publications into containers for works of art that should be viewed not as content, but as "signs that convey ideas … not things in themselves but symbols or representatives of things."[17] These aesthetic strategies rely upon notational systems and structures such as diagrams, charts, and lists, leading art historian Eve Meltzer to argue that the theoretical discourse of structural linguistics can be both "thought and *felt* " through the mechanistic grids underlying these notational forms.[18] It is possible to read conceptual works as affective responses to a world view in which pre-existing systems and institutions produce identity categories. When messy bodies and emotions emerge from the gaps of conceptualist grids, they resist identification with a symbolic order – such as the cultural codes determining inclusion and exclusion from national groups.

The identities and social roles worked out in Véhicule's linguistic space were understood by the artists to be more than points on a structuralist grid;

instead, they were defined in relation one to the other. Conceptual paradigms of "art-as-information" encouraged visual artists to conceive of publishing on Véhicule's press as an act of networked communications, or a complementary mode of public address to exhibition activity.[19] Véhicule's press was first acquired in 1972, along with a photo-typesetting machine, to print the aforementioned "Special Pornography Issue" of Tom Dean's *Beaux-Arts*.[20] The magazine was an assemblage project following a Fluxus model wherein artists prepared their own contributions as paste-ups conforming to a standard page size. Contributors then sent their work on to Dean who would create the films and print them using an offset lithography process. *Beaux-Arts* magazine was loosely modelled on General Idea's FILE *Megazine*, first published out of Toronto in 1972. Dean also drew inspiration from collage-based assemblage magazines circulating in international concrete poetry and correspondence art networks at the time. The listing of contributors' names in the table of contents and masthead of *Beaux-Arts* creates associations then and now between people who would otherwise not physically meet. In keeping with the predictions of Marshall McLuhan, that electronic communications technologies would erode national sovereignties, the magazine aspires to a multi-locational conception of space in which language use is decoupled from territory or ethnic ancestry.

The pages of *Beaux-Arts* combined explorations of visuality and sensory perception with themes of sexual liberation. Sex and sexuality were treated as codes, or modes of communicating the perceptual limits of repressed desires. For instance, the "Summer 1972" issue of the magazine prints the overtly erotic content of General Idea's "Orgasm Renewal Project" (a graph on which to record the frequency of one's orgasms) next to "Les Coins," a series of photographs taken by Serge Tousignant that explore the perceptual effect of shifting camera positions. In each frame, the perspective subtly shifts as a few pieces of tape in the corner of the artist's studio transform into the image of a three-dimensional cube. Although the content of General Idea's erotica and Tousignant's photographs differs significantly, they both formally address the issue of how images signified for a viewer/reader through a mediated experience.

Tom Dean was able to reach a francophone readership in 1972, when student-run *Médiart* magazine published Chantal Pontbriand's review of *Beaux-Arts* magazine. Both publishing venues called out to readerships with a common countercultural sense of geography, arising from libidinal networks of associative belonging. In the pages of *Médiart*, Pontbriand lists Dean's address, the technical specifications for contributors, price, and distribution details as an open invitation for her francophone readership to contribute content to *Beaux-Arts,* with an emphasis on reversing their sensorial experience of corporate advertising and public messaging. Despite the dominance of English-language content, Pontbriand describes the magazine as a bilingual project; furthermore, the unedited nature of the compilation implies that the readership attracted to the magazine is not equivalent to the national public targeted by cultural policies promoting the linguistic equivalency of official bilingualism.

One might ask why I am spending so much time describing the relationship between a pornographic magazine and a student-run magazine when there is a well-known poetry press and poetry-reading series that could form the basis of a study of "literary" events at Véhicule Art. Most writing about the early 1970s at Véhicule Art, Véhicule Press, or Vehicule Poets is anecdotal and considers visual arts and literary production to be separate undertakings with minor mutual influence or effect on artistic or poetic production.[21] Furthermore, existing literature tends to focus on the period following 1975, leading book scholar George L. Parker to describe Véhicule Press as a "marginal" regional alternative to the major English-language publishing houses located in Toronto.[22] My own approach to unarchiving literary events moves away from issues of language use and lineages of poetic tradition to look instead for crossovers between the visual arts and poetics in the early 1970s. In this period, words and images move across media, explore mutable sexualities, and alternate kinship structures as they work outside of a historical narrative of linguistic divide.[23] I draw from Carolyn Bayard's comparative study of artistic and poetic forms in Quebec and Canada, which identifies Véhicule Art as one site among a network of parallel galleries and publishers where expanded literary forms and conceptualism in the visual arts interfaced in indirect ways. For instance, she argues that seemingly distinct developments in English- and French-language concrete poetry, open-form poetics, and multimedia and oral performance can be read transculturally if viewed as common engagements with language as a historical and anthropological force. For Bayard, the arrival of an international modernism in the "two Canadas" in the 1960s is characterized by the "reign of the signifier,"[24] that is, by a moment when both English-language and French-language artists, writers, and performers were leaving behind an understanding of words and images as mimesis, or the reproduction of things in the world, and instead adopting structuralist models that approached language as a system in which semantic meaning arose through a network of relations between signifier (image/text) and signified (mental image).[25]

The linguistic space I am looking for existed prior to structural changes in 1975, when Véhicule's press transformed into its own separate legal entity, Coopérative d'Imprimérie Véhicule, and established Véhicule Press as a poetry imprint. As the gallery's first press manager, Dean resisted an organized reporting structure and avoided formalized financial records, thus making the historical linguistic space I seek even more challenging to find within the gallery's administrative archive.[26] When the first federal Local Initiatives Program grant awarded to the gallery was extended in July 1973, a revision of the bylaws officially established "Véhicule Press" as a division of the gallery's operations.[27] The bylaws determined that fundraising and day-to-day accounting were to be maintained separately and that these would be consolidated with the end-of-year accounting for the gallery. The minutes also show that the gallery appointed Annie Nayer as the new manager of Véhicule Press, her first task being to register the entity in "the legally required manner."[28] Curiously, their lawyer then recommended that the name Véhicule Press "be dropped."[29] In July 1974, the same year in which Simon Dardick appears on the list of members in the meeting minutes, Véhicule Press finally purchased "Tom Dean's press," with a loan from the gallery for $400 to be repaid in instalments of $50 over a period of six months.[30] "Véhicule Press" then became defined as an imprint for English-language poetry, one of the many entities making use of the printing equipment owned and operated by the Coopérative d'Imprimerie Véhicule.

Signs of a Linguistic Space: Un Évantail d'Expériences

The founding members of Véhicule Art named the gallery after a spatial metaphor: a vehicle as a thing, substance, or medium that facilitates transportation or consumption.[31] This imaginative space materialized through the joint efforts of American immigrants and English-speaking Canadian nationals, who, alongside their francophone colleagues had earlier participated in *Opération Fourrage*, a moment of cultural activism via aesthetic protest against the patronage role played by Quebec's Ministry of Cultural Affairs.[32] A slippage between languages and, therefore, cultural references was actively fostered at the gallery in its early years, and just as much effort was expended in the administrative life of the gallery in producing bilingual publicity, grant reports, and meeting minutes.

Lake remembers that in the year during which the gallery was transforming from an informal discussion group into a physical entity, she and fellow-artist Milly Ristveld hired a lawyer and wrote a legal charter, codifying their "pie in the sky" ideals in order to meet the eligibility requirements for funding from the Canada Council of the Arts and the Local Initiatives Program managed through Manpower and Immigration.[33] It is notable that the operational bilingualism at Véhicule Art appears to have been one of their ideals in praxis, rather than a condition of "official bilingualism" imposed by federal funding agencies. Policies of decentralized governance, championed by Prime Minister Pierre Elliott Trudeau, meant that federal funding sources simultaneously imposed administrative protocols and encouraged the artists to define their venture through participatory and egalitarian organizational techniques borrowed from "counter-institutional" experiments of the 1960s ("free" schools, etc.).[34] In keeping with the countercultural belief in "free" spaces, the imperfect, voluntary bilingualism at Véhicule Art worked as something practised on a personal, individual level. Administrative decisions at Véhicule Art were shaped by aspirations for a free space, just as this ethos encouraged the eclecticism of event programming in the early years. Ranging from formalist painting to drag performance and poetry readings, the gallery gained a reputation in both the French and English press as a site for post-minimal, performance, and process-based forms of conceptualism not encountered elsewhere in the city. Nonetheless, a common grammar between the activities at Véhicule Art and the poetry, performance, and multimedia work associated with the Quiet Revolution did not go unnoticed at the time, as there is a record of at least one critic speculating upon "ideological connections."[35]

Photographs dating from the early 1970s show neon lettering mounted above the street-level entrance of the gallery. This use of glass tubing, which illuminates when electricity passes through an inert gas, recalls conceptual strategies that engage with standardized industrial materials as a means of diffusing authorship. The viewer of modern art is thereby transformed into a reader of semiotic codes. Flanked by sagging awnings and crooked hand-lettered "Vente/For sale" posters, the neon lights also position the aesthetic space of the gallery in relation to a crowded visual field of advertising and public signage on the street. Although subdued in comparison to surrounding marquees for nightclubs and restaurants bordering Saint-Laurent Boulevard, their glowing lights still evoke a desire to engage with street-level mass entertainment forms and language use that mixes and blends as bodies move along crowded sidewalks. In 1960s and 1970s Quebec, language had a symbolic value associated with unequal social status. Therefore, the choice of language for a public sign had a political implication. For an outsider, the sign above Véhicule's door would have suggested the gallery was a francophone organization. As translation studies scholar Sherry Simon has observed, when languages blended at this time, the insertion of English into French was considered an unwelcome invasion, whereas the converse often signified as progressive politics.[36] Because the gallery's neon sign predates the passing of Bill 101, The Charter of the French Language (1977), which legislated unilingual French-language public signage, the surrounding signage in this downtown streetscape would have been predominantly English. However, its address, 61 rue Sainte-Catherine Street Ouest, locates Véhicule Art in close proximity to La Librarie Tranquille, at 69 rue Sainte-Catherine Street Ouest, the legendary bookshop where the Refus Global manifesto was launched in 1948.[37] Therefore, the neon sign works to associate the gallery with an avant-garde tradition of internationalism and creative and intellectual freedom in Quebec while simultaneously presenting an alienating position for a public who defined their sense of community in terms of English-language usage.

Inside the gallery, Lake and studio-mate Bealy were producing and exhibiting works at Véhicule Art that explored the signifying relationship between text and images, and objects as their referents in the world. This mutual interest would lead them to organize the exhibition *Sound as a Visual/Visual as Sound – Le Visuel comme le son / le son comme le visuel*.[38] Lake and Bealy were both fascinated by the way notations on a page could work as a transferable language between mediums as different as film, music, dance, and sound recording – as in the examples set by the Judson Dance Theatre or John Cage's performance scores.[39] Furthermore, Lake and Bealy organized the exhibition through the mailing list and referral system published as an Artists' Directory in General Idea's *FILE Megazine*. This artist collective (AA Bronson, Jorge Zontal, and Felix Partz) published their magazine in order to showcase the activities of a communications network encompassing Canadian conceptual artists and concrete and visual poets working in dialogue with international artistic and literary modernisms.[40] From the late 1960s on, members of General Idea pursued design and printing work at Coach House Press. Their magazine was also developed in close collaboration with artists and writers involved with Vancouver's Intermedia Society. The directory features Marshall McLuhan, writers such as Roy Kiyooka, Gerry Gilbert, and Victor Coleman, as well as Coach House authors such as bpNichol and Steve McCaffery, who drew inspiration from Fluxus performance scores for their own collaborative sound poetry compositions as the Four Horsemen. These last two appear in FILE *Megazine*'s Artists' Directory in 1973, shortly after the listings for Suzy Lake, Allan Bealy, and other members of Véhicule Art were included.

When the French-language press announced *Sound as a Visual/Visual as Sound*, it was used as an example of how audience participation was a means to communicate difficult forms of experimental art to a mass public. Nonetheless, it is also possible to interpret the reception of the exhibition in terms of the embodied experience of relational systems of signification. Critic Gilles Toupin described the show as "un évantail d'expériences qui furent envoyées par plusieurs artistes de différentes parties du monde. On y trouve des images en relation avec des trames sonores, de la poésie concrete juxtaposé à des sérigraphies, des oeuvres commandées par bandes sonores ou par telephone, des jeux lumineux et sonores, des pieces mues grâce à l'énergie électrique, etc."[41]

Toupin's focus on how the works oscillated across a space where communications technologies attain equivalency with the aesthetic forms of high art suggests that *Sound as a Visual/Visual as Sound* united multiple mediums through a structural model – photographs index objects in the "real" world just as sound recordings and telephones index voice; concrete poetry emphasizes the act of reading as a visual process because the reader's attention is drawn to the signifying properties of iconic visual and verbal signs, and synaesthetic and kinetic works similarly activate the body as a multi-sensory organism responding to the environment.[42]

The exhibition was organized through an international open call with submissions continuing to arrive after the show opened. As a result, the remaining documentation in the archive is incomplete and details must be confirmed elsewhere. For instance, paste-ups for what look like posters for the exhibition promote a reading by Québécois poets Michel Garneau and Raôul Duguay. Though this event is not included in the chronology compiled by Concordia University Archives, both Suzy Lake and Endre Farkas remember the reading by Garneau (if not that of Duguay) taking place.[43] Images of works are captured on the contact sheet without reference to an author; however, one work is worth discussing in relation to the linguistic space produced at Véhicule Art, especially as the anonymity of the work thwarts attempts to identify the ancestry or language group of the creator.[44] Two words are stencilled onto the transparent glass of a window in the gallery: "Ouvrez" and "Lift." Outside the window, we see a gridded parking lot, surrounding modernist high-rises, and older industrial buildings typical of the downtown district. The words make visible the function of the transparent glass as a barrier, just as the imperfect translation and word play reminds us that as Vincent Bonin has observed, at Véhicule Art, "language is not transparent."[45] Instead, the window-words emphasize the sensory act of looking, thereby sharing authorship with a reader-participant who senses that their body is spatially constrained by a position marked "inside" through its opposition to an "outside." The ability to act on any desire to move between these positions or to allow for the body to fully merge with the two separate spaces is likewise contingent upon knowledge of English or French (or the facility to move between both).

Gaps in the Grid: Un Art de Non-Lieu

When Véhicule Art's linguistic space interfaces with other kinds of bilingualisms, this positioning according to linguistic grouping is further complicated. Roy Kiyooka's *Poetry/Video/Text* event took place at the Véhicule Art gallery in December 1973. Although English would have been the commonly held language that allowed him to interface with the group, his bilingualism was marked instead by code-switching into Japanese. Moreover, Kiyooka's acute awareness of the tensions regarding identity, language, and territory in Canada and Quebec is made clear in one of his *Transcanada Letters* addressed to Véhicule Art members Claudia Lapp, François Déry, and Suzy Lake. While making arrangements for the reading in Montreal, he asks, "and if the Parti Quebecois get in / will i then need a 'passport' to travel from one strange / country to another?"[46]

Like the window work discussed above, Kiyooka's intermedial performance event emphasized a world contained within the gallery space, without directly addressing political programs linking identity to language and territory. Photographs of the event show Kiyooka hunched over a table reading.

A flute and a tape recorder lie before him. Seated to his right is Annie Nayer. Behind them both, dancer Vicki Tansey strikes poses atop a ladder.[47] Stephen Morrissey, a student of Richard Sommer and one of the first poets to participate in the reading series at the gallery, documented the event in his diary, revealing how Kiyooka combined process-based actions with recording technologies. The reading collaged together accounts of his personal migrations with key references of international modernism; however, on the gallery windows, the national imaginary produced within pages of *artscanada* magazine formed a barrier to the outside world. That said, it is a barrier through which the light filters into Véhicule Art's linguistic space imbued with marijuana smoke: "walked in and Richard was playing his flute – after a while Roy, Japanese, around 50 5′8″ I'd guess, grey hair, as [someone was] sticking pages of Arts Canada [*sic*] onto the windows with masking tape, while Vicki danced – Roy's woman recorded it all on a videotape – lasted about 1/2 hour – then we all moved upstairs to hear a reading, a mixture of Gertrude Stein and Samuel Beckett that Roy put together to read with his girl while Vicki danced again – Richard played the flute and it was really a nice effect – then back downstairs where Roy read letters he's written and they were very personal about his life, letters to his children and friends and parents – they were really … fine – before Richard had offered me a toke but I don't smoke"[48]

Morrissey's detailed observations – noting Kiyooka's height, hair colour, and ethnicity – reveal the degree to which fixed identity categories were operative at the time, as do his comments upon "women" as determined by a possessive relationship to men. His uncensored thoughts indicate how the linguistic space at Véhicule Art was not so much free from these pervasive cultural restraints as opened up – a space within which these categories could be recognized and contested.[49] In his own performance, Kiyooka worked against a fixed sense of Japanese-Canadian identity by telling the personal stories he would later collect in his book *Transcanada Letters*, which includes memories of his time teaching at Sir George Williams University in the late 1960s. In this period, Kiyooka crossed linguistic lines and disciplines, exhibiting hard-edged paintings at the Galerie de Siècle alongside the predominantly French-Canadian, internationalist neo-Plasticien painters while simultaneously working with George Bowering to organize the Sir George Williams Poetry Series. These social scenes place Kiyooka at the confluence of conflicting interests. As Camlot has observed, the reading series revitalized English-language writing in the city through a dissonance produced between "competing versions of literary modernism" and varying degrees of Canadian nationalism.[50] A further sense of belonging to a transnational geography could be inferred from Kiyooka and Bowering's personal connections. As Gregory Betts has noted, their poetry series favoured "Vancouver's aesthetic interests,"[51] such as collagist modes and a sense of localism developed through Black Mountain College poetics.[52]

Kiyooka's movement between language groups at this time, as well as his sensitivity to tensions between parochial nationalisms and international artistic and literary avant-gardes, reflected his reticence around claims to origin in cultural nationalist programs. Despite an avowed admiration for René Lévesque as his "all-time favourite politician,"[53] Kiyooka avoided taking a political position contingent upon national identity. Instead, he located himself in relation to modernist ideas of an autonomous aesthetic realm. Kiyooka's blocking out of the windows at Véhicule Art with pages of *artscanada* suggests that the utopian linguistic space at Véhicule Art was contingent upon a concrete belief in the autonomy of art, the limits of which could be tested through a conceptualist approach to language and cultural codes.

Kiyooka's performance took place inside an exhibition featuring works by Suzy Lake and Allan Bealy. A common theme shared by all three was the relationship among concept and its material form, and the affective bonds this relationship can create within personal memory.[54] Gilles Toupin's review of the show remarks, "On croirait même que Suzy Lake écrit ses mémoires à l'aide de signes et d'indices dont on se ferait fort de dénicher les points d'identité au reel."[55] It was at this moment that Lake began to produce serialized photographic portraits arranged in a grid, which resemble those produced by Roy Kiyooka in the same period. In the work *A One Hour (Zero) Conversation with Allan B.* (1973), Lake systematically documents the performance of identity in the activities of everyday life. The gridded structure reminiscent of a contact sheet contains images of Lake, depersonalized by the white-face makeup worn by mimes, as she performs affective moments throughout a conversation with Bealy.[56] Several frames are circled and singled out as if they were ideal performances of femininity, ready to be enlarged and reproduced. This photographic series can be compared to Kiyooka's similarly gridded photo series, *Long Beach BC to Peggy's Cove* (1971). As it is printed across eighteen pages inserted between the personal letters compiled in *Transcanada Letters*, the pictorial record of cross-country mobility disrupts a fixed understanding of Japanese-Canadian identity.

For his part, Lake's partner in dialogue, Allan Bealy, used Véhicule's press to playfully bridge the relationship between concept and material form across visual and literary spheres. Between 1973 and 1975, five issues of Bealy's *Davinci* magazine included contributors such as George Bowering, Endre Farkas (then Andre), Artie Gold, Suzy Lake, David McFadden, Stephen Morrissey, Opal L. Nations, Françoise Sullivan, and Bill Vazan, as well as Fluxus contributors such as Klaus Groh, William Gaglione, and Dick Higgins stemming from contacts made through *Sound as a Visual/Visual as Sound*. Each issue of *Davinci* played with the visual presentation of texts alongside images. In No. 4 (Autumn 1975), the table of contents listing the names of contributors is displayed next to a torn segment of an index taken from another source.[57] This is a clever reference to little magazines as affective sites of poetic community, where the texts "index" the presence of the poets' bodies to the page as an imaginary site. Bealy similarly produced chapbooks under a separate imprint, Eldorado Editions, as a conceptual project that established an association between his friends, the manual labour of the photomechanical printing process, and the street-level culture of an automat 24-hour diner open below the gallery.[58]

When collected together, these books, magazines, photographs, news clippings, and administrative ephemera allow present-day viewers to perceive a linguistic space fostered at Véhicule Art prior to 1975. The material and social relations that produced this free space worked as a countermeasure to the link between language, territory, and social identity in political programs that proscribed official bilingualism in Canada and provincial legislation that protected the status of French as the language of public life in Quebec. Instead, space at Véhicule was constructed like a language. Véhicule Art's linguistic space prompts its historically distanced visitors to consider nationhood and national identity as something constructed through language and the repetition of myths. As Eve Meltzer observes, the "linguistic turn" of conceptual art aligns with the Derridian notion that "in the absence of a centre or origin, everything [becomes] discourse."[59] Affect, emotion, desire, and fantasy took shape in a space that neither fits with a Québécois neo-nationalist project nor reinforces a federalist model of bilingualism and biculturalism. It is a linguistic space, constructed from archivally indexed traces of events, activities, and social relations, which may only now be recognizable from the present-day perspective of globalized circulation routes and transnational mediascapes.

NOTES

1 "Véhicule: Alternative Space, Alternative Attitude, New Situation," *Médiart* 9 (September 1972): D1–D8.

2 Jacques Derrida, *Archive Fever: A Freudian Impression,* trans. Eric Prenowitz, (Chicago: University of Chicago Press, 1995), 45.

3 The Musée d'art contemporain was founded as a state institution in 1965 as part of the provincial cultural policy enacted by the Liberal government under the leadership of Jean Lesage during the period known as the Quiet Revolution.

4 Fernande Saint-Martin, "La Situation de l'art et l'identité québécoise," *Voix et Images* 2.1 (1976): 26. The article is signed with the official title of "directrice du Musée d'art contemporain" and reflects statements made earlier in response to the exhibition Québec 75, curated by Normand Thériault at the Musée d'art contemporain.

5 Barry Lord drew on Marxist-Leninist and Maoist theory to advocate for a "people's art" through NC Press, the publishing arm of the Canadian National Liberation Movement. Barry Lord, *The History of Painting in Canada: Towards a People's Art* (Toronto: NC Press, 1974), 213.

6 See Elaine Pigeon, W.H. New, and Jason Garrison and Tomas Waugh for a discussion of "the Main" as a metaphorical site of drug culture and sexual ambiguity in the work of authors Michel Tremblay and Leonard Cohen, and filmmaker Frank Vitale. Elaine Pigeon, "Hosanna! Michel Tremblay's Queering of National Identity," in *In a Queer Country: Gay and Lesbian Studies in the Canadian Context,* ed. Terry Goldie (Vancouver: Arsenal Pulp Press, 2001), 27–49; W.H. New, *A History of Canadian Literature,* 2nd ed. (Montreal and Kingston: McGill-Queen's University Press, 2003); Jason Garrison and Thomas Waugh, *Montreal Main: A Queer Film Classic* (Vancouver: Arsenal Pulp Press, 2010).

7 Quoted in Craig J. Peariso, "The 'Counterculture' in Quotation Marks: Sontag and Marcuse on the Work of Revolution," in *The Scandal of Susan Sontag,* eds. Barbara Ching and Jennifer A. Wagner-Lawlor (New York: Columbia University Press, 2009), 155, 169n19.

8 Jonathan D. Katz, "Allen Ginsberg, Herbert Marcuse, and the Politics of Eros," in *21st Century Gay Culture,* ed. David A. Powell (Newcastle: Cambridge Scholars Publishing, 2008), 13. José Esteban Muñoz has also applied his theory of disidentification to pre-Stonewall and "preidentiarian" activations of *eros* in *Cruising Utopia: The Then and There of Queer Futurity* (New York: New York University Press, 2009).

9   An example of the combined exhibition and publishing projects undertaken be GRAA is *Quebec Underground, 1962–1972* (Montreal: Éditions Médiart, 1973), which was both a three-volume publication reprinting over 1,000 pages of press clippings and other ephemera from arts and literature scenes of the 1960s in Quebec, and an exhibition and launch-party performance event at the Casa Loma nightclub located a few blocks away from Véhicule Art.

10 Jean-Phillipe Warren, "Fondation et production de la revue Mainmise (1970–1978)," *Mémoires du livre/Studies in Book Culture* 4.1 (autumn 2012), www.erudit.org/revue/memoires/2012/v4/n1/1013326ar.html (accessed 26 May 2014).

11 Arno Mermelstein, "Maid in Canada," *Beaux-Arts* Special Pornography Issue (1973): 38–9.

12 A.A. Bronson, *From Sea to Shining Sea: Artist-Initiated Activity in Canada, 1939–1987* (Toronto: The Power Plant, 1987), 71.

13 Herbert Marcuse, *Essays on Liberation* (Boston: Beacon Press, 1969), 8–9.

14 Suzy Lake quoted in Diana Nemiroff, "A History of Artist-Run Spaces in Canada, with Particular Reference to Véhicule, A Space and the Western Front," MA thesis (Montreal: Concordia University, 1985), 136.

15 P027 Véhicule Art (Montréal) Inc. fonds, 1972–1983, Concordia University Archives, Montreal, Québec.

16 This hovering between aesthetic states in the archives of artist-run centres has been noted by Vincent Bonin in Vincent Bonin, ed., *Documentary Protocols/Protocols Documentaires 1967–1975* (Montreal: Leonard & Bina Ellen Gallery, 2010).

17 Lucy R. Lippard, "The Dematerialization of Art," in *Changing: Essays in Art Criticism* (New York: Dutton, 1971), 255–76.

18 Eve Meltzer, *Systems We Have Loved: Conceptual Art, Affect, and the Antihumanist Turn* (Chicago: University of Chicago Press, 2013), 11.

19 Nemiroff, "A History of Artist-Run Spaces in Canada," 143–5.

20 Two issues of the magazine had already been published in the spring and summer of 1972. The equipment was purchased using funds Dean had received as an individual artist from the Canada Council for the Arts toward publishing the third, and final, issue of *Beaux-Arts*.

21 *The Vehicle Poets* (Montreal: Maker Press, 1979); Ken Norris, ed., *Vehicle Days: An Unorthodox History of Montreal's Vehicle Poets* (Montreal: NuAge Editions, 1993); Victoria Stanton and Vincent Tinguely, eds., *Impure: Reinventing the Word* (Montreal: Conundrum Press, 2001); Tom Konyves and Steven

Morrisey, eds., *The Vehicule Poets Now* (Montreal: The Muses Company, 2004); Jason Camlot and Todd Swift, *Language Acts: Anglo-Québec Poetry, 1976 to the 21st Century* (Montreal: Véhicule Press, 2007).

22 George Parker, "Trade and Regional Book Publishing in English," in *History of the Book in Canada: 1918–1980, Vol. 3*, ed. Carole Gerson and Jacques Michon (Toronto: University of Toronto Press, 2004), 177.

23 For a more comprehensive list of publishing activity in this period, see Nemiroff, "History of Artist-Run Spaces in Canada," 146–7.

24 Caroline Bayard, *The New Poetics in Canada and Quebec: From Concretism to Post Modernism* (Toronto: University of Toronto Press, 1989), 7.

25 Bayard, *The New Poetics in Canada and Quebec*, 7–9.

26 See Véhicule Art (Montréal) Inc. Minutes, 10 March 1973. P027 Véhicule Art (Montréal) Inc. fonds, 1972–1983.

27 Véhicule Art Inc., and its press, received a total of $103,000 over a period spanning a year and a half, from February 1973 to June 1974. Nemiroff, "A History of Artist-Run Spaces in Canada," 143.

28 Amendment to Vehicule Art By-Laws, 1973 Meeting. P027 Véhicule Art (Montréal) Inc. fonds 1972–1983. Around this point, Guy Lavoie and Willie Wood also entered the scene as pressmen.

29 Véhicule Art Inc. Meeting, November 1973. P027 Véhicule Art (Montréal) Inc. fonds 1972–1983.

30 Procès Verbal Réunion, 30 juillet 1974. P027 Véhicule Art (Montréal) Inc. fonds 1972–1983.

31 The founding members were Suzy Lake, Gary Coward, Tom Dean, Andrew Deutkewych, Dennis Lucas, Kelly Morgan, Gunter Nolte, William Vazan and Milly Ristvedt who worked alongside Henry Saxe, Jean-Marie Delavalle, Francois Déry, and Serge Tousignant. Nemiroff, "A History of Artist-Run Spaces in Canada," 125.

32 *Opération Fourrage* plays with two meanings of the word "fourrage" in French: it connotes the plant-based diet of farm animals, such as hay, but in Québécois slang it also connotes sexual relations. Véhicule Art is considered to have emerged from social ties and aesthetic affinities formed around the 1971 conceptual art exhibition, *45°30' N-73°36' W* exhibition at the Saidye Bonfman Centre for the Arts and Sir George Willams Art Gallery. However, an article in *Médiart* emphasizes instead the protest-event, *Opération Fourrage,* also occurring in 1971, where approximately twenty to thirty artists organized to submit identical bales of hay (*bottes de foin*) to a jury for the survey show

"Exposition des créateurs du Québec" organized by the Ministère des affaires culturel. Strict restrictions were placed on the size of the work in order to facilitate touring the province, and artists perceived this as insensitivity to new artistic forms on the part of the cultural ministry, which functioned as a patron of the arts. Discomfort also arose regarding the "packaging of art as a national product" implied in the relation between a cultural ministry, artistic production, and the definition of a national identity – a situation further complicated by the "importation" of Dennis Young from Art Gallery of Ontario as judge. The article in *Médiart* describes the hay bale as a national symbol associated with a period before the Quiet Revolution, "la dernière qualité d'une culture malade." Tremblay-Chamberland, "Treize à table, au menu "une botte de foin," E-1. See also, Nemiroff, "A History of Artist-Run Spaces in Canada," 134.

33 Suzy Lake, interviewed by Hélène Sicotte, 2 December 1994, P0007-11-0153 Véhicule Art (Montréal) Inc. 1972–1983: Suzy Lake [sound recording], 1 Microcassette (1 hr. 50 min. 31 sec.), Concordia University Archives, Montreal, Quebec.

34 Diana Nemiroff, "Par-al-lel," in *Sightlines: Reading Contemporary Canadian Art*, ed. Jessica Bradey and Lesley Johnstone (Montreal: Artextes Editions, 1994), 180; Bonin, ed., *Documentary Protocols (1967–1975)*, 44–5.

35 Robert Johns, "Québec Underground," *Artscanada* 2 (May 1973): 74.

36 Sherry Simon, *Translating Montreal: Episodes in the Life of a Divided City* (Montreal and Kingston: McGill-Queen's University Press, 2006), 40.

37 *La Librarie Tranquille* was at this address from 1948 to 1974. *Entre l'auteur et le lecteur: l'archive.Group de recherches et d'études sur le livre au Québec*, GRÉLQ (Montreal: Université de Sherbrooke, Sevice des bibliothèques et archives, 2015), 35

38 *Sound as a Visual/Visual as Sound* took place at Véhicule Art from 1 March 1973 to 18 March 1973.

39 Suzy Lake, interviewed by Hélène Sicotte, 2 December 1994, P0007-11-0153 Véhicule Art (Montréal) Inc. 1972–1983: Suzy Lake [sound recording], 1 Microcassette (1 hr. 50 min. 31 sec.), Concordia University Archives, Montreal, Quebec.

40 Suzy Lake, Allan Bealy, and other members of Véhicule Art such as Henry Saxe appear in the "Artists' Directory," which was printed in the three issues of FILE released in 1972. FILE 2.1&2 (April/May 1973) includes a photograph of Steve McCaffery. bpNichol has a listing in the Directory of FILE 2.3 (1973) in which he requests images of "Clouds, images of H's, Dick Tracey in non-comic strip."

41 Gilles, "Quand le son et l'image…," *La Presse* (8 March 1973): Arts et spectacles, C2. Contributor's translation: "an eclectic array of experiences were sent in by several artists from different parts of the world. We see images in relation to soundtracks, concrete poetry juxtaposed with silkscreens, works commissioned by audio tape or telephone, light and sound events, kinetic works powered by electricity, etc."

42 A poster for the exhibition, and images in the archive confirm these participants in the show: dancers Liza Doolittle and Margaret Dragu; filmmaker Norman McLaren; Gary Lee-Nova, Gerry Gilbert, and Don Druick, all associated with Vancouver's Intermedia Society; W.O.R.K.S. (Clive Robertson and Paul Woodrow), who performed Fluxus pieces as a process of identity transfer; a contribution from Felix Partz of a recording of people urinating at General Idea's headquarters; Italian concretist Ugo Carrega; and German neo-dada artist Klaus Groh. The Chronology of Activities prepared by Concordia University Archives also lists the following as participants: Pierre Thibaudeau, Marjolaine Robert, Ron Tunis, Allan Bealy, Joe Bodolai, Ugo Carrega, Jerome Cebelak, Cyne Cobb, Serge Garant, Thomas Haynes, Otto Joachim, Dennis Lukas, Saundra Legault, Ed Slopek, Cork Marcheschi, Ian Murray, Gino Pallidini, Northwest Mounted Valise, Jacques Palumbo, John Plant, Chuck Stanon, Janos Urban, and Marjolaine Robert. P027 Véhicule Art (Montréal) Inc. fonds 1972–1983.

43 Both Endre Farkas and Suzy Lake remember the reading by Michel Garneau taking place. E-mail from Suzy Lake, 4 June 2015. Endre Farkas, interviewed by Felicity Tayler, 9 February 2015, *SpokenWeb*, http://spokenweb.concordia.ca/oral-literary-history/andre-farkas-interview-february-9th-2015/ (accessed 3 October 2015).

44 Anonymous contact sheet from the exhibition file. P027 Véhicule Art (Montréal) Inc. fonds 1972–1983.

45 Vincent Bonin, "Language Is Not Transparent: Translating Conceptual Art in Montréal," in *Traffic: Conceptual Art in Canada 1965–1980*, ed. Grant Arnold and Karen Henry (Vancouver: Vancouver Art Gallery, 2011), 38.

46 Roy Kiyooka, "Dear Claudia, Francois and Suzie, 10/21/'73," *Transcanada Letters* (Vancouver: Talonbooks, 1975), n.p.

47 Anonymous contact sheet from the exhibition file. P027. Véhicule Art (Montréal) Inc. fonds 1972–1983.

48 Stephen Morrissey, Wednesday/December 19th/1973, Book 35. Diaries, 1963–1991. Stephen Morrissey Literary Papers, 1963–2014, Rare Books and Special Collections, McLennan Library, McGill University, Montreal.

49 Karis Shearer, in chapter 7, further discusses these gendered hierarchies of poetic community as they were performed in Vancouver.

50 Jason Camlot, "The Sound of Canadian Modernism: The Sir George Williams University Poetry Series, 1966–74," *Journal of Canadian Studies* 46 (Fall 2012): 31.

51 Gregory Betts, "We Stopped at Nothing: Finding Nothing in the Avant-Garde Archive," *Amodern* 4 (2015), online, http://amodern.net/article/nothing/ (accessed 10 August 2017).

52 See Deanna Fong's chapter 2 for an account of poetic modes and social scenes particular to Vancouver.

53 Roy Kiyooka interviewed in *Roy K. Kiyooka: 25 Years* (Vancouver: Vancouver Art Gallery, 1975), n.p.

54 *Suzy Lake and Allan Bealy* took place at Véhicule Art from 2 to 22 December 1973.

55 Gilles Toupin, "Suzy Lake, Allen Bealy," *La Presse* (8 décembre 1973): C18. Contributor's translation: "One has the impression that Suzy Lake writes her memoirs using signs and clues, which we aspire to connect to reality and thereby understand her identity."

56 Georgiana Uhlyarik, ed., *Introducing Suzy Lake* (Toronto: Art Gallery of Ontario; London: Black Dog Publishing, 2014), 50.

57 *Davinci* 4, 2.1 (Autumn 1974)

58 Eldorado Editions issued a series of modest chapbooks: Ian Ferrier's *From YR Lover Like an Orchestra*; Endre Farkas's *Szerbusz*; Tom Ezzy's *Arctic Char in Grecian Waters*; and Claudia Lapp's *Dakini*. The Eldorado was a restaurant where they could eat a cheap meal alongside sex workers and homeless people. Patrons would be served a hot meal through a vending-machine apparatus. Endre Farkas, interviewed by Felicity Tayler, 9 February 2015.

59 Derrida quoted in Meltzer, *Systems We Have Loved*, 18.

9

____

Listening to the Unscripted
Aura and Experience in Irving Layton's Televisual Archives

JOEL DESHAYE

During an archived 1964 television appearance by poet Irving Layton on *The Pierre Berton Show*, Layton said to Pierre Berton, "it's easy to understand the public I witness."[1] Without an authorized typescript of the interview, without a text to see, listeners might be confused by the homophone: Layton might have meant the two words "I witness" or the one word "eyewitness" (as in, "the public eyewitness" that has a function of witnessing). If I were to elaborate on the context, I think I could disambiguate what he said.[2] But the purpose of mentioning this case now is to draw attention to the ambiguity of sounded words, especially when they are uttered spontaneously, in the moment; then recorded, as on television; and then archived, maybe forever. How then does witnessing change? How do we watch, "read," and transcribe archival television? Television usually has a script, even live television such as *The Pierre Berton Show*, but such shows involve performance, and performances can deviate from the script. And, like performances, archives are full of surprises. By that, I mean the unexpected discoveries that are often the result of what Thomas Osborne calls the archive's "indeterminacy,"[3] or the effect of opening an archive to the public and to a future in which someone might find something that was there all along.

My "find" in this case is a 1978 Layton TV appearance that includes commercial breaks without commercials – an irony resonant with implications for profit-driven television that is taken out of the studio and the home to be archived in a public institution. Instead of commercials, the image cuts to two minutes of blackness and silence, but the silence is interrupted twice by intermittent unscripted dialogue and other surprises that seem to qualify archival television as different from television viewed at home.[4] The inclusion of unscripted dialogue when the image can be interpreted as "blacked out" or even redacted from the public broadcast raises questions: How does the experience of the archive change when the viewer unexpectedly becomes a listener? To what extent does television remain public when it includes a comparatively private dimension that the original audience would not have seen or heard? A tacit assumption in these questions is that the private and public spheres are not separate but superimposed. One might think that listening is more private than watching: no one goes out in public to listen to an album; we go to *see* a concert or *watch* a movie – but the archive changes the context so that "behind the scenes" becomes effectively public, evoking some of the excitement of being in a crowd and adding a surprisingly social dimension to the "lonely existential labour"[5] of working in an archive. In my case, the lack of a script or authorized typescript is affective and conceptually revealing – the archive generates a response from the visitor by simulating a space out of sight, blinding the public or public eyewitness (one word) and reinforcing the privacy of the archive. In an age of increasing archival publicity and Internet celebrity, this minor discovery reveals and underscores the interplay of spheres and the sometimes unexpected interchangeability of one for the other.

Layton was and is a major figure – one of those rare poets who was a star, and whose persona became embroiled in his private life and even in the archive. Beginning in 1956, Layton became special as the first Canadian poet to add television to his regular exploitation of mass media, and later he attempted film too.[6] As strategically self-promotional as he was in these media, Layton was also remarkably preoccupied by his sought-after fame in a comparatively private discourse: he made carbon copies of many of his letters so that one was often saved for the archives. Unlike Osborne's example of the former Soviet state's KGB archive, which was so well guarded that it needed to contain no redactions of KGB activities and was never intended to have a public audience,[7] much of Layton's was never intended to be secret. His archive is *performative* in the sense of being related to role play, spectacle, and publics, and it lacks some of the credibility and authenticity of a once-secret archive. Layton's personas live not only on TV but also in his archives, and in this context an unscripted moment in the television archive is like going behind the scenes – not with the commercial escort of the "extras" on a movie viewed at home, but with the all-access pass to a greater authenticity that archives promise and may sometimes provide.

A pass implies a restricted area. The relationships between secrecy, privacy, and publicity in the context of the archive are fascinating partly because the archive spatializes the other concepts. Archives historically need a place. Jacques Derrida suggests that the place of the archives, "this place where they dwell permanently, marks this institutional passage from the private to the public, which does not always mean from the secret to the non-secret."[8] A simplified history of archives is that, before the modern, liberal, public archive, there was the sovereign or totalitarian archive, which consisted of secret records in a private space.[9] Even today, of course, secret records are stored in public archives; some historians joke that finding them is like being invited to enter a door if its location can be guessed and if permission may be granted.[10] An archive is no longer secret when the public knows it exists, though it might remain private even in our modern era, as with Michael Ondaatje's papers at Library and Archives Canada, which I was not permitted to see – possibly for good reason. Archivists and historians have explained the competing rationales of the "right to privacy" and the "right to know" in cases when donors to public archives are "alive and active."[11] In spite of the desire for access to records, private or public, the archive remains a place of privacy, even security, and, I would venture, is likely to retain a private space for scholarship regardless of what happens to its square footage and its vast physical holdings in libraries, universities, and other institutions.

The archive is becoming somewhat virtual, with related increases in potential publicity. Harriet Bradley points out that most modern archives are "public records in a private space,"[12] even if in the case of someone's letters they are also private records in a public space – another sign of the easy interchange of public/private. As I learned in my research on celebrity in the modern world, privacy tends to drift toward publicity.[13] Technology and its cultures encourage us, more and more, to behave as we wish celebrities would behave, giving up privacy for the social gains of publicity. Layton's intentionally archivable letters may be described as public, not private, and insofar as his archives are at publicly funded universities in Canada, they are public records in a public space. But rather than focus on the university archives' public dimension, we must consider the only remaining drift, which is out of the public space of the archives and into the variable space of the archival scholar or visitor – the drift downstream, so to speak, as we download and stream archival material to our computers at home, in other private spaces, or in another public space, such as the classroom. Bradley describes "an inversion of the public/private relationship as the contents of the great storehouses of the public sphere flow into the living spaces of private individuals."[14] I would add only that archives often remain gated – the stream and flow only a trickle, the privacy tap still mostly closed.

The issue of access is crucial to archival theory in the age of the Internet. Defending newer conceptions of the archives, those of Derrida and Michel Foucault, against conservative critics such as Geoffrey Elton, Andrew Prescott argues that "the challenge to become more accessible, to attract new audiences, to explore diversity and identity and to seek out the alienated and forgotten is a challenge which has sprung directly from the new body of theory, and cannot be fully understood without reference to it."[15] Prescott wants marginalized stories to be heard, and Derrida asks rhetorically, "Aren't these stories to be had everywhere?"[16] The truth is, no, they are not. Even with Layton, hardly a marginal figure, you cannot see most of his appearances or hear most of his broadcasts on the Internet. You can see some clips from the CBC, but rarely full programs, unless you go to the CBC's headquarters in Toronto and negotiate for help from their archivists. Linda Morra, whose work appears in chapter 1, observes that the CBC Digital Archives has (at the time of writing) few search tools or finding aids; these "archives" offer to the masses a superficial though centralized repository of broadcasts, whereas a separate set of more thorough archives exists for scholars who can travel and spend time with the materials themselves – different audience, different archive.

The program at the heart of my essay is available as a digital file for viewing at Concordia University's special collections, but it is not available online at the time of this book's publication. When I asked if I could arrange to download it for study at home, the answer was a polite but firm "no" – the unofficial reason being a concern about copyrighted materials reaching the Internet. Some archives want, or are obliged by donors, to restrict access to in-house viewing, perhaps to ensure a role for archivists at a time when policymakers in the age of the Internet might think of archives as obsolete. I imagine, too, that delivering such content online might also require staff members to have the time and expertise for digital video editing and website design and maintenance. Or, if archival footage is to be thorough and unedited, then bandwidth or download limitations (almost but not quite a thing of the past) might affect longer clips; the one I've mentioned is an hour long. Digital formats have also dramatically increased the size of some holdings, even as remediation redoubles efforts to keep up to date with technologies when digital permanence is not yet a reality. At public archives, in Canada at least, archivists have neither enough time nor enough colleagues and other "resources" to deal with a true opening of the archives, and, in a double bind, the opening might be used as a rationale for closing physical archives; in other words, the Internet could in theory make other spaces obsolete.

While Layton was often eager to appear current, partly through his engagement with new media, he was nevertheless accustomed to speaking out for poetry and other traditions, as he did in every talk that I can remember hearing – always in the archives, because he died just as I was becoming a student of his poetry. Bradley argues that we need "a telling of what it is like to be using an archive, working in the archive,"[17] and one of my purposes here is to deliver such a tale, as she does. Bradley contrasts her work on the "pleasures, seductions and illusions of archival work"[18] with that of Osborne, who focuses on its ordinariness. The archive is, of course, an often especially personal library – a "special collection" that can replicate the banality of everyday life in its schedules and scraps, but can also evoke eurekas. I have experienced both, and perhaps the ordinariness makes even a small discovery seem disproportionately meaningful. The "thrill"[19] makes a thrill-seeker of the archival scholar. It has biased my view of the unscripted dialogue that I have already mentioned, and it increases the meaningfulness of Layton's disappearance during the commercial break.

The story I want to tell of Layton's publicity and privacy on archival television is based on a 1978 appearance on the *City Lights* TV show hosted by Brian Linehan in Toronto. (Linehan was a "show-biz interviewer,"[20] and *City Lights* was "an in-depth Citytv celebrity-interview show" that ran from 1973 to 1989[21] and featured a wide range of American and Canadian celebrities.) The occasion was the recent release of Layton's book *Taking Sides* (1977), a collection of his political prose, and the show's first topic of discussion was Layton's letter to the editor to defend Louis Malle's new 1978 film *Pretty Baby*, which features a very young Brooke Shields playing a sometimes-nude attraction for the historical brothel photographer E.J. Bellocq of New Orleans. Layton and Linehan related the movie to an early memory of Layton's, his growing up partly around an area in Montreal, now centred on de Bullion Street, that contained a brothel and a synagogue. The stage was set for a show that depended on an ideological clash of assumptions – that sexuality should be on display, in public, or that it should be private. Layton defended the movie, certainly because he liked the beauty of the women, certainly because he wanted to be provocatively contrarian, but possibly also because he identified with Shields and the other celebrities because of their exposure.[22]

The discussion between Layton and Linehan focuses on place, especially the place of the brothel, a space or place of both exposure and protection (compared to the street) whose qualities relate it to the archive. In a 1967 lecture on "Other Spaces," Foucault named the brothel as an example of heterotopia – an illusion of utopia, or "a space as perfect, as meticulous, as well arranged as ours is messy, ill constructed, and jumbled."[23] Heterotopias are what Prescott calls the "highly stylized expressions of the society's power and social structures,"[24] and, as one such "expression," the archive is sometimes used to rationalize the causes and effects of history and to make sense of the status quo. The "arrange[ment]" of documents itself suggests order and completeness. Likewise, a brothel seemingly allows the "mess[iness]" of sex and sexual relationships to be ordered and cleaned up in a process of simple transactions.[25] Although the brothel–archive analogy could be dismissed outright, I can agree with it in another respect: going to the archives is often like accepting an invitation to invade someone else's privacy, or at least the illusion of privacy, which is all the more germane if the material originates with a star, as it does with Layton. In chapter 3, Katherine McLeod mentions an episode of CBC-TV's *Extension* in which Phyllis Webb plays at psychoanalyzing Al Purdy. Archival research is analogous: it lets us free-associate with its raw materials, even as we also play the role of the analyst privy to another's uncensored thoughts and expressions.

Layton, however, was always playing with his own privacy, and seemed to derive some satisfaction – and attention – from public displays related to his personal life. As someone whose fifth wife was almost fifty years younger than him, Layton controversially (of course) dismisses the controversy of depicting Shields as a sexual figure at the age of only twelve in *Pretty Baby*. Commanding the stage with a series of provocative statements, Layton concludes: "It [the movie] has nothing to do with pornography. When people see the film – if it finally does get released by the censor-morons who can't tell a work of art from an adenoid, you know – they're going to be terribly disappointed because they're going to find that there's no pornography, and no sex, and nothing to titillate them, nothing to excite them."[26] Not believing a word, Layton's host, Linehan, responds first with a pause and an amused look on his face, and then drawls, "Alright." They then talk more about the film in the context of de Bullion Street (which became the title of a poem in Layton's *Here and Now*, 1945), and Layton generalizes the discussion by quoting Robert Frost and saying that his own poetic images are, like Frost's, "a momentary stay against confusion."

Layton's appearance on *City Lights* was an hour long, so they needed to break for commercials, and this is when the archival footage goes unexpectedly (also confusedly) behind the scenes. The archival footage indicates the breaks without including the commercials, which is also the case for Linehan's 1986 interview with Martin Short, which Vanessa Rodriguez has seen and described: "Once the cameras were off, they behaved like two young boys whose mothers had left them alone. Short scooted up to the edge of his seat and whispered excitedly during every commercial break."[27] The archive got the footage not because someone donated a recording from TV. The archive got something closer to the original tape, from the point of the final cut of the program itself. (I do not know the provenance of the tapes that were digitized for the archive, but they may have come from Linehan himself or from the Film Reference Library, to which Linehan donated hundreds of videos and sound recordings, plus thousands of documents.[28] Without wanting to call Linehan's integrity into question, I do also wonder whether his show – which was known for his meticulously collected information about celebrities – typically recorded celebrities when they might have thought themselves unheard or temporarily off camera.) In both of the first two commercial breaks, the camera turns off. The screen goes black, Layton and Linehan disappear, and there is silence. The darkness and silence are only part of the surprise.

Another surprising part is the rare sound of those working to create televisual broadcasts. During the first commercial break, in the darkness, Layton's voice almost instantly fades in, out, and in again as someone turns a volume knob; Layton is chatting with Linehan but the volume is too low to hear the exchange. A third quiet voice recognizably says, "Say a few words for us," presumably to request a sound check. The volume is adjusted upward as Linehan responds, "Yes. Irving Layton. *Taking Sides*. We've been talking about Montreal." Then they quickly fade out again. There is a long pause. Some fabric, presumably, makes noise against a microphone. Another silence – then the mic noise repeats, but louder. "Brian, say hello please," says a voice. Linehan says, "Irving, the man with the camera is Andreas Blackwell. Andreas Blackwell, Irving Layton." "Hi," comes Andreas's voice – the voice of a younger man – "I really enjoyed … your little talk about death." What Blackwell meant by this "little talk" is uncertain, because it does not appear on the program. He might be referring to something else that happened off-camera, without being recorded. This lack attests to the inevitable incompleteness of all archives – an incompleteness that, as Karis Shearer notes in chapter 7, prompts rapt listening and interpretive work to figure out the total "picture" behind the scenes of an event's planning and the archiving of that planning. Notably, the voice of "the man with the camera" is also a sign of the "creative labourers"[29] at work in, not on, television. Layton, Linehan, and their original viewers might have had a break during the commercials, but Blackwell was working. Jason Jacobs writes: "I do not think that I am alone in wanting to see and account for the significance of the way things work behind the scenes. Television archives, then, need to be mindful not only of the present immediate problems of storing and sorting the material we watch, but also those materials that are relevant to the processes that make watching possible at all."[30] Here on *City Lights*, the cameraman's appreciative remark to Layton suggests that fan-like behaviour is normal even for people in the industry who often work with celebrities. It also reveals the fundamentally produced nature of television. From my own perspective as an archival researcher, hearing Blackwell's remark about "death" was retrospectively chilling, because it was a floating signifier heard in the virtual darkness of the archive that Derrida associates with "a haunted house."[31] Although I hope that Blackwell, seemingly a young man in 1978, is alive and well today, he and his fellow-workers are like ghosts in the archive – usually unseen, rarely or barely heard, but part of the untold history that the archive preserves.

Then the sound drops out and I hear the reference tone that usually accompanies a visual test pattern. *Beeeeeeeeeeeeep*. At the conference that invited an earlier version of this chapter, Gary Barwin's presentation on bpNichol included a playback of Nichol's extraordinarily long and beep-like intonation of the word "breathe," which I heard as uncannily like the reference tone.[32] One might say that Nichol's "breathe" shows how the breath is a symbolic and yet also real "reference tone" of life; however, one might also hear the reference tone as an echo of the morbid sound on an electrocardiogram monitor that signifies a flatlining patient. What a coincidence that the sound followed mention of Layton's "little talk about death"! The reference tone also reminds me of those late nights and early mornings, now seemingly far in the past, when there was nothing on TV, as in nothing being broadcast except for a test pattern. Today, "nothing on TV" is only figurative; television is always on – "on demand" – with no off-air times and no beginning or end except to individual programs. There was an irony, therefore, to hearing the reference tone in the middle of the show. It was, if not also a ghostly and floating signifier, an ambiguous sign. The reference tone is a standard of comparison for sound, just as the test pattern is for colour and sharpness. It is an auditory benchmark and mark of stability, but it does little to balance me when an archival *viewing* transforms into an almost purely *auditory* experience of uncanny disorientation – a moment when, without images, there is confusion about what will come next and when.

This breaking for commercial was also poignant, given Layton's future confusion in his old age. Derrida claims that "the archive should *call into question* the coming of the future,"[33] and that it is "not … a question of the past"[34] (author emphasis). When I am in Layton's archives, I always remember that he died after a prolonged experience of dementia and memory loss. I am thinking back from my time in the archives to Layton's death, but I am also thinking ahead from the date of Layton's text to his future death.[35] His late-life memory loss is in my mind even though on *City Lights*, in 1978, Layton was a youthful sixty-six and unquestionably sharp – until the second commercial break. This time, there is mic crackle or fabric noise, and Layton's voice returns first, without an image. We hear him ask his host, in a voice almost timid compared to his persona's clarion timbre, "Is this a half an hour program?" The host answers, "I think we're going to go on, if you will," and then the mic cuts out. In the two minutes of silence and darkness that followed, I wondered when the voices with their images would return, and I *felt* more than understood that Layton and I were both disoriented, *lost in time*. Perhaps I exaggerate; Osborne admits the possibility that archival reason or method is to "[seek] out the obscure detail or the uninteresting fact," but he counters that discovering the mundane is "a distinctive way of making visible the question of power itself."[36] Although Layton seemed to be driving the conversation at the start of the show, we see – no, we *hear* – that Linehan is making the decision (under the guise of a hospitable question) to exploit Layton's potential to draw, grab, and hold an audience. Then, surprise, we're back to the show – but not before the uncannily disembodied voices, the eavesdropping, and the aura of an unscripted and unedited moment combine to leave me thinking I had heard something special.

One reason it is special is that it was an *automatic* transition from public to private realms, a transition that was not voluntary for me or, presumably, for Layton and Linehan and the others present with them. When the video advances into the commercial break, it moves me from the archive of public records to the archive of private records, and, given the expectation that either commercials or the return to the show is imminent, I had no reason to stop watching and listening. In print archives, an item such as a personal letter that is mistakenly included among public records is sometimes classified as an "estray" or "fugitive" item.[37] When such an item is found, a donor may be alerted, and repositioning of the item is decided upon. If I were to find it, I might be able to discern its comparatively private nature simply by the enclosure of the document itself (a perfumed envelope, for example), and I could choose after deliberation not to open it. Although movies and TV are textual in the secondary senses of the word, watching television and film inside or outside the archive differs from reading text because the temporality, the pace, is decided by the director and the propulsive nature of the medium. If you have a recording, you can press "stop" and think, but the default is to continue. In the textual archive, you must decide and act to continue. Prescott asks whether "archives have a distinctive textuality which marks them apart" from other collections of texts, and he concludes (more confidently than I would) that the answer "has to be 'no.' Archives are texts (with all the complications, significations and difficulties implied by that term) like any other texts."[38] Their textuality means that "the use of techniques more generally associated with literary criticism can result in a far richer engagement with the cultural world of the historic text."[39] I generally agree with this assessment, but the temporality of the *motion picture archive* suggests that a distinction should be made between the flow of archived temporal-media artifacts and the relative stasis of those in print archives. Archives of television, film, and radio – media that might record outtakes, bloopers, unscripted dialogue, and other fugitive items and then present them automatically – therefore pose a problem. Should an archivist be expected to cut or otherwise edit the unintended recordings and store the parts separately? Or do we assume that Layton and Linehan have, in effect, signed a waiver by participating in such a public medium?[40] Does the same assumption apply to cameraman Andreas Blackwell? In my little example, on the surface, Layton and Linehan reveal nothing that is personal in their unscripted dialogue, but they could have said something much less innocuous, and the archival record could have automatically revealed unwitting indiscretion, thereby placing responsibility upon whoever discovered it.

Such discovery is potentially ethical and moral, but for me on this occasion it was affective and experiential. Chris McRae, listening with his eyes closed to a recording of a famous 1964 Miles Davis concert at the Philharmonic Hall in New York City, says, "I may as well be in the Philharmonic Hall with my eyes closed. Listening. Feeling."[41] When I stare at a black screen, waiting for something to happen, and then listen to voices I was not meant to hear, I am transported behind the scenes, behind the seen, and share a moment of disorientation with Layton.

The experiential nature of this archival find evokes another concept related to archives: the aura. Antoinette Burton's *Archive Stories* (2005) is meant "to begin to diffuse the aura which now more than ever surrounds the notion of 'real' archives"[42] in contrast with archives that are virtual, oral, or otherwise unconventional. This diffusion could be accomplished by opening up the concept of either the archive or the aura. This chapter has already described some of the ways in which our understanding of the archive has changed because of televisual and Internet technologies, but the auratic dimension of the archive warrants further consideration, too. McRae asks, "Can I return to the performance through recordings and archives?"[43] He argues that it is possible to "listen for aura" by "listening for ... disruptions as potentially meaningful and instructive performative moments"; he claims to "hear the possibility for applying this concept of aura, what [Walter] Benjamin refers to as a unique quality of presence held by an aesthetic phenomenon, to the unlikely example of a recorded music performance."[44] I wonder if Layton's exchange with Linehan during the commercial break counts, especially as a kind of "disruption" of a performance. It is not in itself a performance, nor was it intended as performance, but it does feature a celebrity accustomed to performing, and it evokes the happy accidents that make individual performances special. It also has the thrill of the backstage experience, which is exciting to fans because it can be unscripted and seemingly authentic. Like his homophonic "I/eyewitness," Layton's off-camera question invites questions and our own answers, and our participation through interpretation and transcription can be auratic. His off-camera question is also exactly the type of material one looks for in the archives: something unpublished or, in this case, unscripted and unseen. To the active listener, it has an illusion of aura, which is not experientially different from aura itself.

I know that I am implicated in, partly responsible for, the aura I am finding in Layton's unscripted moments not exactly *on* television but *off*. Active listeners and scholars in mass-media archives act as fans, seeking the rare moment of personal meaning and interpretive power in any text that has a private side – whether the unpublished material or the accidental recording, the side that the public cannot usually see. Solitary listening only emphasizes the sense of privacy, and, like privacy, restricted access makes archives special. I know, too, that I might be thought of as a conservative critic by drawing attention to privacy and valorizing the sometimes-restricted area of the archive, but there is a more flexible attitude at work in my thinking of the archive as a performative space. A mass-media archive seems inevitably performative; any demonstration of its contents will involve performance. When McRae asks (as quoted above) whether he can "return to the performance through recordings and archives," he implies that the answer is "yes." This may be, but perhaps the answer to this question is determined by the conditions informing our encounter with the archival record of the event. The event, as Jason Camlot and Katherine McLeod explain in the introduction to this book, "is the unreachable element that incites desire and hope in the researcher," what might be compared to the Lacanian *petit objet a*, the inciting of desire. The various political positions implied by these conflicting desires seem to corroborate the Foucauldian theory of the archive as an idealized space, one that is not easy to realize.

The archiving of television is like the production of movies available for home purchase on the format of the day, with all their behind-the-scenes footage, outtakes, blooper reels, and director's commentaries; however, archived television differs because such moments have not been selected by a producer. To the extent that visitors to the archive control their own experiences of playback, these visitors become the producers, or reproducers. Without such control, they are on a roller coaster through that "haunted house," subject to the thrilling or chilling affect of the mass-media archive. Partly for this reason, we cannot, and might not want to, bring all those moments home with us. Most of them are stored, not complete but substantially so, only in the privacy of their own home, the archive, which remains a crucial place despite the connective technology of the Internet. When we look back at Layton after considering all of these changes in accessing past recordings of television, Layton might be a face on the screen and, at the same time, a voice of publicity whose style and experience as a literary celebrity can help us understand the continuing reconceptualization of the archive.

NOTES

1   Irving Layton, *The Pierre Berton Show,* CBC Television, item AT02, digital file-name AT02 64 01, Irving Layton fonds, Concordia University Libraries Special Collections, Concordia University, Montreal, 1964.

2   He said, more fully, "I am in a sense writing a public poetry or reading a public poetry because it's easy to understand the public I witness [or 'eyewitness']. I can throw in a couple of jokes and make them laugh." Although he did not say much more about the public here, he seemed to be disparaging the public for their superficiality, turning their scrutinizing gaze back upon themselves. Further details about this quotation and its broadcast, though not the homophone, can be found in an essay of mine, "Irving Layton's Televised 'Public Poetry' and *The Pierre Berton Show," Canadian Poetry: Studies, Documents, Reviews* 73 (2013): 32–53.

3   Thomas Osborne, "The Ordinariness of the Archive," *History of the Human Sciences* 12.2 (1999): 55.

4   Julia Noordegraaf writes more about the distinction between television and archival television: "Once broadcasting materials enter the archive, they lose their *liveness* and their connection to the home as viewing space." Julia Noordegraaf, "Who Knows Television? Online Access and the Gatekeepers of Knowledge," *Critical Studies in Television* 5.2 (2010): 5. Furthermore, to describe television that is preserved only as audio, Phil Gries uses the term "archival television" as I do; it is "illustrated radio with the visuals left to our imagination." Phil Gries, "Archival Television Audio: Surviving Television Broadcast Soundtracks Representing Lost TV Programs (1946–1972)," ARSC *Journal* 41.2 (2010): 252.

5   Jason Jacobs, "The Television Archive: Past, Present, Future," *Critical Studies in Television* 1.1 (2006): 18.

6   In the late 1970s, Layton commented at least a few times on TV that filmmak-

ers were the new poets. Peter Mallet produced a film in 1980, possibly made for TV, about Layton's reading and explaining Joseph Conrad's *Heart of Darkness*, though I don't know if it was ever released or aired; Layton later appeared in *Irving Layton: Poet* (1986) and in a short film that borrows the title of his poem "A Tall Man Executes a Jig" (1986). Earlier, Layton was pictured briefly in the NFB film *Ladies and Gentlemen... Mr Leonard Cohen* (1965).

7   Osborne, "Ordinariness," 56.

8   Jacques Derrida, "Archive Fever: A Freudian Impression," *Diacritics* 25.2 (1995): 10.

9   Osborne, "Ordinariness," 55–7.

10   Barton J. Bernstein, "A Plea for Opening the Door," in *Access to the Papers of Recent Public Figures: The New Harmony Conference,* ed. Alonzo L. Hamby and Edward Weldon (Bloomington: Organization of American Historians, 1977), 84.

11   Alonzo L. Hamby and Edward Weldon, "Introduction," in Hamby and Weldon, *Access to the Papers of Recent Public Figures,* 1. In the context of public officials in the United States, Barton J. Bernstein argues that some "categories of 'privacy' are dangerously broad" and that "public officials, especially the President, have already waived certain claims of 'privacy' by encouraging selective intrusions to create a useful public-political image. The press is inundated with pictures and 'news' of the official, with wife and children, all smiling and loving, attending church; or vacationing on the ski slopes; or receiving and "giving gifts." Bernstein, "A Plea for Opening the Door," 86, 87–8. Although Ondaatje has never invited such "intrusions" as far as I know, Layton has to some extent – as when he was happily photographed with his new wife Harriet Bernstein for *The Globe and Mail* in 1978 – and both are public figures (not "officials") who have donated their papers to public archives. Zena Cherry, "Poet Layton Marries Movie Publicist," *The Globe and Mail* (24 November 1978). Their writing is published, engages with concepts of privacy and publicity, and depends in part on the reputation or public recognition of the author, and so they must expect public interest – including scholarly interest – in their creative processes, including editorial work and correspondence with editors, agents, and mentors about their writing. Hamby suggests that, in addition to a right to know what private dealings our public officials might have, we "have a moral claim to the papers of public figures whose activities may have done much to determine the way we live and the kind of country we have." Alonzo L. Hamby, "Unseen Sources: A Historian's Dilemma," in Hamby and Weldon,

Access to the Papers of Recent Public Figures, 15. In the field of literature, do we also have a claim to the literature-related papers of public figures who have donated to public archives and whose activities might have influenced literature, culture, and, yes, even our country? Although it is against some of my interests, and although my work is often read as a debunking of privacy, I want to defend the concept even as I watch its remarkable retreat from the modern world.

12 Harriet Bradley, "The Seductions of the Archive: Voices Lost and Found," *History of the Human Sciences* 12.2 (1999): 110.

13 Joel Deshaye, *The Metaphor of Celebrity: Canadian Poetry and the Public, 1955–1980* (Toronto: University of Toronto Press, 2013), 23.

14 Bradley, "Seductions," 117.

15 Andrew Prescott, "The Textuality of the Archive," in *What Are Archives? Cultural and Theoretical Perspectives: A Reader*, ed. Louise Craven (Farnham, U.K.: Ashgate, 2008), 49.

16 Derrida, "Archive Fever," 13.

17 Bradley, "Seductions," 109.

18 Ibid.

19 Ibid., 110.

20 Bertrand Marotte, "The Electric Circus," *Ryerson Review of Journalism* (1 March 1985): Web, par. 2, https://rrj.ca/the-electric-circus/ (accessed 15 July 2016).

21 Vanessa Rodriguez, "Life of Brian," *Ryerson Review of Journalism* (16 March 2007): Web, par. 1, 15, https://rrj.ca/life-of-brian/ (accessed 15 July 2016).

22 I explain such identifications at length throughout my book, *The Metaphor of Celebrity*, one example being Gwendolyn MacEwen's identification with T.E. Lawrence.

23 Michel Foucault, "Of Other Spaces," trans. Jay Miskowiec, *Diacritics* 16.1 (1986): 27.

24 Prescott, "The Textuality of the Archive," 32.

25 Foucault mentions the archive only in passing in his "Other Spaces" lecture, and in greater depth in *The Archaeology of Knowledge* (1972) and "The Life of Infamous Men" (1979).

26 Irving Layton, *City Lights*, interviewer Brian Linehan, CBC TV, VT-06, Bay 14, Concordia University Special Collections, Montreal, 1978. Subsequent quotations from Layton and others on the program refer to this citation.

27 Rodriguez, "Life of Brian," par. 2.

28 Ibid., par. 56.

29 Jason Jacobs, "The Store of the Worlds: Television's Extraordinary Archives," *Journal of British Cinema and Television* 8.2 (2011): 185.

30 Ibid., 186.

31 Derrida, "Archive Fever," 55.

32 Gary Barwin, "From Archive to Newhive: Using Historical Recordings to Create *H for It Is a Pleasure and a Surprise To Breathe*," conference presentation, Can Lit Across Media Conference, Concordia University, Montreal, Quebec, 5 June 2015, n.p.

33 Derrida, "Archive Fever," 26.

34 Ibid., 27.

35 In his Freudian imagining of the archives, Derrida conceives of "the future *as ghost*." Ibid., 53.

36 Osborne, "Ordinariness," 59.

37 Philip P. Mason, "The Archivist's Responsibility to Researchers and Donors: A Delicate Balance," in Hamby and Weldon, *Access to the Papers of Recent Public Figures*, 31.

38 Prescott, "The Textuality of the Archive," 47.

39 Ibid.

40 See also Bernstein, "A Plea for Opening the Door," 87.

41 Chris McRae, "From 'All of Me' to 'All of You': Listening for Aura," *Cultural Studies-Critical Methodologies* 13.2 (2012): 123.

42 Antoinette Burton, "Introduction," in *Archive Stories: Facts, Fictions, and the Writing of History* (Durham: Duke University Press, 2005), 6.

43 McRae, "From 'All of Me' to 'All of You,'" 120.

44 Ibid., 115. McRae's example of "a recorded music performance" is ambiguously phrased. He probably meant "recorded musical performance," but he might have meant "performance of recorded music," and indeed he does treat the recording as the performance itself. At the Can Lit Across Media Conference (5–6 June 2015), Karl Jirgens wondered in one of the conversations whether the "unarchiving" of events could itself be performative, and he noted the storytelling elements of my talk. If unarchiving is a retelling of history, and especially if the history is of a performative medium such as television, then performative unarchiving is an appropriate concept.

10

Traces of a Feminist Literary Event
Women and Words, 1983

ANDREA BEVERLEY

It was called Women and Words, and, Brianne's friends said, it was
historic. A thousand women, boiling with ideas and energy and ire.
– Maureen Brownlee, *Loggers' Daughters*[1]

At the height of the second-wave feminist movement, a literary event called
"Women and Words/Les femmes et les mots" assembled an unprecedented
number of women writers, publishers, journalists, and academics in Vancouver, to discuss issues related to "women" and "writing" in Canada. This chapter considers the archived audiovisual recordings of Women and Words as
one way in which the conference resonates beyond the summer of 1983. We
might say that any literary event hopes to reverberate beyond its initial moment: event organizers anticipate impact. However, the women who organized Women and Words were especially intent on the idea that their event
would be generative in the long term. The recordings they produced were
part of that vision. In fact, the relatively extensive Women and Words
archive allows us to track the organizers' hopes for the event's impact, which
includes their aspirations for its audiovisual footage. In addition to describing the literary event itself and how its legacy has been characterized
in Canadian literary scholarship, this chapter focuses on how the women

behind Women and Words conceived of their own media archive-making. I argue for the importance of Women and Words in contemporary Canadian cultural history and anticipate future mobilizations of its audiovisual traces as potential extensions of the organizers' profound desire to create feminist communities and networks. In many ways, my project partakes of the long-standing feminist historical aim to recuperate under-represented voices while maintaining a healthy skepticism vis-à-vis the idea of an accessible, authentic past. Focusing on the recordings and on the archive enables a broader consideration of the processes and material conditions through which literary events are conceived, remembered, and mobilized across time.

The Women and Words fonds at Simon Fraser University contains a wide array of primary documents through which the Women and Words event can be ascertained. My analysis is informed by close reading of archival texts such as minutes of numerous organizing committee meetings, correspondence between organizers and participants (including invited writers), promotional materials in different forms (posters, pamphlets, press releases), grant applications for conference funding, post-conference feedback forms from attendees, transcriptions of conference recordings, receipts from sales of conference cassettes, and clippings of newspaper coverage of Women and Words. The archive also contains a decade's worth of material produced by the West Coast Women and Words Society (the organizing body of the conference) following the 1983 event, some of which harkens back to the conference. In addition to these archival documents, Women and Words can be reconstructed through its published outputs, namely an anthology and proceedings, and through its commemoration in interviews and literary critical texts. Intriguingly, it also figures in a recent creative text. In Maureen Brownlee's 2013 novel *Loggers' Daughters*, characters attend a fictional version of the Women and Words conference.[2] This is interesting in relation to the conference organizers' aspirations: fictionalization in a future novel is an output that they may not have anticipated. I begin and end this chapter with quotations from Brownlee's novel as a reminder that archives of literary events may be repurposed in unforeseeable ways. The idea that Women and Words can pop up unexpectedly in this manner so many decades later invites us to imagine what it might mean to remobilize the recordings from this literary event in equally creative ways.

Women and Words was an impressive feat. The organizing committee began formal meetings at least a year and a half before the actual conference.[3]

They officially registered as a non-profit organization called West Coast Women and Words Society in March 1982 and spent the next eighteen months amassing countless volunteer hours and $110,000.[4] Finally, the Women and Words/Les femmes et les mots conference took place in July 1983 in Vancouver on the campus of the University of British Columbia. The conference brought together approximately 900 women involved in literary activity in Canada; they were writers, journalists, publishers, and academics.[5] The schedule was full. From Thursday, 30 June, to Sunday, 3 July, there were forty-four panels and workshops, four literary readings (sixteen authors total), three short theatre pieces, and opening and closing plenary sessions. The workshops and panels made up the bulk of the programming. Well-known Canadian writers Margaret Atwood, Nicole Brossard, Maria Campbell, Marian Engel, Dorothy Livesay, and Carol Shields were among the specially invited session participants, of which there were 125.[6] Sessions were designed to cover a plethora of practical and theoretical concerns, with topics such as History of Feminist Presses and Magazines, Language and Language Theory in Women's Writing, Inadequate Coverage of Women's News, Writing and the Erotic, and Writing from a Native Woman's Perspective.

As Pauline Butling notes, Women and Words' "long term impact shows up in follow-up activities," some of which I will enumerate here.[7] While organizing the conference, the West Coast Women and Words Society was also putting together an anthology for which they received over a thousand submissions from 300 writers.[8] Following the conference, they published proceedings entitled *In the Feminine: Women and Words/Les femmes et les mots. Conference Proceedings.*[9] The conference site also provided a formative moment for the editorial collectives that went on to found the bilingual, feminist periodical *Tessera* and enact the feminist reinvention of the journal *CV2.*[10] Additionally, Women and Words was the catalyst for the West Word Summer Writing Workshop for Women, which ran from 1985 to 1993. In fact, the West Coast Women and Words Society was active in organizing readings, fundraisers, and other one-off projects (such as a project for Vancouver's centennial) until their dissolution in 1998. In short, Women and Words was a touchstone cultural moment with significant effects[11] due to the content it generated, the collaborations it fostered, and the impact it had on individual attendees.[12]

Smaro Kamboureli's recent theorizations of change within the field of Canadian literature provide vocabulary through which to understand the significance of events like Women and Words as well as the contemporary scholarly interest in such events. Kamboureli identifies a primary feature of contemporary Canadian literary scholarship to be its tendency to "circumvent the literary" in critical acts of "outward mobility," analyzing what lies "beyond the discipline's purview as proper subject."[13] My chapter is a case in point and is akin to current research on literature-related conferences such as investigations of the 1994 Writing Thru Race conference,[14] Pauline Butling and Susan Rudy's charting of poetic events in *Writing in Our Time*, my previous research on the 1988 Telling It conference,[15] McTavish's film documentary on the 1963 Vancouver Poetry Conference, and Jason Camlot's and Karis Shearer's work on the 1963 Foster Poetry Conference and 1963 Vancouver Poetry Conference, respectively.[16] There are undoubtedly a number of other critical interventions that could be added to this list, as well as conferences and events yet to be rediscovered. Some of these sites may constitute what Kamboureli calls "emergent events" that are "operating as nodal points."[17] She notes that change within the field of Canadian literature has not been a sudden paradigm shift. Rather, change has occurred over time as the cumulative outcome of "events that exemplify the emergence of different ways of knowing."[18] Recalling such events as "nodes" emphasizes the fluctuating network formations in which they participate as well as their unique, uneven temporal positionings.[19] Specific sites that may or may not be noticed by the discipline itself pop up here and there over time, involve different intersecting communities, have both noticeable and invisible ripple-like effects, and eventually (in a non-progressivist way) lead to change in the larger discourse of Canadian literature.[20]

Kamboureli names Women and Words (in which she participated) as an example of an "emergent event."[21] She specifically notes its impact on growing feminist, Indigenous, and anti-racist perspectives, reminding readers that "if the iteration of gender, race, and ethnicity has long reached the point of operating virtually as a cliché, a strategy (in part) of scholarly accountability, it was not too long ago when these categories of subjugated subjectivities were relegated entirely outside university culture and critical discourses, and in the margins of the social realm."[22] Other critical texts also flag Women and Words as an important early venue for the articulation of intersectionality.[23] Some of the contemporaneous newspaper coverage of the conference specifically highlighted the contributions of women writers of colour. For instance, Jane Rule published an article in the *Globe and Mail* entitled

"Writer's Conference Recognizes Natives" and Dorothy Livesay's account suggested that "the most stimulating accent heard at the conference was that of our Native women and recent immigrants from the West Indies."[24] It is clear from the archives that the conference organizing committee did hope to offer a platform for marginalized women. Post-conference feedback reports from attendees contain comments akin to Livesay's above.[25] This is not to suggest that the conference *exemplified* profound diversity and took *tremendous* strides toward anti-racist feminist action in Canada. As Kamboureli reminds us, change in Canadian literary spheres generally results *not* from tremendous strides but from the "ripple effect" or "the impetus such emergent moments create to cross different thresholds"[26] among those for whom the emergent event has been "an unquiet force."[27] As an example, Kamboureli asserts that the contributions related to race and Indigeneity made by Makeda Silvera and Maria Campbell at Women and Words constitute "interventional gestures that, along with other things, gradually created the conditions that made possible ground-breaking events like the Writing Thru Race conference and changes in the field at large."[28]

While some retrospective mentions of Women and Words refer specifically to its discussions of intersectionality, or "double colonization,"[29] others reference it more generally as one example of the feminist poetics of the time.[30] Women and Words was certainly not an isolated event; Kamboureli's nodal imagery reminds us to conceive of it as one intersection point among many. The 1980s were punctuated by memorable conferences that addressed women's writing in Canada. For example, the Dialogue Conference at York University in 1981 resulted in the notable publication *Gynocritics: Feminist Approaches to Canadian and Quebec Women's Writing*, in which Barbara Godard first surveyed the country's feminist literary criticism.[31] I have already mentioned the 1988 Telling It conference, evoked as "the first conference to address the intersections of gender, race, and sexuality."[32] The following year, the Third International Feminist Book Fair in Montreal left its mark in turn, as a "watershed in feminist cultural politics."[33] Conjuring this lively period also means discussing the interactions and collaborations between Québécoise women writers and women writers outside Quebec in relation to feminist language theory. The title of the Women and Words published proceedings – *In the Feminine* – gestures toward the "writing in the feminine" and "écriture au féminin" movements at the heart of those collaborations.[34] Introductory remarks in the proceedings highlight the papers that "bring the news from

Quebec, where women writers and critics have been performing a detailed feminist analysis of language, in the process uncovering new forms for the expression of women's experiences."[35] Thus, some retrospective comments on Women and Words focus on its importance for "writing in the feminine" since the conference was a venue at which many English-speaking women writers encountered Quebec feminist language theory for the first time.[36]

In sum, we can assert that critical texts that mention Women and Words position it in relation to histories of women's writing, feminist poetics, and/or intersectionality, which is not to forget the first-person accounts of individuals' personal experiences of the conference. Pauline Butling's summation of Women and Words notes all of the above, mentioning participants' "radical feminist texts," discussion by women writers of colour, and the presence of Québécois feminist theorists.[37] Later on, in *Writing in Our Time*, Butling offers a more personal take on Women and Words. She recalls feeling buoyed up, encouraged, humbled, inspired, empowered, and launched.[38] My intention here is not to confirm or canonize the characteristics for which Women and Words has been remembered, nor do I suggest that Women and Words is famous and lauded near and far. On the contrary, many of the critical texts mentioned above refer to the conference only in passing, rarely devoting more than a few sentences to it. But the references are there, providing evidence that this feminist literary event did move beyond its initial temporality with "ripple effect."[39]

In an interview on teaching about poetic events, Karis Shearer, like Kamboureli, uses the image of the ripple to describe the effects of Women and Words, the Vancouver Poetry Conference, and the Long-liners Conference, the three events on her syllabus. She notes that, "those 'brief' events produced so many texts, so many ripples and possible lineages that could be followed up on."[40] The archives clearly demonstrate that the organizers of Women and Words always anticipated that the event would be more than a three-day phenomenon; "ripples" and "lineages" were part of their raison d'être. This was not merely an event to "celebrate" women's writing, but an event intended to foster collaboration and change among and for women writers.[41] In planning documents, the organizers repeatedly name the creation of networks as a key outcome for the 1983 event. The very first "report" on the conference idea dates from March 1982 and states, under "Concept of Conference," that they seek not only to "bring together" women but to "build an effective system of communication" with the conference acting as a "foundation for this network."[42] Consequently, the official constitutional documents of the West Coast Women and Words Society articulate one of the society's "purposes" as being "to establish and maintain a network of communications between and among women concerned and/or connected with women's writing."[43] In a mail-out to invited participants, the organizers specify that they have designed the conference program in part to "build cross-field information and network support."[44] In a media release, this is articulated as "develop[ing] a resource network from coast to coast."[45] Clearly the conference organizers hoped to birth a pan-Canadian, feminist "textual community," to borrow a phrase from Danielle Fuller, who uses the term to delineate communities that form around texts and are concerned with writing, editing, publishing, and "the way textual practices are valued."[46] The conference was meant to catalyze this textual community, the West Coast Women and Words Society could sustain it over time, and the myriad ripples were its manifestations. An exuberant December 1982 letter from the Women and Words office proclaims, "the society is already an effective networking agency, with many possibilities in the future."[47]

Yet despite the clear intention to be *more than* a one-off event, and despite the many *textual* traces of Women and Words mentioned above, it still matters that there was an actual gathering of hundreds and hundreds of women in July 1983. As I have argued elsewhere (in relation to the founding of the Feminist Caucus of the League of Canadian Poets), revisiting foundational events in Canadian women's writing involves taking into account lived/remembered moments of affective, in-person community.[48] As Shearer points out, the "highly collaborative and performative" nature of poetic events means that they will inevitably "always exceed any ability to document them."[49] But we do have relatively extensive documentation about the Women and Words conference, including audiovisual recordings of the event. This medium (of recorded footage) necessarily documents the event in a different way than the proceedings, photos, or minutes that emerged from that weekend. They are extra-textual and unprocessed in their unedited state.[50] In the remainder of this chapter, I turn my attention to these recordings, focusing in particular on the committee's decision to record the events, the dissemination of the recorded material immediately following the conference, and the potential for the recordings to be unarchived today.

The idea of recording Women and Words was present from the outset of conference organizing.[51] By June 1982, a year before Women and Words, the conference programming committee recommended to the larger group that the conference be taped.[52] Eventually, a subcommittee under the productions committee was devoted to organizing the technical aspects of recording and photographing the event.[53] This, like the conference itself, was an ambitious endeavour. Women and Words hired three students through a $7,000 Canada Summer Jobs program grant to be in charge of recording the conference, transcribing select sessions, and compiling a list of tapes that would be available post-conference.[54] Women and Words also reached out to relevant organizations in a collaborative move that took them beyond their own textual community. They contacted artist-run centre Western Front, feminist arts and media centre Women in Focus, local co-op radio, local TV station CKVU, and the National Film Board (NFB) to garner interest in recording and/or disseminating audiovisual material from the conference.[55]

Though there is evidence that some organizers questioned the decision to record ("it might have an inhibiting effect on the participants"), the task seems to have been integrated into the overall plan from its inception.[56] Who did they imagine as the audience for this footage and through what platform would that audience access it? In the Canadian Women in the Literary Arts Google Group post that alerted me to the existence of this archive, Maureen Brownlee mentioned that the conference organizers had initially hoped that Women and Words would result in a documentary film; hence the contact with the NFB, which was at one point "interested enough to take a look at the project."[57] Though there were plans in 1992 to produce a documentary on Women and Words that would incorporate ten-year-old footage from the event, I have not yet found evidence that the videotapes were ever used post-conference.[58] Some of the audiotapes, however, were edited and disseminated right after the 1983 event, on the radio and through tape sales, which I discuss in more detail below. Overall, the audio and audiovisual representations of Women and Words were meant to benefit those who were not in attendance. Men constituted one such group. When certain (male) voices in the Canadian public sphere complained about being barred from the conference, the Women and Words organizers responded to their complaints in part by inviting them to access recordings after the fact.[59]

The decision to exclude men from Women and Words was controversial among the Women and Words organizers and controversial in the media. Well before the conference, the Women and Words team debated whether or not men should be admitted to fundraising events. For instance, when the fundraising committee suggested a women-only dance to the project committee, there was enough disagreement about the women-only aspect that they decided to bring the decision to a larger, general meeting.[60] In relation to the conference itself, the issue of men's involvement surfaces repeatedly in meeting minutes over the summer of 1982, as at a June meeting when "Mens [*sic*] involvement was discussed, whether or not and how much if at all. no [*sic*] conclusion was reached."[61] At a meeting in early August 1982, organizers were split over five different ideas of how to handle men's attendance, ranging from "conference open at all times to men, except when inappropriate to specific programming" to men being welcome during "evening programming only."[62] A decision was made by vote in late August to allow men to attend public evening events but not daytime conference programming.[63] By February 1983, this decision had been fully integrated: even the presence of a "male technician" as part of a national media crew had to meet with prior approval from the workshop facilitators and panelists.[64]

In media coverage of Women and Words, the women-only decision met with some scorn, in response to which the recordings became a tool of refutation. A *Vancouver Gazette* report on the conference quotes Betsy Warland explaining that men were excluded from the programming in order to "'maximize exchange between women.' Warland noted that anyone interested would be allowed tapings of the conference."[65] This possibility did nothing to reassure Max Wyman who, in an article entitled "Word from the Women Is Clear: Men Aren't Wanted," stated, "I don't really care that audio and video tapes will be made of the proceedings as an archive, and will be available eventually to anyone who wants to consult them. Or that there are also plans to publish a book. None of that compensates for not being able to be there to witness the interplay of lively individual minds on important issues; and to watch ideas grow."[66] Other journalists were similarly offended: Frank Jones of the *Toronto Star* opined that the women-only decision was a blow to freedom of the press and an example of "the kind of sexual hostility being fostered by women's studies programs."[67] Such responses call to mind the media coverage of the 1994 Writing Thru Race conference, an event that limited some programming to Indigenous writers and writers of colour.[68] Without diminishing the particularities of each conference and context, I am pointing out that these textual communities organized conferences whose enrolment restrictions met with mediatized controversy and scandal. Of course there were, in both instances, rebuttals to these critiques and subsequent scholarly historicization and theorization of each.[69] At the time of Women and Words, letters to the editor in direct reference to Wyman's complaints were published under the headline "Women-only rule was proven right."[70] Marian Engel, as a guest columnist for the *Toronto Star*, published an article entitled "Words flowed freely without men" days after the conference. "Was it right to leave out men? I think so," Engel writes. "The emphasis was feminist and the reporters who are sent to cover feminist events are often sent to fight them. More important is the fact that without a male presence the sessions were frank, free and open."[71]

Whatever we think of Women and Words' decision to limit participation to women, it is clear that the recordings were a small element of public rebuttal to naysayers. The idea, so vehemently rejected by Wyman, was that people who could not (for whatever reason) attend the conference might want to access it through recordings. For this reason, the Women and Words conference proceedings includes a list of eleven audiotapes for sale, as managed by the Women and Words "Audio Tape Sales Committee."[72] Though the group might have hoped to garner some extra income from the sales, they were warned that selling cassettes would not be lucrative.[73] Records in the archives indicate that thirty-seven tapes were sent out to about twenty different individuals between November 1983 and December 1985.[74] At least four of these individuals acquired the recordings on behalf of institutions: the publishing house les Éditions de la Pleine Lune, the Kermode Friendship Society, the Metro Toronto Library Board, and the archives of the VOICES for Lesbian Survival. While it is possible that there were tape sales without archival traces, it seems more likely that Women and Words simply did not receive many more orders for their tapes.[75]

Though the distribution of these recordings was not extensive, these transactions remain intriguing in the context of considering the traces of the literary event. It is compelling to imagine these recordings arriving at their various destinations, as if downloaded into households, organizations, or libraries, their subsequent impact difficult to quantify since we do not know who listened to them or how they responded. The introduction to the Women and Words conference proceedings obliquely suggests that the contents of the audiovisual recordings differ significantly from the written outputs: "Many of the oral presentations, while covering important ground and provoking lively discussion, did not translate well onto the written page ... Some workshops were too specific or practical to appeal to a wide audience; others were very personal in nature, intended for a much more intimate setting than the pages of this book."[76] This comment is meant to explain why the proceedings cannot document the totality of conference content. It is similar to an underlying point in Camlot's and Shearer's analyses of the 1963 conferences and in Wyman's complaint: accessing text or media that ostensibly captures a literary event is not the same as participating, nor is it the same as reading written outputs. There are differences among the content of the live event, the recordings, and the text, as well as differences among the experiences of attending, listening, watching, or reading. A further layer involves realizing that in the case of Women and Words, even the noun "recordings" falsely implies a cohesive, definitive set of audiovisual materials. In reality, there were different types of original recordings that have been transcribed (for proceedings), duplicated (to disseminate), edited and remixed (for radio), earmarked for future commemorative endeavours (film or TV), and archived (for preservation).

This many years later, the Simon Fraser University Library Special Collections and Rare Books holds boxes of videotapes and cassettes not only of the July 1983 conference but also of other West Coast Women and Words Society events. Indeed, the idea that recordings would be archived is explicit even on the consent forms that participants were asked to sign.[77] "The Women and Words videotapes will be archival material," proclaim the minutes from a meeting held a few weeks after the conference.[78] Multimedia recordings can be difficult to access within archival settings, given the speed of technological change, and limited institutional budgets for digitization or for the upkeep of older machines. For that reason, media archeology labs that maintain functioning obsolete hardware and software become indispensable[79] unless archived media are systematically migrated onto ever-renewing formats and platforms (and "the migration [would] continue so long as we care about these semi-tangible artefacts of cultural heritage"[80]). But the potential for the Women and Words recordings to be usefully unarchived is great. In their introduction to this book, Camlot and McLeod propose the verb "unarchive" to describe the possible mobilization of media traces of literary events, and in chapter 5, Catherine Hobbs suggests that archival material is repurposed in the present. Methodologies of unarchiving (Camlot and McLeod), repurposing (Hobbs), or "unarresting" (Morra)[81] are not rooted in any naïve desire to construct a real, true, complete, authentic story from the past. Yet, it is true that the Women and Words recordings will enhance our contemporary knowledge of the event by providing us with *more* and *different* material than that which was textualized. For example, during my most recent visit to the Women and Words archive, I listened to a 1983 recording of eminent professor and biographer Patricia Morley leading a workshop on traditions and new directions of Canadian women writers. This workshop does not appear in any form in the published conference proceedings, nor does another discussion I listened to on "Creating Alternative Structures: Mentors, Networks, Reading/Writing Support Groups." The latter showcased conference co-organizer Victoria Freeman describing the obstacles encountered by the Women and Words founders as they sought support for the event. The content of these two cassettes represents a small percentage of Women and Words' audiovisual materials waiting to be unarchived.

Beyond increasing our collective understanding of what happened at this landmark event, unarresting the audiovisuals of Women and Words is also appealing because of what Camlot calls the "certain degree of magic" inherent in recordings of live events.[82] Without glorifying or idealizing recordings, we might still assert their capacity to transmit some of the vibe, tension, energy, affect, and tone of the moment. The atmosphere at Women and Words was reportedly quite memorable. According to Jane Rule's report, "the audience is what made this conference not just another academic exercise … Increasingly the audience took over the discussion periods with an energy which grew as the hours passed."[83] Maureen Brownlee's literary representation of Women and Words in her novel also attributes a unique vibe to the conference. Adare, the protagonist of *Loggers' Daughters*, has "never experienced such extraordinary exuberance."[84] It is "electric" and "exhilarating."[85] In Brownlee's fictionalized version of Women and Words, characters wonder at the dynamism of the event. In the novel, the conference also figures as part of the plot line involving Adare's relationship to her daughter and both of their relationships to feminism. This evokes the generational tropes (waves, mothers/daughters) often used to discuss feminist history. The question of representing connections between present, past, and future feminisms echoes the question of what we *do* with archival traces. The overlap lies in the assertion that neither have to do with wholesale rejections nor linear reconstitutions of past originary moments. Reactivated, the Women and Words recordings will augment our understanding of that

1983 event. But their unarresting will also then inhabit our present moment and produce ripples across generations that we have yet to imagine, like the novel that emerged in part from Brownlee's own archival visit. In other words, a remediated mobilization of the priceless original footage from Women and Words would further our understanding of this groundbreaking event, extend the conference organizers' fierce desire for impact, and intervene across generations in our historical present. The audiovisual traces of this feminist literary event are therefore both waiting to be embraced and ready to be repurposed.

Acknowledgments

For their contributions to this essay, I would like to thank my colleagues at Mount Allison University, the Mount Allison University President's Research and Creative Activities Fund, the librarians and archivists at Simon Fraser University Library's Special Collections and Rare Books, and the organizers and participants of the Can Lit Across Media conference. This research was supported by the Social Sciences and Humanities Research Council of Canada.

NOTES

1   Maureen Brownlee, *Loggers' Daughters* (Fernie, BC: Oolichan Books, 2013), 196.

2   In fact, I was alerted to the existence of the Women and Words fonds at SFU through a comment that Brownlee posted on a Canadian Women in the Literary Arts GoogleGroups online discussion thread.

3   "The Westcoast Women and Words Society." Box 1, Folder 3, Women and Words fonds, Simon Fraser University Special Collections and Rare Books Library, Vancouver, BC, 16 June 2015. (Hereafter referred to as: W&W fonds, SFU Special Collections and Rare Books Library.)

4   Joan Meister, Letter to Registrar of Companies, 23 March 1982. Box 1, File 3, W&W fonds, SFU Special Collections and Rare Books Library, Vancouver, BC, 16 June 2015.

5   This number is indeed approximate. The conference proceedings peg attendance at "over 1000." Ann Dybikowski, et al., eds., *In the Feminine: Women*

and Words/Les femmes et les mots. Conference Proceedings (Edmonton: Longspoon, 1985), 9. The anthology states "over 800." West Coast, "Preface," in *Women and Words: The Anthology/Les Femmes et les mots: Une anthologie,* ed. West Coast Editorial Collective (Madeira Park: Harbour Publishing, 1984), n.p. The attendance undoubtedly surpassed the organizers' initial expectations: at a committee meeting in September 1982, they planned for 500 attendees. "Programme Committee Minutes," 1, 17 September 1982. Box 1, File 4, W&W fonds, SFU Special Collections and Rare Books Library, Vancouver, BC, 16 June 2015.

6 Jane Rule, "Writer's Conference Recognizes Natives," *The Globe and Mail* (9 July 1983): E14.

7 Pauline Butling, "Who Is She? Inside/Outside Literary Communities," in *Writing in Our Time: Canada's Radical Poetries in English (1957–2003),* ed. Pauline Butling and Susan Rudy (Waterloo: Wilfrid Laurier University Press, 2005), 154.

8 West Coast, "Preface," n.p.

9 Dybikowski et al., *In the Feminine.*

10 Daphne Marlatt, Interview by Heather Milne, in *Prismatic Publics: Innovative Canadian Women's Poetry and Poetics,* ed. Kate Eichhorn and Heather Milne (Toronto: Coach House Books, 2009), 245; Kathy Mezei, "*Tessera,* Feminist Literary Theory in English-Canadian and Quebec Literature, and the Practice of Translation as Betrayal, Exchange, Interpretation, Invention, Transformation, and Creation," in *Mapping Literature: The Art and Politics of Translation,* ed. David Homel and Sherry Simon (Montreal: Véhicule Press, 1988), 48; Butling, "Who Is She?" 154.

11 Anne-Marie Wheeler, "Issues of Translation in the Works of Nicole Brossard," *Yale Journal of Criticism* 16.2 (2003): 425; Larissa Lai, "Corrupted Lineage: Narrative in the Gaps of History," *West Coast Line* 34.3 (2001): 40.

12 For instance, Di Brandt describes her experience of Women and Words in the following terms: "It was like a dream for me, being there at all, meeting so many Canadian women writers. Feminism was no longer an idea but a group of women talking, working together. It was like a dream, the beginning of feeling connected to other writers, women, becoming part of a women's community." Di Brandt, "Letting the Silence Speak," in *Language in Her Eye: Views on Writing and Gender by Canadian Women Writing in English,* ed. Libby Scheier, Sarah Sheard, and Eleanor Wachtel (Toronto: Couch House Press, 1990), 55.

13 Smaro Kamboureli, "Shifting the Ground of a Discipline: Emergence and

Canadian Literary Studies in English," in *Shifting the Ground of Canadian Literary Studies*, ed. Smaro Kamboureli and Robert Zacharias (Waterloo: Wilfrid Laurier University Press, 2012), 1, 14,

14 Smaro Kamboureli, *Scandalous Bodies: Diasporic Bodies in Canadian Literature* (Waterloo: Wilfrid Laurier University Press, 2009); Larissa Lai, *Slanting I, Imagining We: Asian-Canadian Literary Production in the 1980s and 1990s* (Waterloo: Wilfrid Laurier University Press, 2014); Scott McFarlane, "The Haunt of Race: Canada's Multiculturalism Act, the Politics of Incorporation, and Writing Thru Race," *Fuse Magazine* 18.3 (1995): 18–31.

15 Andrea Beverley, "The Oral, the Archive, and Ethics: Canadian Women Writers Telling It," in *Basements and Attics: Explorations in the Materiality and Ethics of Canadian Women's Archives*, ed. Linda Morra and Jessica Schagerl (Waterloo: Wilfrid Laurier University Press, 2012), 153–66.

16 Jason Camlot, "Le Foster Poetry Conference (1963)," *Voix et images* 40.2 (Winter 2015): 59–75.

17 Kamboureli, "Shifting," 16, 26.

18 Ibid., 10.

19 Ibid., 11, 26.

20 Christl Verduyn, "Critical Allegiances," in *Critical Collaborations: Indigeneity, Diaspora, and Ecology in Canadian Literary Studies*, ed. Smaro Kamboureli and Christl Verduyn (Waterloo: Wilfrid Laurier University Press, 2014), 228–30.

21 Kamboureli, "Shifting," 10; Kamboureli, "In the Second Person," in *Women and Words: The Anthology/Les Femmes et les mots: Une anthologie*, ed. West Coast Editorial Collective. (Madeira Park: Harbour Publishing, 1984), 81–3; Kamboureli, "Dialogue with the Other: The Use of Myth in Canadian Women's Poetry," in Dybikowski, *In the Feminine*, 105–9.

22 Kamboureli, "Shifting," 15; 25, 273fn18.

23 Daniel Coleman and Donald Goellnicht, "Introduction: 'Race' into the Twenty-first Century," *Essays on Canadian Writing* 75 (2002): 11–12; Myrna Kostash, Interview by Margery Fee, Sneja Gunew, and Lisa Grekul, "Myrna Kostash: Ukrainian Canadian Non-fiction Prairie New Leftist Feminist Canadian Nationalist," *Canadian Literature* 172 (2002): 125; Daphne Marlatt, "Introduction: Meeting on Fractured Margins," in *Telling It: Women and Language across Cultures*, ed. The Telling It Book Collective (Vancouver: Press Gang Publishers, 1990), 16; Enoch Padolsky, "Ethnicity and Race: Canadian Minority Writing at a Crossroads," *Journal of Canadian Studies* 31.3 (1996): 139.

24 Dorothy Livesay, "The Talking Women." Box 3, File 19, W&W fonds, SFU Special Collections and Rare Books Library, Vancouver, BC, 16 June 2015. This is a photocopy of an article that seems to have been published in *B.C. Gulfways* in July 1983.

25 Linda Hale and Dorothy Kidd, "Report on Conference Evaluations," 28 September 1983. Box 4, File 6, W&W fonds, SFU Special Collections and Rare Books Library, Vancouver, BC, 16 June 2015.

26 Kamboureli, "Shifting," 10.

27 Ibid., 12.

28 Ibid., 273fn18.

29 Pauline Butling, "(Re)Defining Radical Poetics," in *Writing in Our Time: Canada's Radical Poetries in English (1957–2003)*, ed. Pauline Butling and Susan Rudy (Waterloo: Wilfrid Laurier University Press, 2005), 25.

30 Alessandra Capperdoni, "Voyage autour de la traduction: The Translator as Writer and Theorist," in *Trans/Acting Culture Writing, and Memory: Essays in Honour of Barbara Godard*, ed. Eva C. Karpinski, Jennifer Henderson, Ian Sowton, and Ray Ellenwood (Waterloo: Wilfrid Laurier University Press, 2013), 202; Marlatt, "Interview," 245; Heather Milne, "Writing the Body Politic: Feminist Poetics in the Twenty-First Century," in *Public Poetics: Critical Issues in Canadian Poetry and Poetics*, ed. Travis V. Mason, Bart Vautour, Christl Verduyn, and Erin Wunker (Waterloo: Wilfrid Laurier University Press, 2015), 66.

31 Barbara Godard, "Mapmaking: A Survey of Feminist Criticism," in *Gynocritics: Feminist Approaches to Canadian and Quebec Women's Writing. Gynocritiques: Démarches féministes à l'écriture des Canadiennes et Québécoises*, ed. Barbara Godard (Toronto: ECW Press, 1987).

32 Pauline Butling, "One Potato, Two Potato, Three Potato, Four," in Butling and Rudy, *Writing in Our Time*, 33.

33 Julia V. Emberley, *Thresholds of Difference: Feminist Critique, Native Women's Writings, Postcolonial Theory* (Toronto: University of Toronto Press, 1993), 79.

34 Susan Knutson, *Narrative in the Feminine: Daphne Marlatt and Nicole Brossard* (Waterloo: Wilfrid Laurier University Press, 2000), 194.

35 Dybikowski, "In the Feminine," 10.

36 Marie Carrière, *Writing in the Feminine in French and English Canada: A Question of Ethics* (Toronto: University of Toronto Press, 2002), 12; Danielle Fuller, *Writing the Everyday: Women's Textual Communities in Atlantic Canada*

(Montreal and Kingston: McGill-Queen's University Press, 2004), 99; Heather Milne, "Writing the Body Politic," 66.

37   Butling, "Re-Defining," 25.

38   Butling, "Who Is She?" 152.

39   Kamboureli, "Shifting," 10.

40   Karis Shearer, interviewed by Sina Queyras, "Teaching the Poetic Event," *The Poetry Foundation* (29 April 2011), www.poetryfoundation.org/harriet/2011/04/teaching-the-poetic-event (accessed 2 March 2019).

41   "West Coast Women and Words Society August 25, 1982 Minutes," 4. Box 1, File 1, W&W fonds, SFU Special Collections and Rare Books Library, Vancouver, BC, 16 June 2015.

42   "Women and Words – A National Conference, First Report," 1–2. Box 1, File 1, W&W fonds, SFU Special Collections and Rare Books Library, Vancouver, BC, 16 June 2015.

43   "Constitution of the West Coast Women and Words Society," 1, 23 March 1982. Box 1, File 3, W&W fonds, SFU Special Collections and Rare Books Library, Vancouver, BC, 16 June 2015.

44   Unaddressed form letter for speakers, 4 May 1983. Box 1, File 21, W&W fonds, SFU Special Collections and Rare Books Library, Vancouver, BC, 16 June 2015.

45   Undated (pre-conference) media release. Box 2, File 16, W&W fonds, SFU Special Collections and Rare Books Library, Vancouver, BC, 16 June 2015.

46   Fuller, "Writing the Everyday," 246.

47   Emma Kivisild, Letter to Penny Williams, 16 December 1982. Box 1, File 20, W&W fonds, SFU Special Collections and Rare Books Library, Vancouver, BC, 16 June 2015.

48   Andrea Beverley, "Affects, Archives, Chapbooks: Sara Ahmed and the Feminist Caucus of the League of Canadian Poets," *Canadian Literature* 223 (Winter 2014): 88–91.

49   Shearer, "Teaching the Poetic Event."

50   Echoing the argument that Jason Camlot makes in chapter 6 about the Gustafson recordings collection, audiovisual recordings of the Women and Words conference also "warrant the development of a robust online platform to enable critical access to the many hours of literary historical sound" they contain.

51   "Women and Words – A National Conference, First Report," 4. Box 1, File 1,

W&W fonds, SFU Special Collections and Rare Books Library, Vancouver, BC, 16 June 2015.

52 "WCWW – Minutes of Meeting 15 June 1982." Box 1, File 1, W&W fonds, SFU Special Collections and Rare Books Library, Vancouver, BC, 16 June 2015.

53 "Women and Words/Les femmes et les mots – General Meeting," 2, 28 April 1983. Box 1, File 1, W&W fonds, SFU Special Collections and Rare Books Library, Vancouver, BC, 16 June 2015.

54 "Women and Words General Meeting," 1, 30 March 1983. Box 1, File 1. And "Project Committee Minutes," 20 April 1983. Box 1, File 1. And "Project Committee Meeting Minutes – March 9, 1983." Box 1, File 4. W&W fonds, SFU Special Collections and Rare Books Library, Vancouver, BC, 16 June 2015.

55 "WCWW – Minutes of Meeting 15 June 1982." Box 1, File 1. And "Anthology Committee Meeting," 2, 28 June 1982. Box 1, File 2. And "Publicity Committee Minutes," 2, 1 February 1983. Box 1, File 4. And "Women and Words – Publicity Committee Meeting," 1, 12 January 1983. Box 1, File 4. And unlabelled minutes, June 1983. Box 1, File 4. W&W fonds, SFU Special Collections and Rare Books Library, Vancouver, BC, 16 June 2015. Thanks to Felicity Tayler for pointing out potential connections with Western Front even before I found evidence for it in the archive.

56 "West Coast Women and Words Society August 25, 1982 minutes," 3. Box 1, File 1, W&W fonds, SFU Special Collections and Rare Books Library, Vancouver, BC, 16 June 2015.

57 "Publicity Committee Minutes," 2, 1 February 1983. Box 1, File 4, W&W fonds, SFU Special Collections and Rare Books Library, Vancouver, BC, 16 June 2015.

58 "A Proposal for a Tenth Anniversary Video Documentary of Women and Words," February 1992. Box "WCW&W – 97 shipment I," File "Board Minutes & Correspondence from Nov. '89," W&W fonds, SFU Special Collections and Rare Books Library, Vancouver, BC, 18 June 2015.

59 In *Spaces Like Stairs*, Gail Scott mentions some men's anger over not being allowed to attend Women and Words. Gail Scott, *Spaces Like Stairs* (Toronto: Women's Press, 1989), 69.

60 "Women and Words/Les femmes et les mots – General Meeting," 2, 28 April 1983. Box 1, File 1, W&W fonds, SFU Special Collections and Rare Books Library, Vancouver, BC, 16 June 2015.

61 "WCWW – Minutes of Meeting 15 June 1982." Box 1, File 1, W&W fonds, SFU Special Collections and Rare Books Library, Vancouver, BC, 16 June 2015.

62 "West Coast Women and Words Society," 3, 4 August 1982. Box 1, File 1,

W&W fonds, SFU Special Collections and Rare Books Library, Vancouver, BC, 16 June 2015.

63 "West Coast Women and Words Society August 25, 1982 minutes," 4. Box 1, File 2, W&W fonds, SFU Special Collections and Rare Books Library, Vancouver, BC, 16 June 2015.

64 "Project Committee Meeting Minutes – February 15, 1983," 1. Box 1, File 4, W&W fonds, SFU Special Collections and Rare Books Library, Vancouver, BC, 16 June 2015.

65 "Women Meet to Find Means of Greater Involvement in Arts," *Montreal Gazette* (6 July 1983): C6.

66 Max Wyman, "Word from the Women Is Clear: Men Aren't Wanted," *The Province* (29 June 1983).

67 Frank Jones, "They Fight Sexual Discrimination in 'Women Only' Feminist Workshops," *Toronto Star* (1 June 1983): A2.

68 As Larissa Lai explains, "The 'controversy' around Writing Thru Race focused on the conference policy that restricted its daytime events to First Nations writers and writers of colour, a practice that had been used, in various configurations, in social justice movements from the 1970s onward to create discursive space for those historically marginalized by the forces of racism, sexism, classism, homophobia, colonialism, or other oppressions." Lai, *Slanting*, 218.

69 In relation to Writing Thru Race see, for instance, Scott McFarlane, "The Haunt of Race: Canada's Multiculturalism Act, the Politics of Incorporation, and Writing Thru Race," *Fuse Magazine* 18.3 (1995): 18–31, and Smaro Kamboureli's *Scandalous Bodies*. Additionally, Kamboureli, Lai, and Miki co-organized a 2015 colloquium entitled "Twenty Years of Writing thru 'Race': Then and Now."

70 Helene Da Silva and Bob Amussen, "Women-only Rule Was Proven Right," *The Province* Box 3, File 19, W&W fonds, SFU Special Collections and Rare Books Library, Vancouver, BC, 16 June 2015.

71 Marian Engel, "Words Flowed Freely without Men," *Toronto Star* (8 July 1983). Box 3, File 19, W&W fonds, SFU Special Collections and Rare Books Library, Vancouver, BC, 16 June 2015.

72 Dybikowski, "In the Feminine," 227–8; "Project Meeting/Women and Words," 3, 22 July 1983. Box 1, File 4. And "Minutes of the General Meeting of the Westcoast Women and Words Society," 2, 14 September 1983. Box 1, File 5. W&W fonds, SFU Special Collections and Rare Books Library, Vancouver, BC, 16 June 2015.

73 "Project Committee Minutes," 2, 23 November 1983. Box 1, File 4, W&W

fonds, SFU Special Collections and Rare Books Library, Vancouver, BC, 16 June 2015.

74 Lorraine Chan, Letter to Viola Thomas, 25 October 1983. Box 5, unnumbered file called "W&W Audiotape Requests," W&W fonds, SFU Special Collections and Rare Books Library, Vancouver, BC, 16 June 2015.

75 Not only were sales minimal but the paperwork also suggests that sales management was sometimes inefficient. One customer wrote in October 1984 to inquire about an order placed months earlier: "PLEASE GIVE THIS YOUR IMMEDIATE ATTENTION. I can't afford to lose $20.00!" Isabel Andrews, Letter to Gloria Greenfield. Box 5, unnumbered file called "W&W Audiotape Requests," W&W fonds, SFU Special Collections and Rare Books Library, Vancouver, BC, 16 June 2015.

76 West Coast, "Preface," 9.

77 Among other items, participants were asked to assent to "the audio tape(s) of the workshop(s)/panel(s) I participated on remaining in the possession of the West Coast Women and Words Society as a part of their archives." Letter to participants, 25 July 1983. Box 4, File 1, W&W fonds, SFU Special Collections and Rare Books Library, Vancouver, BC, 16 June 2015.

78 "Project Meeting/Women and Words," 3, 22 July 1983. Box 1, File 4, W&W fonds, SFU Special Collections and Rare Books Library, Vancouver, BC, 16 June 2015.

79 The Media Archaeology Lab at the University of Colorado at Boulder, for instance, seeks to "both preserve and maintain access to historically important media of all kinds – from magic lanterns, projectors, typewriters to personal computers from the 1970s through the 1990s" (mediaarchaeologylab.com/about/). It is important to note that Media Archaeology Labs, and media labs in general, are not only utilitarian sites that facilitate access but also spaces of creative production, and institutional spaces to be historicized and theorized. For example, the scholarship of Darren Wershler, Jussi Parikka, and Lori Emerson does this work, as in their joint project "What Is a Media Lab?" See whatisamedialab.com (accessed 1 March 2019).

80 Jason Camlot, "Historicist Audio Forensics: The Archive of Voices as Repository of Material and Conceptual Artefacts," *19: Interdisciplinary Studies in the Long Nineteenth Century* 21 (2015), www.19.bbk.ac.uk/articles/10.16995/ntn.744/ (accessed 2 March 2019).

81 Linda Morra, *Unarrested Archives: Case Studies in Twentieth-Century Canadian Women's Authorship* (Toronto: University of Toronto Press, 2014).

82 Camlot, chapter 6 in this volume.

83 Rule, "Writer's Conference."

84 Brownlee, *Loggers' Daughters*, 196.

85 Ibid., 196, 197.

11

Salvage Modernisms
Indigenous Knowledges, Digital Repatriation, and Reconciliation

DEAN IRVINE

Salvaging Dark Days

Installed in April 2011 on an electronic billboard on Skwxwú7mesh (Squamish) territory at the foot of the Burrard Street Bridge in Vancouver, the public artwork *Digital Natives* invited artists and writers from across North America to contribute to a series of sixty text messages (limited to the 140-character Twitter format). Each displayed for ten seconds and interrupted the loop of corporate advertisements. Members of the public were also invited to tweet @diginativ and thirty of these responses were selected and broadcast. Curated by Lorna Brown and Clint Burnham, the billboard erected a digital commons for exchange between natives and non-natives and staged an intervention into technologies of modernity that include advertising's colonization of public space. By taking back the concept of the "digital native" from new media, Brown and Burnham strategically appropriated – or, perhaps, decolonized – a term coined during the dot-com boom that has come to signify a generation that was "born digital," one that coincides with the rapid proliferation of digital technologies toward the end of the last century.

Where the *Digital Natives* project speaks to the contemporary production of literary and artistic public spaces for Indigenous and non-Indigenous communicative exchange, I want to return to another time on the West Coast, a century earlier, when these communities engaged in the collaborative production of Indigenous ethnography and auto-ethnography. Considering these collaborations from the early to mid-twentieth century, I turn to digital remediation and return of Indigenous cultural heritage as a strategy to counteract long-standing literary-historical and anthological narrativizations of the historical gap between the death of Mohawk author E. Pauline Johnson/Tekahionwake in 1913 and the renaissance in Indigenous writing in Canada at the end of the 1960s. This half-century or so is commonly known as the "barren period"[1] of Indigenous writing, the "dark days"[2] of residential schools, and the "nadir" of Indigenous–white relations.[3]

Reasons cited for the apparent decline in Indigenous writing include government control of the Indigenous population through policies of assimilation, education, and displacement. These policies have left a devastating legacy that continues to haunt the nation; their revenant has returned with each act of testimony collected by the Truth and Reconciliation Commission (TRC). However, what most have uncritically assumed is that these policies were actually successful in wiping out Canada's Indigenous literatures from the early to mid-twentieth century. By accepting the dark-days narrative in literary histories and historical anthologies, we have, in effect, ratified a program of assimilation and ignored Indigenous peoples' histories of resistance and survival, restructuring them in a narrative of capitulation and disappearance.[4] In other words, where government policy may have failed to achieve its assimilationist objectives, cultural institutions and practices have been instrumental in the suppression of Indigenous cultural production from this period.

If not an actual lacuna in literary production but a stubborn blockage of cultural memory, the so-called dark period in Indigenous literature is the product of a literary-historical narrative that has been recklessly inattentive to the material conditions of Indigenous cultural production. Certainly the available historical anthologies of Indigenous literature and orature in Canada for this period have either omitted selections or represented it with retrospective works of life writing and as-told-to narratives that date from the 1960s and later. Robert Dale Parker states the problem quite plainly in *The Invention of Native American Literature* (2003) when he says, "of course … Indians were writing and sometimes publishing … and more Indians would have written if more were published."[5] But what and where were Indigenous authors publishing? Thomas King admits that although "there appears to be a gap of some fifty-odd years in which we do not see Natives writing," because there seem to be no Indigenous novelists, short-story writers, or playwrights from this period, there were in fact many "making speeches, producing articles, writing poetry, stories, and autobiography." He goes on to say that while we have yet to recover this material, it is probable that most of the writing of Indigenous peoples from this period appeared in periodicals or may remain in archives and the hands of ancestors.[6] This chapter speaks in part to the stories of those periodicals and family archives. It also speaks to the ways in which technologies of modernity – whether newspapers and magazines, or compact discs and digital repositories – mediate the inscription and storage of Indigenous knowledges. Under these conditions, unarchiving is a process of telling stories both about how such Indigenous knowledges are transmitted across generations, languages, and cultures and about how the histories of print and audio technologies become part of each telling of these stories. While the effects of such technologies are co-extensive with imperial expansion, these mediated archives of Indigenous knowledges are not merely accumulations of colonial memory. These stories and their mediations tell us not only about adaptations of Indigenous languages, stories, rituals, and customs to imperial technologies but also about their appropriation and transformation by emergent, modernist modes of Western cultural expression – both literary and ethnographic.

The phantasmatic dark period in Indigenous literature in North America coincided with the disciplinary emergence and subsequent institutional ascendance and dominance of salvage ethnography. Premised on the assumption that assimilationist policies and the corrosive forces of Western imperial modernity would inexorably bring about the cultural demise of Indigenous peoples, the practice of salvage ethnography reflects what James Clifford calls a "desire to rescue something 'authentic' out of destructive historical changes."[7] Yet salvage ethnographers never conducted fieldwork to produce "authentic" documentation of how Indigenous peoples actually lived under the conditions of imperial modernity but rather generated nostalgic projections, phantasms of how they might have once lived in a premodern state. Among the most forceful critiques of the salvage paradigm can be found in Edward Said's *Culture and Imperialism*, where he identifies these ethnographies as nothing more than histories of European colonial thought. More nuanced, I think, is the recent anthropological work of John Sutton Lutz on Indigenous auto-ethnography in which he reads the simultaneity of "conflict and consent, collaboration and coercion"[8] embedded in the social and economic exchanges transacted between Indigenous and non-Indigenous peoples in the historical production of ethnographic and auto-ethnographic narratives.

Digital Repatriation

By rejecting the ethnographic salvage paradigm and instead adopting practices of digital repatriation that use participatory computer-based technologies of digitization, transmission, preservation, and curation, we may find ways to reinitiate and rethink collaborative exchange between Indigenous and non-Indigenous communities. Collaboration has often been a mask worn by practitioners of cultural appropriation, so it stands to reason that any program of digital return needs to be wary of the legacies of Indigenous and imperial relations. Located at the conjuncture of Indigenous knowledges and new-media technologies, I have been gradually and cautiously developing a pilot project to allow practitioners to collaborate with Indigenous communities on the West Coast of BC to remediate literary and cultural history, so that the material and social mediations of Indigenous and non-Indigenous communicative exchange can be read anew. This collaborative project calls attention to the survival of Indigenous cultural heritage not just as remnants of imperial histories but also as a continuing series of multiply mediated modes of oral, script, and ritual performances that extend over a century. Crucially, I am working to implement participatory strategies of engagement that see Indigenous communities actively involved in the curation, remediation, and digital repatriation of their own cultural heritage. Digital repatriation thus signifies far more than McLuhanite understandings of remediation as the reciprocal relationship between old and new media: it facilitates and participates in the social and political processes attached to the return of Indigenous cultural heritage and conservation of traditional knowledges.[9] Most importantly, digital repatriation must be enacted in recognition of Indigenous social, political, and cultural sovereignty; it must not be a symbolic gesture, but rather an act of return that is "predicated on reciprocity and respect" and that enables "self-representation and reclamation of ethnographic authority."[10]

I am ever mindful of the latent neo-imperialism of digital technologies, a phenomenon that has accumulated significant scholarly attention, principally constellated by the critical theory and practice of digital race studies[11] and post-colonial digital humanities.[12] The practice of digital repatriation could easily run the risk of crossing over to neo-imperial territory were I to adopt a policy of uncritically promoting open access to Indigenous content under the ideologically misaligned intentions of Western notions of cultural property and public domain. With the mass digitization of ethnographic materials collected, translated, and published in the early twentieth century – as evidenced by their availability in digital repositories such as Google Books, the Internet Archive, and the HathiTrust – public domain runs the risk of legislating a new phase of salvage ethnography. And along with the concurrent digitization of indigenized modernist texts in the public domain, the recirculation of salvage ethnography looks to recolonize and expropriate Indigenous cultural heritage in digital media. This understanding of public domain reveals acute blind spots in Western ideas of cultural property, which chronically fail to accommodate non-Western systems of knowledge circulation and preservation. In effect, public domain threatens to re-enact early twentieth century cultural policy that rendered Indigenous knowledges and art as part of a linguistic and aesthetic commons available for expropriation by non-Indigenous peoples. Instead of a return to salvage ethnography in the guise of new media, I am proposing the digital return and repatriation of Indigenous cultural heritage not to facilitate open access but to safeguard traditional knowledges in collaboration with Indigenous communities and in observance of the cultural protocols that regulate circulation and preservation.

At a time when neo-imperial and neo-liberal conceptions of public domain and open access see the recirculation and reappropriation of Indigenous texts and objects online, this initiative addresses how to redress the effects of early salvage ethnography and artifact expropriation, how to adopt repatriation protocols appropriate to the curation of Indigenous cultural heritage, and how to respect Indigenous conceptions of the commons. By understanding the need to indigenize the repatriated commons, I pursue new paths in critical race and post-colonial studies by entering into activist interventions into the digital humanities and its material and ideological investments in technologies of imperial modernity. In doing so, I have followed the lead of and started to collaborate with several leading North American digital repatriation initiatives – such as Mukurtu, Local Contexts, Intellectual Property Issues in Cultural Heritage, and the Sustainable Heritage Network – whose ethical, respectful, and reciprocal collaborative work is indicative of efforts to decolonize the institutional relationships between Indigenous and non-Indigenous agents.

What follows in this chapter is a story about different modes of collaboration with and by Indigenous communities – from the salvage ethnography of the early twentieth century to the return of Indigenous cultural heritage to traditional practitioners in the present. Each part of the story speaks to the different ways in which technologies of modernity mediate the inscription and storage of Indigenous knowledges. This story begins a century ago on the West Coast of British Columbia – at a time when Indigenous communities engaged in the collaborative production of ethnography and auto-ethnography.[13] At the same time as the emergence of an indigenized modernism practised by non-Indigenous British Columbian poets, novelists, playwrights, musicians, and librettists (such as Carroll Aikins, Hubert Evans, Hermia Harris Fraser, Dorothy Livesay and Barbara Pentland, Bruce McKelvie, Frank Morrison, Howard O'Hagan, Constance Lindsay Skinner, A.M. Stephen, and Sheila Watson), Indigenous elders recited their narratives to a host of salvage ethnographers – some of them professionals, most notably those who followed Franz Boas out west, and others amateurs. The story I am telling concerns two such amateurs, Eloise Street and her mother Sophia White Street, and their collaboration with Stó:lō Chief William K'HHalserten Sepass. Between 1911 and 1915, Chief Sepass recited a cycle of poems to Sophia, who translated them aloud into English from the Halq'eméylem language. These oral translations were transcribed and edited by Eloise, who assembled a manuscript and then laid it aside for nearly thirty years.

Salvaging Modernism

Canadian non-Indigenous authors who appropriated and adapted Indigenous art, orature, and ethnography produced literary works of salvage modernism that plundered the cultural heritage of Indigenous peoples. Similar to their ethnographer counterparts, salvage modernists searched for an authenticity evacuated from Western literatures by the progressive forces of imperial modernity. These non-Indigenous appropriations of Indigenous cultural goods expose a site of contradiction at the advent of modernist literary culture in Canada. Salvage modernisms oscillate in a dialectic between the modern and the primitive, such that Indigenous peoples, their cultures, and their art become objects of fetishization and commodification in the practice of non-Indigenous primitivist aesthetics. This dialectical formation sees Indigeneity not as an antinomy of modernity but as an intermediating element in the indigenization of an incipient modernism in Canada and, in particular, an emergent Indigenous literary and print culture on the West Coast.[14]

Contrary to still prevailing critical assumptions that Canadian modernists merely participated in "historical and ideological erasures" through the "exclusion of Canada's indigenous populations,"[15] I want to contest this narrativization and propose a counternarrative that recognizes how a version of early modernist literary production in Canada – specifically the phenomenon of salvage modernism – is predicated upon the representation and collaborative participation of Indigenous peoples and communities. Salvaging modernism from its colonialist and imperialist dispositions necessitates coming to terms with the period's appropriations, adaptations, and intercultural mediations of Indigenous cultural heritage. In other words, the negotiation of terms of reconciliation between Canada's Indigenous and imperial cultures is a necessary precondition to the decolonization of a critical and literary-historical practice that has been given to the historical erasure of Indigenous literary production.

After the "modern symbolism"[16] of the Canadian expatriate avant-garde of fin-de-siècle Boston and New York, but before the cosmopolitan poetics and metropolitan little magazines of post-war Toronto and Montreal that most histories mark as the beginnings of literary modernism in Canada, the indigenization of Canadian modernism took place far from the urban centres "in regions on the colonized peripheries of the world's empire-driven modernity."[17] Set in the littoral spaces of empire and staged at the encounter between colonial and Indigenous communities, the discourses of primitivism and modernity that circulate in the literature of Canada's West Coast at the turn of the century inform the aesthetic and ideological constellation of what Lynda Jessup calls "antimodern modernism."[18] That same modern–antimodern contradiction inhabits salvage modernism's intercultural iterations of imperial–Indigenous contact and exchange.

Art historians have already done much in excavating the tightly packed ground of modernist aesthetics and primitivism in Canada, principally in connection with Emily Carr and members of the Group of Seven.[19] Not unlike the field of literary production, the visual arts of the early to mid-twentieth century have been characterized as a period of creative decline for

Indigenous peoples in Canada. Although Indigenous artists continued to produce through this period, the narrativization of Indigenous peoples in Canada as a disappearing race in government assimilation policy carried over to cultural institutions and practices. Instead of the modernist period in Canadian art history being commemorated as a time when native artists such as Frederick Alexie, a Tsimshian carver and painter, and Chief Joe Capilano (Sa7plek), a Squamish carver, produced works, it is principally commemorated as a time when non-Indigenous artists (such as Carr, Edwin Holgate, A.Y. Jackson, and Anne Savage, among others) gained recognition for their appropriation of Indigenous culture as subject matter for their canvasses. Members of the Group of Seven and its affiliates regularly refused to acknowledge the influence of Indigenous artists on their work, even when they painted villages whose architecture was dominated by the work of native carvers. Unlike the avant-gardes of early twentieth century Europe – Fauvism, Cubism, and Expressionism – and their often explicit acknowledgment of the African and indigenous appropriations that informed their work, the avant-garde in Canada claimed to have nothing to learn from Indigenous artists.[20] Rather, Canadian non-Indigenous artists trained in the primitivisms of the European avant-garde believed that they could employ these modes to translate local Indigenous cultural artifacts into a modernist aesthetic.[21]

What non-Indigenous artists encountered in Canada's West Coast was not what they considered art – it was the raw material for their art. At this time, Indigenous art was recognized by cultural institutions not as art but as ethnography; it was not collected as art by the National Gallery of Canada until the mid-1980s.[22] According to cultural policy of the period, Indigenous art and orature were treated as natural resources – that is, resources to which it was commonly held no individual Indigenous person could make a singular claim and, therefore, could be freely colonized and extracted for use by non-Indigenous ethnographers and creative practitioners. This systematic refusal to recognize Indigenous artistic production as art and to salvage it instead as ethnography – namely the material and immaterial cultural heritage of a people whose "disappearance" was overseen by state policies of assimilation – cleared the way for the indigenization of modernist visual art and literature in Canada. Salvage modernism, whose primitivist modes attempted to translate Indigenous cultural artifacts and knowledges into a modernist aesthetic, furthered the assimilation of Indigenous cultural heritage into a dominant imperial culture.

Salvage Technologies

With the rise of newspapers in the 1940s and 1950s such as the Native Brotherhood of British Columbia's *Native Voice* (1946–97), founded by Tsimshian editor Jack Beynon, along with Squamish leader Andrew Paull's *Thunderbird* (1949–55) and *Totem Speaks* (1953), the publication of the little magazine *Indian Time* marked a pivotal moment in Indigenous print culture. Published by an Indigenous man, Doug Wilkinson, and edited by a non-Indigenous woman, Eloise Street, *Indian Time* was a mimeographed magazine out of Vancouver issued at irregular intervals from 1950 to 1959. Wilkinson, a Sioux who appears on the masthead and signs his editorials Sohany, describes the program of the magazine as one devoted to "land rights, health, general welfare, agriculture, fishing, equal education for all Canadians, preservation and revival of native arts and culture" (1). Among the preservation efforts initiated by the magazine was the publication of English translations of Indigenous orature. Beginning with the January 1951 issue, *Indian Time* serialized a cycle of poems by Stó:lõ Chief William K'HHalserten Sepass. Street serialized a manuscript she had assembled under the title "The Songs of Y-Ail-Mihth." In the late 1940s, prior to the *Indian Time* serialization, Street had published an article about the cycle and an excerpt in the *Native Voice* as well as additional excerpts in early issues of *The Smoke Signal*, the mimeographed newspaper of the Federated Indians of California, which was edited by a Mountain Maidu woman named Marie Potts.[23] *The Smoke Signal* provided an important model for Street's own editorial work on *Indian Time*.

Street was by no means alone or unique among Canada's amateur salvage ethnographers of her generation, many of whom wrote about the Indigenous peoples on the West Coast. In 1911, the same year that Street and her mother initiated the process of translation and transcription of the Sepass cycle, Pauline Johnson published the first privately printed edition of *Legends of Vancouver*, which she describes in her foreword as "legends ... told to me personally by my honoured friend, the late Chief Joe Capilano ... These legends he told me from time to time, just as the mood possessed him, and he frequently remarked that they had never been revealed to any other English-speaking person save myself."[24] The most highly regarded non-Indigenous amateur ethnographer active at this time in Canada was Charles Hill-Tout. His strong relationships with Salish communities led to the publication of his best-known work, *The Native Races of British North America* (1907);

his legacy as an anthropologist has been vigorously defended and partly restored by the recovery of Hill-Tout's field reports from the late-nineteenth and early-twentieth centuries in Ralph Maud's four-volume collection, *The Salish People* (1978).[25]

In her efforts to find a publisher for the Sepass cycle, Street suffered the scorn of Canada's anthropological elite. After Chief Sepass's death in 1943, she submitted the manuscript to Lorne Pierce of Ryerson Press – the same publisher who produced the early collections of Canada's major mid-century anglophone modernist poets. Based in part on a recommendation from anthropologist Marius Barbeau that "accused Street of embellishing and romanticizing the original stories," Pierce rejected the manuscript "on the grounds that it was not considered to be authentic."[26] Because "Street later confessed to having elaborated upon several of the stories," it may seem logical to dismiss the poems outright as inauthentic, corrupt, appropriative, or fraudulent.[27] But it would not get us any closer to understanding the practices of amateur salvage ethnography and their intersection with literary adaptations of Indigenous cultural heritage, the emergence and dissemination of primitivist modes of modernist art among the European and North American avant-gardes, and the pervasiveness of the phenomenon of white Indigeneity in Canada's early to mid-century modernist and middlebrow literary cultures.

To speak of white Indigeneity in early to mid-twentieth century Canada surely brings to mind the figure of Grey Owl, the faux-Indigenous name adopted by British-born environmentalist and author Archibald Belaney. Unlike amateur ethnographers of the West Coast, Grey Owl enjoyed a large readership during his lifetime; he became the epitome of the early to mid-century's "middlebrow purveyors of Indianness,"[28] as Sherry Smith calls them, not only since he marketed himself as an environmental activist and commodified himself as an idealized "ecological" or "green" Indian but also since he has been read since his death and the revelation of his imposture. Grey Owl was not an ethnographer, but his posthumous positioning as a non-Indigenous figure who appropriated an Indigenous identity calls into question the "authenticity" of his life and writings, which is precisely the kind of questioning non-Indigenous amateur ethnographers were subjected to by the likes of Boas, Sapir, and Barbeau. The amateurs were open in their admission of having taken poetic licence with their subject matter. They explicitly wanted to distance their work from institutionalized ethnography published in such series as the annual reports of the Smithsonian's Bureau of American Ethnology or the Anthropological Division of the Geological Survey of Canada. In other words, they fashioned themselves as middlebrow ethnographers, at once aware of the anthropological methods pioneered by Boas and his followers – and that these modes of collection and dissemination were recognized at the time as best practices for linguistic, sociological, or cultural analysis – but also aware that these modes were not especially well suited to the popular tastes of their reading public.

Questions of authenticity pervade the reception history of the Sepass poems. The cycle has been circulated in multiple versions over six decades: serialized in *Indian Time*, published in two mimeograph editions issued by the magazine in 1955 and 1958, collected in print versions in 1963 and 1974, and most recently republished in a new commemorative edition in 2009. Each presents variations and invites different practices of reading in accordance with its medium, apparatus, and projected publics. From mimeographed magazine to full-colour hardcover, the cycle has undergone subtle but significant changes in its evolution from a text over which Street made proprietary declarations in claiming it as a gift from Chief Sepass and copyrighting it under her own name to one that, in its most recent iteration, is issued by a non-Indigenous publisher of Indigenous works, transfers copyright to the Sepass family, names Chief Sepass as a co-translator, and corrects Street's transliterations. Each new version of the cycle progressively seeks to claim greater legitimacy, authenticity, and authority. This evolution has attempted to move the cycle on a trajectory toward the kind of institutionalized ethnography practised by Boas and his followers. Contrary to the well-minded intentions of the cycle's publishers, this trajectory has effectively led to its assimilation into the institutional structures and practices of salvage ethnography. While it may seem counterintuitive to think that anyone could seek to safeguard cultural heritage without continuously regenerating new publics, I want to suggest that continued attempts to attribute authenticity and authority to the cycle without accounting for its inception at the colonial encounter between agents of Indigenous and imperial cultures are counterproductive. Rather than trying to mask its mediation by non-Indigenous agents, I am more inclined to read the cycle as a profoundly compromised set of documents that speak to the unresolved conflicts and contradictions of modernist primitivism and salvage ethnography.

Conspicuously absent from later printed versions of the text is Street's initial characterization of the cycle as a modernist translation. Only in the earliest mimeographed versions from the 1950s does she describe her transcription of the recitation as "a sort of free verse, rather like waves washing on a beach, rolling in and withdrawing, rolling in again and again ... Sequence followed sequence in this manner, the phrases always having an uplift of voice at the end, which had the effect of drawing the listener on with a sense of continuance – of something never quite finished – again like the sound of waves."[29] With her "free verse" analogy, Street engages in another translative act, an intersemiotic translation of Indigenous oral tradition into modernist poetics. While her mother Sophie was responsible for the translation, Street was the one who transcribed the poems in which she claims "each line had the same syllable length as his original, and had the same stresses."[30] Although the irregular line lengths in the Street translation and transcription do give the impression of a wavelike motion, it seems highly suspect that the translated poems maintain absolute fidelity to the syllabics and rhythms of the originals. There is no way of ever knowing because Street recorded no transcription of the source language; this is one way in which her transcription practices differed substantially from the salvage methods employed by professional ethnographers. Even so, her import is clear enough: for Street, the poetics of an Indigenous oral performance is coincident with modernist poetics – in other words, these poems are emblematic of the conjuncture of imperialist and Indigenous histories that Glenn Willmott calls "aboriginal modernity," in which "modernism ... may be grasped as a form of aboriginal expression."[31] To put it another way still, Willmott's "aboriginal modernity" is a variation on salvage modernism.

Rather than leap to Carl Sandburg's wry observation that "the Red Man and his children committed direct plagiarisms of the modern imagists and vorticists,"[32] I take Willmott's point to "recognize aboriginal modernity and imperialist modernity to be variations on a single historical struggle" in which modernist "primitivism [is] understood as a discourse of *translation* between apparently unlike or uncommunicative alternatives" (author emphasis) – that is, between "imperialist and aboriginal cultures."[33] Although Street hardly thought of herself as a practitioner of modernist primitivism, she is all the same its apologist in the Sepass translation. Contradicting the firm belief that her English version of the Sepass cycle fully captures the original, the translation exposes not the equivalence but the incommensurability of two modernities, the subaltern repressed and displaced by the hegemonic. It exhibits more than unresolvable differences between the linguistic and cultural codes of source and target. Its translation and transliteration of Indigenous traditional knowledge is mediated by imperialist technologies of inscription and storage mobilized by practitioners of salvage ethnography and modernist primitivism alike – that is, technologies predicated upon the capture of cultural heritage of what they believed to be a vanishing people. Rather than reconciliation, the unsettling sense of "something never quite finished" that Street remarks on in Sepass's recitation of the cycle is uncannily apposite to its unexpected telling of the always incomplete story of modernity – for the story of these poems and their modernist translation is a narrative about ongoing negotiations over cultural goods and transactions between agents of Indigenous and imperial histories. The act of reconciliation between Indigenous and imperial cultures is perpetually deferred in the Street-Sepass version of the poem cycle.

To recognize that the Sepass cycle and *Indian Time* are part of both Indigenous and modernist print cultures in Canada is to move at once beyond the narrativization of the early to mid-twentieth century as no more than a barren period in Indigenous cultural history and away from conceptions of modernism in Canada and elsewhere as merely complicit in a hegemonic, transnational, imperial culture that appropriated Indigenous art in the name of a primitivist aesthetic. This is not an apologia for the primitivist modernism practised by non-Indigenous authors and artists, but it is a call to acknowledge the localized, west coast formation of salvage modernism at the intersection of imperial and Indigenous print cultures and the intermediation of imperial and Indigenous modernities in the translation of the Sepass cycle and the production of *Indian Time*. With few literary contributions from contemporary Indigenous authors, *Indian Time* never definitively moved beyond its project of salvage ethnography. This is the impasse that Dorothy Livesay identifies in a review of the early issues of the magazine in which she commends "Indian themes occupying the attention of translators like Hermia Fraser and Eloise Street," but asks, "What about the young Indians today who have within themselves a strong creative impulse? Will it find outlet in the carrying on of tradition, the faithful and necessary work of revivifying and bringing to light the dying motifs, the unwritten songs of the people? Or is there already some restiveness among them, a feeling that they should not be constrained by tradition?"[34] What Livesay effectively asks is whether there are among Indigenous authors at mid-century some emergent modernists. A leading and loaded question to be sure, but one that invites further interrogation of critical assumptions about mid-century modernist literary culture.

Beyond Salvage

With Longhouse's 2009 edition of *Sepass Poems*, the century-old collaboration between its Indigenous orator and non-Indigenous translator and editor entered into a phase of return that coincided with a global movement toward the involvement of Indigenous communities as principal agents and partners in initiatives to safeguard their cultural heritage. Although *Sepass Poems* started off principally as a print-based project, Longhouse issued a CD recording of its glossary of Halq'eméylem words, spoken by Vivian Williams of the Cheam First Nation. When I contacted Longhouse to obtain a copy of the recorded glossary, I inquired about the passing indication on its website that there were plans to release an audio recording of the poems "in the oral tradition with traditional Coast Salish drumming and song."[35] That query precipitated a collaborative pilot project involving Ann Mohs of Longhouse, members of the Sepass family, and Editing Modernism in Canada (EMiC; editingmodernism.ca), which led to EMiC funding an audio recording of the 2009 edition of the cycle – recited by Gabriel George, great-grandson of Chief Dan George of the Coast Salish, with traditional drumming and songs by members of the Sepass family.[36] These audio components of the Sepass project gesture toward the digital transformation of "intangible cultural heritage," as defined by the 2003 UNESCO Convention. Among the notable features of the new audio recordings are their multi-track vocal layerings and ambient sound effects and, as a result, these are not exclusively recitations in "the oral tradition with traditional Coast Salish drumming and song."[37] They are, for the most part, far more typical of the sound technologies and recording techniques available to Indigenous technicians and artists working together in a twenty-first century digital studio. This is yet another "media translation"[38] of the poem cycle, another remediation; it is not a restoration of lost authenticity but an accretion of digital audio effects intermixed with traditional drumming and song. Digital repatriation need not mean a return to the past; it may incite a break with tradition, an adaptation in tune with our digital times.

Rather than perpetuate the salvage paradigm that situates Indigenous cultural heritage prior to modernity, this digital collaboration between Indigenous and non-Indigenous partners is based on the premise that Indigenous peoples and cultures "are not outside of the modern, *they are integral to what makes the modern possible.*"[39] As Lisa Nakamura demonstrates in her research on Navajo women who worked between 1965 and 1975 as circuit makers for Fairchild Semiconductor, the industrialization of these Indigenous women "produced a complicated identity whose formation relied on the idea that the tribe could be modern, even hypermodern" through the rebranding of their "traditional, premodern artisanal handiwork" as blanket weavers and jewellery makers in the service of electronics manufacturing for computers.[40] To exclude Indigenous peoples from narratives of technological modernity reinforces stereotypes about their inability to adapt, the corollary of which is the implication that they are subject to assimilation into a dominant, technologically advanced Western culture. While Nakamura's investigation of early computer hardware manufacturing among the Navajo is far from an example of a respectful and collaborative economic exchange between non-indigenous and indigenous agents, it still underscores the ways in which adaptation to the conditions of technological modernity and territorial occupation is an integral component of the story of Indigenous peoples' engagement with an industrialized Western culture.

The audio recording of the Sepass poem cycle inserts Stó:lō cultural heritage into the technological apparatus of the digital recording industry. It marks the beginning of a collaboration between the Street and Sepass families to curate a comprehensive, web-based multimedia digital exhibit of the cycle. After working with Longhouse and EMiC on the audio version, the Street and Sepass families[41] have agreed to continue this collaboration on the joint curation of a digital exhibit of the Sepass cycle that implements the cultural protocols and Traditional Knowledge (TK) labels/licences introduced by Mukurtu and its partner project Local Contexts. Mukurtu (mukurtu.org) is a content management system with customized sharing and access protocols as well as TK labels and licences – all designed to protect Indigenous cultural heritage. Its Drupal-based system not only allows users to add and share text, images, audio, and video but also permits them to attach specific access and sharing protocols to digital objects that facilitate decisions about how to circulate content – whether restricted to authenticated and variously differentiated types of Indigenous users or open to the public. The TK labels and licences recognize that Indigenous communities have particularly sensitive access and use expectations with respect to cultural heritage. Because TK access procedures protect digitized items with community-specific, gender, age, seasonal, and other restrictions, they are crucial to the governance and circulation of sacred and ceremonial material. Unlike the appropriative collection practices of salvage anthropologists – whose collaborations with Indigenous agents led to the deposit of traditional knowledges in state-controlled archives, museums, and publications – TK sharing and access protocols encourage the "reciprocal curation" of digital cultural heritage.[42] Critical to this curatorial practice is the expectation that the exhibit will be built upon a web-based platform that actively resists the salvage paradigm, one that is supported by an institutional and organizational infrastructure committed to decolonization and Indigenous sovereignty, so that sovereign Indigenous scholars, programmers, and technicians may take over the design and implementation of the technologies that facilitate digital repatriation.[43] Heeding Len Findlay's exhortation to "always Indigenize!"[44] and establishing policies that protect against the assimilation of Indigenous cultural production into a repository of salvage modernism, the exhibit aims to respect and enact Indigenous conceptions of the commons and adopt protocols appropriate to its "reciprocal curation" in collaboration with Indigenous families and organizations.

An indigenized commons works to decolonize digital technologies, render their adoption by Indigenous users in accordance with community-led efforts to preserve and revitalize traditional knowledges, and counteract the imperial legacies and neo-imperial effects of the digitization and dissemination of salvage ethnography under the mandate of public domain. Indigenizing an exhibit such as this as a digital commons is an act of repatriation, a return of Indigenous sovereignty over cultural and technological domains. A century ago, salvage ethnographers and modernists captured Indigenous oral heritage with the recording tools of an imperial culture. Repatriation necessitates not only the restoration of sovereign authority over that material to communities of origin but also the reciprocal act of developing web-based technologies in partnership and consultation with Indigenous stakeholders to provide the means to execute that authority through access and sharing protocols. The

TK label/licence functionality and access protocols described above represent one means of decolonizing technologies of modernity and a mechanism of repatriating Indigenous digital cultural heritage.[45]

The exhibit aims to feature materials currently in the possession of Bill Sepass, the great-grandson of Chief William Sepass, which include his great-grandfather's papers and photographs as well as Eloise Street's original handwritten notes and manuscripts. It will reproduce the mimeographed texts, photographs, and drawings published in *Indian Time* and under the magazine's imprint in the 1950s; display publisher's correspondence from the 1940s through the 1970s and other papers preserved by Street's son and grand-daughter; make available Gabriel George's audio recording of the cycle; and document stories by members of the Street and Sepass families about their ancestors and about the stories that intertwine them. In addition, the exhibit will present related early to mid-twentieth century ethnographic material, most notably the unpublished manuscript of Diamond Jenness's field notes from a 1936 interview with Chief Sepass, which include "sketches of stories" that are "versions that differ entirely in form and significantly in plot" from those later published by Street.[46] Rather than attempt to recuperate the authenticity of the Eloise Street–Sophia White Street version, the digital exhibit will present material that speaks to the intercultural mediations of the Sepass cycle across and through different technologies of inscription and storage – from fountain pen to web-accessible repository. In making all extant versions available, the collective and cumulative stories that they tell and retell will situate the cycle in relation to a century-long process of media translation, which begins with and returns to the recitation of the poems in the oral tradition. How that oral tradition is transformed by both modernist-primitivist and Indigenous print cultures over the course of a hundred years is one of the ways in which the exhibit can attest to the historical and historicized mediations of technological and cultural modernities.

If the editions of the Street-White version have reinscribed a series of variations on the intersecting narratives of salvage modernism and ethnography, the exhibit will offer an opportunity to consider how digital repatriation may contribute to the national project of reconciliation between Indigenous and non-Indigenous cultures in Canada – which, according to the TRC, requires an "awareness of the past, acknowledgement of the harm that has been inflicted, atonement for the causes, and action to change behaviour."[47]

This is not to say that the exhibit must strictly condemn the Street-White version as a colonial project of salvage ethnography and modernism, but to suggest that its assembly foregrounds such narrativizations of imperial-Indigenous relations as a necessary part of its story. To tell that story as an act of repatriation and reconciliation – to cite the evidentiary collection practices of the TRC – is at once to assert that "previously inaccessible archival documents are critically important to correcting the historical record" and to give "equal weight and greater voice to Indigenous oral-based history, legal traditions, and memory practices."[48]

By creating an online environment in which materials preserved by the Street and Sepass families may be curated collaboratively by their source communities, the indigenized commons that I am describing seeks to stage the repatriation of the Sepass cycle in relation to the history of its intercultural mediations. Instead of dislocating Indigenous cultures from the land to digitization labs, members of the Stó:lō Nation will be employed in the digitization of local materials on their own land. Rather than enacting the neo-liberal policy of "accumulation by dispossession,"[49] or repeating the fallacies of salvage ethnography that attempted to preserve a premodern Indigenous culture, the exhibit looks to promote modes of collaboration that mobilize digitization and semantic-web technologies. It is imperative to stop the extraction of cultural resources from Indigenous communities and to work to conserve the lineages of local, communal, and familial provenances.

NOTES

1 Penny Petrone, *Native Literature in Canada: From the Oral Tradition to the Present* (Toronto: Oxford University Press, 1990), 95.

2 Armand Garnet Ruffo, "Out of the Silence – The Legacy of E. Pauline Johnson: An Inquiry into the Lost and Found Work of Dawendine – Bernice Loft Winslow," in *Literary Pluralities*, ed. Christl Verduyn (Peterborough: Broadview, 1998), 212.

3 Cecilia Morgan, "Performing for Imperial Eyes: Bernice Loft and Ethel Brant Monture, Ontario, 1930s–1960s," in *Contact Zones: Aboriginal and Settler Women in Canada's Colonial Past*, ed. Katie Pickles and Myra Rutherdale (Vancouver: University of British Columbia Press, 2005), 70.

4 Leslie Dawn, *National Visions, National Blindness: Canadian Art and Identities in the 1920s* (Vancouver: University of British Columbia Press, 2005), 274.

5 Robert Dale Parker, *The Invention of Native American Literature* (Ithaca: Cornell University Press, 2003), 83.

6 Thomas King, "Native Literature in Canada," *Dictionary of Native American Literature* (New York: Garland, 1994), 357–8.

7 James Clifford, "Of Other Peoples: Beyond the 'Salvage' Paradigm," in *Discussions in Contemporary Culture*, ed. Hal Foster (Seattle: Bay Press, 1987), 160.

8 John Sutton Lutz, *Makuk: A New History of Aboriginal-White Relations* (Vancouver: University of British Columbia Press, 2008), 24.

9 Scholarship on the subject of digital return and repatriation of Indigenous cultural heritage is vast and perpetually evolving; for a selection of sources that have influenced my thinking, see Jane Anderson and Kimberly Christen, "'Chuck a Copyright on It': Dilemmas of Digital Return and the Possibilities for Traditional Knowledge Licenses and Labels," *Museum Anthropology Review* 7.1–2 (Spring–Fall 2013): 105–26; Kimberly Christen, "Does Information Really Want to Be Free? Indigenous Knowledge Systems and the Question of Openness," *International Journal of Communication* 6 (2012): 2870–93; Kimberly Christen, "Gone Digital: Aboriginal Remix and the Cultural Commons," *International Journal of Cultural Property* 12.3 (2005): 315–45; Kimberly Christen, "Opening Archives: Respectful Repatriation," *American Archivist* 74 (Spring/Summer 2011): 185–210; Ira Jacknis, "Repatriation as Social Drama: The Kwakiutl Indians of British Columbia, 1922–1980," in *Repatriation Reader: Who Owns Native American Remains?*, ed. D.A. Mihesuah (Lincoln and London: University of Nebraska Press, 2000), 266–81; Patrick Moore and Kate Hennessy, "New Technologies and Contested Ideologies: The Tagish First Voices Project," *American Indian Quarterly* 30.1–2 (2006): 119–37; Amber Ridington and Kate Hennessy, "Building Indigenous Agency through Web-Based Exhibition: Dane Wajich: Dane-zaa Stories and Songs: Dreamers and the Land," *Museums and the Web 2008: Proceedings*, www.archimuse.com/mw2008/papers/ ridington/ridington.html (accessed 29 August 2017); Robin Ridington, Jillian Ridington, Patrick Moore, Kate Hennessy, and Amber Ridington, "Ethnopoetic Translation in Relation to Audio, Video, and New Media Representations," in *Born in the Blood: On Native American Translation*, ed. Brian Swann (Lincoln: University of Nebraska Press, 2011), 211–41.

10 See Kate Hennessy, "Virtual Repatriation," 5–6; and Kate Hennessy, Natasha Lyons, Stephen Loring, Charles Arnold, Mervin Joe, Albert Elias, and James

Pokiak, "The Inuvialuit Living History Project: Digital Return as the Forging of Relationships between Institutions, People, and Data," *Museum Anthropology Review* 7.1–2 (2013): 44–73.

11 See Tara McPherson, "Why Are the Digital Humanities So White? or Thinking the Histories of Race and Computation," in *Debates in the Digital Humanities*, ed. Matthew K. Gold (Minneapolis: University of Minnesota Press, 2012), 139–60; Lisa Nakamura, *Cybertypes: Race, Ethnicity, and Identity on the Internet* (New York: Routledge, 2013); Lisa Nakamura and Peter Chow-White, eds., *Race after the Internet* (New York: Routledge, 2013).

12 See Adeline Koh, "Digititzing Chinese Englishmen: Creating a Nineteenth-Century 'Postcolonial Archive,'" *Verge: Studies in Global Asias* 1.2 (Fall 2015): 25–30; Roopika Risam, "Beyond the Margins: Intersectionality and the Digital Humanities," DHQ: *Digital Humanities Quarterly* 9.2 (2015), www.digitalhumanities.org/dhq/vol/9/2/000208/000208.html (accessed 25 June 2016); Risam, "Diasporizing the Digital Humanities: Displacing the Center and Periphery," *International Journal of E-Politics* 7.3 (2016): 65–78; Risam, "Other Worlds, Other DHs: Notes towards a DH Accent," *Digital Scholarship in the Humanities* (February 2016), http://dx.doi.org/10.1093/llc/fqv063; Risam, "Revising History and Re-authouring the Left in the Postcolonial Digital Archive," *Left History* 18.2 (Fall/Winter 2015): 35–46.

13 Anthropological scholarship on the salvage ethnography of Barbeau has enjoyed a protracted and robust tradition, one that has in recent years placed greater emphasis on their collaborations with Indigenous interpreters, translators, and co-authors.

14 Scholarship on the international modernisms of Europe and the United States and their primitivist modes is well established and extensive. More recent is the emergence of scholarship on the crossovers between international modernisms and indigenous North American literatures and cultures, with examples such as J.J. Healy, "Wrestling with White Spirits: The Uses and Limits of Modernism and Postmodernism in Aboriginal and Native American Literary Contexts," *Australian and New Zealand Studies in Canada* 12 (December 1994): 31–50 and Helen Carr, *Inventing the American Primitive: Politics, Gender, and the Representation of Native American Literary Traditions 1789–1936* (New York: New York University Press, 1996), among others.

15 Gary Boire, "Canadian (Tw)ink: Surviving the White-Outs," *Essays on Canadian Writing* 35 (1987): 3, 4–5.

16 D.M.R. Bentley, "'The Thing Is Found to Be Symbolic': *Symboliste* Elements

in the Early Short Stories of Gilbert Parker, Charles G.D. Roberts, and Duncan Campbell Scott,"' in *Dominant Impressions: Essays on the Canadian Short Story*, ed. Gerald Lynch and Angela Arnold Robbeson (Ottawa: University of Ottawa Press, 1999), 44.

17 Glenn Willmott, *Unreal Country: Modernity in the Canadian Novel in English* (Montreal and Kingston: McGill-Queen's University Press, 2002), 51.

18 Lynda Jessup, *Antimodernism and Artistic Experience: Policing the Boundaries of Modernity* (Toronto: University of Toronto Press, 1991), 6.

19 See, for example, Ann Katherine Morrison, *Canadian Art and Cultural Appropriation: Emily Carr and the 1927 Exhibition of Canadian West Coast Art – Native and Modern* (Vancouver: University of British Columbia Press, 1991); Douglas Cole, *Captured Heritage: The Scramble for Northwest Coast Artifacts* (Vancouver: University of British Columbia Press, 1995); Gerta Moray, *Unsettling Encounters: First Nations Imagery in the Art of Emily Carr* (Vancouver: University of British Columbia Press, 2006); and Paige Raibmon, *Authentic Indians: Episodes of Encounter form the Late-Nineteenth-Century Northwest Coast* (Durham and London: Duke University Press, 2005). The scholarship that has proliferated on primitivism and modernism in early to mid-century Canadian visual art has seen its much smaller counterpart in the literary field. Of western Canadian non-Indigenous modernist authors whose work adapts and appropriates First Nations cultural heritage, only the canonical fiction writers such as Howard O'Hagan and Sheila Watson have sustained a body of criticism that documents their debts to traditional Indigenous songs, stories, and art. Of Indigenous authors from the early twentieth century, scholarship has concentrated on two major Indigenous women authors – Mourning Dove and E. Pauline Johnson (Tekahionwake) – who shared ambivalent relationships to collaborative authorship, imperial modernity, and modernist aesthetics.

20 Dawn, *National Visions, National Blindness*, 256.

21 Gerta Moray, "Emily Carr and the Traffic in Native Images," in *Antimodernism and Artistic Experience*, ed. Lynda Jessup (Toronto: University of Toronto Press, 2000), 73.

22 Dawn, *National Visions, National Blindness*, 314.

23 Terri Castaneda, "Making News: Marie Potts and the *Smoke Signal* of the Federated Indians of California," in *Women in Print: Essays on the Print Culture of American Women from the Nineteenth and Twentieth Centuries*, ed. James P. Danky and Wayne A. Wiegand (Madison: University of Wisconsin Press, 2006), 77.

24 E. Pauline Johnson [Tekahionwake], *Legends of Vancouver* (Vancouver: Privately printed, 1911), vii.

25 By the 1920s and 1930s, the number of non-Indigenous amateurs who collected and published west coast "Indian legends" expanded to include Alfred Carmichael (*Indian Legends of Vancouver Island* [1922]), Cyrus Macmillan (*Canadian Wonder Tales* [1918], *Canadian Fairy Tales* [1922]), Isabel Ecclestone Mackay (*Indian Nights* [1930]), George H. Griffin (*Legends of the Evergreen Coast* [1934]), and Major J.S. Matthews (*Conversations with Khatsalano, 1932–1954* [1969]). With the exception of Hill-Tout, none of these amateurs has been granted much, if any, notice in ethnographic scholarship, and if they have been mentioned, it has always been with derision.

26 Brendan Frederick R. Edwards, "A War of Wor(l)ds: Aboriginal Writing in Canada during the 'Dark Days' of the Early Twentieth Century," PhD dissertation (University of Saskatchewan, 2008), 17n28.

27 Ibid.

28 Sherry Smith, *Reimagining Indians: Native Americans through Anglo Eyes, 1880–1940* (London: Oxford University Press, 2000), 213.

29 Eloise Street, "Glossary," in *The Songs of the Y-Ail-Mihth*, ed. Eloise Street (Vancouver: Indian Time, 1955), 8.

30 Ibid., 1.

31 Willmott, *Modernist*, 7.

32 Carl Sandburg, "Aboriginal Poetry II," *Poetry* 9.5 (February 1917): 255.

33 Willmott, *Modernist*, 18–19, 13.

34 Dorothy Livesay, "Indian Time," *Northern Review* (Apr–May 1951; Rpt. In *Indian Time* 1.7 (May–June–July 1951): 14.

35 Chief William K'Hhalserten Sepass, *Sepass Poems: Ancient Songs of Y-ail-mihth*, recited. by C.L. Street, ed. Eloise Street (Mission, BC: Longhouse, 2009).

36 Chief William K'Hhalserten Sepass, *Songs of Y-Ail-Mihth, The Ancient Singer: Sepass Poems in Oral Tradition*, recited by Gabriel George (Mission, BC: Longhouse Publishing, 2016).

37 Sepass, *Sepass Poems*.

38 N. Katherine Hayles, *My Mother Was a Computer: Digital Subjects and Literary Texts* (Chicago: University of Chicago Press, 2006), 89.

39 David Gaertner, "Traditional Innovation: The Turn to Decolonial New Media Studies," in *Novel Alliances: Allied Perspectives on Literature, Art, and New Media* (25 November 2014), https://novelalliances.com/2014/11/25/traditional-innovation-the-turn-to-a-decolonial-new-media-studies/ (accessed 25 June 2016).

40 Nakamura, "Indigenous," 924–5.

41 The preliminary arrangements for the initiative have been handled (beginning in 2012) by Ann Mohs of Longhouse, who received endorsements for the project from Gerald Sepass (grandson of Chief Sepass), Bill Sepass (great-grandson of Chief Sepass), Gwynn Harries (son of Eloise Street), Lisa Harries (granddaughter of Eloise Street), and Ron Denman (director, Chilliwack Museum and Archives). I have taken over communication with the Sepass family, and I expect to continue in this role as the project moves forward. While I am pleased to have in place the support of the Sepass family, I have also secured the endorsement of the Stó:lō Research and Resource Management Centre.

42 Christen, "Opening," 193.

43 This exhibit will leverage a wider network of collaborative relationships among non-Indigenous agents and institutions invested in practices of digital repatriation – Intellectual Property Issues in Cultural Heritage, the Reciprocal Resource Network, and the Sustainable Heritage Network – that have already developed partnerships with and within Indigenous communities to implement digital technologies that enable ethical, respectful, and participatory acts of collaboration. It will also extend that network to involve Indigenous organizations, most notably the Stó:lō Research and Resource Management Centre and the First Nations Technology Council in British Columbia.

44 Len Findlay, "'Always Indigneize! The Radical Humanities in the Postcolonial Canadian University," *Ariel* 31.1–2 (2000): 307.

45 One proposal for the development of the platform would see an open-source codebase of the Modernist Commons (modernistcommons.ca) – a digital repository, modular editorial workbench, and publishing platform for critical editions designed by Editing Modernism in Canada (EMiC) in partnership with Islandora (islandora.ca). Although EMiC has been instrumental in helping to fund the audio version of the poem cycle, its participation in the repatriation of Stó:lō cultural heritage must begin with an act of reciprocation. Instead of throwing open the Modernist Commons to Indigenous material from the early to mid-twentieth century, it is imperative that the exhibit resist the absorption of Indigenous knowledges into a digital commons whose principles of use and access are predicated on Western copyright law and conceptions of intellectual property.

46 Crisca Bierwert, *Brushed by Cedar, Living by the River: Coast Salish Figures of Power* (Tucson, AZ: University of Arizona Press, 1999), 104.

47 Truth and Reconciliation Commission of Canada. *Canada's Residential Schools: The Final Report of the Truth and Reconciliation Commission of Canada, Vol. 6: Reconciliation* (Montreal and Kingston: McGill-Queen's University Press, 2015), 3.

48 Ibid., 162.

49 David Harvey, *Cosmopolitanism and the Geographies of Freedom* (New York: Columbia University Press, 2009), 68.

PART THREE

Archives of the Present

12

Is the TRC a Text?

CLINT BURNHAM

My teachings come from the mouths of people whose ability to
read was basic at best ... yet they were unequalled in their ability
to relate a story, a story that flowed like water in a stream, soothing,
calming, then at times angry, raging like rapids released from the
icy grip of winter.
– Duncan Mercredi, "Achimo"[1]

Even in the worst catastrophe, there is something unknown
and cherished to be discovered.
– Lee Maracle, *Memory Serves: Oratories*[2]

In this chapter, I explore what it means to talk about the TRC as a text, arguing, specifically, that *The Survivors Speak,* an archive of TRC testimony, can be productively approached as a work of literature. Here I am already blurring some distinctions (for example, what is the difference, if there is one, between "text" and "literature"?) and I will keep doing so, speaking of the testimony's status as an archive and of its relation to the TRC as an event (but also a performance); thinking of the digital, mediated, and visual culture aspects of *The Survivors Speak*; and making an argument for the concept of "orature" as a useful way in. My working thesis is that the literary – or the

Canadian literary – both is and is not an adequate criterion for understanding or interpreting *The Survivors Speak*. It is an important or adequate criterion in the strategic/canonical sense that I want to argue for the aesthetic value of the testimony qua orature. But to call *The Survivors Speak* literature is also inadequate – and here the reasons are more complex. In the fitting sense of any *negative* critique, my critique is in solidarity with, but also questions, anti-colonial and decolonizing politics and methodologies. To declare the testimony as literary is a move in danger of losing sight of the specificities of its event: the archival and performative natures of the testimony on the one hand, and the colonial question not only of the literary but also, specifically, of *Canadian* literature on the other.[3]

From 2009 until 2015, members of the Truth and Reconciliation Commission (TRC) toured Canada, taking testimony, in private and public sessions, from survivors of residential schools.[4] The schools themselves, first established in 1883 with the last ones closed in 1996 (these being industrial schools in the Northwest), had the frank purpose of assimilation, of "killing the Indian in the child."[5] Over 150,000 students attended the residential schools, almost always under compulsion of law: 86,000 survivors are still alive today and 6,750 testified at the TRC hearings.

Documentation from the TRC was first released in an interim report, and the historical document *They Came for the Children* in 2012. Then, at the culmination of the Commission's activities on 31 May–1 June 2015, a 388-page *Executive Summary* and a 260-page selection of testimony, *The Survivors Speak*, were released. In December 2015, a further eight reports were issued, including historical surveys of the residential schools, the northern and Métis experiences, a report on missing children and graves, and calls for actions. All of the reports are available as freely downloadable PDFs and, with the exception of *The Survivors Speak*, the 2015 documents were published by McGill-Queen's University Press in soft and hardcover.

The Survivors Speak is divided into thirty-two sections, organized both chronologically ("Life before residential school," "Forced departure," "The end") and also thematically ("Language and culture," "Strange food," "Classroom experience"). Located in the different sections are also photographs of survivors, 112 in total. Within each section, testimony varies in length. Sometimes it is presented as a block quote of five to ten lines, and sometimes it is embedded grammatically into the expository frame that conveys a summary of survivors' experiences to the reader. All quoted testimony is identified in the text with the speaker's full name; the figures in the photographs are likewise identified by full name. All text is footnoted: there are 740 endnotes, which repeat the speaker's name, the date of the statement to the TRC, a statement number, and occasionally a note on translation.

A "media archeology" of *The Survivors Speak* would trace the following events, archives, and media storage protocols. As it toured the country, the TRC solicited testimony at "statement gatherings," which included seven national events (in Winnipeg, Inuvik, Halifax, Saskatoon, Montreal, Vancouver, and Edmonton between June 2010 and March 2014) and seventy-seven local hearings in smaller communities.[6] Testimony was given either in public or in small private, curtained enclaves for audio recordings; much of the testimony was also videotaped. The recordings are now stored at the National Centre for Truth and Reconciliation at the University of Manitoba, and will be available online, depending on privacy agreements signed by survivors. Testimony was also transcribed by a team at the TRC, and a selection made from those transcriptions for publication.[7]

Media theory can also help us understand the process by which *The Survivors Speak* is transmitted from survivors' recorded testimony as a digital publication, and the methodologies at work in this chapter. Here we can think about the archive as a Foucauldian space of gaps and ruptures, but also as that which is "less concerned with memory than with the necessity to discard, erase, eliminate," a matter not of "teleology and narrative closure" but of networks, the temporality of data movement, and, indeed, of testimony itself not as a Lacanian "missed encounter with the real."[8] That is, these tropes of absences and gaps theorized by media critics Sven Spieker and Wolfgang Ernst demand a reading practice that locates gaps in the archive symptomatically in the text. My argument is that a reading practice that engages with a poetics of testimony as orature indigenizes or decolonizes the archive via a formalist encounter with the text. This is no doubt a dense and compact (not to say contentious!) proposition, and I leave it with the reader to determine if I have been successful.

The Critiques

Before discussing and quoting from the testimony more directly, I want to address two different critiques of the testimony, the TRC, and the process of apology, reconciliation, and confession. I will be brief, and specific, choosing not to delve into larger questions of other national TRC processes, the apology industry, or philosophical questions of reconciliation. The first critique – more of a caveat – has to do with the TRC process and other forms of restitution. As part of the Indian Residential Schools Settlement Agreement of 2007 (which itself followed a lengthy history of not only such quasi-governmental inquiries as the Royal Commission on Aboriginal Peoples [RCAP; 1991–96] but also long-standing efforts beginning in 1987 by such groups as the Shubenacadie Residential School Survivors), "two regimes of compensation" were established.[9] The Common Experience Payment was apportioned to anyone who attended residential schools, while the Independent Assessment Process (IAP) adjudicated individuals' claims of harm. Over 38,000 survivors have made claims under the IAP. Specific to our interest here is the fate of testimony at the IAP, which has become a matter of political contention between Canada's federal government, the churches that administered the residential schools, the Assembly of First Nations (AFN), and the TRC itself.

Contentious issues included the confidentiality of submissions to the IAP; the possibility or requirement that survivors would have to give their testimony twice, both to the IAP and to the TRC; and, as former AFN leader Phil Fontaine remarked, the concern that "stories of aboriginal-on-aboriginal abuse at the schools could prove damaging to First Nation communities."[10] While the TRC is calling for IAP transcripts to be transferred to the National Centre for Truth and Reconciliation, others have called for the documents' destruction, and the Catholic Church and the AFN has expressed concerns over issues of privacy. Unlike the IAP transcripts, *The Survivors Speak* is first of all a public archive, digitized and readily accessible online.[11] Some names are redacted, and some testimony has been translated from French or from Indigenous languages, including Inuktitut, Cree, Ojibway, Oji-Cree, Swampy Cree, and Woodland Cree.

If this is a procedural framing or caveat about testimony and the legal pitfalls thereof, my other critique is political, and comes from the work of Indigenous theorists and artists, including Gerald Taiaiake Alfred and David Garneau. In his essays "Imaginary Spaces of Conciliation and Reconciliation" and (with Clement Yeh) "Apology Dice: Collaboration in Progress," Garneau has made the forceful case that "conciliation," rather than "reconciliation," is a more apt term for this process and, especially, that in its focus on emotional statements, allocation of payments, and public display, the

"TRC is a pain generator, a testimony and tear-stained tissue collector," and, most damning, "the official Truth and Reconciliation is primarily a non-Indigenous project designed to reconcile settlers with their own dark history in order that they might live in this territory more comfortably and exploit these lands more thoroughly."[12] Similarly, Taiaiake Alfred has argued for abandoning the "pacifying discourse of conciliation" and using "restitution as the first step towards creating justice and a moral society," a "decolonizing" project rather than one that advances colonialism.[13]

The TRC as Literature, Performance, and Photograph

These are important critiques of the politics and process of the TRC, but in no way do I take them to mean that the testimony given at hearings should be discarded like a "tear-stained tissue," as so eloquently described by Garneau. Rather, I would argue that for precisely those decolonizing reasons – and *not* to reconcile (we) settlers with (our) history, and *not* to make us comfortable – we should use the methods of literary and cultural analysis to interpret *The Survivors Speak*.[14]

One of the ways we should do this is to think of how that document, that PDF, functions as an archive, an archive of a performance, a performance documented with text and photography. Or perhaps it is more accurate to say that *The Survivors Speak* is a guide to an archive (the archive of the TRC), which then preserves a document of a performance of the thousands of performances by which survivors told their stories, narrated their lives, and, in particular, their lives at residential schools.[15] That performance – the range of survivors' testimony – may have been private, only for members of the Commission, or it may have been public. To discuss that performance more closely, I turn to a photograph in *Honouring the Truth, Reconciling for the Future: Summary of the Final Report of the Truth and Reconciliation Commission of Canada*. The photograph was taken by Piita Irniq, himself a survivor.

This photograph depicts two Inuit people giving testimony in Nunavik in 2011. It is an interesting photograph because you can see those testifying (they are not named) and the community from which they come. On the back wall of the community hall is a large painting of an *aiviq*, or walrus, its tusks framing the doorway and mirroring the open coats of the community members; in March, in the North, you keep your coat on, even inside.

12.1 Kuujjuaq community hearing, Nunavik, March 2011.

Prominent in the shot are the tissues mentioned by Garneau – in boxes on the front table and on a chair, in a community member's hands, held to her face.[16] People lean forward to listen: the man in the foreground places his hands flat on the table, as if imploring the Commission members (from whose point of view the photograph is taken) to pay him heed. The man next to him looks thoughtful, perhaps sad, which is the demeanour of most of the community members we can see.

What does it mean to argue that the survivors' giving of testimony is a performance and, further, that we can talk about such performance via a photograph, a photograph that is part of a digital archive of that testimony? The TRC events themselves, as many accounts and video documentations have shown, were highly staged and theatricalized. Even as survivors were guided in their testimony (with explanatory sessions, health support workers, and opening statements by "mentor survivors," if you will), elements of the events, down to Luke Marston's bentwood box, contributed to what Niezen calls an "ontological invulnerability" of the testimony: "as anthropologists have long recognized, [there is] no better way to cut through distractions and focus attention than to convey messages through ritualized performance."[17] Here I also give a nod to the debates that have taken place recently with respect to "liveness," documentation, performance, and the archive in the works of Peggy Phelan, Phillip Auslander, Diana Taylor, and Rebecca Schneider.[18] In *Performing Remains*, Schneider encapsulates this debate over the constructed nature of liveness, the role mediation plays in creating that illusion of liveness, and, further, the role of still photography with respect to performance.[19] This last role is germane to our text – our image-text, if you will – because the photograph is taken by a survivor, who himself appears, in both words and in a photograph, later in *The Survivors Speak*. So the photograph in this case *is part of the performance*, is part of the testimony. This is all the more true if we think of the deleterious role that photography has played in a colonial context. Edward Curtis's work is only the most (in)famous on the subject.[20]

One thing the photograph does is to remind the viewer that the stories and testimony collected in *The Survivors Speak* come from a community, a community or communities that were torn asunder by the colonial forces of residential school education. But community in a broader sense is also present, in the text and in the sheer number of voices – hundreds in total – that, even when collected as a dozen or so for a given chapter, will support one another, disagree, add to the reader's knowledge, and create the reader's knowledge.

But what is this knowledge that is being created? Before turning to the text of *The Survivors Speak*, let us revisit the title of this chapter, which asks the question, "Is the TRC a text?" For some readers, the answer will, thus far, be "no" – I have not really talked about texts; I have talked about a photograph, and some critical-political frameworks. My title refers to the titles of two earlier publications. The first (and most recent) is Warren Cariou's essay "Who Is the Text in this Class? Story, Archive and Pedagogy in Indigenous Contexts."[21] Cariou discusses the complexities involved when Omushkego Cree storyteller and Elder Louis Bird joins Cariou's university class to impart traditional Cree stories. The class has no printed textbooks and allows students to develop their listening and memory skills. When Cariou poses his question, he is inquiring into whether a text can be an oral performance, or the memory of the same. He is also echoing the second publication my title refers to: Stanley Fish's influential book *Is There a Text in This Class?*[22]

At least that was my hunch when a student brought Cariou's essay into a discussion of *The Survivors Speak*. So, leery of my own propensities for bringing everything back to theory, I e-mailed Cariou to ask him.[23] But, yes, he assured me, "when I was writing this piece I was thinking back to [Fish's] work from the '80s, including the stuff on interpretive communities. ... I still think Fish in that era has a good sense of the fluidity and contingency of speech-acts and interpretive communities that fits well with the sensibilities of the Indigenous storytellers I've spent time with."[24] So we already have, thanks to Cariou's appropriation of Fish to an indigenous context, a more fluid notion of what a text can convey: not just the printed word but also, perhaps, orality. To which we can, of course, add the insights of the last thirty years of cultural studies, which allows us to discuss the photograph as text, or "reading a film," and so on, but in a more specific way: can we not see precisely Fish's and Cariou's interpretive communities in the audience in the photograph?

What Do I Mean by "Orature"?

What do I mean by arguing that *The Survivors Speak*, a collection of orature, is a work of literature? It is partly a matter of reading, of interpretation. I want to use the tools of literary analysis to think about this text; for example, consider how little summary, transition, or exposition is to be found in the framing narratives of *The Survivors Speak*. But to speak of the formalism of orature means also to think about the overdetermined nature of the stumbles and repetition that characterize the narrative as structural indices of trauma. It means to think about the way language was simultaneously a form of indoctrination (students were forced to learn English or French) and a site for punishment (for speaking traditional languages). It means to propose a First Nations poetics (to be found, for example, in the stories of Okanagan storyteller Harry Robinson). Finally, in a more universal way, it means to think about orality in general, from its literary representations (William Gaddis, George V. Higgins) to the everyday. These poetic contortions of the oral, then, are a way of thinking about the testimony in terms of a call both for an "indigenist" methodology (Marie Battiste) or even Len Findley's exhortation to "always indigenize!" and for the universalism of the event, in the sense that the poetic characteristics of the text embody the demand on the part of the TRC (its calls to action) for education, for activating

the archive. To read *The Survivors Speak* as literature, as orature is significant, first of all, because of how residential school students were indoc-
trinated, often through the most violent of methods, to abandon their
traditional languages and to learn, speak, and write English or French. Here
is Peter Nakogee: "That's where I had the most difficulty in school because
I didn't understand English. My hand was hit because I wrote on my scribblers, the scribblers that were given on starting school, pencils, erasers, rulers
and that, scribblers, and textbooks that were given. 'Write your names,' she
said, so they don't get lost. But I wrote on my scribblers in Cree syllabics.
And so I got the nun really mad that I was writing in Cree. And then I only
knew my name was Ministik from the first time I heard my name, my
name was Ministik. So I was whipped again because I didn't know my name
was Peter Nakogee."[25] Nakogee's testimony has been translated from the
Swampy Cree, and thus is already, ontologically, an example of resistance
to the residential schools: even though punished as a child, he did not forget
the use of his traditional language. Equally important here is that he is already
writing: Nakogee tells us he "wrote on [his] scribblers in Cree syllabics."
Here is an indication that we must not fall into a primitivist myth of First
Nations or Indigenous orality, seeing orality as intrinsically and exclusively
Indigenous, or, worse yet, naturally so. Rather, if Nakogee's testimony is a
kind of second-order orality (speech about writing), it is also yet more evidence of the important role that Indigenous writing has had, Margery Fee
tells us, since the eighteenth century.[26]

The very real trauma that we are talking about here, in depriving children
of their language, is apparent in Lily Bruce's testimony: "I was just getting
dressed into pyjamas, and I never, I never spoke English. [crying] My auntie
was told to tell me that I wasn't allowed to speak Kwak'wala anymore. I
told her, 'But Auntie, I don't know how to speak English.' And she says,
'Well you're gonna have to learn pretty quick.' [crying] She said, 'From now
on, you have to speak English.' I don't know how long it took me. I kept
my mouth shut most of the time. I'd rather keep quiet than get in trouble."[27]
Bruce's auntie was a student at the Alberni residential school and thus, on
Lily Bruce's first night at the school, was told to impress upon Bruce the importance of speaking only English. As might be expected, crying is mentioned
often in *The Survivors Speak*, over one hundred times (but also, a few times,
survivors mention *not* crying when being strapped, as a point of pride). The
decision of the editors of *The Survivors Speak* to emphasize the crying needs

to be highlighted: it is virtually the only expository signal of affect in the text. It is a choice that reminds us of Garneau's "tear-stained tissue" remark. Here we can also agree with Audra Simpson's trenchant critique of "the reconciliation hustler tour" and where, in another context, she writes that "to be a subject of pity, or sympathy … is not an efficacious model of political subjectivity in an historical field of collective captivity, the condition that some indigenous critics might argue, is the correct approximation of current native 'conditions.'"[28]

Notable here is that Lily Bruce is crying as she tells her story of not being allowed to speak her Kwak'wala language. Bruce's crying breaks through the temporalities of testimony and archive, and achieves, as we will see in a later excerpt with Benjamin Joseph Lafford's "Wow," a present-ness, a live-ness, an audible now-ness.[29]

The abundance of accounts in *The Survivors Speak* dealing with the loss of language is authoritative. Geraldine Shingoose tells us: "I just remember, recalling the very first memories was just the beatings we'd get and the lickings, and just for speaking our language, and just for doing things that were against the rules."[30] Margo Wylde couldn't speak French, and said: "I felt I was a captive."[31] William Antoine spoke Ojibway and didn't understand English: the teacher "would get mad at me."[32] Marcel Guilboche, Andrew Bull Calf, and Alfred Nolie all describe being strapped for not knowing English.[33] Said Bull Calf, "the only language we spoke was Blackfoot."[34] Calvin Myerion describes the cruel paradoxes: "I was told not to speak my Native language, and I didn't know any other language other than my Native language" and "my brother, who had been there before me, taught me in, said in my language not to talk the language."[35] Percy Thompson recalled being slapped in the face for speaking Cree: "Was I supposed to learn English words, so the nun would be happy about it? It's impossible."[36] Meeka Alivaktuk, who "came to the Pangnirtung school … with no knowledge of English," was slapped on her hands: "That's how my education began."[37]

And yet while Arthur Ron McKay wet himself because he could not at first speak English, "I just kept going and I couldn't speak my language but then I was speaking to boys in the, 'cause they came from the reserve and they speak my language. We used to speak lots, like behind, behind our supervisors or whatever you call it. That's why I didn't lose my language."[38] That Peter Nakogee and Meeka Alivaktuk (and twelve others in *The Survivors*

Speak) testified in their traditional language shows, in however marginal a way, that language loss has not been total. Important, too, is the determination and drive of the survivors, not only to remember and to recount but also to reflect, often acerbically, on that cruel oppression: "It's impossible," Percy Thompson said. "That's how my education began," added Meeka Alivaktuk. "Our supervisors *or whatever you call it*," retorted Arthur Ron McKay. Indeed – what do you call it?

As noted earlier, *The Survivors Speak* is broken up into thirty-two sections, arranged both chronologically and thematically. Each section has a title and typically an epigraph, from one of the survivors' stories. The first section, "Life before residential school," includes the epigraph: "We were loved by our parents." The first story is from Bob Baxter:

When I think back to my childhood, it brings back memories, really nice memories of how life was as Anishnaabe, as you know, how we, how we lived before, before we were sent to school. And the things that I remember, the legends at night that my dad used to tell us stories, and how he used to show us how to trap and funny things that happened. You know there's a lot of things that are really, that are still in my thoughts of how we were loved by our parents. They really cared for us. And it was such a good life, you know. It, it's doing the things, like, it was free we were free I guess was the word I'm looking for, is a real free environment of us. I'm not saying that we didn't get disciplined if we got, if we did something wrong, we, you know. There was that, but not, and it was a friendly, friendly, like a loving discipline, if you will.[39]

Baxter's narrative is typical of *The Survivors Speak*'s first section in how it beautifully captures a prelapsarian past, often what seems to be a time before contact or capitalism, one where traditional land-based practices (hunting, trapping, fishing, gathering) abound, with traditional foods, family life, and, especially poignant, the role of storytelling, songs, and legends. And even here, in remembering a gentle and idyllic past, the narrative itself skips and jumps: "as you know, how we, how we lived before, before we were sent to school." And: "It, it's doing the things, like, it was free we were free I guess was the word I'm looking for." Baxter also delineates the quality of family discipline (if you want to call it that, but he does), again in that beautiful, hesitant way: "I'm not saying that we didn't get disciplined if we got, if we did something wrong, we, you know. There was that, but not, and it was a friendly, friendly, like a loving discipline, if you will."

It is crucial to note how this quotation works in terms of the overall structure of the book (or archive, or PDF …) that is *The Survivors Speak*. The coherence here of a past, a *before*, with the structure of the book itself poses an interpretive conundrum, for we have to keep in mind that *The Survivors Speak* is an arranged narrative. We should not be naïve and expect – or assume – that Bob Baxter necessarily told this story at the beginning of his narrative, or that he told it before anyone else.

I want to hold onto this notion of temporality (what, in structuralist poetics, is called the distinction between story and plot), and turn to a passage from Benjamin Joseph Lafford's account of taking a train to the Shubenacadie residential school in Nova Scotia:

So that morning, we heard the, told my brothers we had to sit over here and wait for the train to come. So we heard a train, we heard a whistle and we said, and my brother said, "Oh, that's the train coming to pick us up, pick us up." I said, "Okay," you know. So when the train came, they put us on, Indian agents put us on, the RCMP put us on the train. Told us to sit over here. So it doesn't matter, so we left from Grand Narrows. Every station we stopped at, there was children. Native children, that had long hair when I looked out the window.

And I went, "Wow, there's more children going on the train, probably they're going the same way as I'm going." So at that time it didn't matter to me, so every station we stopped, there was Native children, girls and boys. And there was RCMP and an Indian agent lining them up, put them on the train, put them on the seats. No one's talking about anything, I didn't know them. Every station, and by the time we got to Truro, there was full of Native people, Native children on the train. Wow, there was a whole bunch of us. Had long hair, you know, had no clothes to take with them.[40]

Again, as with Baxter's narrative, we have here syntax that has been torqued, or broken, or intervened into, with gaps, repetition, elisions: "we heard the, told my brothers." We have temporal shifts: "RCMP and an Indian agent lining them up, put them on the train, put them on the seats." We have deictic references to the telling of the story, that is to say, to its performance: "had long hair, you know"; and interjections that do the same work: the repetition of "Wow, there's more children" and "Wow, there was a whole bunch of us." [41]

These temporal and deictic shifters are both aspects of performance and examples of what Paul de Man, referencing both literary analysis and theatre, calls "anacoluthon," "parabasis," and "buffo." [42] The last two terms come from Greek Old Comedy and Italian *commedia dell'arte*, respectively: the former refers to points at which the Chorus addresses the audience directly, while the latter "is the disruption of narrative illusion, the *aparté*, the aside to the audience, by means of which the fiction is broken." [43] "Anacoluthon," while not deriving from performance or theatre, denotes a syntactic-temporal shift in a narrative, even at the level of the sentence. De Man is using terms from theatre and literature (he cites Proust as an example of anacoluthon). Why should we now bring such a vocabulary to an oral account of what is certainly *not* fiction – what is already, perhaps, oral history?

In some ways, my answer is framed by the question. Precisely because this is a text that contains oral testimony, it is easy, if not predictable, to read it for its Truth (and here I capitalize the noun to denote both the TRC itself and the notion of an actual Truth, not the mutable, or postmodern, truth often bandied about). And the Truth in this testimony, in this orature, then, comes not only from its content, from the accounts of the survivors, but also from the form, from the shifting and temporal cuts, from the "Wow" that brings a child's perception of a train trip, in the 1950s, into the minds and ears of readers in the second decade of the twenty-first century.

Here the work of Lee Maracle may be helpful, not only for ethical or political reasons (the urgency with which we may feel to bring indigenous critical frameworks to bear on indigenous texts) but also for how it both adds a new dimension to how to think about *The Survivors Speak* and offers a useful counterpoint to de Man's stress on the meta-performative. There are two ways in which I read Maracle's notions of oratory, as developed in the oratories, or essays, collected in *Memory Serves:* in terms of the relationship between oratory and memory, and the meta-generic or meta-theoretical way in which Maracle develops her concept of oratory. As developed in the essay or oratory titled "Memory Serves," memory is directional, a matter of reconstruction or remembering, and yet it is not merely a matter of recall, especially in the Salish and Stó:lō traditions of the West Coast. Here the

Stó:lō word/concept *Sqwa: lewel* is significant: felt ideas or felt thought, or, as she expressed it in an oratory in June 2016, "think feel."[44] Further, as she develops the concept of oratory throughout *Memory Serves,* oratory is a master-signifier, "unambiguous in its meaning,"[45] but also a way of "question[ing] the direction from which looking occurs" and "directed at that which is not seen, not known, at what is cherished and hidden,"[46] about "searching for what lies beneath the obvious,"[47] imagining "what direction each of the pathways" leads from others' stories. Finally, like critic Leanne Betasamosake Simpson, Maracle sees stories and oratories as inseparable from theory.

Consider, again, Benjamin Joseph Lafford's first sentence: "So that morning, we heard the, told my brothers we had to sit over here and wait for the train to come." Between "we heard the" and "told my brothers" we only see a comma, an indication that when transcribing Lafford's statement, there was presumably a short pause. Perhaps the missing subject of the predicate "told my brothers" is the "RCMP and an Indian agent" mentioned at other times in Lafford's statement. There is a gap here, a void, which is only apparent if we refuse to see Lafford's memory as unidirectional, if we listen as Maracle calls on us to listen. This gap is also a temporal or syntactic shift, an anacoluthon that forces the reader to reorient themselves, to think about their *direction.* Then, in that same sentence, the deictic shifter "here" does the work of a buffo or parabasis, as with the "you know"s and the "Wow"s elsewhere in Lafford's testimony: they point to the moment of the telling, flattening time, changing the direction of time, bringing the past into the present (into two presents: the present of the performance, of the testimony on 28 October 2011 in Halifax, as well as the present of the text, of the digital archive that is *The Survivors Speak*). The "Wow," the "you know," the "here" *are* here, are saying Wow, are saying Wow to you and to me. The challenge is to allow Maracle and de Man to guide us to what is cherished (Maracle's word) in *The Survivors Speak.* It is the Wow that is cherished.

A formalist analysis as I am proposing here triangulates between the medium-specificity of *The Survivors Speak,* the historical Real of colonialism, and an inscription of that colonialism to be found in the literary qualities of orature. Lafford's "Wow" travels through the time of the archive and its media, resisting the legacy of the residential schools before he even arrives at Shubenacadie, marking that resistance in an archive that itself is unsettled.

Conclusion

I want to be clear here about what I am *not* saying. I am not arguing that the statements of survivors provide the only record of residential schools, nor that such records should be read as typical or paradigmatic of the experiences of Indigenous people in Canada today. There exist many memoirs, statements, and other accounts of those experiences, from Basil Johnston's canonical (if I may put it that way) *Indian School Days* (1988); other novels and memoirs such as Tomson Highway's *Kiss of the Fur Queen* (1998), Richard Wagamese's *Indian Horse* (2012), Bev Sellars's *They Called Me Number One* (2013), and the recent (rough-hewn) and autobiographical *The Education of Augie Merasty* (2015); and documentary films such as *Our Voices, Our Stories* (Barb Cranmer, 2015) to scattered accounts that exist in other volumes (such as Marie Annharte Baker's AKA *Inendagosekwe* [2013]) and the abundance of online records (including but not limited to weweresofaraway.ca). *The Survivors Speak* is, nonetheless, a key document that offers, in its compressed form, a compendium of first-person accounts that can bring both literary and historical (and thus, in both senses, political) nuances to questions of the residential schools and reconciliation. Equally crucial, however, is the need to avoid constructing a new paradigm or stereotype of the suffering Indian, the abject survivor, and to avoid reinforcing a discourse that ignores the strength, courage, and hard work of survivors to get compensation and reconciliation onto the national agenda. As a worker on the Commission reminded me recently, the TRC itself, as a process coming out of the Indian Residential Schools Settlement Agreement, was in effect paid for *by the survivors*. By examining critically the cultural representations of *The Survivors Speak* as archive, as event, as literary text, as performance, and as visual object, we can better understand the impact of the residential schools, and the resistance to that legacy, which continues today.

NOTES

1   Duncan Mercredi, "Achimo," in *Indigenous Poetics in Canada,* ed. Neal McLeod (Waterloo: Wilfrid Laurier University Press, 2015), 17–22, 18.

2   Lee Maracle, *Memory Serves: Oratories*, ed. Smaro Kamboureli (Edmonton: NeWest Press, 2016), 239.

3 The term "orature" was coined by Ugandan linguist Pio Zirimu (d. 1977) in
   the early 1970s. Pio Zirimu used it as early as 1970, at first interchangeably
   with "oral literature," but later defined more precisely to mean "the use of
   utterance as an aesthetic means of expression." Ngũgĩ Wa Thiong'o, "Notes
   Towards a Performance Theory of Orature," *Performance Research* 12.3
   (September 2007), www.ohio.edu/people/hartleyg/ref/Ngugi_Orature.html (accessed 4 March 2019). The term then surfaced in a Canadian context in 1993
   in the first edition of *An Anthology of Canadian Native Literature in English*
   as a category of "Traditional Orature [from the] Southern First Nations." Terry
   Goldie and Daniel David Moses, eds., *An Anthology of Canadian Native Literature in English*, 4th ed. (Don Mills, ON: Oxford University Press Canada,
   2013), iii. Lee Maracle has categorized her texts as "oratory," with "concate-
   nation" between speaker and community privileged over self-expression, for
   "the point of oratory ... to create a passionate feeling for life and help people
   understand the need for change or preservation," but also, crucially, oratory
   is understood in a meta-theoretical sense, as in her "Oratory on Oratory,"
   Maracle, *Memory,* 172, 165, 229–50. Please see the final section of this
   chapter for more engagement with Maracle's oratories.

4 Residential schools were in existence before Confederation, including the
   Mohawk Institute in Brantford, Ontario, which operated from 1834 to 1970,
   making it "the longest operating residential school for Aboriginal people in
   Canadian history." Truth and Reconciliation Commission of Canada, *Canada's
   Residential Schools: The History, Part 1, Origins to 1939: The Final Report
   of the Truth and Reconciliation Commission of Canada, Volume I*, I–IV (Montreal and Kingston: McGill-Queen's University Press, 2015), 66. There were
   eleven schools still operating in the 1990s in Alberta, Saskatchewan, Ontario,
   and Quebec. Truth and Reconciliation Commission of Canada, *Canada's
   Residential Schools: The History, Part 2, 1939–2000: The Final Report of the
   Truth and Reconciliation Commission of Canada, Volume I*, I–IV (Montreal
   and Kingston: McGill-Queen's University Press, 2015), 103. The trajectory
   of residential schools in Canada's north is distinct in many ways.

5 The phrase "killing the Indian in the child" is often "but incorrectly attributed
   to Duncan Campbell Scott, though his actions as the head of the DIA [Depart-
   ment of Indian Affairs] between 1913 and 1932 suggest that he might have
   agreed with the idea." Dan Eshet, *Stolen Lives: The Indigenous Peoples of
   Canada and the Indian Residential Schools* (Toronto: Facing History and
   Ourselves, 2015), 123n11.

6 Truth and Reconciliation Canada, *Honouring the Truth, Reconciling for the Future: Summary of the Final Report of the Truth and Reconciliation Commission of Canada* (2015), 29.

7 In March 2016, I interviewed the editor of *The Survivors Speak*, a former broadcast journalist, who did not wish to be named out of deference to the survivors. As the editor described the process to me, most material came from statement gatherings but also other events, including sharing circles. The interviews were unstructured. Survivors were asked to talk about their residential school experiences, and what they thought about reconciliation. Most of the testimony was collected at national events. After material was transcribed and after a rough selection, material was checked or verified from recordings again. See also Greg Bak, "More Is More: Towards a Theory and Practice for Archival Decolonization" (keynote address, Archives Society of Alberta annual conference, Canmore, AB, 5 May 2016).

8 Wolfgang Ernst, *Digital Memory and the Archive*, ed. Jussi Parikka (Minneapolis: University of Minnesota Press, 2013), 113–14. Ernst draws here on Sven Spieker, *The Big Archive: Art from Bureaucracy* (Cambridge, MA: MIT Press, 2008). A "deep" media archeology would trace a temporality (what Ernst calls a "micro temporality") from testimony to recording, transcription to selection, digital publishing to cloud storage, downloading to interpretation. See also, in this regard, Wendy Hui Kyon Chun, *Programmed Visions: Software and Memory* (Cambridge, MA: MIT Press, 2011).

9 Ronald Niezen, *Truth and Indignation: Canada's Truth and Reconciliation Commission on Indian Residential Schools* (Toronto: University of Toronto Press, 2013), 36, 43.

10 Bill Curry, "Battle Lines Drawn over Preservation of Documents Detailing Abuse at Residential School," *The Globe and Mail* (4 June 2015): www.the globeandmail.com/news/politics/legal-battle-to-preserve-stories-of-residential-school-abuse-to-begin/article24813412/ (accessed 4 March 2019).

11 Of course, there still exists a "digital divide," and access to high-speed Internet connections is one of many infrastructure failings that bedevil remote and First Nations communities. See, for a discussion of Internet media and indigeneity, the public art project and exhibition catalogue, Lorna Brown and Clint Burnham, eds., *Digital Natives* (Vancouver: Other Sights, 2012).

12 David Garneau, "Imaginary Spaces of Conciliation and Reconciliation," *West Coast Line* (Summer 2012): 28–38; David Garneau with Clement Yeh, "Apology Dice: Collaboration in Progress," in *The Land We Are: Artists and Writers*

Unsettle the Politics of Reconciliation, ed. Gabrielle L'Hirondelle Hill and Sophie McCall (Winnipeg: ARP, 2015). A more recent version of "Imaginary Spaces" is in Dylan Robinson and Keavy Martin, eds., *From Arts of Engagement: Taking Aesthetic Action in and beyond The Truth and Reconciliation Commission of Canada* (Waterloo: Wilfrid Laurier University Press, 2016).

13 Gerald Taiaiake Alfred, "Restitution Is the Real Pathway to Justice for Indigenous Peoples," taiaiake.net (accessed 16 February 2016). Essay adapted from *Wasáse: Indigenous Pathways of Action and Freedom* (Peterborough: University of Toronto Press/Broadview, 2005).

14 Taiaiake Alfred has also made the cogent argument that it is a mistake to continue to define Indigenous people in terms of colonialism (see *Cutting Copper: Indigenous Resurgent Practice,* Morris and Helen Belkin Art Gallery, University of British Columbia, 4–5 March 2016, www.belkin.ubc.ca/events/cutting-coppers-lalakenis). Similarly, cheyenne turions has questioned the politics of the call to "decolonize" as also indebted to a colonial logic. Finally, Raymond Boisjoly works out this logic in his koan-like utterance *there is no way that things are supposed to have been.* cheyanne turions, "From Where Do You Speak? Locating the Possibility of Decolonization in Krista Belle Stewart's *Seraphine Seraphine,*" and Raymond Boisjoly, "Questions without Answers: Needs, Justifications, Explanations, Meaning," Wood Land School: Critical Anthology – A Symposium on Directions in Indigenous Contemporary Art, Or Gallery, Vancouver, 11–13 March 2016.

15 Here, by "performances," I mean the testimony of survivors, and not other cultural performances proper (drumming, dancing, music, oration by elders and officials). This characterization of testimony as performance is in no way an argument that the testimony was contrived, inauthentic, or otherwise dubious. Rather, with the greatest respect for the survivors' histories and trauma, it is a way of recognizing their courage and seeking to determine the ethical and political valences of the work they have done in coming forward – including, crucially, the performance of *not attending, not testifying.* Such non-performances have in turn to be distinguished from what Sarah Ahmed calls "nonperformativity." See Sarah Ahmed, "The Nonperformativity of Antiracism," *Meridians: Feminism, Race, Transnationalism* 7.1 (2006): 104–26, and Anna Carastathis, "The Nonperformativity of Reconciliation: The Case of 'Reasonable Accommodation' in Quebec," in *Reconciling Canada: Critical Perspectives on the Culture of Redress,* ed. Pauline Wakeham and Jennifer Henderson (Toronto: University of Toronto Press, 2013), 236–60.

16 Niezen provides a detailed ethnography of precisely the role of tissues, and their collection, at TRC events, noting that they were often ceremonially gathered and, at the close of the event, burned in the sacred fire (Niezen, *Truth*, 65). At the 2016 Chutzpah! festival in Vancouver, for a screening of *Our Voices, Our Stories* (Barb Cranmer, 2015), a documentary on the St Michaels Indian Residential School in Alert Bay, members of the IRSSS (Indian Residential School Survivor Society) were on hand as counsellors, with boxes of tissues. Here we have two problematics: on the one hand, the spectacle of the "suffering Indian," on the other, the way in which survivors are called on to be nurturers for emotion-wrought settlers.

17 Niezen, *Truth*, 67.

18 Rebecca Schneider, *Performing Remains: Art and War in Times of Theatrical Reenactment* (New York: Routledge, 2011). Diana Taylor, *The Archive and the Repertoire: Performing Cultural Memory in the Americas* (Durham, NC: Duke University Press, 2003).

19 Schneider, *Performing Remains*, 90–2, 94.

20 *Umeek* of Ahousaht (Richard Atleo) writes of an Edward Curtis photograph depicting a Nuu-chah-nulth bowman: "I am filled with that familiar sense of fear, oppression, helplessness, and powerlessness that I felt as a small child of seven years when I entered residential school." Pam Brown, et al., OLD IMAGES/NEW VIEWS: *Perspectives on Edward Curtis* (Vancouver: Museum of Anthropology, 2008), n.p. Gwich'in artist and performer Jeneen Frei Njootli has more recently made the forceful argument that Indigenous people have been working with photography since the nineteenth century. See Paul Chaat Smith, "Every Picture Tells a Story," in *Everything You Know about Indians Is Wrong* (Minneapolis: University of Minnesota Press, 2009), 1–6.

21 Warren Cariou, "Who Is the Text in this Class? Story, Archive and Pedagogy in Indigenous Contexts," in *Learn, Teach, Challenge: Approaching Indigenous Literatures*, ed. Deanna Reder and Linda Morra (Waterloo: Wilfrid Laurier University Press, 2016). Grateful acknowledgment is made to the author and editors for very generously allowing me to read the essay in manuscript.

22 Stanley Fish, *Is there a Text in this Class? The Authority of Interpretive Communities* (Cambridge, MA: Harvard University Press, 1980).

23 That is, we supposedly work now in a "post-theory" era. In this context, see Leanne Betasamosake Simpson's description of how "theory works ... within Nishnaabeg thought," which makes it clear, for instance, that she does not mean "theory in a Western context, which by nature is decontextualized

knowledge" and that she is more interested in "our embodied theory, [such as] our Creation stories." Leanne Betasamosake Simpson, "Land as Pedagogy: Nishnaabbeg Intelligence and Rebellious Transformation," *Decolonization: Indigeneity, Education & Society* 3.3 [2014], 1–25: 7, 11, 14. I should add that I would like to trouble the "decontextualized" versus "embodied" antinomy.

24 Warren Carriou, e-mail to Clint Burnham, 30 January 2016. Cariou is implicitly bringing two slightly different concepts of Fish's into his class, his essay, and our e-mail. Fish's phrase "is there a text in this class" has at least two meanings: "is there an assigned text in this literature class?" and "do we assign priority to meaning residing in the text or in readers' interpretations?"; this is "decided," Fish argues, depending on which interpretive community one occupies. Fish, *Is There a Text in This Class?*, 307.

25 Peter Nakogee, Statement to the TRC, Timmins, 9 November 2010, trans. from Swampy Cree into English, in *The Survivors Speak: A Report of the Truth and Reconciliation Commission of Canada* (2015), 48.

26 Here Margery Fee's work is important. See, for example, her chapter "'They Never Even Sent Us a Letter': Literacy and Land in Harry Robinson's Origin Story," *Literary Land Claims: The "Indian Land Question" From Pontiac's War to Attawapiskat* (Waterloo: Wilfrid Laurier University Press, 2015).

27 Lily Bruce, Statement to the TRC, Alert Bay, 4 August 2011 (*The Survivors Speak*, 48–9).

28 Thanks to Warren Cariou for pushing me on the resonance of the "crying" in *The Survivors Speak* and to Smokii Sumac for the Audra Simpson references. See Simpson, "The Chief's Two Bodies: Theresa Spence and the Gender of Settler Sovereignty" (keynote address, *Unsettling Conversations, Unmaking Racisms and Colonialisms: R.A.C.E. Network's 14th Annual Critical Race and Anticolonial Studies Conference*, University of Alberta, Edmonton, October 2014); and Simpson, "Comment: The 'Problem' of Native Mental Health: Liberalism, Multiculturalism and the (non) Efficacy of Tears," *Ethos* 36.3 (2008): 376–9, 379. A clarification is, perhaps, necessary here. As noted in the main text, survivors mention crying more than one hundred times in their testimony; in addition, in six different survivors' testimonies, *they themselves cry*, as noted with "[audible crying]" or "[crying]."

29 At other times in *The Survivors Speak*, the annotation "audible crying" is used.

30 Geraldine Shingoose, Statement to the TRC, Winnipeg, 19 June 2010 (*The Survivors Speak*, 50).

31 Margo Wylde, Statement to the TRC, Val d'Or, 5 February 2012 (*The Survivors Speak*, 47).

32 William Antoine, Statement to the TRC, Little Current, 12 May 2011 (*The Survivors Speak*, 47).

33 Marcel Guiboche, Statement to the TRC, Winnipeg, 19 June 2010 (*The Survivors Speak*, 48); Alfred Nolie, Statement to the TRC, Alert Bay, 20 October 2011 (*The Survivors Speak*, 47).

34 Andrew Bull Calf, Statement to the TRC, Lethbridge, 10 October 2013 (*The Survivors Speak*, 49).

35 Calvin Myerion, Statement to the TRC, Winnipeg, 16 June 2010 (*The Survivors Speak*, 48).

36 Percy Thompson, Statement to the TRC, Hobbema, 25 July 2013 (*The Survivors Speak*, 49).

37 Meeka Alivaktuk, Statement to the TRC (translated from the Inuktitut), Pangnirtung, 13 February 2012 (*The Survivors Speak*, 49).

38 Arthur Ron McKay, Statement to the TRC, Winnipeg, 18 June 2010 (*The Survivors Speak*, 47, 53).

39 Bob Baxter, Statement to the TRC, Thunder Bay, 25 November 2010 (*The Survivors Speak*, 3).

40 Benjamin Joseph Lafford, Statement to the TRC, Halifax, 28 October 2011 (*The Survivors Speak*, 26).

41 There are many moments in the testimony of notable repetition. A few examples include: "My mother opened the letter and I could see her face; I could see her face, it was kind of sad but mad too." Josephine Eshkibok, Statement to the TRC, Little Current, 13 May 2011 (*The Survivors Speak*, 13). "[My father] said, 'I, I will, I will go, I would go in jail, I will go in jail if I didn't let you go.'" Paul Dixon, Statement to the TRC, Val d'Or, 6 February 2012 (*The Survivors Speak*, 15). "I didn't have a wife at the time and I felt that was a good place for her, so I wasn't really fully aware of the, you know, the negative parts of, the parts, negative, negativity of residential school 'cause really, I guess, when I look at the residential school issue, you know I saw, you know, physically, I guess, better than what I experienced at the reserve." [Name redacted], Statement to the TRC, Key First Nation, 21 January 2012 (*The Survivors Speak*, 19).

42 Paul de Man, "The Concept of Irony," in *Aesthetic Ideology*, ed. Andrzej Warminski, (Minneapolis: University of Minnesota Press, 1996), 163–84.

43 Ibid., 178.

44 Maracle, *Memory*, 1–49, 2, 14. Also in conversation with Cyndy Baskin, Toronto, 1 June 2017.

45 Ibid., 161.

46 Ibid., 231.

47 Ibid., 232.

13

The Material of Palinodic Time
Sounding the Voice of Lisa Robertson's Archival Poetics

JESSI MACEACHERN

Introduction: The Poet's Audible Archive

Canadian poet Lisa Robertson, who spent her early years associated with Vancouver's Kootenay School of Writing and has since been involved in feminist and experimental communities across Canada and the U.S., has spent much time in the archives. In particular, she has frequented her own archive, housed in the Simon Fraser University (SFU) Library Special Collections: Contemporary Literature Collection. Access to this archive is restricted,[1] but the materials within proliferate in unexpected ways outside the institutional confines. The 2010 collection *R's Boat*, built on fragments culled from the notebooks housed there, demonstrates the poet's creative intervention in her archive. Further demonstrating the escape of these material traces are the audio and visual recordings of the writer reading the many versions of these poems. These mostly online videos exist variously in catalogues such as PennSound or as yet unindexed search results hosted by YouTube or Vimeo. With each digital iteration of the recitation, the original archival materials are at once repeated and recanted. In Robertson's multiple performances of "Palinode/," a poem from *R's Boat* (2010), it is the ancient palinodic form that begets this paradoxical move. The palinode repeats history in order to recant it; that is, the palinode creates a phantom double in order to deny written history the status of the real. The palinode is an inherently oral form that, by admitting fault with the documents it repeats in negative, prompts rupture and change. In its unique transformation of pasts and futures, the palinodic voice begins to undo the archive.

As scholarly concepts of the archive multiply,[2] the audible remains a tricky category of sensory experience for the researcher. Audio and visual recordings are a relatively new phenomenon in the history of human creative and intellectual production, but the rapid acceleration of technological development has guaranteed that even recent attempts at such records are increasingly difficult to replay. Inside special collections devoted to contemporary writers, audio tapes or reels sit ignored; few libraries any longer house the technology to play them, and even fewer have digitized these materials. Research into the archiving process as it pertains to the audible is a growing field – for instance, Jonathan Sterne's *The Audible Past: Cultural Origins of Sound Reproduction* (2003) is an extensive and impressive examination of the theoretical problem of capturing audio; Jason Camlot and Christine Mitchell's co-edited volume of *Amodern* stages a critical inquiry into the audio recordings of a particular literary event; and in chapter 2 of this book, Deanna Fong investigates the ontological status of the "tiny events" recorded on tape. Rather than concentrate on the material media that preserve traces of the audible in institutional archives, this chapter explores an unarchivization of poetics and voice through a particular mode of poetic production.

The voice, as an ontological category, is of distinct interest here. As Fong writes, "the more we try to pin down a definition of the voice, the more it escapes us; it is neither the exclusive territory of language nor the body, neither a guarantee of interior presence, nor an autonomous force 'out there' in the world."[3] As technology that "both affirms and negates a sense of selfhood,"[4] the voice is a necessary tool for the repetitive (i.e., affirmative) and recantatory (i.e., negative) functions of the palinode. Even before the advent of audio recording, the palinodic voice resonated "across a striated temporality"[5] – denying broadcasted pasts and projected futures in order to resonate within the polyphonic present. Over the course of this chapter, I discuss the peculiar effects of the palinode, a poetic form that recants a previous performance by the same poet. The palinode employs the negative ("It was not I," "No, it was not so") in order to multiply possibility. It is due to its recantatory mode, which denies the framing structures of written history in order to reveal what more has gone unseen or unheard, that the palinode is a tool capable of intervening in the literary archive.

"The archive" is a term I use here to refer, firstly, to actual collections of literary materials housed by institutions and, secondly, to the archive as newly mobilized theoretical concept, such that "archives are not just institutional sites, but also spatio-temporal processes" and that archiving is "an historical, material, and ideological set of practices."[6] The recitation of the palinode affirms the existence of past performances – it is built upon their very traces – through repetition, but it also resolutely discards this past through recantation, in order to intervene in the present possibility of the poem. It is this double movement of affirmation and negation that makes it of particular use to the poet and the reader looking to escape the archive. The classical poet who invented the palinode, Stesichorus, relied on his voice as a compositional tool. These unrecorded and proliferative recitations simultaneously create and de-create the poetic subject, so that the item left for the archive is arguably more phantom than real. The subject of Stesichorus's palinode, Helen of Troy, consequently becomes more phantom than real as well. The localities from which she recites her song are multiplied (i.e., she is in Egypt now) and her previous crimes are negated (i.e., she was never in Troy). The subject of Stesichorus's palinode is the woman and the material effects, within the epic lyric's immaterial archives, of her purported beauty; the subject of the palinode is the resounding material and immaterial effects of the poetic voice.

The Role of Composition and Performance

In a 2015 *Paris Review* interview with Ben Lerner, Eileen Myles describes a different view of the role of voice and performance in composition. Separating the utterance from the written word, Myles insists, "the most exciting thing is to read a poem out loud for the first time. There's a whole kind of inside thing bursting out, and I'm always dying to hear it. I do hear it in my head, but I never read it out loud to myself until I'm in front of people."[7] In this schema, the literary event is the singular vehicle for voice, and the audience is a key factor of its emergence. Lerner, a poet himself, is surprised to hear that, for Myles, performance does not coexist with composition, that Myles does not read the poem out loud when writing it. In fact, the oral, performative practice Lerner considers tantamount to the act of composition, Myles considers "obscene."[8] It is my contention that Myles's use of this word relegates certain compositional practices to defeated zones of exciting possibility. After all, the proper subject of the palinode is certainly obscene: woman and her beauty. My concern is not the sacred voice of Myles's poetics, though that merits much exploration, but the alternate – and obscene – schema Myles invites. It is a schema that exists beyond simple dichotomies such as inside and outside.

In her interview with Lerner, Myles fervently insists the poet's role is one of medium: for a voice that emerges inside the writer from outside the self. "It isn't a literal voice – at all. But there is a murmuring."[9] Poetry, for Myles, is "this old thing mumbling inside" of them.[10] The literary event is an instance of aftermath in the stead of the composition's advent,[11] and the moment that Myles does read their poem aloud is one they consider holy: "What is so great – I'll even say holy – about reading a poem for the first time in front of people is that you're sharing what you felt in the moment of composition, when you were *allowing* something. [author emphasis] When I'm writing the poem, I feel like I have to close my eyes. I don't mean literally, but you invite a kind of blindness and that's the birth of the poem. Writing is all performance."[12] Yet there is not simply an advent and aftermath in Myles's writing. If the event (i.e., the recitation) is accepted as a sacred present in which the poem is uttered, the voice is a vehicle of perpetual becoming: the poem will be *repeated* in future presents, thus recanting the originary event. Myles does not clarify what ontological category the voice fulfills when between events, but it is implied that, through the voice, the poem enters into a differentiated movement of becoming again and again.

The Recitation/Repetition/Recantation of the Palinode

The poem's capacity for perpetual becoming in the presence of receptive bodies especially intrigues me in the case of the palinode, a poetic form with the unique ability to prefigure its audience. It is a form Robertson approaches as "obscene"[13] and a form historically associated with the "blindness"[14] inherent to poetic recitation. The palinode was invented as a form of response and, especially, of recantation. We know it was invented in the sixth century BCE by Stesichorus. Of Stesichorus, we know little except that, prior to writing his palinode, he was blinded by Helen. In order to emphasize the radically negative construction of his palinode's single surviving fragment, I quote Anne Carson's characteristically ex-centric translation: "No it is not the true story. / No you never went on the benched ships. / No you never came to the towers of Troy."[15]

The palinode recants the insult Stesichorus had previously brought against Helen, and the form's legacy unfolds from a miraculous restoration of sight, or (more likely) a performative recantation of insight. Its peculiar form of address – as apology for a previous poetic gesture – infers that the audience has previously engaged with the impoverished mirror image of the present recitation. In a displacement of the creative agency believed to exist between author and reader, the palinode obscures the author-subject in order to foreground a complex ground of composition and performance. The palinode is a passive form, in that the text does not resist having its original body de-created, and is endlessly receptive. Meanwhile, the audience is active, in that they (preformed by the act of apology assured by the form of the poem) decide the degree to which the poem's passive interior will in fact become a spatial or temporal event.

In order to explore the relevance of this classic form to contemporary poetics and politics, I will analyze the many versions of Robertson's "Palinode/" from 2010's *R's Boat* and map the trajectory of the poet's voice through the *material* of palinodic time. Robertson's many collections blur the distinction between visual art and literature, as well as the distinction between prose and poetry. *R's Boat* continues the poet's tendency to explore the sentence, in particular as a unit capable of disrupting narrative and, more importantly, ideas of identity and subjectivity. This follows the experiments of the U.S. writers involved in L=A=N=G=U=A=G=E poetry, as well as the grammatical disruptions of Gertrude Stein. Through this vehicle of the sentence, *R's Boat* examines the poet's own archive housed in SFU Library Special Collections.

It is not the first time the poet has taken to the archive – *The Weather* (2001) fragments historical texts from the British Library – but *R's Boat* is notable for the unique, if "solipsistic" as Robertson admits,[16] return to her own materials. The "Palinode/" that completes the book recants the possibility of unearthing a single author-subject from the materials upturned. This erasure presents a multiplied temporality: the defeated past, unbounded present, and differentiated future of the palinodic form. These are the temporal modes necessary for Stesichorus to soothe Helen's ire, to become no longer blind. With unparalleled lines of relation and possible becoming between these multiple and multiplying temporal locations, Robertson's palinodic text sounds the poetic voice in and beyond the various temporal modes proposed by Myles's earlier schema: the voice that pre-exists the individual writer, the writer's voice that emerges in the act of composition, and the physical utterance that unfolds before an audience. Due to its creative intervention in the archive, Robertson's "Palinode/" recites, recants, and repeats within each of these temporal zones simultaneously. The "final" versions of the poem recant the originary event; simultaneously, these ever-changing versions of the poem repeat the event of the earlier recitations. Due to the record of her performative voice, the unbounded present of the literary event hastens backward to reveal multiple advents in the material traces of previous drafts and scored-out lines, and lunges forward to reveal multiple aftermaths in which the digital phantom of the poet recites, recants, and repeats these traces of a self under erasure.

Accounting for these dizzying lines of temporal tracing are the many versions of Robertson's "Palinode/." It is absent from the early chapbook *Rousseau's Boat* (2004), though the surrounding material is intact and the initial poem "Passivity," uncollected in future versions, foretells much about her use of the palinodic form; it first appears as "Palinodes," with a companion essay, "On Palinode," in the *Chicago Review* (Spring 2006); and the final poem, "Palinode/," appears in the final collection entitled *R's Boat*. *R's Boat* is an expanded and contracted version of the previous phantom-versions of the poem. This dual action, folding outward and inward simultaneously, is a quintessential element of the poet's process: the writing has expanded in that several new poems appear, and has contracted in that earlier lines have now been culled. To the latter point, even the title has been shortened from *Rousseau's Boat* to *R's Boat*. In this decision to provide the initial (the letter *R*) rather than the proper name, Robertson multiplies the identity of the individual who owns the boat (in which one thinks, reads, and/or writes): Rousseau/Robertson/Reader. To recant, in this instance, is to multiply; it is also to open onto the void and allow "the very condition that permits transformation and radical change."[17] These series of expansions and contractions in the material of the poem suggest a way to engage Gilles Deleuze's multidisciplinary theory of the fold, as well as his concept of the event, in the spirit of Elizabeth Grosz's and Rosi Braidotti's feminist appropriations of his proliferative theory, alongside Robertson's own aesthetic critique of radical materiality. In this way, I may posit a use for Stesichorus's fragmented form in unveiling political fictions and destabilizing hierarchical textual relations.

Contrary to Myles's schema of the holy voice that arrives only in the aftermath of composition, Robertson's enunciated phonemes, typographical manipulations, and paratactic subversions resist rather than reaffirm the outer limits of language in order to open onto something else – as Fong does in the Roy Kiyooka archive – onto something beyond logos itself. In fact, Robertson suggests that the inside/outside of a text is a myth that prevents becoming-subjects from possessing agency on and off the page. In an earlier essay, "My Eighteenth Century: Draft towards a Cabinet" (2003), Robertson writes that "the suchness or quiddity of the print on the page, the phoneme on the air, the paratactic fragment, stand in current 'innovative' poetries as material metaphors for the radical outer limits of language as a social medium."[18] Rather than affirm the use of these "material metaphors," Robertson's objective is to critique and interrogate the ways in which this "radical materiality" sustains the "political fiction" of difference.[19] Like Braidotti in her re-figurations of epistemology in *Metamorphoses: Towards a Materialist Theory of Becoming* (2002) and *Transpositions: On Nomadic Ethics* (2006), Robertson refuses the philosophical and psychoanalytical notion of difference (i.e., sexual, racial, or class difference) as pejorative. Locating the middle ground between male/female, white/black, and rich/poor as a zone of potential becoming, Robertson suggests that "the materially radical outer limit is a frontier myth."[20] In a page from "Palinodes," which is absent from the final collection, she echoes this assertion in the line: "The space was not about its edges."[21] I attempt to further dissociate the text from any such modernist preoccupation with edges by blurring the distinction between its material and immaterial forms – thus engaging with its many phantom versions inside and outside the archive, as printed page and as spoken word.

Interventions in the Archive

Robertson's *R's Boat* is an explicit intervention by the poet in her archive. The book develops from a series of indices the poet created during the transfer of her personal materials – or "garbage"[22] – to SFU. Robertson describes the motive behind creating these indices in an interview with Kate Eichhorn: "I wanted to see if I could construct an autobiographical text which was indexical but not self-referential in a narrative sense. I wanted to see what linguistic subjectivity could become in relation to the pure exteriority of the archive."[23] This was pointedly not an attempt to find herself – that is, the poems do not reveal a solid author-subject – but rather, it was an attempt to "leave" the archive,[24] even as her materials were entering it. "Palinode/" further allows this escape. Its recantatory mode provides the means to create a rupture within the material traces left in the archive. Robertson's intervention in the archive is an intervention in the presumed solidity of the archive's potential subject, "of taking that body apart, of distributing it across a surface."[25] The final "Palinode/" is composed of negatively constructed sentences selected from the sixty-nine notebooks housed in the Special Collections. Within its repeated refusals, the reader gleans a sense of the event of composition in the archive: "Though my object is history not neutrality, / I am prepared to adhere to neither extreme."[26] Already, the intervention is suspect – neither historical, nor neutral; it is questioned whether the event of composition came to be at all: "Perhaps this did not occur in a material sense."[27]

Of course, it would be beside the point to suggest there exists a coherent narrative from line to line. These sentences are not about the writing process any more than they are about the author-subject. However, the passivity of the form does not resist the reader's interpellation of meaning and continuity, though it manages, by its recurrent recantation ("It was not I," "No, it was not"), to avoid becoming such a staid object of singular description. Robertson, like Myles, requires the audience to create the event of the poem's becoming. However, the difference for Robertson is the admission that the performative is already always present in the compositional process; within palinodic time, the voice is perpetually involved in recitation, recantation, and repetition.

This complicated temporality carries across the entire book, embodied by the forward slash that follows the title of each of the six long poems. Significantly, this relational mark is multiplied in "Palinode/"; it occurs at the beginning of each page. The forward slash, isolated to its own line, symbolizes the relationship between the text that came before and the text that follows. The typographical mark also symbolizes the relationship between the voice that pre-existed the poem and the voice that reads the poem to an audience. In a page that does not appear in the final version of the poem, approaching the end of the earlier "Palinodes," Robertson writes: "We cannot know a gesture, a page, speech."[28] In this line, she closely aligns these techniques of composition and performance. The page, with its mute words, is enveloped by the embodied gesture and the sounded voice. All three of the aforementioned materials (gesture, page, speech) constitute an event, the purpose of which is to communicate. All three use voice, though not always literally. All three, in one way or another, might escape the scope of a material archive: the gesture if it has not been photographed, the page if it deteriorates, the speech if it has not been recorded. In "Palinode/," these events unfold *in absentia* or, as previously said, as though they "did not occur in a material sense."[29] Though this line about the unknowability (the un-occurrence) of the event does not appear in the final poem, it continues to exist in the archive from which it has escaped. It is one of the *"specific losses"*[30] to which the researcher who seeks to undo the archive must be attuned. This persistent trace of the unknown further confirms the impossibility of forming a coherent account of the life that accumulated among the spatially confined and temporally unbounded archival ephemera.

The archive is the overarching constraint that enables the poet's creative self-erasure. In her aforementioned interview with Eichhorn, Robertson describes the archive as "a tight frame – a bounded frame – in which anarchic variability appears."[31] Here, the poet differs with Eichhorn, whose research rather affirms the order found in the archive and insistently celebrates the work of the archivists and librarians who create indices and finding aids. In contrast, Robertson, investigating the self that persists in exteriority of the archive's constraints, insists that "the order of the archive is a falsity … It's projected, not actual" (381). Similarly, the order of the poems in her autobiographical text is a falsity as well. There is no narrative progression in the six poems of her collection, from "Face/" to "Palinode/," only a self-effacement that underscores the impossibility of knowing the author-subject.

Eichhorn notes in *The Archival Turn in Feminism* (2013) that it has become "commonplace to understand the archive as something that is by no means bound by its traditional definition as a repository for documents."[32] It is seized by contemporary scholars, especially feminist and queer scholars, as "theory, curatorial trope, poetic form, subject of inquiry, and site of research."[33] Within this seizure of new tropological meaning for the once dusty place is the possibility for creative interventions like Robertson's. The story told by the poet writing her autobiography, like the story told by the archivist ordering a special collection, need not conform to a singular truth. Finding aids and indices, rather than preserving absolute identity, might instead be repositories for *gaps* and *absences* in knowledge[34] – much in the way that the palinode contains (and repeats) what is *no longer* being said: what *has been* recited, what *will be* recanted.

Time in the Archive

From the facing inscription of Robertson's "Palinode/," as it appears in *R's Boat*, the form is concerned with time: "This Is the Beginning of Utopia / Its Material Is Time" (68). The difficulty with this description is the degree to which we, as beings in time, ever think of *time* as material. Ahead of Robertson's aphorism, Grosz, in *The Nick of Time: Politics, Evolution, and the Untimely* (2004), confronts this problem head-on by resituating the ontology of time – like that of its frequent partner, space – as the ontology of a material. Thinking of time as a malleable substance further transforms the archive into a site for creative and critical intervention. The material traces are no longer spatially confined, but – as with the palinode – temporally unbounded.

The first page of "Palinode/" is written in the present tense, and, in fact, the speaker is resolutely fixed to the present throughout the poem. The terms of this temporal reality, in which the speaker goes neither backward nor forward, are dependent on something exterior. So, too, is the form of the palinode (a response, a recantation, an apology) dependent on an audience exterior to itself. Robertson writes: "That which can no longer be assumed in consciousness becomes insolvent / Because it doesn't finish I can be present."[35] Does Robertson here refer to the precipitating event of the palinode? In the history of the form, Helen has become phantom and exits the ontology of whoredom. The poet (first, Homer; then, Stesichorus) is struck blind. Considering Robertson's use of the word "insolvent," however, we may wish to insist on a relationship between blindness and debt. For the poet who recants appears to owe the subject something that cannot be paid. If, in fact, debt *is* a synonym for blindness, the palinode is the form in which the poet reassesses their finances.[36] The palinode unravels in a present apart from the mistaken past and the broke(n) future. In writing the palinode, Stesichorus's credit rating is repaired. In archiving her collected papers, Robertson acquires the literal capital necessary to mobilize herself.[37]

Robertson recants her previous forays into the archive (into history, neutrality, and the past) and embraces the present economics of the archived (and subsequently unarchived) page. Affirming this are the changes between this book version of the poem and the "Palinodes" that appears in the *Chicago Review*. For example, in the first page of the final "Palinode/," there are two major omissions: first, two stanzas about the loss of "gods and goddesses";[38] second, a single line that begins in the past tense, "We were animals."[39] The loss here is the same: the gods and goddesses belong to a mythic past to which Robertson sends the stricken tense. Robertson's urgent intervention in the present poses the question of whether or not the palinode, as poetic form, is capable of producing change. Stesichorus's returned sight suggests, yes. Robertson's own investment in the political economy – of the gender politic that has historically forbidden women access to archives, of the racial politic that creates false and violent hierarchies, of the class politic that continues to forbid lower-class individuals access to the city state's policed knowledges – further reaffirms that, yes, palinodic time unfolds as change: whether we mean this in the sense of development (i.e., adolescence) or coinage (i.e., the money clinking in one's pocket).[40] In locating the possibility for *change* in the form of the palinode, I am further interrogating the degree to which the form's three resonances, as recitation/recantation/repetition, land as an event – in the Deleuzian sense of the term. Grosz writes: "Events are ruptures, nicks, which flow from causal connections in the past but which, in their unique combinations and consequences, generate unpredictability and effect sometimes subtle but wide-ranging, unforeseeable transformations in the present and future. Events erupt onto the systems which aim to contain them, inciting change, upheaval, and asystematicity into their order."[41] The eventful text that is the palinode upheaves the phallogocentric legacy inherent in letters in order that a singular woman (i.e., Helen) can figure herself in new ways. From Stesichorus, to H.D. (who writes *Helen in Egypt*), to Robertson (who reads H.D.'s re-visioned epic during her Kootenay years), a line of feminist poetics establishes itself by recanting the previous forms of (masculine) knowledge and establishing new forms of (feminine or *obscene*) performance.

What Is the Event?

In Deleuze, the event exists beyond tidy limits of epistemology. As he writes in *The Fold*, it "is at once public and private, potential and real, participating in the becoming of another event and the subject of its own becoming."[42] The event, like the compositional and performative practice enacted inside and outside Robertson's archive, "does not end; it is incessant."[43] In demonstration of its multiple manifestations and consequences, Lawrence Lawlor carefully unpacks the distinct and inseparable relation between the "event" (with a lower-case *e*) and the "pure Event" (with an upper-case *E*) in Deleuze's *The Logic of Sense,* in which sense becomes the event itself (i.e., the sense-event): "Event (with an upper-case 'E') is not depth; it is opposed to the abyss of chaos; chaos is the unforeseen mixture of bodies, the rumbling of bodies in the depths." Instead, the Event "is the surface," but a surface that "ramifies into many dualities, more than the ones that we have seen, between bodies and incorporeals, between signifier and signified; *there is always more than one surface*" [emphasis added]. This multiplied surface "means that one and the same Event contains potentially a multiplicity of events (now with a lower-case 'e')." These events "are not the surface (not the Event), but 'surface effects' of the mixtures of bodies," and they "are always events of language (or of expression)."[44] These events have the power to enter different temporalities and to exceed the singularity of any one surface: "Unlimited, the event (still written with a lowercase 'e') 'follows the border' or 'skirts along the surface.'" In this way, the two terms are "virtually identical": "The event is always said twice."[45]

Alain Badiou, in "The Nature of the Event in Deleuze," further interrogates the identical nature of these distinct terms with a certain degree of skepticism. Deleuze's ontology of the event seemingly aligns itself with "the linguistic turn of the great contemporary sophists, much more than Deleuze would have wished."[46] Despite the unintentional turn into sophistry, this linguistic introversion is what remains of interest to the present discussion – that is, the inherent connection between the unfolding event of becoming and the recantatory and repetitive language of the palinode. For Badiou, this connection rears its head as "a chimera" and the sense-event becomes, at best, "an inconsistent neologism."[47] However, in the context of the palinode, I think it is possible and useful to read sense differently. Whereas Badiou aligns sense – and, thus, language – with the notion of truth (if not pure Truth, then the apparition of truth), a poet such as Stesichorus or Robertson aligns these vehicles of expression with, instead, the inexpressible and the unsayable. But if the event (with a lower-case *e*) is merely a "surface effect"[48] or trace, Badiou proposes "it can in no way be supported on the side of language."[49] And yet, poets – especially feminist and queer poets – have long been constructing their responses and recantations on such fragmentary traces of becoming. It is the collision of the two terms, the near but incomplete sameness of event (with a lower-case *e*) and Event (with an upper-case *E*), which suggests spoken or written expression as the vehicle of becoming. Moreover, if the event rears from Deleuzian philosophy as a chimera, all the better for a theory of becoming-woman; our feminist theorists have long been fashioning a hybrid and monstrous feminine event capable of upheaving the phallogocentric flow of time.

In her autobiographical text, Robertson sought to "construct a sense of continuous surface, then to shift the surface as minimally as possible so that it would become a gestural event."[50] In "Palinode/," wherein the sequence of recantations and repetitions folds time, the surface has become "omni-distant."[51] If the project of the poem, in fact of the whole book, is to "make an autobiographical book that was not self-referential,"[52] this final poem, as the form suggests, is an admission of failure: "I had no alternative but to become a person."[53] This admission recalls the mistaken narrative perpetuated by the reader's desire and the incipient misrecognition of the phantom Helen on the walls of Troy, after which the poet begins anew someplace rooted deep in the past: "I'm not done with myth yet."[54] The myth Robertson perpetuates is grammatical. Each page in this series is, according to the logic of end punctuation, a single sentence existing in a single temporal plane, though the forward slash that appears at the beginning of each page implies a connection between these, in actuality, grammatically and temporally excessive sentences.

Conclusion: Mobilizing the Archival Event

Robertson's archive continues to proliferate outside the Special Collections of SFU Library, far beyond the print forms of her chapbooks, journal publications, and final collections. The persistence of literary events – that is, the staged reading of a poem by a performer – ensures that multiple versions of the poet's intervention persist, if not materially, at least digitally. With the aid of online projects like PennSound, SpokenWeb, and Archive of the Now, researchers have catalogues of audio and visual recordings available at their fingertips. Without a great deal of expense or effort on the researcher's part, we can travel through the material of palinodic time in order to return to these phonic events. No longer must we rely on the presumed possibility that Stesichorus performed his recantation/repetition/recitation. We may resolutely, by simply entering "Lisa Robertson" into a search engine and browsing the video results in reverse chronological order,[55] find ourselves in August 2014 and the Audiatur festival in Norway, when and where Robertson reads aloud from *R's Boat*.[56] The woman who introduces her has a heavy Norwegian accent, pronouncing her first name as "Liza." Like Lisa and the woman who introduces her with a quote from the book's poem "Face," the following intervention will let us "speak of what actually happens." The palinodic event is repeated in phantom guise so that the material of the archive may begin to skirt the edges of the poem. The following account occupies the "specific intersection of time and place" of one palinodic event in order to draw attention to the subtractions inherent in the becoming of the reciting voice and to acquire from it the *"something else"* capable of producing change.[57]

Robertson reads with the book in hand. And as she reads aloud the line *"A man's muteness runs through this riot that is my sentence"* (all emphases added), a woman with bobbed hair and a nearly full glass of water passes in front of the camera, obscuring the face of the poet. After the line, "What can I escape?" the poet's breath hits the microphone and overloads the signal resulting in a heavy thud. This is the antithesis of the rising inflection that usually indicates when a question is being asked, and yet it performs the same inquisitive function. As she finishes a line that ends with the phrase "cold clammy word," an audience member with shoulder-length golden hair shifts uncomfortably in her seat. The camera then pans to a close-up of two women, one sitting back with a slight smile and one bent forward in deep concentration. Robertson reads, *"I willed myself towards this neutrality. / I have not loved enough or worked."* The smiling woman looks down, and the other snaps her head up quickly. The camera pans back to the poet. There is an intake of breath. *"What I want to do here is infiltrate sincerity."* The final syllables land like the earlier thud of a question mark. The line with which the poet was introduced is repeated, this time by the poet herself, "I must speak of what actually happens."

To the respectful silence of her audience, made up of men, women, and microphone, the poet subtly shakes her head, as though apologizing for what actually happens, and reads, *"I can only make a report."* The poet's brow furrows and her voice catches; she reads, "Sometimes I'm just solid with anger and I am certain I will die from it." The earlier smiling woman's face has returned to the camera and her eyes seem to slide toward the present eye that gazes on this virtual reality, with acknowledgment, each time the poet performs a repetition: "I am satisfied with so little / *I am satisfied with so little*," "*I have not loved enough or worked* / I have not loved enough or worked," "Honeysuckle, elder, moss / *Honeysuckle, elder, moss*," "*I made my way to London* / I made my way to London." The poet says, "I can't say any of these words." Without glancing up, the poet reads, "*I subsist by these glances.*"

Robertson's urgent tone is belied only by its consistency. Her volume remains level, except for the rare moment of a stray breath hitting the microphone and distorting the certain consonants. Only her *Ss* take any time on the tongue, and this seems supremely considered. The room of the reading does not appear in the poem, but the poet's speaking voice does. Robertson writes and reads, "*In the strange shops and streets I produce this sign of spoken equilibrium.*" The poet speaks to the gathered crowd and the digital voyeur, and says, "I speak as if to you alone." The poet recalls, aloud, "I let myself write these sentences." A moment later, the poet recants, "I will not remember only transcribe." The book is now held against her chest like the manuscript at the breast of Virginia Woolf's heroine Orlando. The rising and polite clamour of applause finishes the poem, its compositional event, and its virtual replica, and the present intervention concludes, for this moment, the repetition of these archival poetics.

This video and others continue the proliferation of the writer's archival traces outside the closed constraint of its actual "house arrest" – the term used by Jacques Derrida to define the origins of the archive.[58] Do these lines belong inside or outside the archive? Can their recantation have a real effect on the amassed materials of the official institution? Will this phonic experience remain the same when next replayed? Will this phonic experience remain at all? Furthermore, it is necessary to ask what phantom versions of this performance exist, on the individual recorders held in audience pockets (our phones that pulse in our palms) and within the pencil or pen tracings of material edits in the *advent* and *aftermath* of the event. For those of us in the presence, or present, of these digital repositories or material traces, we wonder whether Helen has, in fact, restored our sight. The palinode allows us to sense the *phonic* experience through renewed *eyes*. The spatial and temporal zones of the archive, the sense-event in which perpetual becoming always already continues before and after the composition and performance, expand in creative ways through this new and ancient recantatory practice.

NOTES

1   A note in Simon Fraser's online finding aid indicates that access to certain materials must be granted by the writer herself.

2   There is a wealth of contemporary research into the institutional space and theoretical trope of the archive. For some sense of the scope of this research, see Carolyn Steedman, *Dust: The Archive and Cultural History* (New Brunswick, NJ: Rutgers University Press, 2001); Carolyn Hamilton, et al., eds., *Refiguring the Archive* (Dordrecht and Boston: Kluwer Academic, 2002); Ann Cvetkovich, *An Archive of Feelings: Trauma, Sexuality, and Lesbian Public Cultures* (Durham, NC: Duke University Press, 2003); Charles Merewether, ed., *The Archive: Documents of Contemporary Art* (Cambridge, MA: MIT Press, 2006); Linda Morra and Jessica Schagerl, eds., *Basements and Attics, Closets and Cyberspace* (Waterloo: Wilfrid Laurier University Press, 2012); Kate Eichhorn, *The Archival Turn in Feminism: Outrage in Order* (Philadephia, PA: Temple University Press, 2013); and Linda Morra, *Unarrested Archives: Case Studies in Twentieth-Century Canadian Women's Authorship* (Toronto: University of Toronto Press, 2014).

3   Deanna Fong, chapter 2.

4   Ibid.

5   Ibid.

6   Michael O'Driscoll and Edward Bishop, "Archiving 'Archiving,'" *ESC/SLC* 30.1 (2004): 3.

7   Eileen Myles, Interview by Ben Lerner, "The Art of Poetry No. 99," *Paris Review* 214 (Fall 2015), 47.

8   Ibid.

9   Ibid.

10   Ibid.

11   I use these terms after Nathanaël, who interrogates the temporal nature of the catastrophal event (i.e., the photograph) in *Sisyphus, Outdone. Theatres of the Catastrophal* (New York: Nightboat, 2012).

12 Myles, "The Art of Poetry No. 99," 48.

13 Lisa Robertson, "On Palinode," *Chicago Review* 51/52:4/1 (Spring 2006): par. 6.

14 Myles, "The Art of Poetry No. 99," 48.

15 Anne Carson, *Autobiography of Red: A Novel in Verse* (Toronto: Vintage Books, 1998), 17.

16 Lisa Robertson, Interview by Kate Eichhorn, in *Prismatic Publics: Innovative Canadian Women's Poetry and Poetics,* ed. Kate Eichhorn and Heather Milne (Toronto: Coach House Books, 2009), 381.

17 Fong, chapter 2 in this volume.

18 Lisa Robertson, "My Eighteenth Century: Draft towards a Cabinet," in *Assembling Alternatives: Reading Postmodern Poetries Transnationally*, ed. Romana Huk (Middletown, CT: Wesleyan University Press, 2003), 389.

19 Ibid.

20 Ibid.

21 Lisa Robertson, "Palinodes," *Chicago Review* 51/52:4/1 (Spring 2006): 21.

22 Robertson, Interview by Kate Eichhorn in *Prismatic Publics*, 381.

23 Ibid., 382.

24 Ibid.

25 Ibid.

26 Lisa Robertson, *R's Boat* (Berkeley: University of California Press, 2010), 71.

27 Ibid., 73.

28 Robertson, "Palinodes," 21.

29 Robertson, *R's Boat*, 73.

30 Fong, chapter 2.

31 Robertson, Interview by Kate Eichhorn, *Prismatic Publics*, 380.

32 Eichhorn, *The Archival Turn in Feminism*, 2.

33 Ibid., 4.

34 This is the contention of Morra, whose examination of Canadian women writers' archives investigates not only the materials in institutional archives but also the traces of what "institutions either refuse to preserve or mislay." Morra, *Unarrested Archives*, 4.

35 Robertson, *R's Boat*, 71.

36 Robertson has long been interested in the financial realities of the body in capitalism. As well, contemporary poetics in general continuously revisit the tangible financial rewards (or punishments) for the practice of writing. There is, for example, Josef Kaplan, *Kill List* (Baltimore: Cars Are Real, 2013) and, even

more recently, Eileen Myles, "Times I've Got Paid," *Poetry Foundation* (21 April 2016), www.poetryfoundation.org/harriet/2016/04/times-ive-got-paid (accessed 4 March 2019).

37 In her interview with Eichhorn, Robertson reveals that the motive for depositing her papers is financial. She requires money for an international move, and creating an archive entails an enticing tax break. Robertson, Interview by Kate Eichhorn, *Prismatic Publics*, 381.

38 Robertson, "Palinodes," 8.

39 Ibid.

40 I am indebted to Caroline Whitbeck for illustrating the multivalence of this word in connection with the palinode. Her dissertation draws this connection in an analysis of the chapter titled "Changes" in Carson's *Autobiography of Red*. Caroline N. Whitbeck, "The Palinodic Strain," dissertation (University of Pennsylvania, 2013).

41 Elizabeth Grosz, *The Nick of Time: Politics, Evolution, and the Untimely* (Durham, NC: Duke University Press, 2004), 8.

42 Gilles Deleuze, *The Fold: Leibniz and the Baroque*, trans. Tom Conley (London, U.K.: Continuum Books, 2010), 88.

43 Lawrence Lawlor, "Phenomenology and Metaphysics, and Chaos: On the Fragility of the Event in Deleuze," in *The Cambridge Companion to Deleuze*, ed. Daniel W. Smith and Henry Somers-Hall (Cambridge, U.K.: Cambridge University Press, 2012), 105.

44 Ibid., 113.

45 Ibid., 114.

46 Alain Badiou, "The Nature of the Event in Deleuze," trans. Jon Roffe, *Parrhesia: A Journal of Critical Philosophy* 2 (2007): 40.

47 Ibid.

48 Lawlor, "Phenomenology," 113.

49 Badiou, "The Nature of the Event in Deleuze," 41.

50 Lisa Robertson, "Lifted: An Interview with Lisa Robertson," Interview by Kai Fierle-Hedrick, *Chicago Review* 51/52: 4/1 (Spring 2006): 52.

51 Robertson, *R's Boat*, 74.

52 Lisa Robertson, "All Sides Now: A Correspondence with Lisa Robertson," Interview by Sina Queyras, *The Poetry Foundation* (18 March 2010), www.poetryfoundation.org/harriet/2010/03/all-sides-now-a-correspondence-with-lisa-robertson (accessed 4 March 2019).

53 Robertson, *R's Boat*, 74.

54 Ibid., 75.

55 This is, in fact, untrue, since searches for "Lisa Robertson" are much more likely to produce results concerning the popular QVC cable network host of the same name. The researcher must add the terms "poetry" and "reading" to her search in order to ensure the correct person is found.

56 This video is hosted by Vimeo, under the Audiatur account, with the title "Audiatur 2014 Day 1 05: Lisa Robertson: From 'R's Boat.'" It runs a total time of 17 minutes and 26 seconds. Audiatur, "Audiatur 2014 Day 1 05: Lisa Robertson: From 'R's Boat,'" online video clip, Vimeo, 4 May 2014, https://vimeo.com/93831274 (accessed 4 March 2019).

57 Fong, chapter 2.

58 Jacques Derrida, *Archive Fever: A Freudian Impression,* trans. Eric Prenowitz (Chicago: University of Chicago Press, 1996), 2.

14
___

Unfolding Echoes
Temporal Frames and Resituated Archives in Digital Poetics

KARL JIRGENS

One of the questions that chapters in this book examine is how archival materials can be reconsidered, and re-presented, through other media. This chapter examines the action of unarchiving older materials and resituating them within the context of contemporary art forms, including digital poetics and digitally enhanced performance installations. It also offers an interpretation based on Gilles Deleuze's notion of the "fold." Among other things, the Deleuzian fold references overlapping layers of time and space. I unfold some of the echoes or folds in the temporal frames and resituated archives found in several contemporary digital-poetic expressions. The resituation of archival materials in contemporary digitally enhanced artistic expression serves to unfold past echoes by engaging five spatio-temporal folds: (1) the original archived event itself and the audience reception of that event; (2) the recording of the event (audio, video, print, photo, etc.), which is then archived for posterity; (3) the resituation of the archived material within a new and contemporary artwork as a kind of echo; (4) the reception of that contemporary artwork by a contemporary audience; and (5) the critical reaction to both the contemporary expression and the resituated archival material.

There are two parallel phenomenologies involved in all five time frames or folds. One involves the effects of the artistic work on the audience's awareness of time. The second involves how the artist's chosen medium manipulates cultural history through what theorists such as Wolfgang Ernst call "microtemporalities," which invite audiences to reconsider cultural memory as it is redefined by digital media. These microtemporalities also align with Deleuze's notion of the fold wherein different temporal layers are overlapped. The five folds listed above affect the way a resituated past event might be newly received by audiences within a fresh artistic statement.

The notion of the fold can be applied to a wide range of contemporary inter-media works that feature not only enfoldments of time and space but also the inter-folding of different media. Several contemporary digital artists create works that resituate public records, historical sources, and/or archival sources by creating hybrid art forms that deploy multiple temporal layers, which serve as a prosthetic extending the audience's memory functions.

This hybridity includes crossovers between fictive/poetic and non-fictive materials. Archived literary events may feature authors reading fictive/poetic works, but the *documentation* of such readings is considered "actual." For example, interviews with such authors recorded for archives are deemed non-fictive. The intention of both kinds of recordings is to provide historical records. But what happens when contemporary authors embed archival materials featuring works or earlier recordings by others into their own contemporary works? For digitally minded creators such as Gary Barwin, Darren Wershler, and Bill Kennedy, as well as Janet Cardiff and George Bures Miller, the types of archival materials are diverse, but when those materials are echoed and recontextualized within a new format, their significance resonates with altered meanings that re-historize archival materials, thereby affecting the significance of cultural memory, the original archived materials, and the new hybrid artworks.

In this chapter's analysis, I am considering both technical artistry and bio-textual elements of earlier records as they are unarchived, resituated inside contemporary pieces, and then reintroduced to audiences. For the purposes of this chapter, I refer to the wide range of archival materials as biotexts. In her entry on "Life Writing" in the *Encyclopedia of Literature in Canada*, Marlene Kadar identifies the multi-purpose term "bio-text," originally forwarded by George Bowering.[1] In my use of this term, biotexts can be archived and can include eyewitness accounts, memoirs, letters, diaries, journals, anthropological data, (auto)biographies, photographs, written and/or oral testimonies, and recordings of interviews with authors/artists or authors/artists performing works.

I am using an expanded definition of archive here to include all sites that feature public records. Archives provide extensions of human memory while serving as echoes of our cultural history. The etymology of the word "archive" arises from the Late Latin *archivum* [singular] and the Greek *ta arkheia*, meaning a place where "public records" are stored, including institutional sites such as city halls, university libraries including digital libraries, or digital domains such as Google, Yahoo, or YouTube. Digital sites include wide arrays of records ranging from atrocities to banal data. Contemporary mobile devices and digital rapid-transfer technologies permit access to digital globospheric archives allowing endless re-enfoldment or recycling of historical materials that can be stored, retrieved, and recirculated. Such technologies redefine all human experience as potentially archivable.

Some artists, such as Gary Barwin, have developed new modes of expression by integrating archival materials, including bio-texts of earlier artists, into their works. Barwin has recontextualized bpNichol's sound poetry and audio-recorded breath, while reinterpreting aspects of Nichol's individual aesthetic. Barwin's piece, "I after H" (from *H: it is a pleasure and a surprise to breathe*), uses bpNichol's audio cassette tape recordings, originally published by Underwhich Editions (Toronto). bpNichol was one of the founders of the company, in 1978. Underwhich recordings were released in limited editions, and their rarity makes them definable as archival. Barwin had to obtain permission from the bpNichol estate to use portions of Nichol's recordings. Nichol's recordings have also been uploaded to digital archival sites such as UbuWeb and PennSound, both serving an archival function by providing public access to audio works, many of which were published or recorded before personal computers became available in the 1980s. In the making of *H: it is a pleasure and a surprise to breathe*, Barwin selected a section of the sound poem "Beast (I dreamed I saw Hugo Ball)" from bpNichol's 1971 audio cassette *bpNichol*. Barwin located a moment where Nichol chants the word "breathing." Using audio technology, Barwin then stretched Nichol's single breath until it was over six minutes long. The signifying function of the re-recorded and resituated "breath" was transformed, as technology posthumously extended its "life." Barwin has enfolded a variety of Nichol's works into his own contemporary audio works.

Barwin acknowledged that Nichol's aesthetics, persona, and biography influenced the composition of his audio-phonic compositions.[2] By resituating Nichols's aesthetic, and his archived audio recordings, Barwin's hybrid works revivify and re-historicize fragments of the sound and mindset of Nichol's artistry, thereby engaging in a *dialogue* with Nichol and his works. Barwin's use of archived materials within his new audio compositions generates unprecedented folds that overlap virtual and actual, past and present, Thanatos (bpNichol/posthumous) and Eros (living/breath). Barwin also performs such pieces before live audiences. The microtemporalities emerging through the five enfolded time frames of Barwin's live performances generate a surreal experience transcending conventional barriers of time-space. Nichol's resurrected voice "participates" in Barwin's live performances. The effect of this technologically enabled "collaboration" between Barwin and Nichol is enhanced by the fact that Barwin knew Nichol personally and studied under him at Toronto's York University. Barwin's audio pieces redefine the meanings of Nichol's unarchived and resituated audio recordings, inviting audiences to reconsider cultural memory as it is redefined by digital media.

Other artists choose more ubiquitous archival sources. Darren Wershler's *Update* (2010), created with Bill Kennedy, uses Facebook status updates as source materials for digitally enhanced poetic expression. The jacket note for *Update* states: "This book will publish unauthorized communications. It will collect content or information using an automated means, employing harvesting bots, robots, spiders and/or scrapers without permission." And, "It will let the dead speak." The inclusion of the voices of the dead indicates that some updates might be from those who have since died. Like Barwin, Wershler and Kennedy create new works by mining archives that might potentially incorporate posthumous voices, once again overlapping the five folds listed at the start of this chapter.

Yet another type of engagement with archival materials is evident in Janet Cardiff and George Miller's walking tours. Cardiff and Miller's tours enfold three prominent features, listed here and then explained in greater detail. The first involves temporal cascades, which extend the audience's perceptual frame. The second, a *trompe l'oreil* effect or auditory illusion, makes it difficult to differentiate between virtuality and actuality, resulting in an irresolvable multistable perceptual oscillation. And the third, the impact of ergodic expression, involves direct audience participation in generating meaning in any digital work, which thereby redefines the roles of "artist," "artwork," and "audience."

Beginning with the first feature, temporal cascades arise when hybrid digital works create resonances oscillating between past and present, generating shifting perceptions of time. Deleuze's *The Fold* speaks of the Baroque technique of shifts in temporal perspectives.[3] Such enfoldments synthesize interior and exterior space, while juxtaposing and overlapping multiple spatiotemporal loci, thereby generating a sense of simultaneity that envelops the audience with overlapping and multiple sensory impressions that expand into diverse branches of possibilities. In contemporary digital poetics, Neo-Baroque enfoldments of the actual and virtual generate manifold, syncretic fugue-like layers of time-space, while destabilizing perception. Inter-media performance/installations, including Cardiff and Miller's walking tours enfold different experiential phenomena atop one another. Such experiential phenomena include visual, auditory, and sensual layers (for example, smell, taste, touch, physical vibrations). Cardiff and Miller choreograph multiple experiential layers, and thereby generate an alternate system of signification.

In his definition of Deleuze's "fold," Simon O'Sullivan speaks of the "superfolds" of language/communication itself.[4] If we recognize various media as types of "language" then, atypical forms of expression can be found within inter-media expression. The overlaps and resulting enfoldments of experiential sensations in Cardiff and Miller's ergodic walking tours generate what might be called an "inflected language" where interior and exterior spaces overlap, typical of Baroque and Neo-Baroque expression. Interior space emerges through the virtual audio track channelled through headphones provided with the walking tour. Exterior space is constituted by the actual streetscape the virtual tour guide asks the audience member to traverse. But interior/exterior, virtual/actual soon become indistinguishable.

A kind of language-within-a-language emerges through the enfoldments of experiential sensations generated by virtual inter-media layered atop the actual streetscape. This language-within-a-language is evident when one recognizes the Neo-Baroque folds of inter-media as another form of language investigating contact points of interior and exterior space. The inflections at such contact points can include linguistic elements of tense, mood, person, number, case, and gender. However, they can also include tempo, rhythm, stress, intonation, timbre, volume, or tone. Inflections become emphatic when interior and exterior signifiers coincide and echo each other. For example, a virtual sound might enhance the meaning of an actual visual object. Further, the multiple audio tracks layered atop each other present overlapping time frames, or microtemporalities.

Any audience members participating in such walking tours experience enfoldments of multiple layers of time or microtemporalities set atop each other in a fugue-like manner. The compositional form aligns itself with Neo-Baroque aesthetics. Deleuze's *The Fold* speaks of Baroque expression less as an essence and more as an "operative function."[5] He explains that the multiple and layered time frames in Baroque expression generate endless openings in meaning as "the Baroque fold unfurls all the way to infinity."[6]

The Baroque aspect that Deleuze speaks of draws from Gottfried Leibniz's theory of the "monad," where each monad reflects the entire universe in a pre-existing harmony. Gottfried Wilhelm Leibniz's (1646–1716) idea of the monad defines any single entity as a reflection of harmonious universal patterns. However, from Neo-Baroque, post-Leibniz, and post-Deleuzian perspectives, the so-called harmony expands into branching bifurcations, open possibilities, and numerous divergences, akin to fractal patterns. Monads can range from atoms to humans, to planets and stars, to the universe itself. Any individual human being can be thought of as a monad, as a microcosmic reflection of universal patterns. In Cardiff and Miller's walking tours, the microtemporality of the artist-as-monad is layered atop the microtemporality of each audience-member-as-monad, with ergodic expression roles of artist and audience overlap. Appropriately, Cardiff and Miller enhance this overlap by anticipating what audience members might think. For example, in "Missing Voice," the narrator–tour guide asks the audience members to move through a dark alleyway that would inspire trepidation in most participants. As if she can read their minds, Cardiff comments, reassuring audience-participants that the alleyway is safe. A similar comment involving images of luggage and references to memory as baggage arises in "Alter Bahnhof." Such comments further overlap interior and exterior time-space. It is as if Cardiff is inside your head, further overlapping the monadic relationship of virtual narrator-artist atop actual audience-participant.

Leibniz was a polymath; among other things, he refined the binary number system that is currently used in all computers. Leibniz also developed the notion of self-similarity, the foundation for Mandelbrot's fractal geometry. The application of self-similarity is evident in Cardiff and Miller's walking tours, which overlay virtual audio recordings of a geographic location atop the same actual location. When audiences experience overlapped, self-similar virtual and actual experiences of such locations, then a temporal phenomenology of infinite regression emerges rendering signifying functions as unstable or multistable.

The socio-political effects of manifold temporal layers in these walking tours forward ethical implications. In his essay "The Common Concept of Justice," Leibniz upholds rebellion against tyranny, while supporting inter-religious and multicultural justice systems. For Leibniz, enlightened self-interest is synonymous with virtue. Unities between self-interest and morality are metaphysical and dependent on love of others. In his *Political Writings*, Leibniz expands on justice and Plato: "Plato in his dialogues introduces and refutes a certain Thrasymachus, who, wishing to explain what justice is, gives a definition which would strongly recommend the position which we are combating, if it were acceptable: for that is just (says he) which is agreeable or pleasant to the most powerful. If that were true, there would never be a sentence of a sovereign court, nor of a supreme judge, which would be unjust, nor would an evil but powerful man ever be blameworthy. And what is more, the same action could be just or unjust, depending on the judges who decide, which is ridiculous."[7] In "Alter Bahnhof," Cardiff and Miller revisit a site that was used for the deportation of victims during the Holocaust. Leibniz's point concerning the necessity of resistance against a powerful tyranny is apparent here. Cardiff and Miller's reference to Plato's cave near the start of "Alter Bahnhof" denotes phenomena outside our immediate field of perception. By overlaying the quotidian experience of daily commuting with a Thanatotic history of attempted genocide, and by asking audiences to revisit a memorial that documents the Holocaust, they resituate an archived history of violence underlying the train station.

The multi-track audio recording and overlays of microtemporalities in "Alter Bahnhof" generate a seamless blend of virtuality and actuality that enfold the unarchiving of disturbing historical event within the context of daily commuting. All of Cardiff and Miller's walking tours resurrect similar disturbing and archived elements, implicitly arguing that we must be mindful of our troubled past. Memory loss must be avoided, and unarchived materials extend memory. Walking tours such as "Wanås," "Missing Voice," and "Alter Bahnhof" resituate histories of brutality, murder, war, and genocide. By folding unarchived histories atop present-day happenstance, Cardiff and Miller engage audiences socio-politically. The Neo-Baroque, fugue-like layering of microtemporalities in these artworks finds precursors in earlier but less socio-politically inclined Canadian artists.

Co-relative Neo-Baroque visual cascades occur in Norman McLaren's film *Pas de Deux* (1968: 13′ 22″), an inter-media piece incorporating music, dance, and cinematography. Film critic Alain Dubeau explains that McLaren recorded *Pas de Deux* using high-contrast stock film, with a step-and-repeat printing technique that generated seemingly stroboscopic microtemporalities.[8] The film begins with solo movements by ballerina Margaret Mercier, who dances with multiple overlapping images of her "self" created by McLaren's step-and-repeat print technique. At eight minutes into the film, she is joined by danseur Vincent Warren. They perform a pas de deux with further microtemporal, seemingly stroboscopic overlapping kinetic images of the two dancers. McLaren's *Pas de Deux* creates a visual temporal cascade enfolding second-by-second transitions or microtemporalities creating kinetic echoes that contribute to multistable perceptual shifts.

The second feature, *trompe l'oreil* or auditory illusions or multistable perceptions, are generated by layering virtual recordings atop actual sounds. In Cardiff and Miller's digitalized walking tours, the actual and the virtual layers of sounds seem undifferentiated. Cardiff provides the following "Note on Walking tours" from her website:

The format of the audio walks is similar to that of an audioguide. You are given a CD player or Ipod and told to stand or sit in a particular spot and press play. On the CD you hear my voice giving directions, like "turn left here" or "go through this gateway," layered on a background of sounds: the sound of my footsteps, traffic, birds, and miscellaneous sound effects that have been pre-recorded on the same site as they are being heard. This is the important part of the recording. The virtual recorded soundscape has to mimic the real physical one in order to create a new world as a seamless combination of the two. My voice gives directions but also relates thoughts and narrative elements, which instills in the listener a desire to continue and finish the walk.

All of my walks are recorded in binaural audio with multi-layers of sound effects, music, and voices (sometimes as many as 18 tracks) added to the main walking track to create a 3D sphere of sound. Binaural audio is a technique that uses miniature microphones placed in the ears of a person. The result is an incredibly lifelike 3D reproduction of sound. Played back on a headset, it is almost as if the recorded events were taking place live.[9]

The fugue-like overlapping layers of sound and the accompanying enfoldments of virtual and actual can confuse audiences and result in multistable perceptions of auditory space. The virtual might seem to be actual, or vice versa. A disorienting sense of defamiliarization coupled with a sense of hyperreality results from the seamless enfoldment of actual and virtual. Such technologically generated ambiguities directly affect the audience's experience of the phenomenology of time.

U.S. theorist Don Ihde comments on digital illusions in his *Postphenomenology and Technoscience: The Peking University Lectures*: "At this point I want to make a large leap to an example set now related to technologies. While the use of visual 'illusions' has the advantage of initial clarity and ease to demonstrate multistability as a phenomenological result of variational analyses, these illustrations also have the disadvantage of being all too simple and all too abstract."[10] Using technology to overlap auditory sensations generates oscillating multistable perceptions of virtual and actual. Necker cubes generate similar multistable perceptual oscillations.

The brain alternately perceives A or B as the closest or farthest. Both seem possible. Necker cubes provide analogues for multistable perceptions in digital audio works that generate *trompe l'oreil* effects or auditory illusions that result in irresolvable multistable perceptual oscillations when actual and virtual seem indistinguishable. Such illusions generated by indistinguishable sound layers generate pseudo-schizophrenic experiences.[11]

The third feature, inter-media performances requiring direct audience engagements, can be identified as ergodic. Espen Aarseth, in *Cybertext: Perspectives on Ergodic Literature*, defines ergodic expression as any that requires direct audience participation to generate meaning or an artistic statement.[12] Cardiff and Miller's digital walking tours with their temporal cascades, multistable perceptions, and ergodics enhance the resituation of unarchived materials by enfolding present and past, living and dead, actual and virtual, thereby generating socio-politically engaged temporal phenomenologies.

Michael R. Kelly has noted that the intentionality of the observer must be included in any discussion of temporal awareness.[13] By enfolding virtuality atop actuality, and by resituating disturbing unarchived information in their walking tours, Cardiff and Miller manipulate the time-consciousness of the audience-observer as subject. To take part in these walking tours, members of the audience as participants must partly surrender their "intentionality" to the

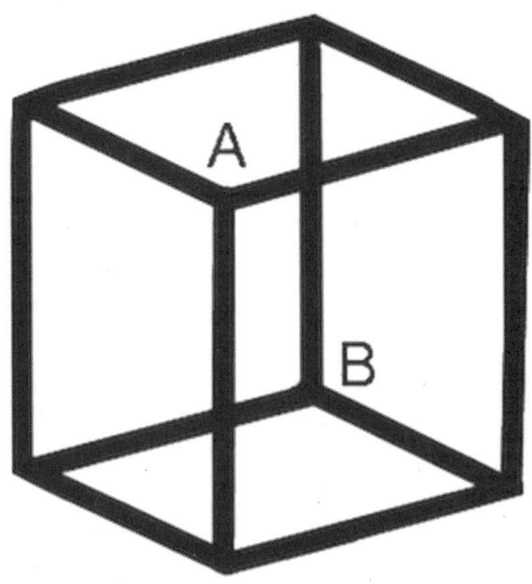

14.1 Example of a Necker cube.

tour guide. Then, the audience-participant is led through a landscape *and* a timescape. Kelly, in line with Husserl, argues that the phenomenon of time is inseparable from the audience-as-subject. Ergodic audience-participants are both agents and subjects.

Cardiff and Miller manipulate perception until the participant has the multistable perception of being both inside and outside of time, both audience and subject of the artwork. This enfoldment of interiority and exteriority is typically Neo-Baroque. Technology as prosthesis opens an uncanny psychic dimension that manipulates the audience's senses. These walking tours revolutionize techniques of writing, theatre, and performance art through their manifold temporal layers, auditory illusions, and ergodics that demand direct audience participation. These walking tours include audio-generated experiences of ghosts, torture, murder, and war. For example, the bucolic woodland setting of the "Wanås" walking tour resituates archival materials in the form of bio-textual memoirs recounting the history of a military battle near Knislinge, Sweden. In the "Missing Voice" walking tour, one finds oneself in the Spitalfields district of London, England, while virtual "footsteps" follow one through the neighbourhood once terrorized by Jack the Ripper. With "Alter Bahnhof," one is led through a train station to an archival public casement that includes accounts of deportations to death camps during the Second World War. The resituated bio-textual archival materials within these artistic compositions affect the audience's time-consciousness while raising ethical concerns. I will expand briefly on Cardiff and Miller's "Wanås" and "Alter Banhhof."

"Wanås" or "Into the Woods" (1998) is an early example of a series of approximately two dozen walking tours composed by Cardiff and Miller. Situated adjacent to the Wanås Foundation at Knislinge, Sweden, this tour is set in the wooded Swedish countryside near a medieval castle. The tour is fourteen minutes long and includes directions by Cardiff as "tour guide." This pre-recorded performance-installation includes a multi-layered and cross-temporal audio-scape. Enfolded audio layers include a pre-recorded female voice singing as if within the forest, while a male voice responds to her. An older female storyteller's voice recounts a memoir involving the plight of two lovers. Cardiff's voice as tour guide provides continuity and a sense of direction, but soon digresses to recount events during the war, including a pre-recorded historical account of resistance fighters taking refuge in underground tunnels. Such histories include unarchived bio-textual narratives recounting actual events of roughly half a century ago. Overlapping audio tracks include sounds of nature, birds' wings, and animals rustling through the leaves, adding a pre-recorded layer of virtual nature sounds atop actual nature sounds. The virtual and actual are easy to confuse, and the result is a peculiar intensification of the acoustic environment that creates a sense of hyper-reality alongside numerous eerie references to death.

During the "Wanås" tour, other voices come and go while Cardiff's voice slips beyond its tour-guide function by interviewing the pre-recorded disembodied voices about their dreams. A pre-recorded male voice gives an eyewitness account of attacks by soldiers and his escape into the forest. Cardiff's voice then conveys dreamlike memories that shift to nightmarish recollections of death and corpses ravaged by ravens and rats. Such death imagery coincides with a walk through a graveyard near the end of the tour. Art critic Gary Michael Dault provides the following eloquent account of his experience of the tour: "I press Play. I jump out of my skin. The hair stands up on the back of my neck and my scalp prickles. There are birds twittering *inside my head*. And suddenly, so close she's *inside me*, the precise but sensuous voice of Janet Cardiff says to me, to us, 'My mind is full of images from this place and another time' … A car drives by on the gravel road, just to my right! A thrill of fear. Brief flare of rising anger at the disturbance. You look quickly to the right and … there is no car. The car is *inside your head, too*, on the CD … The resulting 3-D sound is so spectacularly realistic it is astounding. Everything is so, you feel as if your brain were as big as the sonic world you walk. That acoustic car, for example, almost ran me over." [all emphases added].[14] Dault's sense that the narrator's voice is "inside" him echoes my earlier comments about the convolution of interior and exterior space, typical of the Neo-Baroque when it enfolds actuality and virtuality. Pre-recorded and unarchived echoes of war experiences layered atop each other within a graveyard establish a dynamic tension enhancing the symbiotic relationship between audience and artist, with audience serving as both agent and subject. Without the audience's direct (ergodic) participation, the piece could not happen. But the audience must subject itself to the will of the tour guide. As both subject and agent, the audience experiences a multistable perception of itself as both within and outside of time, as both audience and subject of a performance. The tour eventually winds back to its starting point where one returns the audio equipment. By embedding echoes of the past through unarchived bio-textual accounts and memoirs, this walking tour layers several microtemporal folds that invite audiences to reassess an aspect of the region's cultural past. The ironic juxtaposition of bucolic woodland and military strife enhances multistable perceptual oscillations between present and past, actual and virtual, vital and mortal, asking the participant as both audience and ergodic agent to consider the ethical implications of contemporary tranquility layered atop a history of war. For those interested, the "Wanås" online website provides a short essay, an excerpt from the audio track, and an excerpt of the audio script.

The "Alter Bahnhof Video Walk" (2012) was part of dOCUMENTA (13), and is set within a train station in Kassel, Germany. Audiences borrow an iPod with earbuds from a checkout booth and are guided through the station. This tour differs from previous ones by including pre-recorded audio *and* video. As with earlier walking tours, virtual and actual realities overlap. The tour guide's voice recommends a path paralleling exactly the pre-recorded video path on the iPod. It is almost as if the audience is recording events in the station, while simultaneously being the subject of the same video.

The audience-participant is directed to "follow" a group of previously recorded musicians who move through the station on the iPod screen. Meantime, a line spoken by the virtual guide compares memory to the baggage one tows behind oneself while commuting. Just as the line is spoken, a virtual image appears in front of one on the iPod screen featuring a young female traveller towing a wheeled travel bag through the station [2:58–3:05]. The tour guide's comment on baggage serves as a reminder that we carry memories with us. One might also note that digital technology can *extend* memory function. In *The Extensions of Man*, Marshall McLuhan explains that all tools extend bodily functions. He notes that radio, television, and the Internet extend the human central nervous system around the globe.[15] Pursuing McLuhan's maxim, it is evident that books, computers, or digital recordings can extend human memory. During this pre-recorded virtual tour, fugue-like temporal layers of memory, including the actual train station, overlap the seemingly extemporaneous pre-recorded "recollections" of the narrator-as-tour-guide, as well as the uncovering of several historical or archival bio-textual sources. We hear the pre-recorded narrative of an older German male eyewitness recalling bombings during the Second World War: "The sound was terrible. The bombs fell. The houses collapsed … Every house was burning. And the next morning, bodies lying in the street. Arms, legs, everything was lying around" [3:12–3:35]. "Alter Bahnhof" includes other unarchived materials. The narrator-guide announces: "Let's go over to that trolley thing. I read about this. It's a monument to commemorate the Jewish people that were shipped to the camps from this station. The artist worked with school children who researched and then wrote the stories about the deported people. Then, they wrapped these stories around the stones, and put them here in the bins" [3:37–4:06]. The iPod shows a book's pages turned atop a glass and wood casement (the "bin"). The casement is a public archive that includes a book of short biographies with photos of death-camp deportees. The video reveals the stones inside the casement wrapped in papers, each inscribed with a deportee's biography. The tour-guide-as-narrator resumes: "They boarded the trains on platform 13. Let's see if we can find it. Go to the right, through the doors, out onto the platform. This is platform 3. Stop. I like that strange bicycle rack over there. Looks like a sculpture. Go to the right, onto the main platform. It's snowing. Let's stop and watch the trams right here. Trains have always frightened me in ways. They're so big and loud. Like some prehistoric animal" [4:33–5:26]. The enfoldments of *actual* train-station sites and the *virtual* site images on the iPod provide almost identical, coincidental views. Pre-recorded virtual sounds are indistinguishable from actual sounds. The absent dead are evoked by the presence of the case-ment archive-as-monument. One is surrounded by commuters. This juxtaposition of virtuality atop actuality creates a sense of *mise en abyme*, a temporal phenomenology of infinite regression, rendering signifying functions as unstable or multistable. The ergodic quality of the work and the meta-artistry enfold and overlap the functions of audience and artist. The comparatively benign routine experience of a busy train station is contrasted with unarchived accounts of deaths from the Second World War. The narrator-guide returns to the image of baggage while reflecting on the *gravitas* of history: "How do other people deal with memories they don't want? Do they just close the suitcase?" [6:20–6:26].

We might prefer to forget some baggage-as-memory, but we do so at our peril. Disturbing histories of human aggression are important to recall if we wish to avoid them in future. This tour unarchives the Thanatotic underlying quotidian experience by unfolding microtemporalities, including commemorative books featuring photos of war victims, stones wrapped with bio-texts of the dead, and audio-recorded eyewitness recollections of mangled bodies. While guiding the audience through the cavelike train station ·by using an iPod video, the tour guide's voice speaks of watching television the night before, coupled with a philosophical reference to Plato's cave. The coincidence of virtual and actual, cave and station, television screen and iPod video screen establish a super-folded inter-media language. Using the analogue of Plato's cave, Cardiff and Miller shift the audience's perception from daily commuting to violent genealogies that might otherwise go unnoticed. "Alter Bahnhof" retrieves cultural memory through rediscovered archives by unfolding narratives of past and present through overlapping microtemporalities, or stories within stories.

In *Digital Memory*, Ernst comments on how history is related to memory and auditory experience: "But history as a cognitive dimension is bound to narrative acts (be it literary writing, oral poetry, or visual stories). Auditory evidence (as achieved in the past), though, asks for an alternative approach:

media-archaeological re-enactment, leading to a different temporal regime of auditory memory."[16] If the phenomenology of time, or temporality, is shaped by media and their structural frameworks, then through their enfoldment of the seemingly banal experience of a commuter at a train station underlain with horrific events during the Second World War, Cardiff and Miller reintroduce audiences to an alternate or "different temporal regime of auditory memory" through their embedding of unarchived materials. Their website includes a summary, a list of participants, and an 8.27-minute excerpt from the full 26-minute "Alter Bahnhof" walking tour. Jussi Parikka reads Ernst's analytic approach to media archaeology through the impact that a recording apparatus has on the making of memory: "Ernst outlines that media archaeology is less about telling stories or even counter-histories (leaving open the relation of media archaeology to Foucault's genealogy, which insists on the political function of counter-histories). Hence, it is more about how stories are recorded, in what kind of physical media, what kind of processes and durations – and as such, its focus is on the archaeology of the apparatus that conveys the past as fact not just as a story."[17] Cardiff and Miller's walking tours deploy a unique archaeology through the digital apparatus of binaural recording and reconsider the mundane "story" of daily commuting by re-historicizing the past. This deployment of media for socio-politically engaged archaeological purposes overlaps microtemporal genealogies that demand a reassessment of our cultural past. Parikka emphasizes that "Ernst wants to see media archaeology as an investigation into intensive microtemporality that forces us to reconsider cultural memory combined with an understanding of the technical memory as an active process instead of a stable, permanent memory."[18] Cardiff and Miller's walking tours are all relatively brief performances and, as such, are ephemeral process-works. The walking tours enfold meta-memories or memories-within-memories featuring multistable auditory perceptions (recalling the nature of the *trompe l'oreil*, and its visual analogue, the Necker cube). Because the tours are kinetic, they mimic or echo the movement of time itself, suggesting that cultural memory is ephemeral and mutable, and that ethical implications should be periodically reconsidered.

Through the five folds described at the start of this chapter, artists such as Barwin, Wershler, Kennedy, and Cardiff and Miller generate echoes or microtemporal realms that re-evaluate cultural memory. The abilities to record, archive, re-record, retrieve, and unarchive materials create metamorphic memories. Archived materials evoke a sense of permanence, but when unarchived, their signifying function shifts. By juxtaposing unarchived materials with quotidian experience, these digital artists gesture to an awareness that *all* human experience has the potential to become archival matter. These artists gesture to the significance of being self-conscious creators *and* subjects of our own cultural histories.

NOTES

1   Marlene Kadar, "Life Writing," in the *Encyclopedia of Literature in Canada*, ed. W.H. New (Toronto: University of Toronto Press, 2003), 662.

2   Such as in Barwin, "From Archive to Newhive: Using Historical Recordings to Create *H for it is a pleasure and a surprise to breathe*" (presentation, Can Lit Across Media: Unarchiving the Temporal Literary Event, Concordia University, Montreal, 5–6 June 2015).

3   Gilles Deleuze and Felix Guattari, *Anti-Oedipus: Capitalism and Schizophrenia,* trans. Robert Hurley, Mark Seem, and Helen R. Lane (Minneapolis: University of Minnesota Press, 1983), 21.

4   Simon O'Sullivan, "Fold," *DeLeuze Dictionary*, www.simonosullivan.net/articles/deleuze-dictionary.pdf (accessed 8 June 2017).

5   Gilles Deleuze, *The Fold: Leibniz and the Baroque*, trans. Tom Conley (Minneapolis: University of Minnesota Press, 1992), 3.

6   Ibid.

7   G.W. Leibniz, *Leibniz: Political Writings*, trans. Patrick Riley (Cambridge: Cambridge University Press, 1988), 46–7.

8   Alain Dubeau, *Guide to the Cinema(s) of Canada* (Westport, CT: Greenwood Press, 2001), 168.

9   Janet Cardiff, "Note on Walking-tours," www.cardiffmiller.com/artworks/walks/# (accessed 8 June 2017).

10 Don Ihde, *Postphenomenology and Technoscience: The Peking University Lectures* (Albany: SUNY Press, 2009), 16

11 For more about pseudo-schoizophrenic experiences, see Karl Jirgens, "Digital Mediations: Janet Cardiff and George Bures Miller's Schizo-Phenomenologies," *Wi: Journal of Mobile Media* 9.1 (2015), http://wi.mobilities.ca/wp-content/

uploads/2015/02/Karl-Jirgens-Digital-Mediations-Janet-Cardiff-and-George-B%C3%BCres-Miller%E2%80%99s-Schizo-Phenomenologies.pdf (accessed 4 March 2019).

12 J. Espen Aarseth, *Cybertext: Perspectives on Ergodic Literature* (Baltimore: Johns Hopkins University Press, 1997), 3.

13 Michael Kelly, "Phenomenology and Time-Consciousness," *Internet Encyclopedia of Philosophy,* Web: www.iep.utm.edu/phe-time/ (accessed 8 June 2017).

14 Gary Michael Dault, "Once upon a Time, at a Castle in Sweden, an Artist from Alberta Told Stories to Trees," *Canadian Art Magazine* (Spring 1999): 41–2.

15 Marshall McLuhan, *The Extensions of Man* (New York: McGraw-Hill, 1964), 1, http://cdn.robynbacken.com/text/nw_research.pdf (accessed 8 June 2017).

16 Wolfgang Ernst, *Digital Memory and the Archive*, ed. Jussi Parikka (Minneapolis and London: University of Minnesota Press, 2013), 172.

17 Jussi Parikka, "Media Archaeology," in *Digital Memory and the Archive*, ed. Jussi Parikka (Minneapolis and London: University of Minnesota Press, 2013), 7.

18 Ibid., 16.

15

Excerpt from an Audio Recording
(from a presentation at the TransCanada conference
at the University of Toronto)

JORDAN ABEL

15:19:35   Hey, everyone. This might take me a moment. So please talk amongst yourselves. Stand up. Stretch. Do whatever you need to do. [Inaudible]

15:21:25   Hi, everyone.

15:21:28   My name is Jordan Abel.

15:21:32   I am a Nisga'a writer from Vancouver, BC.

15:21:39   I identify this way because for many Indigenous peoples, these kinds of national identifications can indicate one's home, one's friends and family, and one's position within Indigeneity.

15:21:49   Likewise, these kinds of national identifications can often also be an indicator of which community (or communities) we are accountable to.

15:21:59   For example, Layli Long Soldier identifies as a "citizen of the Oglala Lakota Nation."

15:22:07   Louise Erdrich identifies as being of both "Chippewa" and "German-American" descent.

15:22:15   N. Scott Momaday identifies as being "Kiowa."

15:22:19   Neal McLeod identifies as being "half-Cree, half-Swedish."

15:22:22   Marie Annharte Baker identifies as being "Anishinabe (from the Little Saskatchewan First Nation in Manitoba)."

15.1 Cover of *Totem Poles* by Marius Barbeau.

15:22:29   That being said, these kinds of national identifications do not always adequately account for the complexity and plurality of Indigenous identity.

15:22:34   For some Indigenous peoples they simply do not tell the whole story.

15:22:39   For example, when I say that I am NISHGA, you might assume that I grew up in Kincolith, BC, like my grandparents.

15:22:43   You might assume that when I say that I am NISHGA, that I speak NISHGA.

15:22:47   You might assume that my writing reflects on NISHGA knowledge, NISHGA worldviews, and NISHGA understandings.

15:22:54   Then again, you might not assume any of those things.

15:22:59

15:23:01   A few years ago, during the City of Vancouver's Year of Reconciliation event, I was at a dinner meeting at a restaurant on Water St.

15:23:06   I was one of a few poets that was commissioned to write a poem in response to the Truth and Reconciliation Commission.

15:23:10   The initiative was called Reconciliation through Poetry. The work that the poets were engaging with was meant to honour the work of Chief Robert Joseph.

15:23:15   At the dinner meeting, the poets (along with a few administrators) talked with Chief Robert Joseph, exchanged stories, discussed what reconciliation meant for both Indigenous and non-Indigenous peoples.

15:23:22   After a while, Chief Joseph directed his attention to me and asked me where I was from.

15:23:26   I told him that I was NISHGA and that my grandparents were from Kincolith.

15:23:30   After a few moments, he said "you're not really Nisga'a.

15:23:33   Some of my friends are Nisga'a.

15:23:36   Do you know how I can tell?

15:23:38   If you were really NISHGA, you would have said Niska.

15:23:43   With a *K* sound.

15:23:45   Niska.

15:23:47   You said Nishga.

15:23:50   With an S.H. sound."

15:23:53   You know, I didn't really know how to respond to that.

15:23:55   My grandparents are Nisga'a.

15:23:59   My dad is Nisga'a.

15:24:03   But to a certain extent, he was right.

15:24:07   I wasn't born in Kincolith.

15:24:11   I was born in Vancouver, moved when I was very young, and essentially grew up in Ontario.

15:24:15   Does that make me less Nisga'a?

15:24:19   And what does it mean anyway to be Nisga'a? With a *K* sound.

15:24:24   And what does it meant to be NISHGA? With an *SH* sound?

15:24:32   What does it mean to be Nisga'a, but to have grown up removed from the Nisga'a community?

15:24:39   What does it mean to be Indigenous if your relationship to community has become severed somehow?

15:24:46   What does it mean to be both an intergenerational survivor of residential schools and an urban Indigenous person?

15:24:52   I think these are the questions that I've been struggling with my whole life.

15:24:54   I want to tell you about my life for the purposes of openness and accountability and transparency.

15:24:59   I think especially now when there have been so many thoughts and questions about how we define Indigeneity and who or who does not count as Indigenous.

15:25:09   I'm telling you about my life because I am accountable not only to the Nisga'a community,

15:25:14   but I am also accountable to the communities of intergenerational survivors of residential schools

15:25:19   and the communities of urban Indigenous peoples.

15:25:26   I'm accountable to the communities of dispossessed Indigenous peoples

15:25:32   who are not able to find their way back to their communities because of an ongoing legacy of colonial violence.

15:25:37   I am accountable to myself

15:25:40   and I hope to talk openly about my subject position within the scope of Indigeneity.

15:25:43   Colonialism has had and continues to have a profound impact on Indigenous peoples.

15:25:49   And some of that legacy of violence has been discussed at length, some of that legacy of violence remains silenced.

15:25:53   Here's a scene from my life.

15:25:56   I am 22 years old.

15:25:59   It's 2007.

15:26:03   I am an undergraduate at the University of Alberta in Edmonton.

15:26:06   I am studying English.

15:26:09   According to my official transcripts, I have taken Art History, American Literature, Astronomy, Sociology, Spanish, Children's Literature, Literary Theory, and Creative Writing.

15:26:17   But to this point in my academic career, not one book by an Indigenous author has been assigned in any of my classes.

15:26:22   In fact, at this point in my life, I have never even met another Nisga'a person.

15:26:26   I mean, I've known some Ojibway people when I lived here in Ontario, and some Cree people when I lived in Alberta.

15:26:30   But the Nisga'a are from northern coastal BC.

15:26:35   At least that's what I hear.

15:26:38   That's what I've read.

15:26:42   That's what I've been told.

15:26:46   But I've never been there.

15:26:49   I've never had the opportunity to get there.

15:26:53   So here I am.

15:26:56   A young Nisga'a person who has not only never met another Nisga'a person in his entire life, but is also painfully

15:27:03   (and I mean really hurtfully, deep-down pain in your heart kind of hurting)

15:27:08   aware of the hole in his life where Nisga'a knowledge and understandings belong.

15:27:12   At that point, I think, the only book I had ever read by an Indigenous person was *Green Grass, Running Water* by Thomas King, and that was at least somewhat accidental.

15:27:20   I didn't read it because it was written by an Indigenous author.

15:27:24 I read it because someone had casually mentioned that it was good.

15:27:29 And it was good.

15:27:33 And sometime after I'd read that book I asked myself why I didn't know anything about the Nisga'a people.

15:27:39 Why didn't I know anything about myself?

15:27:44 Why is it that I grew up in Ontario but I was born in BC?

15:27:48 Why have I spent all my life not knowing the Indigenous side of my family?

15:27:53 So being at least a somewhat dutiful student at the time, my first instinct was to go to the library.

15:27:59 So I went off to the library and I started to look for books using the search term Nisga'a.

15:28:04 The first book I found was *Totem Poles* by Marius Barbeau.

15:28:08 You know, I honestly don't know what I expected this book to be.

15:28:13 But when I opened it up, there were stories about the Nisga'a people.

15:28:17 Which Barbeau spelled Niskae. N. I. S. K. A. E. (again, the k sound)

15:28:21 As opposed to Nisga'a which is spelled N.I.S.G.A.'A.

15:28:25 But there were stories!

15:28:28 There was some hint of Nisga'a knowledge here!

15:28:33 I didn't articulate it in this way when I was going through this process, but what I was looking for was a doorway into Nisga'a knowledge and nationalism.

15:28:40 And without knowing any Nisga'a people

15:28:44 (or, I think importantly, understanding why I didn't know any Nisga'a people),

15:28:49 Barbeau's work was in fact a doorway even if it was ultimately a deeply distorted colonial representation of Nisga'a knowledge and Nisga'a world views.

15:28:57 *Totem Poles* was an imperfect entry point and I had no other way in.

15:29:01 And Barbeau's book was filled with photographs of totem poles, and stories from the Indigenous peoples of the Pacific Northwest.

15:29:07	But instead of providing me a pathway to Indigenous knowledge, Barbeau's work opened another doorway.
15:29:12	I began to wonder why I didn't know any of these stories.
15:29:17	Why didn't I know any of the Indigenous peoples in my family.
15:29:23	In my book *The Place of Scraps*, the main narrative revolves around the role Marius Barbeau played in dismantling Nisga'a culture
15:29:29	(along with many other nations in the Pacific Northwest)
15:29:34	by the buying (and often stealing) of totem poles and other cultural items from struggling communities
15:29:39	(and very often struggling community members).
15:29:44	I make that distinction because in many cases he did make some kind of arrangement with an individual within the community, but it wasn't a community decision.
15:29:53	In the narrative of *The Place of Scraps*, it also becomes clear that Barbeau essentially stole a totem pole from the community that my grandparents were born in,
15:30:01	and there is a narrative thread in which I remember encountering this totem pole at the Royal Ontario Museum when I was a child without knowing or understanding its significance in my life.
15:30:10	It's actually just a few blocks away from here.
15:30:14	That, more or less, is the main narrative of *The Place of Scraps*.
15:30:19	But when people have talked about why precisely I use erasure in this book, I think most people end up missing a key detail.
15:30:25	Their suggestion that my erasing of Barbeau's words in some ways replicates Barbeau's own attempted erasure of Indigenous peoples is, absolutely, part of it.
15:30:33	That by removing totem poles and taking advantage of struggling communities, Barbeau was actively contributing to colonial erasures.
15:30:37	Yes, I think this is true.
15:30:41	But the detail that is missing
15:30:45	– the reason why Barbeau's text is so important to this work –
15:30:51	is also because Barbeau's writing was the first imperfect glimpse I had into Nisga'a culture,

15:31:00 and that *The Place of Scraps*, in addition to being about Marius Barbeau and Salvage Anthropology, is also about what it means to be an intergenerational survivor of residential schools,

15:31:15 it's about what those experiences can look like,

15:31:21 and it's about having no choice but to learn about your own family history through the now-debunked work of a dead white anthropologist.

15:31:30

15:31:35 Here, I think we've arrived at a good moment to pause for a second and to talk about Indigenous identity and position because it is helpful, I think, to frame urban Indigenous experiences and experiences of intergenerational trauma through these theoretical frameworks.

15:31:40 And to subsequently understand these lived experiences as not only being manifestations of Indigenous identity and position

15:31:46 but also as being deeply misunderstood and under-theorized categories of Indigenous identity.

15:31:52 As Bonita Lawrence theorizes in her book *"Real" Indians and Others*,

15:31:57 Indigenous identity is best thought of "as a negotiated and highly contested set of realities."

15:32:03 The way I've been thinking through Indigenous identity, then, is quite similar to Bonita Lawrence's thinking:

15:32:10 Indigenous identity can be thought of not so much as being fixed or static, but instead as being fluid, shifting, relational, "multifaceted and at times ambiguous."

15:32:16 In Deanna Reder's introduction to *Learn, Teach, Challenge*, she privileges the term "position" over the term "identity" as one that "undermines the object/subject dichotomy and makes visible the lines of relationship that affect one's perspective."

15:32:27 Reder's suggestion here to think through position rather than identity has been really useful for me,

15:32:35 and I think, importantly shifts the conversations about identity away from the problematic discourses of authenticity.

15:32:43 My purpose in this talk is to address my positionhood as both an Urban Indigenous person and an Intergenerational Survivor of Residential Schools.

15.2 Dad, mask.

15:32:52

15:33:00 Before I move on to the next slide, I just want to preface this section by saying that I am sharing these details with you not because I particularly like to share these things.

15:33:10 In fact, some of these details are still quite painful to share.

15:33:16 But I feel the need to share them with you in this context because I think it is important to understand what the experiences of an intergenerational survivor of residential schools can look like,

15:33:27 and where the difficulties are with communicating this type of lived experience to both Indigenous and non-Indigenous peoples

15:33:34 who may not have any idea of how these lived experiences are different from their own understandings of what Indigenous experiences look like,

15:33:43 or even what counts as Indigenous lived experience.

15:33:50 This is my Dad.

15:33:55 His name is Lawrence Wilson.

15:34:01 I have met this man once in my life.

15:34:06 When I was 23.

15:34:11 He was the first Nisga'a person I've ever met.

15:34:17 He was a carver and a painter. He carved this mask. And this mask.

15:34:23 He lived in Vancouver for most of his life and mostly worked as an artist.

15:34:27 Here is a photo of him painting a frog.

15:34:32 This painting is currently hanging on my wall in Robson.

15:34:37 Here is the finished frog.

15:34:41 Here is my mom and my dad.

15:34:46 Catherine Abel on the left.

15:34:50 Lawrence Wilson on the right.

15:34:53 They met sometime in early 1980s, and I was born on April 13th, 1985.

15:35:00 In an affidavit from the Provincial Court of British Columbia between my mother and my father dated May 8, 1996, the fourth line reads as follows:

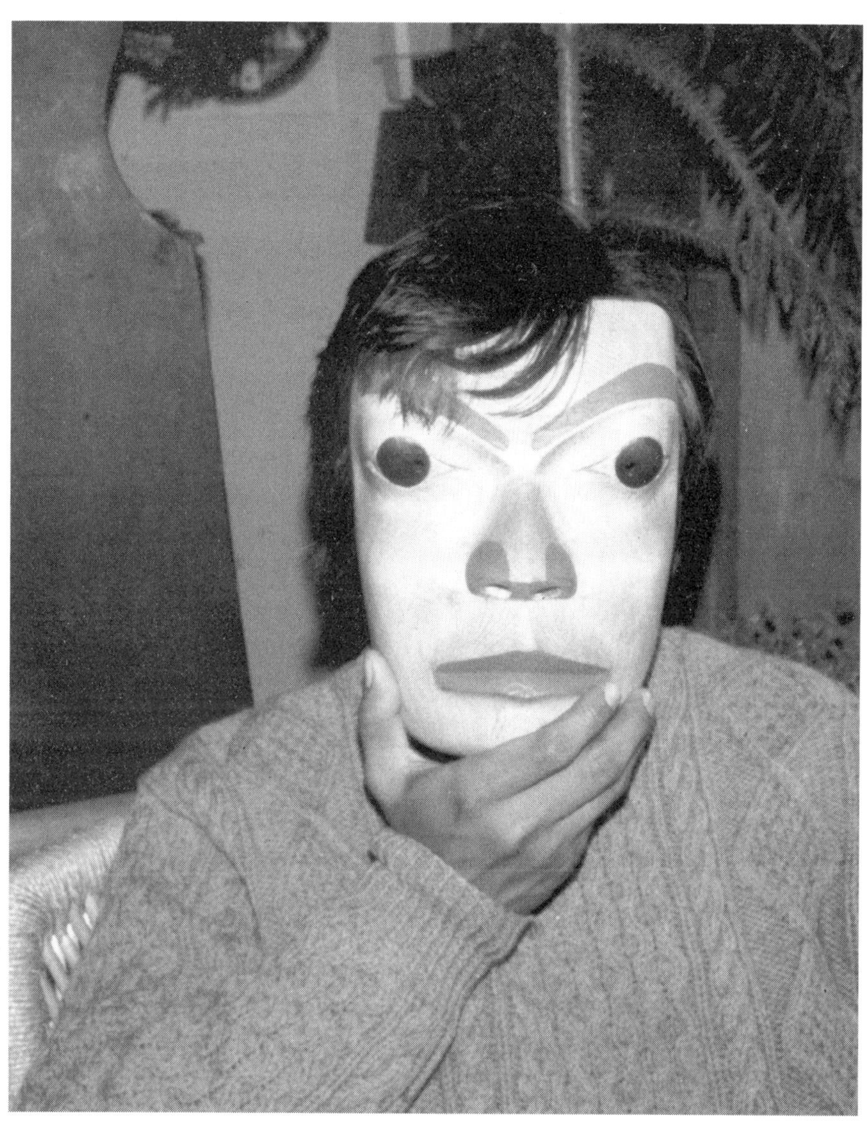

15.3 Dad, mask2.

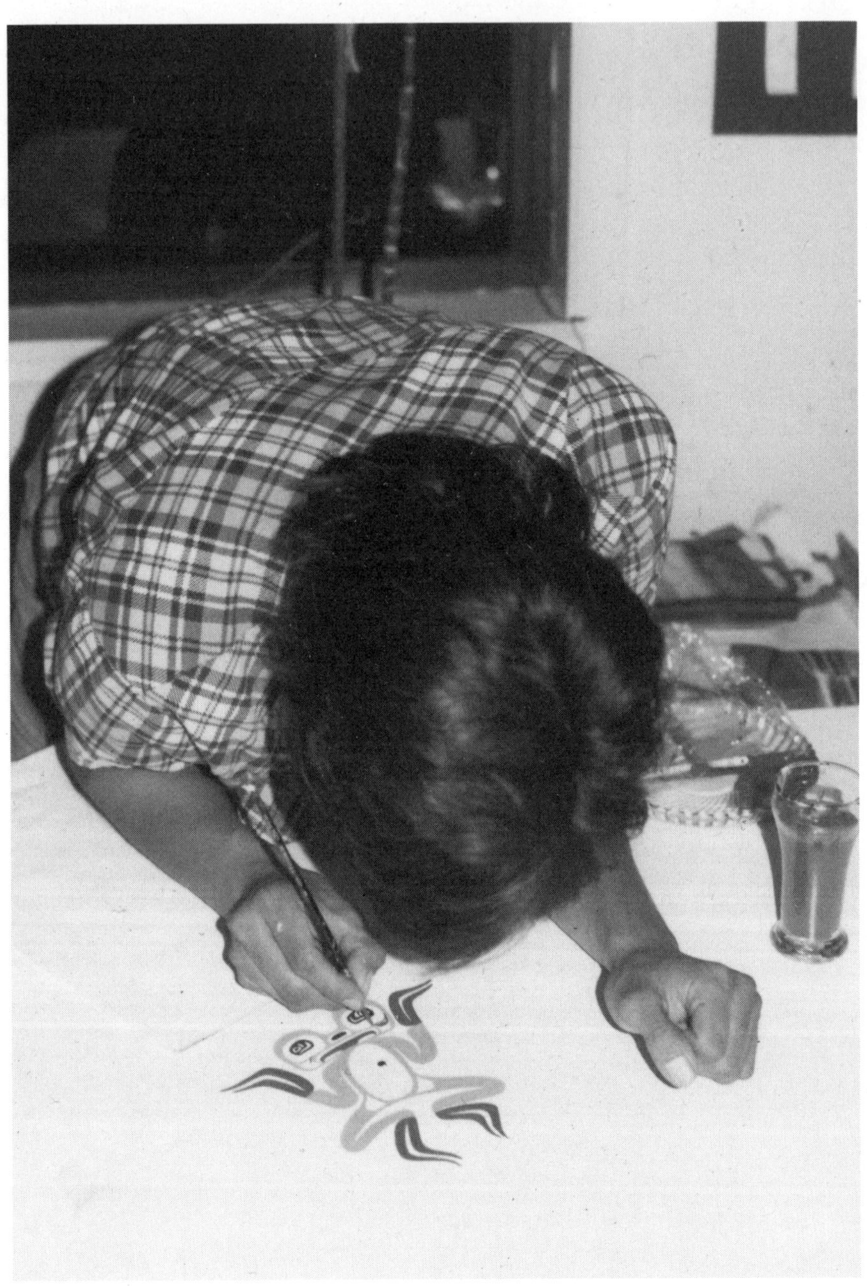

15.4 Dad, painting frog.

15.5 Frog.

15:35:10   On June 15, 1987, Ms Abel was advised by Detective Michael
            Miller of the Vancouver Police Department that Mr Wilson
            was under investigation for a possible sexual assault against
            a 15-year-old girl.

15:35:19   Line 5 reads: On June 16, 1987, Ms Abel was advised that
            Mr Wilson had, in fact, been charged with a sexual offence
            against a 15-year-old girl.

15:35:30   Thereafter, nothing was heard from Mr Wilson.

15:35:36   He neither exercised his access pursuant to the terms of the
            Order of May 21, 1987, nor contacted Ms Abel in any way.

15:35:41   Line 6 reads: In the Fall of 1987, Ms Abel confirmed her in-
            structions to us to continue to act as her agent as she no longer
            resided in the province of British Columbia.

15:35:49   Her instructions were that we should notify Ms Abel of any
            inquiries from Mr Wilson or attempts to contact her so that
            she could make appropriate arrangements for the exercise of
            the access to which Mr Wilson was entitled by Court Order.

15:35:59   Line 7: Ms Abel provided our office with her forwarding office
            following her departure from the province of British Columbia.

15:36:07   Line 8: We have received no inquiries from Mr Wilson, or
            anyone acting on his behalf,

15:36:15   with respect to the matter of access to the child, JORDAN SKAI
            WILSON ABEL, born April 13th 1985, since the date of our
            appearance in court on her behalf on May 21, 1987.

15:36:24   Line 9: At the time of Mr Wilson's disappearance in June of
            1987, to the best of my knowledge and belief, Mr Wilson has
            been in receipt of income assistance benefits for a period of
            some years and was not in a position to provide support.

15:36:35   That fact, combined with his disappearance, resulted in our
            recommendation to Ms Abel not to pursue Mr Wilson for
            child support.

15:36:42   Given that she continues to have no knowledge of his
            whereabouts

15:36:48   or financial circumstances,

15:36:51   the likelihood of any family support from Mr Wilson is too
            remote to justify the costs associated with pursuing such
            an action.

15.6 Mom and Dad.

15:36:58   The affidavit summarizes my mother's departure from BC,
15:37:05   the sexual abuse committed by my father,
15:37:11   and his subsequent disappearance.
15:37:18   But what the affidavit leaves out is that Lawrence Wilson,
15:37:25   shortly after becoming a father,
15:37:30   was also emotionally and physically abusive.
15:37:34   In a letter that my mother wrote to me around 2008, she says
           that "when [she] was 7 or 8 months pregnant,
15:37:43   Lawrence revealed [to her] that his father [and my grandfa-
           ther] had been violent to his mother [my grandmother],"
15:37:50   that he had "broke her leg, knocked out teeth, etc."
15:37:55   Later, she writes that "not too long after Jordan had come
           home from the hospital" that "Lawrence's behavior changed."
15:38:02   She notes that [Lawrence] became pathologically jealous, and
           that he "began to take out his anger physically on objects –
15:38:10   threw a chair and broke it, crashed the baby's drying rack over
           the empty crib and then clubbed [her] over the head while
           [she] was breastfeeding."
15:38:19   Later, she writes that she "finally got up the nerve to suggest
           that '[they] weren't working out and should live separately.'

15:38:28   Lawrence, apparently, took such great offence to this that he knocked [her] on the floor and smashed a large clay ashtray over [her] head.

15:38:38   [According to the letter], he took off on his bicycle right after that."

15:38:45   Here, she notes that she departed immediately afterwards for Victoria where her brother lived and stayed there for two weeks to recover.

15:38:53

15:38:54

15:38:55

15:38:56

15:38:57

15:38:58

15:38:59

15:39:00

15:39:01   My first memories are of Ontario.

15:39:05   I lived with my mother.

15:39:11   None of the Indigenous side of my family was around.

15:39:15   She had told me that my father had disappeared

15:39:19   and that there was no way to contact him.

15:39:24   It turned out that this was mostly true.

15:39:30   I grew up not knowing and not understanding

15:39:35   why it was that I was completely disconnected from any Nisga'a people.

15:39:41   When I finally decided that I needed to figure it out,

15:39:46   I was eventually able to track down my father and several of my aunts and uncles.

15:39:52   But it was over the phone with my aunt Bonnie that everything in my life started to make sense:

15:39:57   why the Indigenous side of my family didn't talk to each other,

15:40:01   why I felt so isolated,

15:40:05   why everything was so broken.

15:40:10   She told me quite plainly that both my grandparents were survivors of residential schools.

15:40:16   In fact, they met each other in the same residential school.

15:40:22   She told me that the best she could describe it was that her parents,

15:40:26   that my grandparents,

15:40:29   had learned how to be parents from residential schools,

15:40:33   that all of that sexual, physical, and emotional abuse they had been taught in residential schools essentially raised them.

15:40:39   And that when it was time for them to become parents themselves they passed all of that abuse down to my father's generation.

15:40:46   I think, for the first time in my life, I understood why I didn't know any of the Nisga'a side of my family.

15:40:53   I understood why my experience of Indigeneity was primarily based around confusion, disconnection, and isolation.

15:41:01   I began to understand that even though I never attended residential schools

15:41:06   that my life had actually been profoundly impacted by an intergenerational trajectory of violence,

15:41:12   and that the violence perpetrated by those schools doesn't just stop after the schools were closed

15:41:19   or after the apology was issued.

15:41:22   My position –

15:41:25   as an urban Indigenous person growing up in the city without a connection to my home community and as a person impacted by intergenerational trauma –

15:41:34   is one of disconnection and lack.

15:41:39   The reason why I ended up turning to Barbeau's book for Indigenous knowledge can,

15:41:45   I think,

15:41:48   be traced directly back to the legacy of violence created by Indian Residential Schools policy.

15:41:57   Here, I'd like to turn to a piece in *The Place of Scraps* called "The Silhouette of Pole on the Shore of Nass River."

15:42:03   The beginning page is, again, an excerpt from page 442 from *Totem Poles* by Marius Barbeau.

15:42:11   The second page of this piece is then an erasure of the excerpt from page 442.

15:42:17 Here, you can see my focus on the parentheses in the original excerpt.

15:42:23 Here, on the third page, there are just the parentheses.

15:42:28 Here's the 4th page.

15:42:33 And the 5th.

15:42:39 In the final page of this piece, we ultimately arrive at another excerpt.

15:42:44 The erasures in this piece flow forward and backward and intersect in the middle.

15:42:51 Stephen Collis has called this intersection point a hinge page.

15:42:58 The page in question, of course, is the middle page with the parentheses.

15:43:02 Here, there is a moment in the piece where the erasures from the first excerpt meet up with the erasures from the last excerpt.

15:43:10 The erasures, in this case, work in both directions.

15:43:15 The concept of the hinge, here, is really useful I think because it ties together

15:43:22 and in a certain way stabilizes

15:43:26 the points of intersection between Marius Barbeau's anthropological work in the first excerpt and my historic fiction masquerading as Barbeau's work in the final page.

15:43:34 The hinge page (as it is constructed in this piece)

15:43:40 appears a few times throughout *The Place of Scraps*

15:43:44 where it symmetrically balances two sides of a poem and the hinge appears precisely in the centre.

15:43:50 However, I would argue that there are also asymmetrical hinges in *The Place of Scraps*

15:43:56 and they are centred around the material excerpts from Marius Barbeau's work.

15:44:02 Here, again, is the first page from the poem.

15:44:06 What I would like to suggest is that this page is a kind of asymmetrical hinge that on ONE SIDE of this excerpt

15:44:12 holds my experience and position as both an intergenerational survivor of trauma and lived experience as an urban Indigenous person

15:44:19   AND ON THE OTHER SIDE of the excerpt holds my dismantling of colonial authority and simultaneous articulation of an Indigenous voice.

15:44:27   Here, every moment in which a material excerpt comes up in *The Place of Scraps*,

15:44:32   the moments that precede that excerpt are also the moments in which I, as the author, am attempting to grapple with my own experiences as an Intergenerational survivor.

15:44:41   The moments that precede these excerpts are the moments where I am forced to search for Indigenous knowledge through Marius Barbeau

15:44:50   because of the ways in which intergenerational trauma has impacted my ability to connect directly with members of my community.

15:44:57   What I'm trying to get at is that I think you can read these asymmetrical hinges

15:45:03   (and the materiality of Barbeau's work)

15:45:09   as attempts to represent both the lived experiences of intergenerational trauma and the experiences of urban Indigenous peoples.

15:45:15   After all, what does it mean to be an intergenerational survivor of residential schools?

15:45:20   What does it mean to be an urban Indigenous person?

15:45:26   What does it mean to be Nisga'a?

15:45:32   What does it mean to be Indigenous?

15:45:37   What counts as lived Indigenous experience?

15:45:42   What doesn't?

15:45:46   What does it mean to be an Indigenous person without a connection to a home community?

15:45:51   What does it mean to attend to the communities of dispossessed Indigenous peoples who don't have access to the knowledges and languages of their nations?

15:46:00   And who is allowed to answer these questions?

15:46:04   Thank you.

15:46:09   [Inaudible]

16
___

The Archive in Motion

DARREN WERSHLER

In figure 16.1, an object for consideration:

This is a Harold Innis "Toronto School" hockey card – or rather, a digital image of one. The card was created by Charlene Vachon, a PhD student in communication studies at Concordia University, around 2001. I scanned the image that appears in this book from the one that serves as the bookmark in my copy of Innis's *Empire and Communication*. It is not necessarily a "literary" object, but it is not entirely excluded from that realm either. For the purpose of this essay, it can easily stand in for a digital file made from any piece of small-press ephemera, like a chapbook or broadside. I have chosen it as my object here for two reasons. Firstly, this card was printed about the same time as I was busy pumping out digital ephemera for the Coach House Books website. During the time that I was senior editor (1997–2002) at the press, Coach House became the first publisher in the world to produce simultaneous full-text print and digital editions. And secondly, each day when I left work at Coach House for home, I would walk past (and occasionally through) Innis College at the University of Toronto. So it is appropriate that the digital file I produced when I scanned the Innis hockey card lies at the crux of a very Innisian argument about whether or not online repositories of digital documents are archives in any meaningful sense of the term.

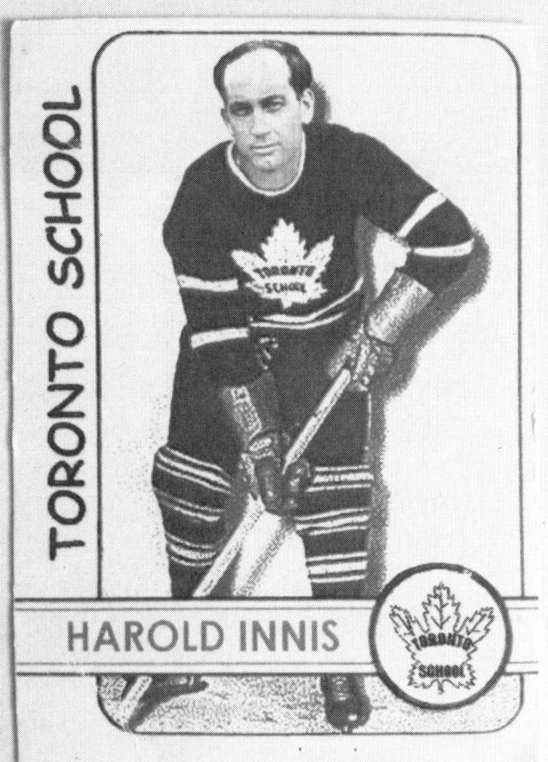

HAROLD ADAMS INNIS

1894-1952

Harold Innis was a Canadian economist and a pioneer historian of economics and communication, who introduced the 'staple' theory of economic development.

Innis received his PhD in Economics from the University of Chicago, where Robert Park and George Herbert Mead were teaching communication. Innis spent his teaching career at the University of Toronto, where Innis College was named in his honour in 1964, twelve years after his death.

In the latter years of his life, Innis turned his attention to the study of communications. Innis divided media into two 'biases': time-binding media, such as manuscripts and oral communication, which have limited distribution potential, and space-binding media, such as print and the electronic media, which are concerned with expansion and control.

Selected Bibliography
Empire and Communications, 1950
The Bias of Communication, 1951

Ripley's
Believe It or Not!

The student newspaper at Innis College is called the Innis Herald!

16.1
Harold Adams Innis, Toronto School hockey card (front and back).

In order to determine the influence of a given medium in its cultural and historical setting, Innis argues, it is necessary to consider its properties in relation to the tensions that it embodies between space and time. The relative emphasis on time or space will imply a bias of significance to the culture in which it is imbedded."[1] As Paul Heyer notes, the concept of bias that Innis employs has nothing to do with the most common use of the word (as in "liberal media bias"), which concerns content. What interests Innis is the influence that form exerts over content.[2] The use of the word "bias" in relation to the cutting of cloth is a better analogy: cloth moves and stretches more readily along its bias (the diagonal to the lengthwise grain and crosswise grain) than in other directions. What follows from this analogy is that every distinct medium will permit some actions more easily and make others more difficult to accomplish.

A given medium may be time-biased – that is, it "may be better suited to the dissemination of knowledge over time than over space, particularly if the medium is heavy and durable and not suited to transportation."[3] The primary purpose of time-biased media is to address some future audience. Striving for the stabilization of meaning over time, its purpose is to produce continuity, regularity, and tradition. Conversely, media may be space-biased, and better suited "to the dissemination of knowledge over space than over time, particularly if the medium is light and easily transported."[4] Space-biased media aim for the ubiquity of particular information in the present. Such media is particularly well suited to the needs of empire, which require an efficient means to circulate regulations and protocols over an empire's territory as quickly and clearly as possible in order to maintain and consolidate power. From this perspective, the stability of a political regime depends on its success in finding a balance between growing (space-bias) and protecting and nurturing what is already in place (time-bias); to lose that balance is literally to lose the balance of power. We could also think of this tension in terms of the need to find a balance between storage (time-biased) and transmission (space-biased) media.

The contemporary mania for storing, filing, and archiving is itself the result of a tension between the use of time-biased and space-biased practices in the workplace. Cornelia Vismann, the media historian who has paid the most attention to the subject of files, filing, and record-keeping, writes that for the last several centuries at least, "the phantasmal belief that files can and are meant to record all governmental proceedings and happenings in their entirety has fueled the categorical imperative of Western administrations to make records and keep files."[5] The emergence of the importance of the telephone to business practices is a classic instance of a space-biased medium challenging a time-biased regime, only to be followed by a doubling-down on the time-biased medium to ensure stability: "This new non-script based means of communication threatened the existence of files insofar as it had the potential to usurp extra- and intra-administrative communications from the documentary universe of the written word. To prevent this from happening, record keeping was implemented as a bureaucratic principle. From then on files began to pile up all over."[6] The mania for digital record production is yet another reaction to the proliferation of paper records, and has produced similar results.

Contemporary exhortations to both business and individuals to "go paperless" are thus part of a very long tug-of-war about what a given medium is good for at a particular time and place. The relative functions of media may change considerably in this process; Dykstra et al. argue that "as electronic systems assume the archival role, the role of paper will continue changing from an archival medium to an active and vital communication medium, filling gaps in current technology."[7] So the question at hand is: what are the relative properties of digitized ephemera during this process of change?

Contemporary discussions centred around media repositories almost always emphasize the importance of preservation and continuity. Digital media are much, much better suited to the rapid and profligate circulation and transfiguration of information than to the preservation of it. Circulation is the "across" in the title of this book. As Jason Camlot and Katherine McLeod point out in the introduction to this book, circulation concerns the distribution and transmission of cultural objects across media and media formats, which transfigures both the objects in circulation and the culture around them. As a result, we should probably temper our enthusiasm for the use of phrases such as "digital archive" and begin thinking about how we can use digital collections to circulate and propagate information before its dissolution and disappearance. Let's begin with the premise that the bias of digital ephemera requires a different perspective, beginning from the microtemporal scale of digital processing.

Microtemporalities

What are microtemporalities? In "The 'Cinematographic Snapshot,'" Maria Tortajada uses the term to describe the discursive field that emerged around the nineteenth-century invention of the snapshot, especially as explored by Étienne-Jules Marey in *La Méthode graphique*. At the end of the nineteenth century, "instantané" meant both very rapid shutters and the images obtained by means of a short exposure. In a word, the photographic image referred to the instant not only as the very brief moment of the photographed action but also as the instantaneous moment of the taking of the photograph.[8] From very early in its history, popular discourse imagined the photographic image as more than a static object. It is also a relationship between the duration of a technical process (in this case, illumination and exposure) and the speed of its subject's movement. The instant is a fraction of a second in length – a microtemporal phenomenon.

German and North American media theorists have devoted significant amounts of their attention to microtemporality. Sybille Krämer has carefully described this aspect of Friedrich Kittler's work in "The Cultural Techniques of Time Axis Manipulation."[9] The most recent and sustained discussions of microtemporality are in the work of Wolfgang Ernst, collected as *Digital Memory and the Archive* and translated into English by Jussi Parikka.[10] Wendy Hui Kyong Chun's "The Enduring Ephemeral, or the Future Is a Memory" provides a third major touchstone.[11]

Chun's work in "The Enduring Ephemeral" historicizes the material origins of computer memory in mercury delay lines and Williams tubes (similar to the CRTs that, until the last decade, were the basis for TV and computer displays) in order to make a number of important points. Memory is not a synonym for storage: it is an active process, meaning that memories must be held in order to keep them from fading.[12] Computer RAM (Random Access Memory) requires a steady electrical current in order to hold anything, and even flash memory has a limited number of read-write cycles.[13] In other words, electronic memory is possible only because signals can degenerate. To place something into computer memory is also always to threaten it.[14]

Chun's arguments proceed from and return to Ernst's observations about the specific temporal qualities of digital media. A digital file exists as a moment in time because it is constantly refreshed. Cycles of regeneration and degeneration in the flow of electronic signals provide its structure. The constant refreshing of such signals results in what Chun terms the "enduring ephemerality" of digital media. This is a never-ending "battle of diligence" that is responsible for the uncanniness we all feel about digital memory.[15] What you want to disappear as quickly as possible is there forever, and the resources you desperately need to complete your work invariably disappear before you can make a local copy of them.

In an interview with Jussi Parikka, Ernst provides an aphoristic summary of the larger point: "Technological media have a distinct quality: They are in their medium-being only in operation ('under current')."[16] In other words, the sense that we have of electronic media and digital media as material is a function of the constant motion of electric current. Microtemporalities, or "minimum temporal moments," become "time-critical" for the success of digital communicative acts (whether internal, between machines, or between humans and machines) because of their extreme sensitivity and susceptibility to "intrusion, irritation and manipulation." Because these events almost always transpire below the threshold of human cognition, "the true archaeologists of time-critical knowledge are technical media themselves."[17] Parikka sums up his thoughts about this point again, in his introduction to *Digital Memory and the Archive*: "Microtemporal approaches refer to archives in motion."[18]

This is where I want to reassert the importance of Innis's work to this matter. Innis emphasized that understanding a given society's relationship to media involves discerning where its dominant media forms fall in terms of the tension between temporal and spatial biases. I would contend that if Parikka is correct, and digital archives are archives in motion, then we need to conceive of them more in spatial terms, as acts of circulation and transfiguration, rather than in temporal terms, as objects for preservation. Chun comes closer to this realization than Ernst, concluding that "repetition becomes a way to measure scale in an almost inconceivably vast communications network."[19] If microtemporalities are always also spatialities, this has serious implications for what we mean when we speak of the "digital preservation" of anything, or try to imagine our activities as scholars in terms of building "digital archives." Space-biased media are excellent at the rapid, promiscuous promulgation of ideas over vast areas. As such, they frequently play a role in the construction of empires of various sorts. However, their inherent instability also means that they just as frequently play a role in the undermining of those same empires.

Many librarians and archivists continue to see digital media as largely circulatory in its biases: "The recognition of digitization as a preservation strategy is a relatively new and still-controversial concept within the cultural heritage community, which has generally viewed digitization activities as a form of copying for easier and broader access."[20] The language that Paul Conway uses to describe the moment when the Association of Research Libraries officially recognized digitization as a preservation strategy in 2004 suggests that they did so grudgingly, "recognizing the sheer impossibility of redoing digitization work as technology evolves and acquiescing to the notion that technology capabilities and standards are sufficiently mature for the task at hand."[21] Conway goes on to observe that the cultural heritage community neither needs nor can afford "preservation-quality digitization" in all cases, and predicts that the eventual outcome will be that digital collections managed by librarians and archivists will be, like their print counterparts, small, expensive, and few in number.[22] Many people in many walks of life will digitize materials for preservation, but whether those digitized works are selected as being worthy of digital preservation by any given institution is another matter. So, given that the resources of our traditional memory institutions are already under strain, and will probably never want nor be able to preserve the bulk of digital and digitized cultural materials, does circulability add anything to the odds of a digital file's survival?

Circulation vs. Retrieval

When we imagine how to preserve something digital, our most common answers tend to be spatial. A well-preserved digital object is one that exists in many different locations at the same time. The acronym of the digital preservation program at Stanford University Libraries is exemplary in this respect: LOCKSS – Lots of Copies Keep Stuff Safe.

The founders of LOCKSS, Vicky Reich and David S.H. Rosenthal, distinguish between the way that an archive functions and the way that networked digital preservation tools function. Where archives drastically limit access to maximize the protection of materials that are difficult to replicate, digital systems combine the process of making their materials available with the action of preservation. The result is that what is preserved is not original but rather a range of distributed copies, each of which, by the very nature of digital copying, will have slightly different characteristics. As a result,

Julia Martin and David Coleman reason that "the very notion of a permanent or fixed archive may have to give way to an ecological preservation system that (paradoxically perhaps) is in a state of constant change."[23]

Outside of the friendly confines of the homebrew LOCKSS server network, in the world of daily practice (say, BitTorrent or other forms of file circulation), things get even worse. Dispersing something is no guarantee of being able to retrieve it, especially in the form in which it left your computer in the first place.

Implications

When we study objects in a networked digital milieu, we are considering not so much an archive of things as a set of circulatory practices that define a particular economy. This realization should affect what we choose to study and how we study it. For example, posing questions about the absolute origins of a digital object might not be particularly productive. Investigating what sorts of subjects, institutions, and communities came into being by virtue of its circulation, and what sorts of marks they left on its various surfaces, will probably produce more interesting results. In other words, the study of digital ephemera will likely be non-hermeneutic, because it will focus on how externalities determine its meaning rather than on the specific value of its symbolic content.

Digital storage and preservation is possible, of course, but not easy, because it works against the biases of the medium. Organizations like the Internet Archive labour against the grain of the digital to save things over longer periods of time (at least in theory), but it is difficult, uncertain, and requires vast financial resources and the coordination of a large, dispersed pool of volunteers to do at all. The result is far from unambiguously useful, as Bruce Sterling observed in his 2010 transmediale festival keynote, "Atemporality for the Creative Artist": "termite mounds of poorly organized and extremely potent knowledge, quantifiable, interchangeable data with newly networked relations. We cannot get rid of this stuff. It is our new burden, it is there as a fact on the ground, it is a fait accompli."[24] Someone else will have to sort it. Someone else will have to provide the metadata. And that is the best-case scenario.

I am convinced that we are simply going to lose *most* of the material that is already digital. Flat-out gone, as in Library of Alexandria gone. Geoffrey

Bilder, director of strategic initiatives at Crossref, a not-for-profit member organization that develops infrastructure and tools to prolong hyperlink functionality and works to connect scholarly literature to Wikipedia, says that the average lifespan of a hyperlink is six years.[25] Estimates for the life of a web page vary: forty-four days, seventy-five days, one hundred days.[26] And this is all before any third-party attempts to store or save online documents.

Deep Infrastructure

When an organization like the Internet Archive succeeds, a whole new set of problems emerges, along with potential solutions. Early Internet enthusiasts had predicted increased accessibility for all, and open markets that would allow for small players to compete on a global stage. The contemporary reality is an Internet of increased vertical integration, where single large entities like Google, Amazon, Apple, Facebook, and Microsoft have displaced the lion's share of entire industries. However reluctantly, the Internet Archive is now in a similar position. Most other large Web archives in the world are operated by national libraries, which only collect sites associated with their particular national domain suffix. Jill Lepore has reported that the Web collections of most national libraries depend, in one way or another, on the Internet Archive; for example, in the United States, the Library of Congress contracts out its Web-crawling and collection process to them.[27] This concentration of the world's memory institutions is worrisome because the security of the Internet Archive is far from certain. On 29 November 2016, Brewster Kahle, Internet Archive's founder, wrote in a blog post that Internet Archive was going to create a mirror in Canada as a direct response to the election of Donald Trump as president. As Kahle notes, other than natural disasters like earthquakes, the biggest threats to memory institutions are legal regimes and institutional failure ... which brings me to the matter of infrastructure.[28]

One of the major documents in the history of digital preservation is a report produced by a twenty-one-person task force entitled, "Preserving Digital Information: Report of the Task Force on Archiving of Digital Information."[29] One of its core recommendations is "the need for deep infrastructure." The Report argues that digital preservation is not a clearly defined problem that can be solved by tweaking a set of technical variables. Instead, it is a problem of creating a society-wide set of systematic supports – where none existed before – that will be capable of moving our cultural records into the future *and* managing collective anxieties about this process.[30] This is no small feat, as Susan Leigh Star indicates in "The Ethnography of Infrastructure," because infrastructure is largely relational, emerging out of established communities of practice, with their attendant and often-idiosyncratic technologies and methods. "Nobody is really in charge of infrastructure," and it is mostly invisible until it breaks down at a crucial moment.[31]

Crucially, there is also a significant social component to infrastructure, managed by public policy. Chief among the necessary support structures that the "Preserving Digital Information" report recommends is "national policy efforts," followed by "legal and institutional foundations," along with the need for the involvement of "professional societies" and "the appropriate organizations and individuals."[32] In theory, national policy emerges from legislation that creates institutions that deploy particular instruments to enact the policy in question, but that works best at a moment when there is broad consensus on the value of a "big government" with a mandate to launch and maintain programs in the name of the public good. The current neo-liberal tendency, especially in the U.S., but to some extent in Canada as well, is to download the operation of any such programs to the private sector, and let the market decide whether or not the program is worth maintaining (and, in some notable cases, to actually work to dismantle established practices and policies, like net neutrality, and to close national research facilities and archives, and so on). The global overreliance on the Internet Archive is a fair indicator that the construction of a robust digital information preservation infrastructure has not occurred, and that there is little will to do so, despite decades of sober warnings about the consequences. We are left with a field populated, on one hand, by underfunded individuals and institutions like libraries and NGOs, proceeding as best they can, and, on the other hand, by a number of intensely competitive tech companies, all hoping that their proprietary standard will be the one that establishes a monopoly. The only clear outcome is a massive loss of digital files and, in many cases, their contents.

I mentioned at the start of this chapter that the Innis hockey card was produced at the same time that we were trying to develop a hybrid print-digital business model at Coach House. This begs the question of what happened to all of the dozens of digital literary editions we produced. The answer (which should be unsurprising by now) is that they are nowhere to be found on the Coach House website (chbooks.com). The Coach House mirror site that we established on the website of Library and Archives Canada seems to be functioning to some extent, because individual titles, like NICHOLODEON-LINE, the digital edition of my own first book, whose publication led to my assuming the role of editor at the press, appear there after a Google search (think about this: Google is a better finding aid for the Government of Canada's own website than the government's search engine).[33] But there is no way to find any evidence of this title through Library and Archives Canada's own search box, or even by working backward through the directories in the URL. Nor is there any sort of index of the other Coach House digital editions, which are probably there somewhere. At one point, Coach House also had a mirror site at the McGill Library Rare Books and Special Collections site, though I can find no evidence of its survival. Internet Archive (archive.org) captured 583 impressions of the Coach House website between 5 April 1997 and 4 July 2017, so once again, it has the most complete set of files, though many links are broken, and some scripts and animations are missing.[34] Everything is optimized for 640×480 pixel displays and is coded in a limited Web palette, so the pages look small and awkward on today's screens. But it is there, and its survival depends on the vagaries of archive.org's continued funding. There are some physical copies of a limited portion of these files; we also burned a small number of CD-ROMs featuring the entire contents of the Coach House website in 1997 (*Resurrection: Coach House Books year one*) and 1998 (*Coach House Y2OK*). Some of these copies are in the holdings of various university libraries and archives, but whether or not they are still readable is another question.

We did a substantial amount of policy writing at Coach House Books as well. At first, it was necessary for the survival of the press as an entity. It may seem bemusing today, but the Literary Press Group (LPG) of Canada blackballed Coach House Books in the early months of 1999 because of the existence of our online publishing program. It took a lot of writing and a lot of social engineering before we were invited to reapply the following year (our Open Letters to the LPG are preserved as part of Internet Archive's Wayback Machine).[35] But even before being blackballed, we had been working with an NGO called TERLA, The Electronic Rights Licensing Agency (now defunct), to develop a plan for an equitable and pragmatic system for protecting the electronic rights of all Canadian authors. We were attempting to produce nothing less than a working precedent for a digital collective copyright system that would serve the Canadian literary community. We were developing templates for agreements between writers and e-publishers, and between publishers and their Internet service providers and site hosts. Before the existence of Creative Commons, we tried to imagine what licensing systems for electronic publishing might look like. We suggested the creation of both a blanket licensing system that would pay writers out of a common royalty pool and an "Electronic Lending Right Program" to mirror the Canada Council for the Arts' popular and successful Public Lending Right Program. We spent a lot of time talking with officers at the federal and provincial arts councils, and argued for the creation of granting programs for electronic publishers. All of this is documented at archive.org, but nowhere else.[36]

In order to continue this policy work beyond the press, I found it necessary to co-found a consulting firm with Mark Surman, Tonya Surman, and Sarah Knox called The Commons Group. In 2001, Mark and I were commissioned to write "Electronic Publishing: Guide to Best Practices for Canadian Publishers" for Library and Archives Canada, and the document still exists on their website.[37] To make the case to a general audience, Mark and I also co-wrote a book titled *CommonSpace: Beyond Virtual Community*, which concerns the beginnings of Web 2.0 and what we would now refer to as "social software."[38] Though this small body of policy writing is more widely available than the electronic texts it was designed to promote and protect, and though it represents the first attempt by a Canadian literary press to help formulate policy around the production of digital literature, digitization for preservation, and digital preservation, it has largely been forgotten.

Though born-digital objects seem doomed to this sort of precarity, there is a potential upside for objects that have been digitized, like the Innis hockey card. Intimidating as it might seem, Ernst writes that his "technoascetic" anti-anthropocentric media archaeology is "just another method we can use to get closer to what we love in culture."[39] As long as the analog sources of digitized objects remain in storage, we have more than the best of both worlds. Ernst, after Kittler, believes that analog media, particularly audio media, reproduces the Real when it plays back: "There is no 'historical' difference in the functioning of the apparatus now compared to then (and there will not be, until analog … is finally completely replaced by the digitized transmission of signals); rather, there is a media-archaeological short-circuit between otherwise historically clearly separated times."[40] Though the idea that there is "no 'historical' difference" between instances of playback strains credulity, playing back heritage media like the tapes documenting a 1960s readings series available at spokenweb.ca may well produce some sort of uncanny relation with the past. The digitization of the object accomplishes something else. We are not yet very good at describing what that "something else" of the digital actually is, but I suspect that its uncanniness has to do with potential reach (and unexpected returns) rather than durability.

In order to temper our expectations of what digitization can accomplish, we need to reassert the space bias of digital media, shifting popular vocabulary around digital ephemera away from preservation and continuity to circulation and transfiguration. And if we want any of our contemporary digital production to be saved and accessible outside corporate firewalls, we need to work harder on a public version of the deep infrastructure that the cultural preservation community has been calling for repeatedly over the last two decades. This is more than an academic issue – it has pedagogical implications, policy implications, and financial implications. Huge swaths of research over the last decade and a half were funded under the rubric of "building digital archives," with almost no attention paid to questions of sustainability. In most cases, such projects are "digitizing for preservation" without actually undertaking much in the way of digital preservation itself.[41] Vint Cerf, vice-president of Google, spoke bluntly about this subject in 2015: "We are nonchalantly throwing all of our data into what could become an information black hole without realising it. We digitise things because we think we will preserve them, but what we don't understand is that unless we take other steps, those digital versions may not be any better, and may even be worse, than the artefacts that we digitised."[42] Digitization for preservation is much easier than digital preservation, which requires considerable commitment on a cultural level. But that is not happening to a sufficient degree, because infrastructure is hard. As a result, there are serious ethical and pragmatic questions that we need to address, even as the frantic digitization continues all around us, with a few large players hoovering up the few profitable segments of all that activity. (As I write this, Elsevier, the most notoriously acquisitive force in contemporary academic publishing, has just purchased bepress, one of the major players in the production of open-access software for the creation and management of academic institutional repositories, moving them ever closer to a complete vertical integration of the academic publishing process.[43]) What we do and how we describe it needs to change. And we need to think about what we have already thrown away, whether we meant to or not.

NOTES

1 Harold Adams Innis, *The Bias of Communication/Introd. by Marshall Mcluhan* (Toronto: University of Toronto Press, 1951), 33.

2 Paul Heyer, *Harold Innis* (Critical Media Studies) (Lanham, MD, and Toronto: Rowman & Littlefield, 2003), 61.

3 Innis, *The Bias of Communication*, 33.

4 Ibid.

5 Cornelia Vismann, "Out of File, Out of Mind," in *New Media, Old Media: A History and Theory Reader*, ed. Thomas Keenan and Wendy Hui Kyong Chun (New York and London: Routledge, 2005), 97.

6 Ibid.

7 Richard H. Dykstra, et al., "Persistent Paper: The Myth of 'Going Paperless'" (AMIA Annual Symposium, 2009), www.ncbi.nlm.nih.gov/pmc/articles/PMC 2815440/# (accessed 4 August 2016).

8 Maria Tortajada, "The 'Cinematographic Snapshot': Rereading Etienne-Jules Marey," in *Cinema Beyond Film: Media Epistemology in the Modern Era*, ed. François Albera and Maria Tortajada (Amsterdam: Amsterdam University Press, 2010), 85.

9 Sybille Krämer, "The Cultural Techniques of Time Axis Manipulation: On Friedrich Kittler's Conception of Media," *Theory, Culture & Society* 23.7–8 (2006): 93–109.

10 Wolfgang Ernst, *Digital Memory and the Archive*, Electronic Mediations (Minneapolis: University of Minnesota Press, 2013).

11 Wendy Hui Kyong Chun, "The Enduring Ephemeral, or the Future Is a Memory," *Critical Inquiry* 35.1 (Autumn 2008): 148–71.

12 Ibid., 195.

13 Ibid., 196.

14 Ibid., 197.

15 Ibid.

Jussi Parikka, "Ernst on Time-Critical Media: A Mini-Interview," 18 March 2013, https://jussiparikka.net/2013/03/18/ernst-on-microtemporality-a-mini-interview/ (accessed 5 August 2016).

17 Ibid.

18 Jussi Parikka, "Archival Media Theory: An Introduction to Wolfgang Ernst's Media Archaeology," in *Digital Memory and the Archive*, ed. Jussi Parikka,

Electronic Mediations (Minneapolis and London: University of Minnesota Press, 2013), 17.

19 Chun, "The Enduring Ephemeral," 100.

20 Paul Conway, "Preservation in the Age of Google: Digitization, Digital Preservation, and Dilemmas," *The Library Quarterly: Information, Community, Policy* 80.1 (2010): 65.

21 Kathleen Arthur, et al., "Recognizing Digitization as a Preservation Reformatting Method," *Microform & Digitization Review* 33.4 (2004): 171–80.

22 Conway, "Preservation in the Age of Google," 65.

23 Julia Martin and David Coleman, "Change the Metaphor: The Archive as an Ecosystem," JEP: *The Journal of Electronic Publishing* 7.3 (2002): http://quod.lib.umich.edu/cgi/t/text/idx/j/jep/3336451.0007.301/—change-the-metaphor-the-archive-as-an-ecosystem?rgn=main;view=fulltext (accessed 6 March 2015).

24 Bruce Sterling, "Atemporality for the Creative Artist," 25 February 2010, www.wired.com/2010/02/atemporality-for-the-creative-artist/ (accessed 4 September 2016).

25 Yoona Ha, Victor Grigas, and Jan Novak, "Preserving Wikipedia Citations for the Future: Geoffrey Bilder," Wikimedia Foundation, 1 June 2015, https://blog.wikimedia.org/2015/06/01/preserving-wikipedia-citations/ (accessed 4 September 2016).

26 Mike Ashenfelder, "The Average Lifespan of a Webpage," Library of Congress, 8 November 2011, http://blogs.loc.gov/thesignal/2011/11/the-average-lifespan-of-a-webpage/ (accessed 4 September 2016).

27 Jill Lepore, "The Cobweb: Can the Internet Be Archived?" *The New Yorker*, 26 January 2015, www.newyorker.com/magazine/2015/01/26/cobweb (accessed 4 September 2016).

28 Brewster Kahle, "Help Us Keep the Archive Free, Accessible, and Reader Private," 29 November 2016, Archive.org, https://blog.archive.org/2016/11/29/help-us-keep-the-archive-free-accessible-and-private/ (accessed 25 May 2017).

29 Task Force on Archiving of Digital Information, Donald Waters, and John Garrett, (co-chairs), "Preserving Digital Information: Report of the Task Force on Archiving of Digital Information" (Washington, D.C.: Commission on Preservation and Access and the Research Libraries Group, 1996).

30 Ibid., 6.

31 Susan Leigh Star, "The Ethnography of Infrastrucrture," *American Behavioral Scientist* 43 (1999): 382.

32 Archiving, in Waters, and Garrett, "Preserving Digital Information," 47.

33 www.collectionscanada.gc.ca/eppp-archive/100/200/300/chbooks/online/ nicholodeon/index.html (accessed 2 August 2017).

34 https://web.archive.org/web/19970401000000*/chbooks.com (accessed 2 August 2017).

35 See "An Open Letter to the Literary Press Group of Canada," April 1999, https://web.archive.org/web/20010906152511/http://www.chbooks.com:80/ articles/open_letter_to_lpg.html (1999); and "An Open Letter to the Literary Press Group," September 2000, https://web.archive.org/web/20011101120336/ http://www.chbooks.com:80/articles/open_letter_to_lpg_2.html (accessed 2 August 2017).

36 https://web.archive.org/web/20011101130301/http://www.chbooks.com:80/ articles/manifesto_for_elc.html (accessed 2 August 2017).

37 www.collectionscanada.gc.ca/obj/p13/f2/01-e.pdf (accessed 2 August 2017).

38 Darren S. Wershler-Henry and Mark Surman, *Commonspace: Beyond Virtual Community* ([Don Mills, ON]: FT.com, Pearson Education Canada, 2001).

39 Ernst, *Digital Memory and the Archive*, 72.

40 Ibid., 57.

41 Conway, "Preservation in the Age of Google."

42 Ian Sample, "Google Boss Warns of 'Forgotten Century' with Email and Photos at Risk," *The Guardian*, 13 February 2015, www.theguardian.com/technol ogy/2015/feb/13/google-boss-warns-forgotten-century-email-photos-vint-cerf (accessed 2 August 2017).

43 Roger C. Schoenfeld, "Elsevier Acquires Bepress," The Scholarly Kitchen, 2 August 2017, https://scholarlykitchen.sspnet.org/2017/08/02/elsevier- acquires-bepress/ (accessed 2 August 2017).

Contributors

JASON CAMLOT's critical works include *Phonopoetics: The Making of Early Literary Recordings* (Stanford, 2019), *Style and the Nineteenth-Century British Critic* (Routledge, 2008), and the co-edited collection *Language Acts: Anglo-Québec Poetry, 1976 to the 21st Century* (Véhicule, 2007). He is also the author of four collections of poetry, *Attention All Typewriters, The Animal Library, The Debaucher*, and *What the World Said.* He is the principal investigator and director of The SpokenWeb, a SSHRC-funded partnership that focuses on the history of literary sound recordings and the digital preservation and presentation of collections of literary audio. He is a professor in the Department of English at Concordia University in Montreal.

KATHERINE MCLEOD researches and teaches Canadian literature through sound, performance, and archives. She received her doctorate from the University of Toronto and excerpts from her dissertation have been published in *Mosaic, Open Letter*, and *The Canadian Theatre Review.* She was a SSHRC-funded post-doctoral fellow with TransCanada Institute (University of Guelph) and a post-doctoral fellow with the SSHRC IG-funded SpokenWeb at Concordia University. Her publications on literary sound recordings include a chapter in the book *Public Poetics: Critical Issues in Canadian Poetry and Poetics* and a chapter in the forthcoming collection edited by Linda Morra, *Moving Archives* (Wilfrid Laurier University Press). She is an affiliate assistant professor in the Department of English at Concordia University in Montreal.

———

JORDAN ABEL is a Nisga'a writer from Vancouver. Abel's creative work has recently been anthologized in *Best Canadian Poetry* (Tightrope), *The Land We Are: Artists and Writers Unsettle the Politics of Reconciliation* (Arbiter Ring), and *The New Concrete: Visual Poetry in the 21st Century* (Hayword). Abel is the author of *The Place of Scraps* (winner of the Dorothy Livesay Poetry Prize), *Un/inhabited*, and *Injun* (winner of the Griffin Poetry Prize). Currently, Abel lives in Edmonton where he teaches creative writing and Indigenous literatures at the University of Alberta.

ANDREA BEVERLEY teaches at Mount Allison University (Sackville, New Brunswick) where she is appointed to the English department and the Canadian studies program. Before moving east in 2013, she completed doctoral studies at the Université de Montréal. Her research focuses on Canadian women writers, particularly in relation to feminism, archives, and literary collectives. She has published in *Canadian Literature*, *Studies in Canadian Literature*, *University of Toronto Quarterly*, and *Journal of Canadian Studies*.

CLINT BURNHAM was born in Comox, British Columbia, which is on the traditional territory of the K'ómoks (Sathloot) First Nation, centred historically on kwaniwsam. He lives and teaches on the traditional ancestral territories of the Coast Salish peoples, including traditional territories of the Squamish (Sḵwxwú7mesh Úxwumixw), Tsleil-Waututh (səl̓ilw̓ətaʔɬ), Musqueam (xʷməθkʷəy̓əm), and Kwikwetlem (kʷikʷəƛ̓əm) nations. Since 2007, Clint has taught in the Department of English at Simon Fraser University, where he is a professor and chair of the graduate program. Recent books include *Does the Internet Have an Unconscious? Slavoj Žižek and Digital Culture* (theory, Bloomsbury, 2018), and *Pound @ Guantánamo* (poetry, Talonbooks, 2016). He has published and has forthcoming essays and reviews on Antigone and residential schools, gastronomic colonialism, and Tomson Highway; reviews of the visual art of Dana Claxton, Brian Jungen, and Raymond Boisjoly; and talks on Jordan Abel, *Rhymes for Young Ghouls*, and the Cree mirror; in 2011, he co-curated, with Lorna Brown, the public art project *Digital Natives*.

JOEL DESHAYE is a professor at Memorial University in St John's, Newfoundland and Labrador. His first book, *The Metaphor of Celebrity: Canadian Poetry and the Public, 1955–1980* (University of Toronto Press, 2013), involved Irving Layton and other poets who gained surprising publicity in the latter half of the twentieth century. He has published nationally and internationally on topics related to this book and to media in theory and film specifically. His next book, on the genre of the Western in Canadian literature, develops out of these studies.

DEANNA FONG is a PhD candidate in English at Simon Fraser University in Vancouver, British Columbia, where her research focuses on the intersections of auditory media, event theory, literary communities, and affective labour. She is a member of the federally funded SpokenWeb team, who have developed a web-based archive of digitized sound recordings for literary study. With Ryan Fitzpatrick and Janey Dodd, she co-directs the audio/multimedia archive of Canadian poet Fred Wah, and has done substantial cataloguing and critical work on the audio archives of Japanese-Canadian poet and painter Roy Kiyooka. Her critical work has most recently appeared in *Amodern*, *Digital Humanities Quarterly*, and *The Capilano Review*.

CATHERINE HOBBS is senior lead literary archivist (English language) at Library and Archives Canada, adjunct professor in the English MA program in public text at Trent University (Peterborough, Ontario), and a steering committee member of the Section on Literary and Artistic Archives in the International Council on Archives. A recognized expert in personal and literary archives, Hobbs has participated in or advised global initiatives concerning literary and born-digital archives. Her interest remains in building bridges between literary scholarship and archival theory and practice.

DEAN IRVINE is the founder and director of Agile Humanities Agency, a software, design, and consulting company based in Toronto. He is the author of *Editing Modernity: Women and Little-Magazine Cultures in*

Canada 1916–1956 and co-editor (with Vanessa Lent and Bart Vautour) of *Making Canada New: Editing, Modernism, and New Media*, among other titles.

KARL JIRGENS, former head of the English department at the University of Windsor (Ontario), is the author of four books (Coach House, Mercury, and ECW Presses). He has edited books on the painter Jack Bush, and another on poet Christopher Dewdney, and has edited the "Convergences: Collaborative Expression" issue of *Open Letter* magazine. His scholarly and creative works have been published globally. Jirgens edited/published *Rampike*, an international journal of art, writing, and theory, from 1979 to 2016. He is currently the chair of the creative writing program at the University of Windsor.

MARCELLE KOSMAN is a PhD candidate at the University of Alberta. Her primary area of study is English Canadian literature with a focus on material cultural production. Her dissertation focuses on the print and circulation history of feminist science fiction in Canada, asking what social and political forces correspond to science fiction's increasing popularity among feminist readers and writers in twentieth-century Canada. She is the co-host, with Hannah McGregor, of *Witch, Please*, a fortnightly podcast about the world of Harry Potter.

JESSI MACEACHERN received her PhD from the Université de Montréal. Her essay "The Feminist Poet Re-Creates the Soundscape: The Excessive Noise of Lisa Robertson and Rachel Zolf" is in *Studies in Canadian Literature* 42.2. Her poem "A Number of Stunning Attacks" was longlisted for the 2018 CBC Poetry Prize.

LINDA MORRA is a professor of English at Bishop's University (Sherbrooke, Quebec). She was a former Craig Dobbin Chair of Canadian Studies (2016–17) at University College Dublin. Her publications include *Unarrested Archives: Case Studies in Twentieth-Century Women's Authorship* (University of Toronto Press, 2014), which was shortlisted for the Gabrielle Roy Prize (2015); *Basements and Attics, Closets in Cyberspace: Explorations in Canadian Women's Archives* (2012); and an edition of

Jane Rule's *Taking My Life* (2011), which was shortlisted for the LAMBDA prize (2012). She is currently writing the biography of Jane Rule.

KARIS SHEARER is an associate professor in critical studies at University of British Columbia's Okanagan campus. Her research focuses on literary audio, the literary event, the digital archive, Canadian cultural production, and women's labour within poetry communities. She has published on a range of cultural production, including Sina Queyras's feminist blog *Lemonhound*, George Bowering's little magazine *Imago*, and Michael Ondaatje's *The Long Poem Anthology*. At UBC Okanagan, she directs the Humanities Data Lab and the Poetry Okanagan Sound Archive (POSA) project.

FELICITY TAYLER is e-research librarian at University of Ottawa Library, with a PhD in interdisciplinary humanities from Concordia University in Montreal. Scholarly writing has been featured in anthologies and in *Canadian Literature*, *Mémoires du Livre/Studies in Book Culture*, *Journal of Canadian Art History*, *International Journal on Digital Libraries*, *Art Documentation*, and *Art Libraries Journal*.

DARREN WERSHLER holds the Concordia University Research Chair in Media and Contemporary Literature, and is the co-founder of the Media History Research Centre and director of the Residual Media Depot. He is currently writing THE LAB BOOK: *Situated Practice in Media Studies*, with Jussi Parikka and Lori Emerson.

Index